Architexts of Memory

ArchiTEXTS
of Memory

LITERATURE, SCIENCE, AND AUTOBIOGRAPHY

Evelyne Ender

THE UNIVERSITY OF MICHIGAN PRESS
Ann Arbor

Published in the United States of America by
The University of Michigan Press
Manufactured in the United States of America
☺ Printed on acid-free paper

2008   2007   2006   2005   4   3   2   1

A CIP catalog record for this book is available from the British Library.

Library of Congress Cataloging-in-Publication Data

Ender, Evelyne, 1955–
    Architexts of memory : literature, science, and autobiography /
Evelyne Ender.
        p.   cm.
    Includes bibliographical references and index.
    ISBN-13: 978-0-472-11514-3 (acid-free paper)
    ISBN-10: 0-472-11514-6 (acid-free paper)
    ISBN-13: 978-0-472-03104-7 (pbk. : acid-free paper)
    ISBN-10: 0-472-03104-X (pbk. : acid-free paper)
    1. Autobiographical fiction, English—History and criticism.
    2. Proust, Marcel, 1871–1922. A la recherche du temps perdu.
    3. Woolf, Virginia, 1882–1941—Criticism and interpretation.
    4. Eliot, George, 1819–1880—Criticism and interpretation.
    5. Nerval, Girard de, 1808–1855—Criticism and interpretation.
    6. Autobiographical fiction, French—History and criticism.
    7. Literature, Comparative—English and French.   8. Literature,
Comparative—French and English.   9. Autobiographical memory
in literature.   10. Autobiography in literature.   11. Literature and
science.   12. Memory in literature. 13. Self in literature.
    14. Autobiography.   I. Title.
    PR830.A8E53 2005
    823.009—dc22   2005011743

For Elsa, my mother

Acknowledgments

The book began as part of my American adventure, in the reading room of Sterling library. At Yale University I found colleagues, students, and a treasure house of books that had a decisive influence on my first ideas for a project on memory. I am greatly indebted to Peter Brooks, Michael Holquist, and my colleagues of the "Brain, Mind, Consciousness, and Culture" seminar at the Whitney Humanities Center, as well as to my students in the seminars "Scenes of Childhood" and "Literature and Memory," for listening and sharing their ideas with me at crucial stages of this work. I am grateful as well to Christie McDonald and Susan Suleiman, Barbara Johnson, and Tamar March for their support and for invitations to present my work at Harvard. Nelly Furman, Stephen Dowden, Ute Heidman, Richard Waswo, and Peter Hughes kindly invited me to speak at Cornell, Brandeis, Lausanne, Geneva, and Zurich, respectively. I thank them and the audiences at these universities for their perceptive and provocative comments.

In America, Janet Beizer and Shoshana Felman have helped me with the gift of their friendship and inspired me, through their own work, to respond to the exigencies of this project. I am deeply grateful to Ravit Reichman, who knows almost every page of this text, for her wonderful help in matters of style and content. In Europe, where this project has its intellectual roots, my debt is to George Steiner, who kindly read early versions of this work and offered precious comments, and to Jean Starobinski, whose teachings and work in the history of ideas long ago aroused my intellectual curiosity about the mind. Gregory Polletta cannot be thanked enough—for his unfailing encouragements and for his unequaled Socratic teachings. He read most of this book in manuscript form and responded with invaluable comments and questions, which have found their way into this book in ways I hope he will be pleased to recognize. For conversations about the science of memory and their willingness to help on scientific or medical questions, I want to thank the following researchers and clinicians: Dr. Amy Arnsten, Dr. David Bear, Dr. Robert Kessler, Dr. Jonathan Pollock, and Dr. Ochine Karapetian in Geneva.

Without the generous friendship of Tom Cottle, this book might still be

in manuscript stage. I am forever grateful to him, as well as to my editor
LeAnn Fields, for their confidence in this project. My readers at the University of Michigan Press, Mieke Bal and Nelly Furman, provided me with
provocative, thoughtful, and exceptionally helpful comments. My thanks go
as well to my copyeditor, Richard Isomaki, and to Alina Opreanu, Lynn
Sorsoli, and Loren Wolfe for their insightful and generous help at crucial
stages of preparation of this text. A grant from the Swiss National Science
Foundation afforded precious time to complete the first stages of this
research.

Vahé deserves special thanks for his expert help in computer matters, as
well as for his unshakable faith in his mother's writing abilities. I am more
grateful than words can tell to Taline, for her deep trust in and encouragement of this project. To David I owe most: hours of conversation about the
ideas of this book, and his unfailing patience and confidence in its completion. He knows best what relentless intellectual probing and deep emotion
went into my writing about the wonders of personal memory.

Contents

Introduction

It is well past midnight. He lies awake in bed propped up by pillows, under several blankets and wrapped in fine woolen vests. It is very cold, but he cannot stop writing. He must write, even under such adverse conditions: fighting off the cold in a room where the windows are always closed and the walls are insulated with cork. Discarded pens lie on the floor, and sheets of papers are scattered all over the bed, until his maid and helper gathers them carefully into bundles. Now it is already dawn, and he has fallen asleep, exhausted. The breathing comes harder, and he has already suffered a few episodes of aphasia. The labor of remembering a life is monumental, and death seems very close.

But he has what he needs: pens, ink, paper, and silence. Much silence, because only in silence can the voice that beckons him to writing be heard. The voice is his own childish voice, the voice of a child who first understood that he was doomed to want what would always be behind him. The voice calls to him like Eurydice to her Orpheus; though when he turns toward the past, it seems irrecoverably lost, receding into the abyss of time. But suddenly, miraculously, a taste, a smell, the texture of an object, the cadence of a sound, or an image beckons him—and he remembers. As the old sensation is revived, the past comes back to life, for a time. But, he concludes, the only true paradises are those that we have lost—pleasure is always a thing of the past. There is so much sadness in this truth that it is not a voice that he hears, but actually the prescient sobs of the child that he was. There is a sentimental, or call it a nostalgic, streak in this rememberer.

But nostalgic or not, he knows his true vocation, knows what calls him back to life, what keeps him awake at night: the need to go back to the beginning. Writing will make a clearing in the darkness of time, enabling him to build the set of receding arches that shapes a path, an avenue into memory. It leads, this avenue, to the point where the two lines, of the past and of the present, appear to meet. Then he, the grown, celebrated, secluded Parisian writer, will encounter the child that he was. This is the hardest, but most exhilarating aspect of his journey into writing: for when it comes to childhood, the shadow of forgetfulness is incommensurably larger. What we keep from our childhood—besides the photographs, a few objects, and the stories that others have told us—is so little. This stunning record of times past would never have been born were it not for an unexpected discovery, which revealed that sensory cues can, miraculously, open the way toward recollection. In the absence of this extensive document, our understanding of the phenomenon of autobiographical memory would have been greatly impoverished.

The emblematic story of Proust's discovery is so famous as to barely need recounting. Another boring, unfruitful day has almost elapsed, and the quest for the past seems more than ever doomed to failure. One is offered a cup of lime-blossom tea, accompanied by a plump little cake, a *petite madeleine*. And, as the weary researcher dips the cake into this aromatic beverage, it suddenly happens: an uncanny sensation of pleasure, the question ("where does it come from?"), and the answer, given as the mind is flooded with images of a long gone past. The elixir has transported him back to the village of his childhood, providing the evidence for the solution to the question of how the personal past emerges into consciousness. The particular chemistry of a *tilleul* mixed with a morsel of madeleine has transformed him into a rememberer: he has become someone for whom, to use the psychologist Endel Tulving's description, "remembering . . . is mental time travel, a sort of reliving of something that happened in the past." This experiment, it turns out, can be repeated in varying conditions. Other sensations can similarly produce the phenomenon of recall: the unevenness of a pavement stone, the starched feel of a napkin, a spoon's singing tone, the unexpected hissing of a pipe, the particular slant of a sunset. None of them will be as decisive as that first revelation—which is when the true remembering began, and from which the work unfolded.

The Rememberer's World

Involuntary memory is Marcel Proust's legacy to our experience of remembering. The story of this discovery, recounted in *A la Recherche du temps perdu,* or *Remembrance of Things Past* (as it was until recently titled in English), has largely modeled our representations and conceptions of what autobiographical memory is, of what it can do. Its author, Marcel Proust, has acquired mythical stature. For our culture, Proust is the arch-rememberer, just as the blind Homer is our first storyteller, Shakespeare the supreme dramatist of the human soul, and Jean-Jacques Rousseau the model for modern autobiographers. In his monumental work devoted to memory and human time, Proust presents, in the guise of its hero, a striking embodiment of the "person who does the remembering" whom scientists now call the "rememberer." He represents, in other words, a histrionic, artistically crafted version of the human figure who has come into prominence in studies of autobiographical memory.

In giving pride of place to the rememberer's work of imagination and construction, this book makes a philosophical case about the relation between memory and subjectivity: it argues that our ability to create a record of past experiences provides the foundations of human individuality. When, because of amnesia or dementia, memory disappears, a person's life dissolves into an immediate, purposeless present. Unable to grasp the organizing shapes of her existence, this person will lead an increasingly centerless life, with fits of erratic activity giving way to inertia. For indeed our thoughts, emotions, pleasures, and intentions only acquire an existential relevance when our remembrance casts them in a narrative pattern and creates a self. Adrift in a sea of perceptions and sensations, the amnesiac is reduced to following, mindlessly, the vagaries of her biological fate. The "rememberer," by contrast, who knows how to craft autobiographical memories, is ever ready to grasp and shape a history made of pleasures and pains, as well as of ideas, actions, and projects. Rememberers thus emerge as the heroic figures of this story because of the remarkable feat they accomplish daily, often thoughtlessly and effortlessly: with every memory they construct, they keep the biographical thread that defines their existence and assert their agency as subjects against the force of biological determinism.

"Our memory is like a diary that writes itself," the psychiatrist Jean Delay comments, hinting that for each of us, life is bound up with the creation of a mnemonic diary. In imagining, constructing, scripting our memories, we give a shape and an identity to an existence that otherwise would be no more than a welter of disorganized physiological and perceptual events. Despite all we now know—with our increasingly refined grasp of the brain's neurology and biochemistry—about the somatic underpinnings of mental processes, remembrance is a triumph of the mind. As Jonathan Franzen adduces in conclusion of his essay "My Father's Brain," "the will to record indelibly, to set down stories in permanent words seems to me akin to the conviction that we are larger than our biologies" (107).

While my argument is ultimately philosophical, it emerges from the context of current scientific thinking about memory: the first inspiration for this book comes from rereading Proust in light of the recent debates in memory studies and from sharing his own curiosity and wonder about personal remembrance. His *Recherche* tells us that the creation of an autobiographical memory is nothing short of an amazing feat—a dazzling performance involving wonderfully elaborate mental and verbal skills. To respond to the promptings of involuntary cues is to discover a world in which we are alive with sensations, feelings, and human bonds. Remembrance, he shows, is the best care one can give to a self and the means of our psychic survival. It is also a miracle of engineering: the remembering mind stitches together, in a unique fashion, from a simple image to a scene, the most complex combination of thought, emotion, and words.

It should come as no surprise, then, that even as talented a writer as Proust needed to be schooled in the art of remembrance, by other authors such as George Eliot and Gérard de Nerval. Their mnemonic experiments, in *The Mill on the Floss* and in "Sylvie," help us see how in the mysterious process of verbal articulation and imaginative creation, new memories emerge into consciousness from the depth of a somatic, bodily unconscious. With Nerval in particular, we learn about the emotional aura that defines our most cherished memories. While the Proustian conception of memory has a literary genealogy that I trace in this book, it also finds its match, as it were, in the work of two authors who belong to the same era as Proust, Virginia Woolf and Sigmund Freud.

Woolf felt deep admiration for Proust's work, and indirectly and perhaps even unconsciously, set out to rival him (albeit on a very modest scale) with her experimental autobiographical text written close to her death, "A Sketch of the Past." Her comments highlight the crucial role writing plays in the creation and fashioning of personal memories. Thus she explains, after a particularly successful retrieval of a childhood memory: "my memory supplies what I had forgotten, so that it seems as if it were happening independently, although *I make it happen*. In certain favourable moods, memories—what one has forgotten—come to the top." "I make it happen": these words indirectly acknowledge the rhetorical performance that creates the memory, and insist that writing is the instrument of mnemonic construction. An emphasis on forgetting, which we see in Proust as well, is another important feature of Woolf's description, connecting the projects of both authors to Freud's theories of memory. It has been suggested that Freud reinvented psychiatry in light of forgetting.[1] But this is surely too restrictive a claim: on par with Proust, Freud's conception of memory as the overcoming of forgetting signaled a revolution in the overall conception of personal remembrance, as I show in highlighting the phenomenological aspects of his theory. It is indeed from a phenomenological rather than purely psychoanalytical perspective that my study invokes the notion of the unconscious, and that of deferred action (*Nachträglichkeit*).

This perspective accounts for my claim that writers are the exemplary architects of mnemonic scenes. Through their detailed descriptions of mnemonic processes, they reveal the artifices of imagination and rhetoric that bring the past to life. Their intricate sketches thus provide us with scripts for such processes that are especially relevant at a time of a major epistemic and philosophical shift in memory research. In this new conception, the remembering mind or brain is no longer imagined as a library or a storehouse of information; it is, rather, a site of continuous activity, where "neurons that fire together, wire together." This dynamic model of mental processing, influenced by phenomenology and often built around clinical cases, has sparked new interest in the form of remembrance explored by Proust, namely episodic memory.[2] Israel Rosenfield's description is doubly revealing: "When I form an image of some event in my childhood for example, I don't go into an archive and find a preexisting image, I have to consciously form an image" (184). Rosenfield's words illustrate that neuroscientists are now interested in forms of remembrance that used to be the purview of psychologists or writers as well as poets; they also tell us, in the insistent presence of a first-person singular pronoun, that research on memory must now, out of choice or necessity, make room for the subject who does the remembering.[3]

The writers who have a vocation for remembrance have long known about its subtle complexities. In trying to shape mnemonic scenes, they have learned that memories are constructions, that they depend on mood and context, and above all that there is no ready-made template to be found somewhere in the brain that reproduces an initial impress or trace. These writers see best what is always true for us, namely that remembrance is an act of imagination. With its focus on the figure of the rememberer, this book offers its own cases for study: examples of mnemonic experiments that help us figure out how the remembering "I" featured in Rosenfield's description performs the highly complex function that we identify with the phrase "I remember." But these individuals do more than identify the remembering subject; in Woolf's words, they help us imagine "the person to whom things happen." In other words, they offer us evidence for and insight into aspects of human experience that tend to elude scientific description.[4] The rememberers of this book find their mirror image in this person to whom things happen, which is to say that a major theme of this study is that of a human subject in search of consciousness and experience.

Experiencing the Past

Proustian memory is the instrument of this search for consciousness and experience and thus provides a way into a historical as well as philosophical question—a question that Walter Benjamin, in his reading of Proust, identified with the word *Erlebnis,* or "lived experience." Benjamin identified in Proustian memory the symptom of a shift of sensibility in our perception of the world and in the meaning of history. A few preliminary remarks are called for, however, to establish the premises of this investigation into this new meaning of experience undertaken in Benjamin's footsteps.[5] First we need a quick demonstration of what may seem only too obvious, namely that the Proustian moment of involuntary remembrance represents an ordinary human experience—even though in its fullest form it may occur only rarely and sporadically. (Commenting on its contingent nature, Adam Phillips wittily suggests that if one had to choose between psychoanalysis or involuntary memories, the former might be a more reliable aid to recovering a buried personal past.) Proustian memory is simultaneously banal and extraordinary—to the point that a mere reference to it, for example in the first pages of the manuscript for this book, can elicit instant recognition. For not only does Proust provide us with an archetypal story of private recollection, he also invites us to share our own stories, to dwell on the way they flash up, seize us, unfold before us, and, in the process, demand a narrative: I remember that *this* happened, that I was not alone, that the air was warm and fragrant with the scent of roses, that my heart almost ached from love and the surfeit of color and fragrance . . . Proust, ever the arch-rememberer, encourages us to emulate him, to sustain, for as long as is possible, the discoveries and pleasures of an intricate, intimate recollection. Taking him at his word, I argue in this book, partly for heuristic reasons, that Proust has made of this free, self-indulgent exercise of recollection the work of a lifetime, so that the whole architecture of his *Recherche* rests on an involuntary memory, and is built around a few drops of his famous elixir for remembrance, the tilleul and madeleine.

Meanwhile, because it is so ordinary, Proustian memory has become a concept familiar to thousands of people who have probably not read past the first pages of Proust's work or perhaps have never even set eyes on it. What has made him so popular? Perhaps it is his implicit invitation to create, amid the incessant bustle of modern life, moments of much-desired aesthetic stasis. Proust tells us to make allowances for nostalgia, to leave time for introspection and reminiscence, and to think (perhaps all too unabashedly and feelingly) about just ourselves. Proustian memory—or a little solipsistic, hedonistic dreaming for literate metropolitan culture: I offer for proof a bit of ethnographic sampling I undertook over a few months, in the middle of writing this book. A casual glance at the *Boston Phoenix* revealed a publicity item in the food pages on "lemon madeleines" ominously titled "Remember!" It claimed that "a single bite" would send me "spiraling into a Proustian reverie, a temporal trip back through faded memories." My local bookstore sponsored a talk by the famed Alain de Botton, author of *How Proust Can Change Your Life*, in which I learned that his American publisher had asked for a change of title (out of concern that the initial *How Proust Will Change Your Life* promised more than it could deliver). MIT invited André Aciman to lecture on autobiography; he delivered a talk redolent with Proustian moments (something to be expected perhaps from the author of *New Yorker* reportage on his visit to the Proustian shrine of Illiers/Combray). Once a week or so, a jaded, overworked undergraduate would eagerly tell me that he or she knew exactly what Proust had in mind with the story of the tilleul and madeleine and, with just a little prodding, would describe with obvious pleasure a personal experience of *mémoire involontaire*.

With his model of remembrance, Proust has found his way into ordinary life, perhaps not for the best reasons—to warrant a nostalgic streak and a craving for autobiographical confessions in a culture that has sometime been defined as pleasure-driven and inherently narcissistic.[6] Proustian memory is indeed about "me"—about the many individuals or human beings, rather, who must have personal memories and inner lives that are, for them, as rich and significant as the memories treasured by Proust or his forerunners (Nerval and Eliot) or his "rivals" (Woolf and Freud). This book does not, however, document Proust's influence on ordinary rememberers—sociology or cultural criticism lies outside its confines. If I evoke here the popularity of Proustian memory, it is to find validation, in Proust's fashionable success, for the real and very concrete nature of the phenomenon he describes. The world of science provides another form of validation: in their search for a compelling description or illustration of human remembrance, scientists often invoke Proust. One can imagine that researchers steeped in the analysis of complex mechanisms are naturally drawn toward the writer's beautifully crafted descriptions: even a cursory reference to Proust, in an article or book, will open up a space of aesthetic pleasure, of renewed wonder and excitement. Just as a biologist will sometimes stop in wonder at the perfect symmetry of a leaf or the unfolding shape of a shell, the neuroscientist cannot but be struck by the rich details of Proust's descriptions, which can hardly be matched in neural and physiological accounts.

This book shows, however, that scientists do not merely respond to the aesthetic appeal of Proustian memory; they are also attracted to his analysis of how autobiographical memories emerge. Proust pays unusually close attention to the physical and mental mechanisms that define the phenomenon of involuntary memory. He also provides a compelling script for the intellectual as well as emotional underpinnings of a strong mnemonic experience. In a field where numbers are so often the measure of all things, this author stands out with a strong claim for the qualitative nature of mnemonic experience, echoing or adumbrating perhaps, the interest in qualia that scientists such as Oliver Sacks, Gerald Edelman, and Antonio Damasio have shown. Psychologists, too, are drawn to Proust's work. Daniel Schacter, for example, announces that Proust has "foreshadowed scientific research by more than a half-century" and singles out for study the case of the tea and madeleine to highlight the notion of memory cues. He also relies on Proust to argue that personal recollection—this time voluntary—is linked to self-definition and to an enhanced sense of identity (*Searching for Memory*, 28). A recent account in *Scientific American* shows the relevance of the "Proustian phenomenon" for a study conducted by the psychologist Rachel S. Herz on smell, memory, and emotion.[7] Meanwhile, Ulric Neisser, famous for his innovative approaches in cognitive psychology, presents two texts, by Esther Salaman and by Ernest Schachtel, that highlight Proust's exemplary grasp of childhood memories.[8] Reporting on recent advances in research on memory, Stephen Hall compares Tim Tully's fruit flies—the subject of experiments in the creation and inhibition of long-term memory in a neuroscience center at Cold Spring Harbor—with "Marcel Proust's famous narrator."[9]

The connections between Proustian remembrance and science are even more striking in the clinical field. Proust's name appears frequently, for example, in Oliver Sacks's "neurology of identity," a research field primarily concerned with disturbances in cognition, consciousness, and memory. There, the writer seems to have provided the psychological, at times almost physiological, script for reminiscence—for the sudden, miraculous recovery of the past that Sacks witnesses among his amnesiac patients. For Sacks, the vivid memories called forth by L-Dopa, during some seizures, or when the frontal lobes are stimulated electrically are examples of Proustian recollection. As Sacks demonstrates in his "clinical tales," the study of autobiographical memory must occur at the cusp between the physical and the phenomenal world.[10] Yet while Proust's main share in our conception of memory naturally lies on the side of its phenomenology, his experiments seem to have had a clinical impact. For instance, as I discuss in chapter 6, therapeutic gardens are now being designed with the specific purpose of providing olfactory and visual stimuli to ailing rememberers in the hope that a whiff of lilac or the unexpected sight of a rosebush might, just like the aroma of a tilleul, miraculously jolt the ailing mind of an Alzheimer's patient out of oblivion.

But an even more provocative reminder of the presence of Proustian memory in our current clinical discourse came to my attention only recently—this time not as part of therapy, but in what seemed like an analysis of post-traumatic stress disorder. An article in my daily newspaper recounted the flashbacks experienced by a former general after his experience in Rwanda:

> One day, while driving to the beach, Dallaire, a retired lieutenant general in the Canadian Army, saw road workers clearing trees and his mind filled with images of corpses stacked up like cordwood. The memories so overpowered him that he had to stop the car and describe them to his horrified wife and children. Coming across homeless people sleeping on the street, his first instinct is to make sure they are still alive—(because in Rwanda victims of machete attacks are sometimes left half-dead). Smelling fruit in a Montreal supermarket one afternoon, he fainted; in the markets of Kigali, Rwanda's capital, the odor of rotting flesh and rotting fruit mingled in the open air during the slaughter.[11]

The mechanism of involuntary recollection that Proust describes in his *Recherche*—strong, overwhelming reminiscences provoked by sensory cues—is at work here (perhaps even unbeknownst to the author of this description). Instead of being elated by his Proustian experiences, a man who witnessed a terrible war is haunted by them: this is not a rememberer's *paradise*, but his *hell*.

I owe this stark formulation of the underside of personal remembrance to Lou Andreas-Salomé, the philosopher and psychoanalyst whose work on memory and narcissism helped me chart a challenging transition in this book—from Proustian memory as a pleasure to its symptomatic presence as trauma. To say that there are good and bad personal memories may seem like a truism, and to argue that recalling bad memories can work for one's good or even, as psychoanalysts and therapists know, toward healing has become a commonplace. However, the phenomenological descriptions that Proustian memory encourages raise new questions, which bear on the formal features of remembrance that constitute good or bad *mnemonic experiences*. Virginia Woolf helps us see that the same form of remembrance that brings a "happy" past to life might ultimately promote the recovery from the over-

whelming shocks of existence. Indeed, as Adam Phillips suggests, what ultimately matters for the rememberer is that a "symbolic transformation" take
place that transforms "the irruption" of what has been forgotten and had
thus seemed unrepresentable "into a pattern" ("Childhood Again," 153). In
the last chapters of this book, I dwell extensively on what Woolf calls her
"philosophy"—namely her postulation that, as rememberers, we can "work
through" the most overwhelming of shocks through our ability to find a
"pattern" and create mnemonic scenes.[12] Remembering, for Woolf, constitutes a source as well as a validation of our subjective experience.

Although this book was conceived in full awareness of the rapidly growing body of work in trauma studies, it was written to displace some of the
issues fundamental to this field—issues as rich and broad as history, subjectivities, therapy, and ethical responsibility.[13] For while the questions and
debates surrounding trauma have yielded a rich body of work, there is
nonetheless a crucial need for a more precise understanding of how personal
memory works. The "imperative of memory" that ultimately justifies and
defines trauma studies depends on the validation of personal recollection as
a mode of access to histories.[14] An implied belief in memory represents the
cornerstone, the very premise of the testimonies that speak to traumatic
experiences. Yet there is a sense that this belief has turned memory into
something of a commonplace: as a necessary feature in the recollection of
trauma that warrants no further examination on its own terms.[15] This book
responds to the "commonplace" of memory, then, by placing the foundational moment of remembering at the heart of the matter. For if we are to
truly understand the work that memory does, it is particularly important to
enrich our comprehension of the now familiar concept of memories as constructions. As the first five chapters of this book show, pressing on this
metaphor will take us right to the heart of crucially important assumptions
or questions about our reliance on private testimonies—assumptions about
the truth-value of personal remembrance and questions about the dividing
line between truth and fiction.

As my project was already well under way, a scandal and controversy
emerged around the book *Fragments: Memories of a Wartime Childhood*,
written by Binjamin Wilkomirski and presented as an autobiography.[16]
Wilkomirski's groundbreaking and moving account of children's experiences in Nazi camps was rewarded with several prizes given by Jewish associations—until it was demonstrated that the book was only a fictive reconstruction, based on readings. The author had never himself been part of the
events he described, nor had he witnessed them. How could so many readers, including professional historians, have been fooled into believing that

his memories were authentic? While this book does not tackle directly this stunning case of confusion between truth and fiction, its analysis of mnemonic constructions and their reality effect offers an indirect explanation for why readers were so easily won over by Wilkomirski's autobiographical claim. Given the close and complex ties that bind history to private memory, it has become incumbent on us to refine our understanding of personal remembrance, and to assess more accurately the epistemological challenges such an analysis presents—something that can be done more easily when these questions are staged in the more dispassionate, less morally and politically charged domains of literary studies and of science.

Epistemological Challenges

The idea behind this book was born in the second seminar on testimony that Shoshana Felman taught at Yale—from a question raised on the last day of class, in a recapitulation of our responses to Claude Lanzmann's film *Shoah*.[17] I remember sharing the strong feelings that were elicited by strains of Yiddish in the film, a language whose tonalities reminded me of my parents' own linguistic exile and of my own yearning for a homeland. I remember above all telling the class that I felt we had overlooked the aesthetics of Lanzmann's film—surely they were part of this documentary's overwhelming power. Both the sentimental power and the reality effect of this film, I argued, depended to a greater degree than we were willing to concede on the cinematic medium, on a discourse that involved shots and camera angles and the recording devices of his sound engineers. I remember not pushing my point. However, these two or three early intuitions about personal memory have stayed with me throughout this project: the intersubjective nature of memory, the importance of nostalgia, and above all, the aesthetic element in remembrance.

It took years, meanwhile, until I found an authoritative statement to summarize my thoughts on the aesthetic aspects of remembrance, but I finally read it in Oliver Sacks's clinical study of reminiscence in *The Man Who Mistook His Wife for a Hat* (which I address in my first chapter). Reflecting on the striking reality effect and vivacity of the memories felt by his patients, Sacks turns his attention to their singular phenomenal qualities and concludes: "the final form of cerebral representation must be, or allow 'art'—the artful scenery and melody of experience and action" (148). To say that remembrance, in Claude Lanzmann's documentary, is the product of art, and that there are unexplored "scenic" or "melodic" aspects both to the film and to the actors', or rememberers', performances may seem irrelevant or, even, irreverent—an ill-chosen way to describe the recurrent nightmares of those who experienced or witnessed the worst atrocities.[18] Surely, at a time of ethical summoning, very little can be gained from "problematizing" the nature of personal memory or from "deconstructing" the old category of art versus experience. In this fraught context, an analysis of memory is only relevant if it helps us comprehend something about the rememberer— namely why remembering constitutes for him or for her a way out of trauma and a means of survival. In reading Virginia Woolf's autobiographical proj- ect as a case study in post-traumatic memory in the final chapter of the book, I have gathered elements toward a richer understanding of the beneficial effects of personal remembrance.

Shoah begins with a sad, haunting song—a childhood memory—that seems to express the pain, hope, as well as beauty that can still be found in this world. The rememberer's song speaks of survival, and sings, against all odds, of the courage it takes to be human. I argue in this book that every rememberer carries within himself or herself the mnemonic equivalent of that song. Most often, we look at the "acts of memory" as cultural, histor- ical, and political gestures. But Proustian memory invites to think of the sin- gular and challenging task of the rememberer: the construction of memories endowed with phenomenal qualities that can guarantee their reality and, ultimately, their truth-value. The authors studied in this book teach us that personal remembrance is an aesthetic, as well as a cognitive and emotional, performance.

These claims raise a number of epistemological questions and paradoxes that must be mentioned here, for not only are they central to my argument, they have also determined the shape and the interdisciplinary scope of this book. First, despite our awareness that personal memories are constructed, we naturally assume that they closely correspond to something (an object, an event) that existed (or happened) at some point in time. (When the facts can be checked, and the memory does not correspond to them, we often call the rememberer a liar.) Furthermore, we tend to think of truth and fiction in terms of opposition. However, close examination of the phenomenon of personal remembrance invites us to see these values—truth and fiction— along a continuum. (Personal memories are, then, more or less true.) Finally, the arguments in this study emerge from the claim that personal memories are a highly subjective phenomenon (no one can remember what I remember). How can they be shared, and what is there, in the mnemonic scene's description, that makes us trust the rememberer?

Proustian memory, as can be shown briefly, raises all of these questions, especially once we consider, as we must with Proust, that what we took to be real memories are in fact the products of a fictional, of a fictive, construct. We may accept that personal memories look like "marvelous constructions," brilliant works of architecture born from the depths of our minds (a number of scientists would, I believe, currently endorse this description), but the fact that we are bound to know them, to recognize them only as they emerge from the rememberer's description, is surely more problematic.

Through his ability to create verbal representations of objects and of inner emotional states, Proust provides us in his *Recherche* with invaluable information about autobiographical remembrance; as we know, scientists and ordinary people alike believe in the validity of his descriptions. What if, however, the persuasive power of Proust's memory were not merely *connected to* his art and craft, but *were* his art and craft? Could it be that the construction of memory is predominantly, or perhaps even inherently, of a narrative and scenic nature, and that we respond to its representation as to a text? This issue stares us in the face when we examine the nature of Proust's experiment and consider how true and how convincing we find it—not only as we think about it scientifically, but in our instinctive response to the text.

Thus, although we are well aware of the fictional nature of the story Proust recounts, we respond to his literary representations in every way as if they were true memories. It takes a philosopher and a phenomenological view to unpack this cognitive dissonance: Edmund Husserl would say that our spontaneous, natural belief in the reality of memory images is so strong that it overrides our awareness that we are reading fiction. This is why, no doubt, all budding students of Proust need to be reminded every now and again that the hero of this adventure of the mind is a fictive construct; unlike Sacks's patients, he is not a real person but an imagined figure. Yet we trust Proust's rememberer—even if we know that there is no Combray, but only a village lost on the map of France called Illiers, or that there was never a cup of tilleul, but possibly just tea (as earlier versions of his text suggest)—or perhaps no tea at all. We believe him all the more because the exploration of memory's contents is underwritten by ample and precise phenomenological descriptions. It turns out then that our belief in Proustian memory depends exclusively on the quality of the representations provided by the writer. This simple truth—that we are inveigled, lured into a rememberer's inner world through the elaborate prose of a great fiction writer—gives a new resonance to Sacks's comment about the aesthetic dimensions of reminiscence. If "art" or a certain "scenic" or "melodic" quality of the representation is a defining trait of our memories, then we owe the impression of a life remembered to Proust's remarkable literary talent: it is the *quality* of his recollections, rather than the mere fact of memory, that turns readers into believers.

This book argues that the mnemonic presentations in other writers (Woolf, Eliot) must similarly be taken as true, insofar as they abide by structures and codes that we normally associate with remembrance. Indeed, fictional memories not only *seem* real, they *are* real once we accept that literary representations can present good, convincing analogues for ordinary remembrance. As the masters of make-believe and the supreme creators of imagined worlds, writers no doubt know more about the workings of memory than most of us; as deft manipulators of images, they know how to create a reality effect and how to draw us into a fabled world of their own making. Psychiatrists and psychologists must have intuited this when they gave the name of *confabulation* to the imagined stories that certain amnesiacs instinctively put together when they fail to properly remember an event. The rememberer's art resembles that of the fabulist. With our sophisticated understanding of mnemonic constructions, how can we relinquish our skepticism and still uphold the notion that there might be a kernel of truth in a rememberer's depiction? I explore this question in the chapter "Screen Memories," which traces Sigmund Freud's complex investigation into the truth status of his own childhood memories. Freud, it turns out, puts the sum of his clinical flair in the service of an exercise in discrimination between memory and fantasy only to be reminded that in the end, the rememberer's own sense of conviction offers the only guarantee of a memory's unadulterated authenticity.

Meanwhile, the reason for the epistemological difficulties we face when trying to ascertain the genuineness of a particular memory is very simple: it lies in the fact that memory, like consciousness, is really, in Gerald Edelman's synoptic phrase, "first person matter." Our personal memories are inextricably bound up in the "grammatical" assumption of a first person and thus inherently subjective. Just as I can't dream another's dream, I cannot remember another person's memories. I can hear about them, share them, translate them, reproduce them even—but they have one author, the figure I call a rememberer, who exists by virtue of a first-person singular. Thus, rememberers in this book have said: "I remember a pink-bluish tulip I saw shiver in the sun on a breezy April morning"; "how I waited apprehensively at the top of the stairs for my mother's good night kiss"; "I remember how she glided, a pink and golden ghost, over the green grass bathed in white vapors"; "I remember those large dipping willows . . . I remember the stone bridge." Our private recollections exist by virtue of a grammar and a rhetoric whose combination produces a "memory effect." Swept off our feet by the power of a rhetorical construction, we can be transported to another place, to suddenly recognize, as rememberers, "something that happened to us in the past." When this verbal-mental adventure can be shared, because it has been given a recognizable and convincing shape—either out loud for someone to hear, or on the page for a reader, or in the mind just for oneself—then we have witnessed the advent of a memory and become that someone—a rememberer—for whom, in Tulving's evocative words, "remembering . . . is mental time travel."

Yet this description of personal memory, written in the spirit of current definitions, does not signal the end of all epistemological quandaries. How can science deal with something as subjective as autobiographical recollection, especially once we acknowledge that the architect of memory is also a storyteller? The challenge articulated here is familiar to scientists working on the mind, and is spelled out by Antonio Damasio:

> Multiple individuals confronted with the same body or brain can make the same observations of that body or brain, but no comparable direct third-person observation is possible for anyone's mind. The body and its brain are public, exposed, and unequivocally objective entities. The mind is a private, hidden, internal, unequivocally subjective entity. ("How the Brain," 114)

Proustian memory is itself a "private, hidden, internal, unequivocally subjective entity"; it is a scene and melody created by the first-person narrator particularly adept at convincing us of the reality of his past. It is also the singularly persuasive product of a mental and literary exploration—a thought experiment so successful that it acquires scientific credibility. The study of a sampling of modern texts devoted to explorations of personal memory has convinced me that these epistemological challenges are not necessarily impasses or obstacles, but rather, invitations to take a different approach toward the issue of personal remembrance. The approach that literary memory affords highlights the narrative and textual aspects of remembrance, rather than dismissing them as problematic because they undermine its truth-value. This counterintuitive method assumes, however, another theoretical tenet, which proclaims that memories are only accessible through narrative and, ultimately, through language. Given that we naturally want to believe in the historical veracity, in the "reality," of our memories, this idea may seem too radical, but *Architexts of Memory* insists on this verbal texture, arguing that memories are constructed like a text, and that their particular definition—their qualia—and their reality are bound up with linguistic performances.

Memory's Verbal Texture

Language—not merely as the expression of our thoughts but as a way of symbolizing our emotions—thus figures at the center of this inquiry. Although recent technical advances in brain imaging have provided unique insights into mental processing, no instrument other than language can give us access to the contents of our memories and to their individual thematic and qualitative differences. That our knowledge of all human, personal, and biographical truths is inseparable from narrative is a vision that psychoanalysis has come to accept and that deconstructive philosophy has promoted. Given my focus on concrete examples—on the rememberer, on the texture of memories, and on clinical tales—a psychoanalytic defense of this position is immediately relevant. As a practitioner who works daily with rememberers, Roy Schafer makes a compelling case for narrative. "Narrative," he concludes from his experiences, "is not an alternative to truth and reality; rather it is the mode in which, inevitably, truth and reality are presented" (xiv–xv). Indeed, in studying memory for its personal and biographical aspects, we cannot but confront the complicated, complicating fact that human truths are inherently bound up with our ability to represent them and narrate them. Proust's *Recherche,* as we saw, presents narrative constructions that have such compelling force that they produce the illusion of a biographical truth for even the most astute analysts of memory. This ability is shared by all the writers in this book: they all display, albeit with different strategies, the uncanny persuasive power of the architexture that is the stuff of human recollection. Once we accept that literary texts offer the best examples for the marvelous mental architecture that enables us to construct our past, we cannot but pay attention to the language of our recollection—to its texture, its scenic depictions, and its representations.

In matters of personal memory, there is much to learn, then, from a deconstructive approach, from focusing on the performative aspect of language and on the intimate connection that exists between language and our inner, human world of representations. We use words to do things, to create our inner world and map out our outer world. Our memories are thus really born from a verbal performance, from naming: "I say: a flower! And out of the forgetting where my voice relegates others contours . . . musically arises, the absent from all bouquets." In quoting this famous pronouncement by the French poet Mallarmé, which tells us that it suffices to name an object to see it emerge from oblivion, I draw on the rich heritage of deconstruction and on a philosophical tradition that has singularly complicated the idea that words naturally refer us to things that are "out there" in the world. A deconstructive reading will thus emphasize the word "absent" in Mallarmé's aphorism—to remind us that words, by definition, evoke what is not there.[19] It will also warn us that in spite of our desire for memories vivid enough to give the illusion of presence, it would be wiser to consider that remembrance is our way of summoning up what is absent, what is past and gone. At several points in this book, important questions arise around this simple axiom that remembrance makes objects present in absentia and gives them a "contour" that can only be a mental projection. Only in hallucinations do our memories appear embodied and somehow present.

But although it draws on the epistemological findings of deconstruction, this book does not abide by deconstructive philosophical tenets. It makes too much room for the illusions of presence and reference that deconstructionists so cleverly denounces; it endorses too fully the rememberer's nostalgic wish that the past be revived and be made, somehow, present. To study the issue of reference, I highlight this same, seemingly banal and unobtrusive figure that appears repeatedly in my rememberers' accounts—a flower. For in their mnemonic experiments, Proust, Virginia Woolf, George Eliot, and Sigmund Freud confront the same predicament as Mallarmé with his *fleur*. What does it take to express a personal impression? For these rememberers, just as for Mallarmé, flowers born from simple words serve as emblems of the way imagination and language enable us to apprehend our personal phenomenal universe. Lilacs, hawthorns, cornflowers, poppies; colorful anemones on a maternal dress; the "blue-eyed speedwell in a wood in May"; flowers of the most vivid yellow—these epitomize the aesthetic promise that so often inspires Proustian remembrance. As the focal, salient point of a memory, they also seem to guarantee its reality and become the token of a "true" experience even though their existence is purely textual— a combination of phonemic and semantic features. I show in chapter 8, in reading Nerval through the lens provided by Proust, that the rememberer's poetic use of language enables us in turn to grasp the emotional undertones that lie at the heart of certain memories. Indeed, for us, "readers" or "observers" of another person's memories, the writer's words are the keys to the inner recesses of a mind alive with images, ideas, and above all with affects. Proust conceives of Nerval's words as magical tokens, inviting us to share experiences that are, in Damasio's words, innately "private, hidden, internal" and "unequivocally subjective"—experiences that are memories.

This is why in my interpretation of Mallarmé's aphorism, the stress ultimately needs to fall on the phrase "musically arises": I want to believe, like
Sacks, that in spite of its dauntingly complex structuration and ceaseless
repatterning, the inner landscape of our mind is animated by an "artful
melody."[20] I also want to do justice to the creative nature of memory. The
remembering mind, Proust tells us, "is face to face with something which
does not yet exist, to which it alone can give reality and substance." And
this something, Mallarmé suggests, may be at first no more than a simple
flower, brought into existence by the quasi-musical evocations of that word.

Contrary to appearances, my reliance on Mallarmé's aesthetic meditation for a better understanding of remembrance does not belong to the
premises of this work, but represents the outcome of a sustained analysis of
how writing and remembering mirror each other. It is only in the course of
studying the writers' lifelike mnemonic experiments that the similarities
between a "mental architecture" evocative of memories and the formal and
symbolic processes that we associate with the art of writing became apparent. But through this inductive process, the need to revisit our common
metaphors for remembrance arose, more forcefully than expected. Let me
propose, then, that we conceive of remembrance for a moment (that is, as a
heuristic device designed to enrich our grasp of mnemonic processes) in
terms of writing. To emphasize this writing, however, is not to return to
Freud's *Wunderblock,* the "mystic writing pad" that shows how the "mental apparatus" deals with memory traces; it is, rather, to focus on the complex representations—the "architexture"—constitutive of human remembrance. Old-fashioned as it may seem, this analogy has the advantage of
giving back to memory its profoundly human and subjective dimensions
(only we, humans, can invent characters and symbols to describe our world)
and of highlighting features that the familiar comparison between human
memory and computers fails to encompass. Photographs are often presented
as good analogies for memory because, as Roland Barthes demonstrates in
Camera Lucida, they can present the qualities of a "temporal hallucination"
and thus help us believe in the existence of something "that has been" (115).
Antonio Damasio has used the conceit of a "movie-in-the-brain" as a
"metaphor for the integrated and unified composite of diverse sensory
images—visual, auditory, tactile, olfactory and others—that constitute the
multimedia show we call mind" ("How the Brain Creates the Mind," 115).
But both the photographic and the cinematographic metaphors offer us
greatly stylized and impoverished versions of remembrance, versions that
overlook the phenomenal richness that characterizes Proustian memory.
They also fail to render the richly nuanced emotional underpinnings of

human recollection. In order to account for these, the film's reel would have to be combined with a new, as yet uninvented instrument—a sort of brain scanner that could embed a rememberer's affects into the picture. For whereas a film might capture the aesthetic and formal dimensions of human recollection (its "scenic" or "dramatic" qualities), only the brain scan could give us the melodic quality, the rhythm and pulse, the appeal of the emotions that are part of the memory. But why reach for a new technology when writing offers a ready way of embedding feelings into representations? Memory, this book argues, is a writer, and rememberers are architects so well versed in the art of scripting memories that they produce—spontaneously, naturally—constructions that have the kind of texture we associate with reality.

Questions of form, questions of narrative, and questions of person are at the heart of literature, confronting every writer and relating, crucially, to the shaping of a personal voice and of a persona; in short, they bear on our subjectivity. Indeed, the richest lesson one can draw from writers—and the one I elicit from this extensive investigation into Proustian memory, is that *autobiographical memory is an act of imaginative construction that is constitutive of human subjectivity.* What these italicized words imply is explored in detail in the first chapter, "The Aroma of the Past: Marcel Proust and the Science of Memory"; what they mean, for our lives and for how we remember, is the subject of the remaining chapters.

In exploring this proposition, which endows a creative act with a foundational value, we reach yet another paradox that lies at the heart of personal remembrance: it would seem that we build our present and future through an act of retrospection that embraces the images of the past we have constructed as persuasive fictions—fictions we can live by.[21] In the philosophical section of his book on brain and mind, *Bright Air, Brilliant Fire,* Gerald Edelman states the following: "Human individuals possess selfhood, shored up by emotions and high order consciousness. And they are tragic in so far as they can imagine their own extinction" (176). Sigmund Freud, writing from the opposite perspective, states in his essay on the uncanny that "no human being grasps [the statement "All men are mortal"] and our unconscious has as little use now as it ever had for the idea of its own mortality" (242). Thus these scientists tell us that we need memory to ward off the daunting fact of death, and their philosophical pronouncements confirm my own findings—namely that our desire and need for remembrance express, in one breath, what is the predicament as well as the future of our human condition. Memory speaks of our fear and our tragic awareness of death, but it also attests to our remarkable resilience. As master storytellers, rememberers provide us with what is, according to an expert theorist on subjectivity, the "one possible *récit* . . . that of the extension of time across the body" (P. Smith, 111). The paradox at the heart of personal memory—which tells of our ability to comfort ourselves with fictive, mental constructions born from our wondrous capacity for imagination—makes us all, perhaps, the epigones of the child who whistles in the dark to keep fear at bay. Gérard de Nerval, whose desperate need to remember I study in chapter 7, offers a vivid reminder that autobiographical remembrance can sometimes save a mind from madness or despair, just as it can freeze the rememberer in an autistic nightmare.

We are driven back to the past, we are driven to remember, because it is essential for us, as human beings, to make sense of our lives by connecting to the thread of impressions, feelings, emotions that we have experienced. Memory images provide a fragmentary record of our deepest and most significant emotions, bringing us back to the singular of histories that define each individual's existence. To study remembrance among writers is to discover beautifully crafted narratives that make us see and understand what it feels like to be alive. It is to witness or experience, vicariously, moments when, as W. B. Yeats might say, the "soul clap[s] its hand." The art of memory might indeed represent one of our human responses to a "tragic condition." Were it not for the fact that memories remain so often private and internal, one would want to add the word *memories* to the list of human accomplishments Edelman draws up in the wake of his observations about our tragic consciousness of mortality: "what is perhaps most extraordinary about conscious human beings is their art—their ability to convey feelings and emotions symbolically and formally in external objects such as poems, paintings, or symphonies" (*Bright Air*, 176).

In recent years, personal memory has come to feature prominently in the social, cultural, legal, and medical fields. Ours is an age of fascination with virtual realities, with clones and with artificially created intelligence, preoccupations that paradoxically intersect with a renewed interest in autobiographies, the genre reserved for the depiction of "real stories," for the preservation of the uniqueness and "authenticity" of personal experience. We now have unparalleled resources for storing information in images; words and bytes make us believe that we have entrusted our memories to machines, yet we eagerly chronicle in our newspapers every new step in memory research, in the hope of a magical remedy or vaccine against memory loss. Our present is also repeatedly marked by disputes, in the historical and legal professions, over personal testimonies: by increasing the value and the weight of personal remembrance, we have ignited "memory wars" over the controversial recovery of traumatic memories. Amid this resurgence of cultural interest in memory, it is all the more pressing to reconsider, from the perspective of the humanities, what we know about personal recollection as a subjective phenomenon—not to reject, but rather to take in what modern science has taught us. Thus, despite its focus on the inner aspects of our subjectivities and histories, this questioning belongs in our modern era—because it speaks of a search for the soul at a time of increasing contradictions and anomie. Never before has there been a greater need to reflect on the relation between memory and human experience.

The art of memory, I thus propose, is deeply bound up with our human survival. It is an art that is characteristically human—linguistic, historical, cultural—and it celebrates human consciousness not only in its highest, creative forms but also as part of our responsibility. We gather our memories in view of our future, shaping our existence through the sense that we have given to our past, and thus owe it to ourselves to discover, in the words of Woolf, "the truth about this vast mass we call the world." This truth does not consist merely in the information, however accurate, provided by our senses. It must contain the sum of our autobiographies as well, autobiographies that were built through the memories that both embody and express our subjective responses to the world. As we listen to rememberers and strive to understand what their words symbolize, we will learn to decipher history differently—we will learn to discern, among the accumulated mass of facts that make up our modern, information-driven world, the more precious, more significant human truths. Only then will history speak to us in a new voice, one more filled with poignant meaning, and richer in personal, subjective inflections.

1 • The Aroma of the Past: Marcel Proust and the Science of Memory

And soon, mechanically, dispirited after a dreary day with the prospect of a depressing morrow, I raised to my lips a spoonful of the tea in which I had soaked a morsel of the cake. No sooner had the warm liquid mixed with the crumbs touched my palate than a shudder ran through me and I stopped, intent upon the extraordinary thing that was happening to me. An exquisite pleasure had invaded my senses, something isolated, detached, with no suggestion of its origin. And at once the vicissitudes of life had become indifferent to me, its disasters innocuous, its brevity illusory—this new sensation having had on me the effect which love has of filling me with a precious essence; or rather this essence was not in me, it *was* me. I had ceased now to feel mediocre, contingent, mortal. Whence could it have come to me, this all-powerful joy? I sensed that it was connected with the aroma of the tea and the cake, but that it infinitely transcended it, could not, indeed, be of the same nature. Whence did it come? What did it mean? How could I seize and apprehend it? (Proust, *Swann's Way*, 48; translation amended)[1]

"No sooner had the warm liquid mixed with the crumbs touched my palate than a shudder ran through me and I stopped, intent upon the extraordinary thing that was happening to me." Proust's extended description of a vivid recollection launched by these words has become a cause célèbre in our comprehension of autobiographical memory. With the banal, prosaic act of dunking a cookie (a madeleine) in a hot drink (a tilleul), a new memory is born to the hero of Proust's *Recherche,* and with it, a new vision of how memory works. Proustian memory represents more than a stylistic accomplishment (a new way of articulating remembrance through the notion of *mémoire involontaire*): it reveals a passionate commitment to elucidating the workings of autobiographical memory.[2] Proust's biographical narrative is so tightly intertwined with a scientific and philosophical enquiry that *A la recherche du temps perdu* reads at times very much like a case study or a treatise, even, on the subject of personal remembrance. From the perspective of a science of memory, his work enables us to grasp some of the fundamental features of autobiographical memory: its precarious positioning at the cusp between body and mind, its inherently subjective and dynamic nature, its aesthetic appeal, and most importantly perhaps, its profound connections with our personal identity. The analysis of Proustian memory that I pursue here fulfills a dual role: it provides a summary of this author's contribution to the science of memory, mind, and consciousness, while it also outlines new avenues for investigations into human recollection.

How does personal memory work, how do we recollect our past experiences? These broad and ambitious questions, which have interested experimental psychologists, neurologists, and philosophers for more than a century, are given such an arresting and compelling turn in Proust's descriptions that they remain a source of inspiration in modern science. Directly or indirectly, his inquiry feeds into recent discussions of autobiographical memory, as can be seen in the work of three scientists who have analyzed it from their different specialties. The experimental psychologist Marigold Linton, the neurobiologist Antonio Damasio, and the neurologist Oliver Sacks conceive of memory as a *dynamic process,* a process that enlists the body and the mind in a unique act of creation. Like Proust, they are intrigued by the wonderful brain-work that enables us to revisit the past in all its felt presence, and they focus, in their studies, on a rememberer who "works" to create memories and masterminds mnemonic scenes. In the rich terrain of scientific study of memory, their work stands out as marking a significant shift in interest and attention—away from merely mechanistic or biochemical models toward broader experiential frameworks that involve such concepts as emotion, narrative, and image. They see memory in its concrete existential dimension: initially perhaps as a clinical fact (as is the case when Damasio or Sacks studies amnesiac patients), but also more broadly as an essential feature of human experience. This is why, no doubt, the issues and even the methods of investigation they use can bring them very close, at times, to Proust's discoveries: in studying the phenomenon of personal recollection, he too starts with a physiological and mechanical conception and then embraces a richer model that, in the end, involves emotion, imagination, and narrative.

What I seem to be identifying here is a shift of perspective in memory studies: work that does not focus on the fruit fly or the sea slug, but on a type of memory performance that only human beings appear to be capable of. (The most evolved among mammals may have emotions and perhaps even imagination, but we have no evidence that they can create narratives.) I am also highlighting a mode of inquiry that must necessarily move beyond the confines of a biochemical or cybernetic model: there are psychological dimensions to autobiographical memory, and unmistakable phenomenal aspects. But this broad approach, of a kind that belongs perhaps to a history of science, prevents us from seeing what is, at bottom, Proust's most remarkable contribution to memory studies, namely the description of a particular type of recollection. What we put under the label of "memory" can mean a great variety of things. Calling an object or a person by name, remembering phone numbers, folding a napkin, holding a fork, finding one's keys, finding one's way home, marking an anniversary: in each of these instances we have "remembered," that is, we have relied on a memory. None of these actions describes, however, the kind of memory that Proust put on the map of memory studies when he wrote his *Recherche*. Proustian memory is a scene, a story, an experience; it is intensely personal, embedded in our biography and history; it carves out a sensory, sensual, imagistic moment of a unique kind. Beyond the paradigm shift in the study of memory that Proust's work invokes, there remains, then, a fundamental and very simple fact: Proustian memory is different—exceptionally complex, specifically human, highly subjective, and hard to study empirically. The analysis that I propose here reflects this double awareness: that Proust's new definition of personal memory calls for a new way of approaching the study of memory itself and that it calls, particularly, for a crossing between disciplines, inviting a dialogue between scientific and literary studies.

Proust himself stresses from the start the extraordinary nature of the mnemonic experience he is about to analyze, and in so doing provides us with a crucial aspect of its definition. It is extraordinary, he shows us, not so much because of the exceptional nature of the event (such experiences of involuntary and seemingly total recall are familiar to most of us), but because this sudden, convulsive resurgence of the past, to which he gives the name of *mémoire involontaire,* creates a scene whose existence had remained until then unknown to the rememberer. We witness the birth of a memory that was lost, a memory that was, to all intents and purposes, forgotten.[3] What lies behind this apparent paradox becomes clear once we remind ourselves that in ordinary life, forgetting naturally prevails over remembering. Human recollection is, by nature, extremely selective: only a small fraction of what we perceive and experience is retained. Each of our strong, fully fledged, or "memorable" memories represents, in other words, a significant physiological and mental feat against our innate tendency toward amnesia, against a "forgetting [that] is a truly universal phenomenon" (Weiner, 577). That Proust knew this (if only from experience, and not from studies) is shown in the particular tonality that accompanies each description of a recovered memory: each time, it is seen as a triumph over the prevailing forces of oblivion.

The victory is all the more striking, Proust shows us, because it occurs in the most challenging of contexts: his subject experiences memory in its purest condition and form, without any of the external tools that commonly help us imagine the past. No book, no photograph, and no film even can prompt, or let alone trace, the kind of memory he describes. But his literary voice traces an experience that is internal and occurs in the intimate recesses of the private mind and body. In this way, Proust takes his investigation to a place that is precisely the one that has been invested by the scientists I identified above—a place where a man or a woman is an island unto himself or herself and confronts images of a past that are at once so unique, so personal, and so rich that no artificial medium could hope to represent them. Because its definition is phenomenal (that is, related to sensations) and emotional (its central feature lies in the pleasure that it gives the rememberer), Proustian memory lies beyond the realm of our modern archival resources or cybernetic creations. The experience described by Proust lies outside what modern technologies, however sophisticated, can reproduce, and it could not be captured by video cameras, CD-ROMS, or computers. This is to say also that an analysis of Proustian memory takes us away from quantitative issues (how much can be remembered) or systematic studies (modeling the brain as a sort of machine or computer) toward a qualitative approach. It shows us what it "feels like" to remember; it analyzes the remarkable feat of body and mind that enables us to overcome natural oblivion; it tells us why autobiographical memory is so central a dimension of human existence. But first, it defines a method and a protocol for a thorough investigation of autobiographical memory—a method and protocol that seem to anticipate those developed by Marigold Linton, an experimental psychologist who was among the first to focus on the phenomenon of personal recollection.[4]

Memory Watching: Proust and Linton

In 1972, Marigold Linton set out to explore the contents and structures of autobiographical memory, with the aim of establishing how well (at what rate, how precisely) we remember events of our personal past. She also wanted to analyze what gave certain events the salience that made them endure in memory. Thus for six years, she kept a diary recording events from her own life, while testing every month what she could recall when prompted by the short verbal cues randomly selected from her record. She calls this process "memory watching," and, comparing her investigations to those of an ethnologist or population biologist exploring an island, she declares: "From my vantage point as a population mnemonist the questions to be asked about memories become clear. . . . [They] include: 'What memories survive, thrive, and populate the domain? Whither do they come, where do they go, and what forms do they take during their tenure?'" (51). Linton conceives of her "memory watching . . . as a technique particularly appropriate for obtaining a census of our migratory autobiographical memory" (52). Her metaphors are suggestive: as the inhabitant of an island (herself) who is looking for "live" memories (the birds), she defines the space for a project founded on introspection and establishes, at the same time, the distinction between subject and object necessary to her scientific investigation.

Similarly, in Proust's research the rememberer is his own subject of investigation, and introspection, his method. The text opens onto a scene that shows him in bed, sifting through images and memories as he moves in and out of his sleep. The bed is his island, from which he can, like Linton, observe the memories that fleet in and out of his ken. Relying on memory, imagination, and a few impressions, the half-awakened sleeper reconstructs the topography of a room that becomes his laboratory. This is where he runs his initial experiments and launches an investigation that unfolds across the whole work. Indeed, the Proustian bed is not merely a prop in the unfolding drama that drives a man to stave off death by recapturing the past; it is also the place of crucial discoveries. The figure of the recumbent subject who lies awake in the silence of the night, straining his ear to catch remnants of the past—and feverishly chronicling his visions—provides us with a striking image of the memory researcher at work. The bed is the privileged site for the *gedankenexperiment* that will lead to the capture of memories.[5]

A la Recherche du temps perdu thus documents a study of autobiographical memory that extended over many years and yielded a wealth of phenomenal data on personal recollection. Memory watching defines the engrossing vocation of a narrator who harks after silence in order to recapture the waning music of the past and who presents, in his work, the fair copy of his extensive research. Memory content, of the voluntary and of the involuntary kind, is the matter of the book, and, in the right conditions, the rememberer's observation produces the richest of results. Consider for a moment that the whole of "Combray" (several hundred pages of narrative) springs from one particularly felicitous encounter with a "migratory memory," or that the culminating revelations documented in the last volume and that occur in Paris chart for the time traveler an immense territory that comprises Balbec, Venice, Tansonville, and Combray. These two momentous discoveries are held apart by more than two thousand pages: the tilleul and madeleine belong to the first of the seven volumes, while the triumph of involuntary memory is presented in the last. But the length of the work is a function of the method: the *Recherche* does not offer a set of demonstrations, it charts a process of discovery that spreads over many years and involves many failed trials.

Proust's lengthy work faithfully represents a scientific inquiry founded (as he himself saw) on induction: his researcher has his own method, but no preliminary theory; he needs empirical data to confirm an early intuition.[6] The structure of the *Recherche* thus seems to mirror the slow progression of an investigation that stalled for many years, until the day of the first significant breakthrough—that time when, on savoring his tilleul and madeleine, the rememberer suddenly understood that the essence of autobiographical recollection can only be captured in what Oliver Sacks has called, in his work on reminiscence, "the convulsive upsurge of memories from the remote past" (*Man Who*, 150). With this new discovery, the other earlier findings (culled over long nights, over months and years even of memory watching) blend into the background: involuntary memory becomes the real thing—the phenomenon that, for Proust, epitomizes autobiographical recollection. Linton has not imagined the situation Proust describes: the striking, unforeseen apparition of a new species of memories that will change forever the way in which he conceives of autobiographical recall.

Yet one case is not enough. The researcher needs more data and further assays, which, given the nature of involuntary memories, presents a singular challenge. Founded as they are on fortuitous encounters with sensory cues, these memories cannot be produced at will; they are triggered, each time, by different circumstances. Moreover, as the memory watcher learns in the course of his observations, the first intimations do not always lead to the discovery of a fully fledged memory: many searches fail.[7] Like the biologist who, in Linton's analogy, is watching for birds on her lonely island, the Proustian investigator remains at the mercy of the skies for his discoveries.[8] One fortuitous day, however, on the occasion of a late visit to the Guermantes' home, he suddenly experiences one involuntary memory after another. Stumbling over an uneven stone, hearing the tingling of a spoon, touching a starched napkin, each of these sensations provides him with a chance for a new "assay" *(un essai)* and offers further confirmation: the most vivid of autobiographical memories are the product of such coincidences. A sensory stimulus triggers recall, and somewhere between body and mind there emerges a new, a forgotten memory.

The *Recherche* thus traces a revolution in Proust's understanding of autobiographical recollection: voluntary memory pales or even fails in the light of a form of recollection that can unearth forgotten images and miraculously brings the past back to life. Dipping the madeleine in a spoonful of tea, the rememberer finds a new answer to his earlier misguided quest—misguided because it assumed that memories were born purely from the mind, in isolation from the body. Pure thought is not enough; memory must be seen as well in its somatic and physiological aspects; the thought experiment gives way to the study of memory born from the depth of a physical experience, at the intersection between the outer and the inner world. The island or bed is then no longer the best starting point; a natural context is much more conducive to the kinds of impressions that trigger recollection. Out in the world is where the rememberer is likely to encounter the haphazard cues that can produce, in a flash, the images that show the past in its "true" colors and endow it with a genuine phenomenal richness. Involuntary memory thus provides the solution to the quandary Proust had identified in his earliest draft of the *Recherche*, known as the *Reliquat Proust*:

> For many years I had no recall of our Combray house. All I knew is that I had spent a part of my childhood there. When I wanted to find some image of it, I would prod my intelligence, namely voluntary memory, which in no way gives us our past, because it paints it wholly in a color that is uniform and thus wrong because it draws on the present. In reality, Combray was dead for me. (*Recherche* [Pléiade], 1:1045)

Drawing on our present awareness and our intelligence, voluntary memory, according to Proust, neither involves nor affects us. The closest analogy for this imperfect form of recollection is that of a photograph or a film, which merely unfolds under our eyes and keeps us at a distance from the real, intensely colored experience of the past. But something very different happens, Proust explains to a friend, when we encounter an involuntary memory; there, a scent or a taste can truly reawaken the past, endowing it with a fuller aroma, brighter and more authentic colors:

> Voluntary memory, which is above all the memory of our intelligence and our eyes, will give us merely untruthful aspects from the past; but whenever a scent, a taste re-encountered in completely different circumstances unwittingly reawakens the past, we feel how different this past is from what we seem to remember, and from what was depicted by our voluntary memory with false colors, as by an incompetent painter.[9]

These two statements prepare the major conceptual leap that the writer stages in connection with a cup of tea in the "overture" to the *Recherche*. Pleasure, we thus learn, is the first distinctive mark of this richer mode of recollection, a pleasure that is enhanced "as the whole of Combray and its surroundings, taking shape and solidity, [springs] into being . . . from my cup of tea" (*Swann's Way*, 51). Each successful retrieval of an involuntary memory follows the same carefully delineated pattern: an initial mood of quiescence, the sensory trigger, the sudden and renewed sense of identity that accompanies the recollection, and finally the gradual unfolding of a memory that grows incrementally, through associations, into an intricate, reticular structure of images.[10]

Pondering over the new prominence given to involuntary memory, critics have suggested Proust's preference is motivated, above all, by aesthetic considerations: it enables him to organize his story around a striking revelation, a sort of epiphany.[11] But the overwhelming response this model of remembrance has received among scientists tells us something else. In focusing on the sudden, unexpected release of memory triggered by sensory cues, Proust emphasizes the physiological underpinnings of remembrance and changes the very definition of recollection. He describes how memories are, as it were, captured alive, at the frontier between a physiological and a mental experience—that is, in the very place defined by Oliver Sacks's "neurology of identity" (*Man Who*, viii). Proust's discovery calls for its own metaphor: he succeeded in capturing the moment when a bevy of butterflies flits through the mind, and not the butterflies pinned to a board, frozen and gathering dust. With this, recollection becomes the emergent, dynamic process that is sometimes observed in the neurologist's operating theater or in a clinical setting. When Wilder Penfield found out about the reminiscences that his epileptic patients experienced randomly under electrical stimulation or Sacks observed how L-Dopa and migraines could induce uncannily vivid recollection, they witnessed (albeit under different, namely pathological circumstances) a phenomenon that Proust had first analyzed in showing how memories were born, involuntarily "in response to the powerful mnemonic stimulus of certain words, sounds, scenes, and especially smells" (Sacks, *Man Who*, 151).[12] The revealing word in Sacks's description is "response," because it connects Proust's own epistemology to a current scientific context that is heavily vested in a behavioral model. With his stimulus-response model and his visionary idea that a mysterious chemistry produces remembrance, Proust opened new vistas for the scientific exploration of personal memory.[13]

Tilleul as Dopamine

In Proust's new description, autobiographical recollection is redefined, primarily, as the experience of past perceptions and sensations. This determines, in turn, a shift from a purely psychological conception to one that involves physiological and biochemical aspects. Proust's example doubly emphasizes the physiological origin of memory: in the role it ascribes to bodily sensations and by helping us imagine how the circulation of a certain chemical substance can produce mental images. With the image of "a piece of madeleine soaked in a decoction of lime-blossoms," the writer draws our attention to a (bio)chemical substance that "produces" memories and seems to predict recent findings concerning the chemical triggers of memory (Sacks, *Man Who,* 152).[14] It seems hardly surprising then that, in one of his articles on reminiscence, Oliver Sacks should be able to embrace in one breath the virtues of dopamine and those of Proustian tilleul. Recent research (often directly inspired by Proust) has shown that the cues provided by smell are the most likely to create strong reminiscences. In this light, it seems particularly apt that the first in Proust's series of memory experiments should bear on olfactive memory.[15]

The aroma of the past can be born, meanwhile, from different types of sensations, and the *Recherche* thus offers different recipes for the fabrication of memories. A sensation (a taste, smell, touch, sound, or, very rarely, striking sight) represents, in each case, the key ingredient, the trigger for a mnemonic process. Memory is born from a surprise encounter with a strong impression connected to some material prop: objects of the outer world provoke such mnemonic experiences as are "contained" in the aroma of lime blossoms, the smell of lilac, the feel of starched cotton, the painful shock of a protruding paving-stone, the resounding note of a violin, the tingling of a spoon, the intense color of a sunset.[16] Proust's functional, almost mechanistic model of recollection, with its reliance on stimulus and response, helps us imagine what we mean when we say that we are "cued" into remembering an event or when we speak of memory prompts. But Proust is attentive as well to questions of retrieval. Not every encounter leads to as spectacular a memory as "Combray" and its immensely rich depiction of childhood scenes. Other encounters may produce a much smaller yield, but the patterning is consistent: autobiographical memory always emerges, for Proust, at the intersection between body and mind. Sometimes what looks like a mnemonic cue presents itself to the mind, but nothing can be remembered. Proust excels at conveying, meanwhile, the inherently dynamic nature of recollection. Memories are born in the flash of an instant that summons up our perceptual, emotional, and cognitive abilities, and remembrance, in his description, is an active, creative process—each time a performance, each time a spectacular and unique mental event that effects a miraculous match between sensations, emotions, and images. A physical occurrence determines a mental process; a sensation prompts the mind to produce, through associations, a scene that is registered as a memory. In emphasizing the somatic underpinnings of memory processes, Proust's description seems to anticipate current scientific research that breaks the mold of a Cartesian conception: in his theory, memory occurs somewhere between body and mind.[17]

What Proust saw as well, anticipating later discoveries, is that memory is not a mimetic exercise, but rather a dynamic performance—as Gerald Edelman warns us when he summons up systems that are not merely physiological and thus must be seen as an "ability to repeat a performance."[18] Indeed, by singling out involuntary memory, Proust marks a shift from the older notions of memory as an archive, where memories are stored away to be retrieved at will.[19] In his conception, the mind and the intelligence alone do not give us access to the lived experience of the past: this "real" past is founded on emotion, summoned up through the shock of an impression that sets into motion the work of imaginative construction. By contrast, the images of the past that we cull in a voluntary fashion (from our "stored memories") are not really memories for Proust: like ideas or facts, they are part of our intelligence of the world—but a poor and pale rendering of our past experience.[20] Whenever we rehearse a memory beyond that first involuntary encounter, when we dwell, that is, on "the memory of a memory," we are no longer rememberers, just the historians of our past. Not so, however, when we summon up the past on the promptings of our bodies; there we seem to become newly aware of experience.[21]

A new figure has come into prominence, meanwhile: that of the architect responsible for the mnemonic construction. We do not seek the past, Proust thus insists, we create it. Describing the rememberer's task, he emphatically readjusts his vocabulary and replaces *chercher* (seek) by *créer* (create):

> I put down the cup and examine my own mind. It alone can discover the truth. But how? What an abyss of uncertainty, whenever the mind feels overtaken by itself; when it, the seeker, is at the same time the dark region through which it must go seeking and where all its equipment will avail it nothing. Seek? More than that: create. It is face to face with something that does not yet exist, to which it alone can give reality and substance, which it alone can bring into the light of day. (*Swann's Way*, 49)

The rediscovery of the term *rememberer* to label "the person who does the remembering," by the cognitive psychologist Endel Tulving, highlights the subject's active implication in the mnemonic process; so does Proust's insistence, in his first presentation of involuntary recollection, that memories are the dynamic creation of the remembering mind and not merely a matter of retrieval. In his view, memories are just not "found"—they exist thanks to the subject's active implication in the creative process that gives rise to the mnemonic scene. His *Recherche* thus presents, in the guise of its hero, a striking embodiment of a rememberer. We see him pore over a cup of tilleul, dip his spoon repeatedly to indulge in this potion's evocative aroma and analyze its special chemistry; he freezes at the corner of a Parisian street, disregarding the rain, to inhale the fragrance of the invisible lilacs of his childhood; he repeats again, as in a kind of cinematic playback, the step where his foot hit the stone and took him back to Venice; he lies in bed and covers reams of paper in a frenzied desire not to lose sight of his visions of a past and to say to others, his readers, "I remember." Proust's remembering subject seems in turn devoted, enthralled, fascinated, and sustained by the exploration of his past. He represents, in other words, a histrionic, artistically crafted version of the human figure that has come into prominence in studies of autobiographical memory.

At the same time, in highlighting the active, creative role of the remembering subject, Proust moves beyond a physiological/psychological approach of memory toward an existential/philosophical one. But he also, unwittingly, undermines the categorization of memory that he seemed so keen on establishing. Because creation assumes an intention and because involuntary memory depends on the rememberer's creative, active "intervention" in what looked at first like a mechanical process, it follows that the distinction between involuntary and voluntary memory begins to fade. Contrary to what Proust himself professed, the essence of Proustian memory may well lie beyond his notion of a *mémoire involontaire*, as can be seen in the first pages of his work.

Awakenings

The *Recherche* begins with a memory experiment centered on an experience of amnesia, which leads to a crucial discovery concerning the relation between memory, consciousness, and biography. Analyzing the awakening of his rememberer, Proust charts the progress of a subject who first emerges from his sleep like a man with a "lacuna of forgetting all around him," but gradually gathers enough memories to resume the biographical thread of his life.[22] Under the cover of this first scene, Proust defines in one gesture two distinctive stories that are both of crucial significance for his study of auto-biographical memory: one story is biographical in essence (it sets up the defining, beginning elements of the rememberer's experience), the other is philosophical and scientific (it documents the emergence of subjectivity and consciousness that memory enables). I focus here on the second of these stories, because it further defines Proust's contribution to memory studies and because it strikingly anticipates current neurological research on the self and memory. Watching the awakening of Proust's experimental subject—as he removes, one after the other, the thick blankets of oblivion that sleep had thrown over him—we are led to understand how closely the return to consciousness is linked to remembrance.

What normally happens to us in an instant on awakening—the realignment of our self into a present identity—is unpacked in a description that covers several pages. Leaving the remnants of his dreams behind him, the rememberer comes to awareness in sifting, reconstructing, organizing the images that flit in and out of his mind.[23] Enmeshed as he is amid a kaleidoscopic multitude of mental pictures (a blend of perceptions, dreams, and memories), he must "travel" through layer upon layer of images in an effort to find their context. Each of these hypnagogic images (as these images that arise fleetingly in between waking and sleeping are sometimes called) must be placed within a scene, a scene that in turn must be assigned to the present or the past and then itself fits into an emerging biographical narrative. Memory binds the threads together: it gathers the inchoate, whimsical, and fragmentary images of the awakening mind into scenes that speak of the rememberer's experience, past or present. The rememberer is, like the spider, a master weaver: he spins images into solid structures or scenes that circumscribe a mental space that enables him to capture that most elusive of preys—a self. Morning, night, late afternoon; Paris, Combray, Balbec, Doncières; door, table, window, bed (and which bed?): by reconnecting images and scenes to times and places, he is able to bridge the gaps in consciousness created by sleep.

Memory, we thus learn, enables consciousness. The two faculties go in a circle, and constantly interact: memory needs consciousness, just as consciousness relies on memory. "Not only is it impossible to have memory without consciousness, but equally it is impossible to have anything like a fully developed consciousness without memory," writes the philosopher John Searle in response to recent research on the mind (180). Proust's presentation vividly evokes this intertwining: the birth of his hero through this awakening is the founding moment of the first-person narrative that is the *Recherche*. The making of consciousness as the stitching together of mnemonic scenes sets the paradigm for his fiction. With the maxim "a man who is asleep holds in a circle the thread of the hours, of the succession of years and worlds," Proust thus sets the stage for the unfolding drama of a human existence that is crucially dependent on the faculty of remembrance, for on waking up, this subject must in an instant assume the task of "reading" or deciphering *(lire)* his bearings, his position in the world (*Swann's Way*, 5; translation amended). Our conscious existence is thus woven of one same thread, invisible in sleep, but activated on waking—and that thread is memory, which produces a narrative of the self.

In this scene too, images of the past arise in connection with bodily sensations, confirming that for Proust unconscious or "involuntary" physical events are at the root of autobiographical remembrance. However, the external promptings that trigger involuntary memory have been replaced by sensations that arise from within.[24] A shoulder, an arm, a leg: different parts of the rememberer's body, endowed each with a distinctive sensation, provide him with a first map of past experiences. A "body memory" (Proust calls it *la mémoire du corps*) cues the mind into recollection. It is, however, by reassigning each image to the proper category and scene that the waking subject will eventually "find himself"—that is, he will know who he is and where he is. "I remember, therefore I am," Proust thus tells us, in effect, in his rich demonstration of how the remembering subject finds again and again the necessary moorings that reconnect him to his biography and his identity.

The scene that Proust describes here has literary antecedents: Montaigne and Rousseau both document a return of consciousness, an awakening following an accident in which they demonstrate how memory connects a subject emerging from unconsciousness to the threads of a bodily and mental existence.[25] But Proust's description also looks ahead, toward the kinds of analyses that bear on the "neurology of identity" and have been developed by Oliver Sacks, and after him by Israel Rosenfield and Antonio Damasio. The complex and bewildering combination of impressions (as Proust calls them) or recollections, sensations, and perceptions (as they look to us) presented in this awakening are a perfect instance of Rosenfield's thesis that consciousness arises from "the dynamic interrelations of the past, the present, and the body image" (84). Proust's ideas about consciousness also show an uncanny likeness to the theory Damasio developed in the quest for a neurological definition of consciousness. We cannot experience "extended consciousness," the latter writes, if we are not able to "hold active, simultaneously and for a substantial amount of time, the many images whose collection defines the autobiographical self and the images which define the object" (*Feeling*, 198). To hold these images in mind, to arrange them into a scene, amounts to remembering, and, in so remembering, we become conscious and acquire, as Proust writes, borrowing a term from Jean-Jacques Rousseau, "the sentiment of existence."[26]

Only through memory can the subject answer the questions that assail him or her on awaking (most often fleetingly and subliminally), questions that are, in Antonio Damasio's words: "Where am I? What am I doing here? How did I come here? What am I supposed to be doing here?" (*Feeling*, 203). With his own questioning, Proust's rememberer crosses paths, in a revealing fashion, with one of Damasio's patients, a woman who experiences transient global amnesia during migraines and whose case is featured in *The Feeling of What Happens*.[27] Her diary (an unedited report of an episode of amnesia that hampers autobiographical recollection to the point where, for a moment, she cannot even "retrieve her own name") reveals a state of mind akin to that of Proust's awakening rememberer. She too strives to situate herself in time and space and to reconnect to the thread of her conscious existence and identity. But whereas in his case, images and perceptions seem to fall almost instantaneously into recognizable scenes, it takes this young woman more than an hour until she can regain her mooring. Were she to fail in her mission, she would not know what time, what place, what identity she inhabits and would remain the prisoner of an essentially physiological and mechanically driven existence. In spite of obvious stylistic differences in their accounts and of different etiologies (there is no evidence of a pathology in Proust), the rememberer and Damasio's patient face the same challenge, namely the need to overcome amnesia in order to maintain a sense of the self.[28] In the absence of remembrance, we face our present like a puzzle: "the here and now is simply incomprehensible," concludes Damasio, and "our sense of identity is under serious threat" (203–24). While every awakening represents a search for consciousness, it is only because of our capacity to "carve" autobiographical memories out of the images that pass through the awakening mind that we can fully regain a sense of our identity.

Proust himself is so profoundly interested in this issue that he revisits it several times in his book. A later version of the same experiment, which documents how the rememberer "comes to earth suddenly at the point of awakening," provides another vivid illustration of memory's sway over our subjective life. In spite of its metaphors, or perhaps because of them, Proust's description reads almost like a clinical case-study:

Then from those profound slumbers we awake in a dawn, not knowing who we are, being nobody, newly born, ready for anything, the brain emptied of that past which was life until then. And perhaps it is more wonderful still when our landing at the waking-point is abrupt and the thoughts of our sleep, hidden by a cloak of oblivion, have no time to return to us gradually, before sleep ceases. Then, from the black storm through which we seem to have passed (but we do not even say *we*), we emerge prostrate, without a thought, as *we* that is void of content. What hammer-blow has the person or thing that is lying here received to make it unconscious of everything, stupefied until the moment when memory, flooding back, restores to it consciousness or personality? (*Cities of the Plain*, 1014)

Proust's thesis deserves to be repeated: "memory," he tells us here, "restores consciousness and personality" for a subject, who, without it, is at sea: who on waking up comes out from a "black storm." Is it possible that Oliver Sacks, by all appearances a fine connoisseur of Proust's work, had this passage in mind when he dubbed one of his amnesiac patients "the Lost Mariner"? Suffering from short- as well as long-term amnesia, his mariner can neither form new memories nor retrieve past mnemonic scenes: "He is, as it were . . . isolated in a single moment of being, with a moat or lacuna of forgetting all around him. . . . He is a man without a past (or future), stuck in a constantly changing, meaningless moment" (*Man Who,* 29). In this case, amnesia is not a transient phenomenon but the result of a neurological degeneration often seen in patients who suffer from Korsakoff's syndrome, and it is so severe as to lead to a gradual but dramatic disintegration of his consciousness and personality. The Mariner has lost all bearings and never fully awakens from a confused state in which he merely drifts across a sea of impressions and sensations, unable to anchor himself in time, in space, as well as in his social and his inner world. Such radical amnesia makes him totally unsuited for practical living. He cannot remember ever having met someone before, even his closest relatives or the doctor, and spends his social life faking familiarity and acquaintance with people who are strangers to him. As to relating to himself, he lives under erasure, with not a thread of his biography in mind. Worse even, when asked to keep a diary as a help toward reconstructing his personal story, he is confronted every new day with handwriting (his own) that he cannot identify. The failure of memory is so radical for this patient that the rememberer's best prop—writing—fails him.[29]

The idea that writing can help us keep trace of the past is central to Proust's *Recherche,* but it occurs at a higher, figurative level. In these first pages, for instance, the rememberer is not literally putting pen to paper; however, through a detailed narration in the first person he creates what is his essence, a script of his coming into consciousness. It may have seemed as if this awakening (especially when compared to a case study such as the Lost Mariner's) were merely to confirm Hume's thesis about identity's dependence on memory. (For Hume, life without memory is "nothing but a bundle or collection of different sensations, succeeding one another with inconceivable rapidity, and in a perpetual flux and movement.")[30] But the centrality of writing in the *Recherche* suggests something else: in merging together the writer's and the rememberer's fate, Proust highlights the narrative aspects of personal remembrance. The narrative continuities that memory provides are, for him, indistinguishable from something that, he, as a writer, knows only too well, namely a first-person voice and a style. Whereas Hume assumed the presence of memory as a natural faculty, for Proust it has become a textual and aesthetic construct. It is thus through writing our past (either literally or metaphorically) that we are able to establish the subjective foundations of our existence. As we write-remember our lives, we are able to find, or rather to find again and again (for consciousness is a continuous process except for when we sleep), who we are, in body and in mind.

Meanwhile, a clever stylistic sleight of hand enables Proust to turn the birth of his hero into a programmatic philosophical moment endowed with a universal significance. "Longtemps, je me suis couché de bonne heure": Proust's skillful choice of verbal tense in his famous first sentence of the *Recherche* (a *passé composé* that captures simultaneously the narration of an event and the description of a state) casts the scene in the mode of a repeated process.[31] It is not merely once, but many times that the Proustian narrator has turned these nocturnal awakenings into situations for remembrance, and in this way awakenings are folded into ordinary living. "Je passais la plus grande partie de la nuit à me rappeler" (I would spend the best part of the night remembering), "je restais souvent jusqu'au matin à songer au temps de Combray" (I would often muse over the times in Combray until the morning) are statements that define a sustained investigation into autobiographical recollection, but just as importantly, they make of awakenings a habit, an ordinary condition of our conscious living. They show how profoundly memory is inscribed in our being. Each time we awake and remember, we find our anchoring in time and in space, and resume the narrative thread of our life that defines our identity. Here, the philosophical core of Proust's demonstration comes very close to Hume's fundamental claim that memory is what gives us an identity. Thanks to memory, a multiplicity of sensations (a shoulder that turns, an arm that was asleep, a leg that creates sensual pleasure), woven into the flow of mental impressions that define our consciousness, can be organized into scenes whose succession defines our biography.

Such is the miraculous power of memory that it enables us, at every instant of our waking life, to skip over the abysses of nothingness to resume a sense of identity and of our own existence. Autobiographical recollection becomes then the heartbeat of our mental life: such ceaseless regathering of our perceptions as is afforded through memory provides the crucial narrative thread of our conscious life and identity.[32] Given such premises, it is no exaggeration to claim that in his monumental work, Proust represents the richest record of a stream of consciousness or a spectacular example of a biography—a personal biography built as one vast, intricate, and never-ceasing memory-performance born and created from the rememberer's bed. Here, "the man who . . . holds in a circle the thread of the hours, of the succession of years and worlds" and who, on awakening, weaves his memories with the threads gathered from the depths of his physiological existence becomes naturally a writer, able to capture in his description both the startling pictures and the subtle patterns of our minds (*Swann's Way*, 5; translation amended). Proust's research seems to have deep affinities with Charles Sherrington's idea that "the mind [is] 'an enchanted loom,' weaving ever-changing yet always meaningful patterns—weaving, in effect, patterns of meaning."[33]

Proustian Memory

In demonstrating how closely memory and consciousness are intertwined, Proust establishes the philosophical premises of an investigation focused on the existential dimensions of recollection at the expense of its practical and mundane aspects. It is the quality of certain memory experiences that interests him, and not the indiscriminate quantity of things that a mind can remember (the facts, the skills, the number of events). Remembering, for Proust, defines a way of being in the world; it is what shapes human experience. Waging a battle against amnesia and confusion, and collecting rich samples of personal recollection, the Proustian subject is engaged in a type of mental activity that occupies everyone of us, provided our brains and minds are healthy: he produces a story, or rather multiple stories—each of them a memory—that tell of his encounters with the world. While prominence is given in the *Recherche* to unexpected cues born from the pinprick of a sensation, it remains true that the emergence of a memory scene always depends on the rememberer's active, willful desire to pursue, along a path of associations, the work of construction that leads to a mnemonic scene. To use a familiar metaphor: autobiographical moments "don't just pop up on the screen," they result from a conscious, voluntary act in which the rememberer is actively engaged. Ultimately, the experiment of the tilleul and madeleine and that of the awakening yield similar findings: they reveal, above all, how richly, how consistently we work at gathering impressions, images, and feelings to weave them into memories. While the blurring of the distinction between voluntary and involuntary memory might explain why Proust's categorization never really found its way into science, it also suggests that the interest of defining something called "involuntary memory" may have been essentially heuristic.[34] This imperfect theory enabled a conceptual leap that put a form of memory on the map of memory studies: Proustian memory. Proustian memory is inherently subjective, qualitative as well as dynamic, and it gives prominence to the person who does the remembering.

In Proust's stringent definition, personal remembrance is absolutely individual and unique, for each memory "happens" to a singular body endowed with a singular history.[35] *Petites madeleines* are manufactured by the hundreds in Illiers/Combray, and bags of tilleul, filled with an aromatic mixture of pale dried flowers and leaves, are sold at every counter, but, try as we may, we will never fully inhabit the Proustian past described in the *Recherche*. Similarly, the scene of awakening demonstrates how deeply our memories are connected to our personal, physical experiences of the times and places we inhabit. Indeed, when it comes to autobiographical recollection, *every body* tells a very different story. Sacks uses the phrase "Proustian physiology" to explain that a unique personal narrative, biographical in nature, is contained in every rememberer's body (*Man Who*, 147). Proust's presentations of autobiographical memories are also striking examples of a type of "inner, first person, qualitative phenomenon," which, according to the philosopher John Searle, defines every aspect of our consciousness (5). Quipping on Proust's famous statement that "style is a question of vision," we might indeed say that memory is, in his theory, truly a question of subjective vision, namely of how the world appears or "feels" to each of us. Here Proustian remembrance becomes a purely qualitative state of a kind that philosophers define as qualia.[36] This explains why it is so imperative that the rememberer's world be painted in its "true colors"—that is, with as many of its phenomenal features as can possibly be represented.

Proustian memory is thus a creative, an inspired act that is inconceivable outside of its author's imaginative involvement: the first cue provides merely the first note of a vast symphonic composition. You remember because you smell a whiff of perfume, overhear a melody, touch unawares an object with your hand, catch a view of a bloodshot sunset, or just hear an evocative word. Or you remember because, oblivious of where you are or half-awake, you linger over an image seemingly born from your dreams. Such small pinpricks of impressions and sensations are what fuels the creative work of remembrance that keeps us alive, biographically and consciously. The first vague intimation of a déjà vu, an increasing awareness of the prompt that set your mind racing, and then, at last, the marvelous work of construction that creates the mnemonic scene: this is how memory works for Proust. The remembered content and the rememberer are inextricably linked, and the memory is the single, singular product of a subjective experience. One can imagine that multiplication tables can exist independently of "me," since they will be remembered collectively as shared conceptual abstractions. The skill of riding a bicycle does not depend on me; it can be ridden, that bicycle, indifferently by another.[37] But without the words or thoughts of a recollecting subject, of the *rememberer,* the Proustian memory, the village square of Combray, for instance—as it was felt to be, in all its visual, auditory, atmospheric singularity on a certain morning, by a young child— would not exist.

Surely, no algorithm, no biochemical formula however complex, and not even a Turing machine could capture so complex a mental event, especially given the richness of its phenomenal and emotional underpinnings.[38] This is why, although it is clearly defined in terms of stimulus and response and seems to invite a structural approach, Proustian memory is of no interest to scientists solely vested in functional or reductionist models of the mind. Indeed, as an inherently singular, subjective, and thus nonrepeatable mental event, Proustian memory is hardly conducive to scientific research based on direct empirical observation of phenomena and dependent on repeatable protocols and rigorous controls. In other scientific quarters, it seems, however, that the elusive nature of Proustian memory is not an obstacle but rather a source of inspiration.

Oliver Sacks practices a science that demands that formal models be confronted with personal, physiological experiences. Gerald Edelman, to whom we owe groundbreaking work at the cusp between biological and philosophical theories of the mind, expresses a clear wish for a science that would capture the "first person matter" that defines our consciousness and memory.[39] More recently, as a new wave of research (heralded by, among others, Antonio Damasio and Joseph LeDoux) explores how emotions participate in the brain's functioning, the felt properties of mental phenomena have come to the fore. In these several domains—where the search for models necessarily moves beyond issues of quantification, structures, or algorithms and takes into account the experiential aspects of mental phenomena—Proustian memory invites further research. Such seems to be the case for Oliver Sacks, who in *The Man Who Mistook His Wife for a Hat* is in search of a clinical vision of memory founded on "the relation of physiological processes to biography" (viii).

It is easy to see how the splendidly, almost arrogantly personal memories described at length in the *Recherche* could serve a scientist drawn toward the intimate and singular aspects of the mind's adventures. Proust's descriptions can indeed be read as case histories or "clinical tales" (as Sacks calls the scientific records that found his neurology of identity), and they invite the kind of analysis practiced in neurology or cognitive psychology—an analysis developed inductively around what are often extraordinary cases.[40] Next to research that invokes "schemata, programmes, algorithms," there is a need for another type of insight that helps us grasp what remembrance feels like, a need that Proust's descriptions seem to answer for Sacks (147). Who better than a writer could find the words to describe the specific texture of a memory? Who has more of an ability to represent the "scenic" or "melodic" aspects of remembrance? Proustian physiology enables us to "better understand the essentially personal, Proustian nature of reminiscence, of the mind, of life," Sacks concludes, intimating that for him, Proust's model of personal recollection captures a phenomenon that lies at the heart of our mental life (147).

But Proustian memory represents more than an intellectual discovery; it is also deeply connected to an emotional state—typically (but not always) summed up as an "exquisite pleasure."[41] Most descriptions of Proustian memory call to mind the evocative phrase of Goethe's version of the Faustian wager against mortality: "Verweile doch du bist so schön" (Stay a while, you are so beautiful). They could also be described in the vocabulary of Virginia Woolf as "ecstasies" or "raptures" ("A Sketch," 65–66). Even Sacks's patients, who experience vivid Proustian memories during epileptic seizures, can be overwhelmed by pleasure upon the discovery of a past they thought they had lost. The neurologist writes about Mrs. O'C., for instance, that "the feeling she had was . . . a trembling, profound and poignant joy" (143).[42] In the rapture provoked by reminiscence, Proust finds intimations of immortality; Sacks's patients, meanwhile, would rather endure again the physiological discomforts of a prolonged seizure than give up the privilege of revisiting scenes of their childhood.[43] In the latter's account, Mrs. O'C.'s words seem particularly evocative: "it was, as she said, like the opening of a door—a door which had been stubbornly closed all her life." This rich figure helps us see at once the complex feeling that accompanies remembrance: a combination of anticipation and curiosity, followed by the satisfaction associated with the recovery of something that we thought we had lost forever or that seemed inaccessible. Clearly, the pleasures of Proustian memory involve cognition as well as emotion; they satisfy a nostalgic impulse (the desire to return to certain moments of our earlier existence) as well as a need for mental stimulation or excitement (Proustian memory always comes as a surprise).[44] But it is only by looking more closely at Proust's conception of recollection that we will become aware of another aspect of personal remembrance, an aspect merely intimated by Sacks when he attributes scenic or melodic qualities to Proustian remembrance. On opening that door the Proustian rememberer is given access to a universe of experience that offers itself like a work of art—her work of art.

A Whirling Medley of Stirred-up Colors . . .

Imagine living in a world that is merely black and white, and suddenly finding a secret door that opens onto a landscape richly colored in all kinds of hues. What a pleasure, what a discovery, what a difference! A transition from a "neutral glow" to a "whirling medley of stirred-up colours" is how Proust's rememberer describes the unfolding of first involuntary memory (49). The miraculous advent of a forgotten memory is greeted with the same deep emotion that greets a painting or any other human creation that provokes in us, mysteriously, the recognition of an elusive quality variously defined as beauty, vividness, or color. There lies, in this figure, an implicit invitation to consider another central dimension of remembrance, namely its aesthetic dimension. As it embraces in one "colorful" scene our somatosensory, our cognitive, and our emotional faculties, Proustian memory naturally, spontaneously elicits the rich combination of feelings that works of art can arouse. Memory invokes more than merely our desire for cognition, our intellectual abilities, and our emotions—it summons up all these features at once, in and around a mental image that is the rememberer's work of art.[45] Oliver Sacks suggests as much when he speaks of the "scenic" or "melodic" qualities of Proustian memory. He, however, seems to conceive of these aesthetic dimensions as if they were an emergent property of mnemonic construction—as some elusive quality of memory that becomes apparent when all physiological and formal analyses have been exhausted. I want to argue, on the contrary, that these scenic or "musical" features constitute the very foundation of a mnemonic experience: memory, I believe, is a dynamic process that *emerges from* and *is sustained by* an aesthetic impulse; it is creative in the fullest sense of the term. This discovery assumes, in turn, that a full investigation into the phenomenon of Proustian memory needs to take into account the way each of its representations is staged (as a scene) and patterned (as a melody)—it demands, in short, that we conceive of a poetics of personal memory. What I mean by a "poetics" of memory should become clear over the course of this book.

A tilleul and madeleine, the gossip of Combray and bubbles around water plants, the smell of lilac at a street corner or romance-filled melodies by a fictive composer—each memory in Proust's text is so idiosyncratic and deeply embedded in a personal history that it resists the kinds of generalizations and abstractions that science demands. How can we, then, give universal significance to an experience that is, by definition, among the most subjective and most singular we can imagine? Friedrich Hegel's reflections on aesthetics and history help us make sense of this paradox. Hegel recognized in lyrical poetry the genre that is predestined to give expression to human interiority and subjectivity through its reliance on images that hold a universal appeal.[46] Proustian memory is similarly positioned at the cusp between the most personal and yet the most universal of experiences—that of our being in the world and inhabiting as a self what are its multifarious events and determinations. In embodying the very singularity of human experience and giving it a universal significance, Proustian memory is an aesthetic gesture and a poetic experience in the deepest sense, in that it responds to a need to communicate the singularity of experience at the heart of human existence. Whenever I say, "I remember" and begin to sketch out a Proustian memory, I speak of an experience in which emotion and intellect, body and mind are enlisted together to sing, as it were, of the most private of events—a spot in time when a past moment is brought to life with all the felt properties, the colors, the aroma that only I, you, Mrs. O'C., or Proust's rememberer ever knew. The meaning of this physiological and mental feat defined as personal remembrance is universal, even though its content is irreducibly singular and personal.

It remains true, nevertheless, that the visibility and significance given to different types of memory may vary across cultures, so that Proustian memory may well seem to be a historically and culturally bound phenomenon. But the differences in weight or meaning ascribed to it do not put into question its existence. There may be times or cultures that allow little room for such minute and all too personal (or even seemingly narcissistic) aesthetic experiences, but this would not deny their existence. They would still occur, but perhaps not on quite the same expansive scale that is their trademark in Proust. In a practically oriented existence, Proustian memories are likely to be brushed away as small or irrelevant intellectual or sentimental matter.[47] It surely takes a strong vocation, aesthetic-scientific or clinical, to make of the search for personal remembrance a lifetime project. It may take someone as afraid of loss and death as Proust or someone as curious about the mind and caring about his patients as Sacks. However, the fact that the figure of the rememberer has come into such prominence in the last quarter of the century also suggests that there is something deeply appealing and deeply interesting in a model of remembrance—Proustian memory—that has shifted the emphasis from purely cognitive and mechanistic issues to a realm where the study of mind and brain embraces psychological as well as, ultimately, aesthetic issues.

For a while now, the time has seemed ripe for a rereading, a rediscovery of Proust in terms of his contribution to the science of memory. I take to witness the number of times scientists of the mind or brain have reached, in recent years, for strong metaphors that might convey their own sense that personal remembrance shares some of its qualities with artistic production. Here are just a few examples. In *The Feeling of What Happens,* Damasio writes that extended consciousness is like a "movie-in-the-brain," and core consciousness like (in the words of T. S. Eliot) the "music heard so deeply that it is not heard at all" (172). Sacks, as we know, takes his analogies from the visual arts and from music and relates them to modern technologies for the reproduction of images or sound. "What is the final form, the natural form, of our life's repertoire?" he wonders, enlisting the images of a "film or record, played on the brain's film projector or phonograph" as metaphors for the patterning that sustains our autobiographical memories (146). But writers too offer their share of metaphors to describe remembrance. In the late 1930s, Virginia Woolf consistently argues that remembering is like painting; she also suggests that it is akin to plugging a radiolike device into the wall: a matter of getting on a wavelength that enables us to "listen in to the past" ("A Sketch," 67). Her metaphor may have been more accurate, phenomenologically speaking, than she ever imagined: two of Sacks's patients, Mrs. O'C. and Mrs. O'M., confess to first checking their radios when they heard melodies of their past in their heads. We indeed live in a time when the well-known analogies that cognitive scientists have drawn between minds and computers are in question, and until an algorithm is found that can describe what happens when we remember, we may have to trust the writer's metaphors.

When science, in the words of Jacob Bronowski, "looks for a language which mimics or mirrors the structures of reality," it must often first rely on descriptions that are far removed from the elegant symbolic abstractions that physicists or mathematicians like to develop (47). But in the end, he argues, it is the quality of the "imaginative construction that we put into the laws of nature" that matters most (61). In keeping with such a view, this survey of Proustian memory suggests that a literary approach can serve the purposes of science—not *in spite of* its metaphors, but rather, *because of* them. In reading *A la Recherche du temps perdu* as a treatise of memory we encounter an exceptionally rich imaginative construction of the phenomenon of human recollection. That this construction can be of considerable relevance for a science of memory has been amply demonstrated. There is perhaps no better place to begin to understand what we mean when we say, in common parlance, that we have just felt a "whiff of the past" than to ponder over Proust's well-known experiment: on a dull and ordinary morning, take a spoonful of tilleul, dip into it a little piece of madeleine, observe then the amazing, miraculous power of memory. Not only does it give you the aroma of the past, it brings a self to life in an experience that is at once deeply emotional, intellectual, and aesthetic. We need Proustian memory, the study of amnesia has revealed, because without it, there is no consciousness and no subjectivity; without it, we merely drift in a sea of sensations and unanchored images. Meanwhile, a broader ethnographic view (which would note not only the topicality of Proustian memory, but also our anxious fascination with stories of memory loss in novels or on the screen, and even our growing anxiety about the ravages of Alzheimer's disease) suggests that we live in a time and in places where, more than ever perhaps, we need the reassurance of a form of remembrance that seems to fill us with the sensations of a felt, a palpable reality. What we need perhaps above all is the belief, which Proustian memory embodies, that our personal past cannot get lost amid the purely visual, disembodied images that proliferate on screens. A deep irony, however, underlies such a desire: we seem to have found our anchor as subjects in what is, after all, no more than the careful yet fragile construction of a mental picture. While, like Proust's rememberer, we gather the loose threads of our otherwise inchoate, whimsical, and fragmentary existence into the semblance of a narrative, we live by what is, essentially, a scene and a melody.

2 • Painting the Past: Virginia Woolf's Memory Images

"Science," Gerald Edelman reflects in *Bright Air, Brilliant Fire*, "is concerned with the formal correlations of properties, and with the development of theoretical constructs that most parsimoniously and usefully describe all known aspects of that correlation, without exception" (138). However, the sheer bulk of *A la Recherche du temps perdu* offers a blatant demonstration of the fact that the "first-person matter" of autobiographical memory, if indulged in, will grow into one huge unwieldy monster of phenomenal data that defies analysis. The rememberer can be drawn toward a potentially ever-expanding profusion of material: not only is each image or scene an invitation to further detailing or description, but one memory invites others in its wake. In Proust's vivid metaphor, a first memory, like a paper clip that has been magnetized, will draw into its field a potentially endless sequence of other memories (*Le Temps retrouvé*, 3:716). The richest of histories emerges thus from the proliferation of first-person matter born from a tilleul and madeleine. However, Edelman warns us, "science fails for individual histories even though it may succeed in discerning what is common among twenty chronicles" (138). For a better perspective on autobiographical memory, we must, then, turn to a text that is a chronicle—a text that emphasizes observations at the expense of narrative and presents raw facts rather than interpretations.

Virginia Woolf's "A Sketch of the Past" is shaped like a chronicle centered on the depiction of memories and on the analysis of their creation. She started this project at the prodding of her sister, who urged her to keep a written trace of her personal memories lest she become as forgetful as Lady Strachey. Virginia responded to Vanessa's challenge with a free-flowing manuscript, on which she worked sporadically over two years and which she dropped a few weeks only before her death. Discarding her usual concerns about narrative structuring, Woolf merely juxtaposes short anecdotes about the past with a critical commentary and, occasionally, journal entries. This late work, which she did not revise toward publication, provides a raw, close, and exceptionally insightful record of her own experiments in remembrance. The journal entry of "2nd May" confirms the hazardous, exploratory nature of this project. It also reveals that this rememberer takes a keen interest in the phenomenon of recollection as such and in the representation of memory:

> I write the date, because I think that I have discovered a possible form for these notes. That is, to make them include the present—at least enough of the present to serve as platform to stand upon. I now, I then, come out in contrast. And further, this past is so much affected by the present moment. What I write today I should not write in a year's time. But I cannot work this out; it had better be left to chance. (75)

Woolf's memory experiment, we learn here, is designed in such a way as to produce an alignment between a remembering self and a remembered self, between "I now, I then." Writing becomes the instrument of a staged encounter between a present and a past self, an encounter connected to the emergence of vivid images that speak of memories.[1]

With Woolf's experiment, then, autobiographical memory is disinvested from the body and is removed from the sensory, physiological field to be located, once again, in the mind—or more properly speaking, in the imagination. In "A Sketch of the Past," memory cues, as we shall see, are generated internally by representations that are born from some inner vision.[2] While the experience of memory we owe to Proust is, as we saw, strongly correlated to bodily perceptions, Woolf takes us under a bell jar, where glass walls separate the inner and the outer world, and carves out a separate field of experience devoted to introspection. Under this bell jar, images grow into memories that can be studied in the sealed chamber of a mind.[3] In taking this inward turn, Woolf seems to have rejoined a traditional, classical line of investigation, which conceives of "recollection" as getting knowledge not from the external but from the internal world (Sorabji, 37). But is Woolf's description of memory really backward looking?

I want to argue here that, on the contrary, her description provides us with a fresh understanding of how memory images work at a time when, in the wake of phenomenological influences, images have come into the limelight again in scientific discussions of memory and consciousness.[4] Woolf richly illustrates the link between memory and the faculty of imagination, by letting us see how images enable her to build memory scenes. We have, of course, no other evidence for their existence than her words; for unlike neural patterns, which can be shown on a screen when a perception or a memory occurs, mental images escape our recording, measuring, or imaging devices. Devoid as they are of discernible physical substance, images give us no material proof of their existence.[5] They are also inherently personal and private: short of entering another person's body and history, we will never be able to see what she sees, feel what she feels.[6] Thus, we can only guess at what an image represents or "feels like" for another subject. But as she tells us in "A Sketch of the Past," Woolf believes she is specially gifted with the ability to trace or express, like a photographic plate, the images imprinted on her in the form of memories. Here is how she describes her skills, almost boasting:

> While I write this the light glows; an apple becomes a vivid green; I respond all through me: but how? Then a little owl [chatters] under my window. Again, I respond. Figuratively I could snapshot what I mean by some image; I am a porous vessel afloat on sensation; a sensitive plate exposed to invisible rays; and so on. (133)

In responding to what she sees and hears, Woolf commemorates what are here perceptual as well as aesthetic encounters with the outer word in the form of images. As a description of her mnemonic and literary undertaking, the statement "Figuratively I could snapshot what I mean by some image" is a key element of her analysis. Writers trade in representations; her words show how self-consciously Woolf has made of images her medium. Under a literary author's pen, the notion of "image" means something different from, but not necessarily irrelevant to, what scientists and philosophers mean when they use it. Being made of words, images in literature naturally differ in their substance from the "patterns" or "structures" deriving from sensory modalities that define images for scientists.[7] Nevertheless, for a modernist such as Woolf, these images are more than descriptive ornaments of an outer reality; they are deemed to give evidence of a mental life or a consciousness.[8] They become, in the writer's hands, a verbal approximation of what a memory "feels like." But in fact, whenever we want to share a memory with someone else, each of us must rely on language: we too, just like a writer, will look for the image that expresses what the memory "feels like." This is why Woolf's literary experiment can provide a particularly apt analogy for the phenomenon of remembering: it foregrounds the verbal, textual medium through which mnemonic images are known intersubjectively, as well as, possibly, intrasubjectively. Far from constituting an idiosyncratic mode of remembering, her literary images may well reveal certain paradigms of structure, the general features of a mental architecture that defines the activity of remembering. With Woolf, we can chart some of the first elements and principles of the construction of memory.

Woolf's Mental Time-Travel

The first images that spring from under Woolf's pen are "red and purple flowers on a black ground," and they are the gateway to a world of unique perceptions and sensations that belong to childhood. Unlike Proust's involuntary memories, they appear to be a pure product of the imagination:

> So without stopping to choose my way, in the sure and certain knowledge that it will find itself—or if not it will not matter—I begin: the first memory.
>
> This was of red and purple flowers on a black ground—my mother's dress: and she was sitting either in a train or in an omnibus, and I was on her lap. I therefore saw the flowers she was wearing very close; and can still see purple and red and blue, I think, against the black; they must have been anemones, I suppose. Perhaps we were going to St Ives; more probably, for from the slant of light it must have been evening, we were coming back to London. But it is more convenient artistically that we were going to St Ives, for that will lead to my other memory, which also seems to be my first memory. (64)

Woolf's unusual presentation takes us into the rememberer's mental workshop, where images of the past are assembled into a memory—that is, are fitted into a context and organized as a scene. These colorful flowers constitute the core of a gradually emerging scene drawn through the imagination (she seems to be scanning a picture) and by logical inference (following cognitive schemes).[9] They seem to correspond to what is seen by a very young child sitting on her mother's lap (several pages later she evokes the image of herself as a "baby, who can just distinguish a great blot of blue and purple on a black background," 79). The mother and the child, she thinks, are traveling on a train that, she surmises, takes them from St. Ives to London—for the picture gives the impression of motion, while the particular slant of the light evokes the evening and thus a return from the seaside resort. In the process of this narrative expansion, the flowers have sprouted an additional color: "[I] can still see purple and red and blue." They have also acquired a shape, which can be named tentatively: "they must have been anemones, I suppose." At this point it seems as if the writer has taken over for the rememberer, rearranging the memory in a way that is "more convenient artistically": the trip is now reversed, they are traveling toward St. Ives. But whatever minor readjustments are made, these scattered, unanchored images are made to coalesce in one scene, as a first autobiographical memory.[10] Meanwhile, the next memory, competing with the other in terms of priority and importance (it "also seems to be my first memory"), is introduced with a strong claim for its founding value: it is the "base" on which Woolf's life stands:

> If life has a base that it stands upon, if it is a bowl that one fills and fills and fills—then my bowl without a doubt stands upon this memory. It is of lying asleep, half awake, in bed in the nursery at St Ives. It is of hearing the waves breaking, one, two, one, two, and sending a splash of water over the beach; and then breaking, one, two, one, two, behind a yellow blind. It is of hearing the blind draw its little acorn across the floor as the wind blew the blind out. It is of lying and hearing this splash and seeing this light, and feeling, it is almost impossible that I should be here; of feeling the purest ecstasy I can conceive. (65)

A child lies in bed in the nursery and perceives the outside world as an overlay of noise and of light, from which she distinguishes the rhythmical sound of the waves and the blind's little "acorn" gliding on the floor.[11] A complex perceptual experience, rendered all the more present through the mimetic repetition of rhythm and sound (one-two, one-two), lies at the core of this memory. Sound upon sound, the waves lead to the acorn; for here too the impression is left to expand freely. Woolf's second description is built, like the first, around a central image. This time it is not merely visual, but combines proprioceptive, visual, aural, and kinetic aspects. This rich, layered picture of a memory reminds us, appropriately, that there are mental images for all of our senses: for what we see as well as touch, taste, smell, hear, feel in our bodies or feel as movement. Here again, meanwhile, an early scene of childhood emerges from the associative network of images. But even more clearly than before, the defining trait of this autobiographical memory is perceptual and aesthetic rather than historical. This is why it cannot be precisely situated in a time frame and ends up competing with the other "first memory."

In the end, the predominant note in the orchestration of this memory is not cognitive; it evokes, rather, sensations and affects. This discovery invites us, then, to revise Woolf's conception of memory: in this case, recollection is not a reflexive encounter with the self, between "I now" and "I then." On the contrary, as Woolf herself understands, the self can be submerged by, subsumed under, the power of an impression. "I am hardly aware of myself, but only of the sensation," she writes, and adds, "I am only the container of the feeling of ecstasy, of the feeling of rapture" (67). The memory project is sustained, it seems, by sensory intensities or continuities in sentience that these images render palpable. Contrary to appearances, Woolf's memory watching is not a neutral, disinterested activity; as we have just seen, it is fueled by a combination of intellectual, affective, and aesthetic conditions. Remembrance is thus inextricably linked with the pleasure of certain mental impressions—seeing a scene emerge from a few blots of color or losing oneself in re-created sensations. But this means, in turn, that Woolf's experiment is shaped by underlying intentions or desires and that her project obeys a certain design. What is implied by the notion of a "design" is best understood if we turn to Woolf's own metaphor for remembering: that of painting.

The Search for Childhood Memories

The road to memory lies, for Woolf, in the free association of colored images: as we saw with the first of her memories, the first scene emerges from what were originally blots of color.[12] She herself identifies remembering with picture making: the metaphor describes her search for early impressions ("if I were a painter, I should paint these first impressions in pale yellow, silver, and green," 66) or her desire to evoke the image of her long-defunct mother ("one would have to be an artist. It would be as difficult to do that, as it should be done, as to paint a Cézanne," 85). Thus, Woolf's search for vivid memories is embedded in a literary form of experimentation that aims for a style that must enable her to paint the past. "I dream," she adds later; "I make up pictures of a summer afternoon" (87).

Here is, meanwhile, one of the most striking representations of a memory in "A Sketch of the Past." It seems born from Woolf's desire to emulate a painter (and perhaps from a desire to impress her sister the painter):

> If I were a painter I should paint these first impressions in pale yellow, silver, and green. There was the pale yellow blind; the green sea: and the silver of the passion flowers. I should make a picture that was globular: semi-transparent. I should make a picture of curved petals: of shells; of things that were semi-transparent; I should make curved shapes, showing the light through, but not giving a clear outline. Everything would be large and dim; and what was seen would at the same time be heard; sounds would come through this petal or leaf—sounds indistinguishable from sights. Sound and sight seem to make equal parts of these first impressions. When I think of the early morning in bed I also hear the caw of rooks falling from a great height. (66)

The text of Woolf's early memories grants us access to a universe of sensory perceptions "in the making," a universe that preexists a more elaborate world, in which a knowing, thinking subject would have organized the images into recognizable categories. Woolf's attempt to introduce sound into the picture reveals her overall desire for a synesthetic, holistic impression of the past. But above all, it is the "emergent" quality of the representation that is the most striking. A painterly style—not that of a realist, but rather of a modern expressionist painter—creates a universe endowed with phenomenal features that are initially devoid of clearly defined referential qualities.[13] Perhaps it is this ability to experience (or mime?) perceptions that have an original freshness that reassures Woolf of her success: these must be her first memories. For doesn't the very crudeness of these images guarantee that the impressions lie buried deep in her consciousness, in a place close to her infancy?

Other stylistic resources contribute to the overall impression that the past being revived in these pages of "A Sketch of the Past" is long gone. This is the case when Woolf evokes primitive sensations and a body saturated with sensory and perceptual pleasures. There are times indeed—times of "ecstasy" or "rapture"—when immersion in the sensual intensities is so complete that the rememberer loses a sense of the present and of a self. Woolf herself notes, in impromptu fashion, that she can then enter a field of sensation so powerful that she is merely "the container of a feeling." Here, the defining lines of her conscious recollecting self seem to vanish; so do the boundaries between the inner and outer world. Woolf's description evokes the contours of a primitive subjective entity that is merely the receptacle of sensory input. A self (but can it even be called a self?) emerges that seems boundless and shapeless: what fills it and gives it an identity are the remembered, re-created sensations.

Woolf's third example of a "colour-and-sound" memory, which she describes as "much more robust" and "highly sensual" (this time it includes smells as well), confirms this impression:

> The gardens gave off a murmur of bees; the apples were red and gold; there were also pink flowers; and grey and silver leaves. The buzz, the croon, the smell, all seemed to press voluptuously against some membrane; not to burst it; but to hum round one. I stopped, smelt: looked. But again I cannot describe that rapture. It was rapture rather than ecstasy. (66)

Here again, the memory picture is insistently colored, and it has raw, unprocessed quality. It resembles the stylized, colorful illustrations often found in children's picture books: strong, boldly defined shapes, as well as vivid, bright colors. But the most striking feature of this representation lies in the image of "some membrane" that seems to mark a separation between outside and inside, between the world and the body.

This image of the membrane takes us back to the previous example, the memory from the bed, which gave the rememberer "the feeling . . . of lying in a grape and seeing through a film of semi-transparent yellow." It can be associated as well with the "things" that in Woolf's memory painting looked "globular and semi-transparent" and were "curved shapes showing the light through" or "sounds coming through this petal or leaf." A new configuration emerges, suggestive of the deepest of regressions—to a maternal space. The subject of her remembering is a mere container, or a sack of pleasurable impressions separated from the outer world by a membrane, listening to the breaking of waves—a rhythm that begins to resemble that of a breathing body.[14] In her remembering/writing, the writer gives shape to a self, or rather (since there is no self as yet at this early stage) to a living, sentient being caught at the beginning of her history.

The pleasure the writer experiences in exploring this memory is so acute that any attempt to place such a memory in a chronological, biographical narrative becomes moot. What matters is that the rememberer has found the semblance of a beginning—in images that have taken on the timelessness of a dream. At times, Woolf's memory images are so vague that we cannot make sense of the scene or event that they represent. Perhaps they are the faint traces of "things" that are *almost* forgotten, "things" that can barely be remembered: blots of color on a mother's dress, the powerful rhythm of the sea overheard from one's bed—and prior to that even, the sense of being enveloped in a semitransparent membrane. In this interpretation, Woolf's exercises in memory enable her to reach back to an inner world defined by inchoate, imaginary patterns and not yet fully ordered through language and symbols. Yet if this were to be true, not only would we have found a writer who has lifted the blanket of amnesia that supposedly covers our earliest years, but one who moreover is able to convey an infant's vision thanks to her painterly, experimental style.

The style has created the memories, but the memories themselves obey a certain design: not merely pleasure, but the wish to live life through again from the start, as becomes clear when Woolf writes:

> Instead of remembering here a scene and there a sound, I shall fit a plug into the wall; and listen in to the past. I shall turn up August 1890. I feel that strong emotion must leave its trace: and it is only a question of discovering how we can get ourselves again attached to it, so that *we shall be able to live our lives through from the start.* (67; emphasis added)

A wish to retrace, from the start, the meaningful experiences of a life (that is, those that were marked by "strong emotion") is what shapes Woolf's undertaking. We see it throughout "A Sketch of the Past": when she remembers happy events, the author experiences rapture; when the memory is unhappy (the result of a "shock," as she calls it), it will be worked over and finally acquire sense. Whatever the nature of the memory, writing/remembering is altogether desirable, because it makes sense of an experience. When most of daily existence has the dense, indefinite, opaque quality of cotton wool, a life lived through in memories takes on a meaningful shape. Indeed, the succession of images and impressions creates a "life-line," as she later calls it, which holds the subject in place—or rather in a place where her existence appears to make sense.[15]

But the lifeline needs a point of origin, hence the need to cull the earliest memories and to experience the originating point of a mental life. Whatever prompted it initially, Woolf's memory experiment is ultimately designed to re-create the primal scene from which a life unfolds, a primal scene that speaks of a self-birth and that marks the continuity of sentience. In the book they wrote jointly, Marc and Jean-Yves Tadié (one a scientist, the other a literary critic) argue suggestively that "to write one's autobiography is to find that one's memories come back according to an unconscious qualitative order . . . over which one generally imposes the quantitative measure of a calendar" (169).

Indeed, for Woolf, the content of these early memories matters more, in the end, than their place within a narrative and chronology. Worried as she often was in her fiction about her ability to sustain a good narrative, Woolf seems only too happy, in this case, to discard stories in favor of the rehearsal (made of repetitions and expansions) of a limited number of particularly satisfying, pleasure-filled mnemonic scenes. She thus emerges from this first visionary spell of remembering with a trove of vivid images, impressions, and sensations, most of which evoke a sense of wonder, of a pristine apparition rather than that of a "revisiting." Indeed, it is the *quality*, and not the number, of Woolf's memories that is striking here. In what must have been one of the first systematic studies of childhood memories, the psychologists Victor and Catherine Henri were similarly struck by some features inscribed in the representations of memory. They noted that "a certain number of childhood images, with a relatively insignificant content, were endowed with a considerable figural presence or an intensity of representation, which gave them, without an appreciable reason, a quasi-hallucinatory aspect."[16] It would seem that for Woolf, color has such "figural presence" and represents, most forcefully and vividly, the memory's singular perceptual quality.

Thus, paradoxically, "A Sketch of the Past" shows that the memory's presence—the sense of its reality—does not necessarily depend on wealth of descriptive detail. In Woolf's case, color is more important than the detailed outlining and drawing. In fact, her experiment suggests that it is the very poverty and crudity of the image—an image so poor that it is presented as a mere blob, or as the most primitive of rhythms (one-two, one-two)—that brings the memory to life. In focusing on *how* Woolf represents her memories (and not merely on their content), we are invited to reconsider the mnemonic scene for its qualitative aspects—for its qualia, namely.

Qualia

Qualia, one could then say, are sensuous, perceptual discriminations of a kind that subjects experience when they are conscious. The example most frequently invoked is that of color, as with Edelman, who writes: "Qualia constitute the collection of personal or subjective experiences, feelings and sensations that accompany awareness. They are phenomenal states—'how things seem to us' as human beings, for example the 'redness' of a red object, is a qualia" (*Bright Air*, 114). Proust also draws on the image of color when he wants to highlight the singularity of a memory and express its quale: the past has to have the right color, he declares several times.[17] In this context, it seems emblematic that the last episode he added to his monumental work, as he was coming close to his own death, would show the ailing writer Bergotte staring at a blotch of yellow on Vermeer's *View of Delft*. The dying author recognizes in the vivid visual presence of a corner of yellow wall art's capacity for commemorating the singular beauty of the simplest of objects (*La Prisonnière*, 3:156–57). As Proust's readers, we are urged to consider what it feels like to contemplate, at death's door, the singular "yellowness" of a wall as a painter renders it. And we are reminded that a certain art will reimagine for us—and thus commemorate—a world marked by the rich singularities of perceptions and our experience. Thus, Proust puts his last effort into representing what Edelman described as "a phenomenal state": he shows "how a thing seems to a singular human being" in the example of the "yellowness" of a yellow object. The redness of Edelman's red, the yellow in Vermeer are illustrations of the unique singularity of a human experience; next to them, we can now place the red, purple, and blue flowers on a black ground that constitute Woolf's first memory.

My own experience of such qualia involves a certain, very different shade of yellow; it takes me back to my childhood and my first months at school, days that seemed to have been spent mostly drawing and coloring. I will never forget, I think, the yellow. It had a crisp, bright, almost acidic intensity that of course I cannot properly describe, but that I feel I can still not only *see* but truly *experience*. The town I grew up in had a pencil factory, which produced high-quality items with an unusual concentration of pigments; they supplied our schools with round pencils sheathed in brown-striped wood and with the brightest of points (but I can only see the yellow). Caran d'Ache, their brand name, was one of the first words I learned to read (I still see the scene, my mother and myself sitting in the trolley, the large letters on the side wall of a building that we deciphered together in passing). All this I can reconstruct, but what I cannot will in my mind is the *experience* of the quale itself: I can remember it and record it, as I do here, for documentary purposes. But this reexperiencing of that unique color happens to me every now and again, sometimes not for months or even, it seems to me, for years. I must have colored, as a child, dozens of happy suns, tulips (my most successful flower), and many other things in that yellow. It comes back to me, meanwhile, by sheer coincidence, just like a Proustian involuntary memory, when on very rare occasions my eyes spot somewhere in the visual field a similarly intense and acidic tonality. Sometimes, I also see it unexpectedly in my mind's eye—on a day when I am in an exceptionally sunny mood, or on the contrary (but this is extremely rare) on a drab, cotton wool day to which it seems to add some much-needed color. Then, I just see it again—this yellow from my childhood in its crisp, bright quality. While this quasi-magical conjuring up of a spot of color seems to happen spontaneously, I have considered its invisible determinations—the fact that it is related to certain moods or even ideas (I may have felt it more often since I started this study of autobiographical memory). Given that I am a visual person, it is not surprising that I should be able to chime in so easily with my own example of a "colored" quale. Like Woolf and Proust (whose words I am quoting here), I am inclined to believe that "color can reveal the qualitative difference there is in the way in which the world appears to each of us individually" (*Le Temps retrouvé*, 3:725). But I grant, of course, that qualia are also found in the singularity of a taste and a smell, of an aroma such as Proust's tilleul and madeleine. In fact, I know of an equivalent experience: it involves the combined smell and taste of a certain kind of bread, the aroma of which takes me back to long childhood holidays in the countryside.

It would seem then that my own discoveries can corroborate what I learned from studying Woolf and Proust, namely that the reality we ascribe to memories depends on such insignificant sensual, perceptual discriminations as the particular yellowness of a yellow. "My" yellow has the same value as Woolf's red, purple, and blue: it represents the subjective experience or feeling of a mnemonic image. How rough, however, my evocation of a quale may seem compared to Woolf's lively brushstrokes or Proust's painstaking (and yet mysteriously satisfying) descriptions! It takes a writer no doubt to be able to render in words the very quality, the quale, of a personal memory, and Woolf was undoubtedly right to flaunt her exceptional abilities as a rememberer. *She* knew how to represent the phenomenal qualities of what she saw, felt, and lived in images. She could "snapshot what [she] mean[t] by some image," could be "a sensitive plate exposed to invisible rays," and her images, moreover (unlike most photographs of her time) were truly in color.

A Phenomenological View

Virginia Woolf's metaphors offer a striking perspective on the phenomenon of remembering because it stands between the abstractions of philosophical investigations and the unavoidable materialism of scientific inquiries. In giving such prominence to image making in her conception of memory, she seems to be looking forward to current scientific work that relies heavily on the concept of images for its modelization of mental processes. Antonio Damasio's work appears exemplary in this respect: mental images are a central concept in his theorization of the articulation between brain, body, and mind. In *The Feeling of What Happens,* he conceives of them as an interface between inner bodily processes and the outer world. He thus writes that "images are constructed when we engage objects, from persons and places to toothaches, from the outside of the brain toward its inside; or when we reconstruct from memory, from the inside out as it were" (318–19). In defining the mind in terms of a two-way passage between inside and outside, and in making of images the vehicle of such a passage, the neuroscientist reappropriates a model of consciousness developed by phenomenologists in the last century.[18] But more importantly for our purposes, he conceives of memory as a vector or force that leads to representations: in "reconstructing from memory," we project into images what was originally a perception.

But while this conception of memory seems satisfying enough from a philosophical point of view, it does not answer Damasio's curiosity as a neurologist. We still do not understand, he ponders, how the brain turns "neural patterns into the explicit mental patterns which constitute the highest level of biological phenomenon, which I like to call images." He adds that "this problem encompasses, of necessity, addressing the philosophical issue of *qualia* . . . the simple sensory qualities to be found in the blueness of the sky or the tone produced by a cello" (9). Even if we agree, as phenomenologists have taught us, that images are entities of the mind that are poised between an inside (the body) and an outside (the world), we are not able to describe, with the resources of current science, how a neurological impulse translates into something that feels like a memory. We are left then with the notion that memory is the projection outward of an inner, physiologically created image (while, conversely, our subjective impressions or "qualia" are somehow transferred into neural patterns), without understanding how the bridge is created between brain and mind. Faced with this impasse, my instinct is to turn again to the writer for what she can tell us about how her mind works when she remembers and to consider one more time her conception of the image.

When I remember, Woolf tells us in essence, I am like a photographer and my mind is like a sensitive plate. With these metaphors Woolf does more than capture for us what it feels like to be a conduit for images or neural patterns that move in and out of the brain; she also shares her intuition about the fundamental role that imagination plays in memory processes. Let us go back to the mental scene she describes. "A light glows," "an apple becomes a vivid green," a "little owl chatters"—these are the qualia that she automatically (physiologically as it were) translates into images, thus marking the passage from outside to inside. In speaking of photography, in comparing her mind to a plate, Woolf draws our attention to what is, as phenomenology has taught us, a compelling figure for how our mind deals with images. Jean-Paul Sartre makes this clear when, in his book on imagination he uses this very example, a photographic plate, to tell us that our intellectual apprehension of a mental patterning could "very well be compared to our perception of a picture *as image*" (*L'Imagination*, 149). In other words, for the philosopher Sartre, the best way of addressing the question that puzzles Damasio, namely how do we go from brain to mind, is to think of what imagination enables us to do. It enables us, says Sartre, to read images in such a way that we are not trapped in their medium, but recognize them as representation. Consider an etching or a photograph, he tells us: these are types of images we can apprehend at two levels: *material,* when we focus on the paper, the ink, the texture, the colors, or *symbolic,* as we try to decipher what it represents and recognize the outline of human figures, identify the objects, and perceive the mood it conveys (53). Our minds are trained to slide from the materiality of images to their symbolic aspect: when we see a photograph, we naturally focus on the picture and not the quality of the ink or the paper. Imagination is that faculty which enables us to lose sight of the material aspects of the image and to acknowledge the representation, which has now become "a mental reality." Imagination, in short, enables us to identify the mental, psychical meaning of a physiological, perceptual experience. It makes us "move" from the materiality of a certain neural event and its patterning in the brain to a symbolic meaning in the mind. As Woolf intuited, the photographic plate is indeed what turns us into rememberers.[19]

Meanwhile, in gliding so seamlessly from perception (seeing the vivid green apple, hearing the owl) to memory (the snapshot) Woolf's description emphasizes the immediate, quasi-instantaneous conversion of one into the other. This proximity suggests that, from her perspective, every representation is in truth already a memory—a trace of a perceptual event. In other words, no sooner has the image passed from outside to inside than it is projected outward, as a memory.[20] At the very moment she is taking down—putting on paper—her perception of a vivid green apple, Woolf is actually already recollecting. The same must be true of the "red and purple flowers on a black ground" that materialize in the words that she spontaneously jots down on that first page of her memoir. But in the second case the time lapse—the time it took the photographic plate to show the image—is far longer (she saw it, she thinks, when she was just a baby; she remembers it in her late fifties). Meanwhile, as *we* "read" the pictures that lie behind Woolf's words, we experience, albeit vicariously, the emergence of a mental image. A page of literature, just like a photograph, gives us a chance, when we read it symbolically, to experience the mental *patterning* of a memory.[21] With her red, purple, blue flowers Woolf represents a certain quale for us, and tries to share it with us, against all odds. While, as Damasio reminds us, "images can be accessed *only in a first-person perspective* (my images, your images)" (318), it remains possible to share a verbal description of what it felt like to sit on that maternal lap. What we discover in "A Sketch of the Past" is a first-person voice that narrates, analyzes, and even, as we just saw, "simulates" the emergence of a mnemonic image. Woolf has made us enter an experimental chamber filled with representations that evoke memories.

The Miracle of Analogy

While scientists, as we just saw with Antonio Damasio, are curious about the nature of memory images, the writer naturally wonders how to construct them. From examining "A Sketch of the Past," we know that besides photography, painting constitutes for Woolf a powerful analogy for the experience of remembering. A brief incursion into one of her fictions, *To the Lighthouse,* in which memory is an important theme, can enrich our understanding of this other metaphor. With the figure of the painter Lily Briscoe, Woolf seems to have found an indirect way of exploring the significance of painting as a means of capturing images and memories—and Briscoe is indeed an early, masked version of the rememberer we find in "A Sketch." Woolf ascribed to this figure, who muses in front of her easel on the sources of her artistic vision, thoughts that belong to her own theory on the creation of memories. These thoughts converge around the image of blue paint, which represents, figuratively, the very stuff and matter of memory:

> Lily stepped back to get her canvas—so—into perspective. It was an odd road to be walking, this of painting. Out and out one went, further and further, until at last one seemed to be on a narrow plank, perfectly alone, over the sea. And as she dipped into the blue paint, she dipped too into the past there. (172)

The ideas Woolf casts here in the form of metaphors seem to converge with a number of current scientific tenets on memory. Foremost perhaps is the notion that memory is an active, creative process that follows a certain path (one goes "further and further" on a "narrow plank"), and does not consist in a mere retrieval of some picture inscribed in the depths of the brain or the mind. "Remembering" is (as we saw in a scientist's definition that itself relies on a metaphor) "mental time-travel."[22] Meanwhile, like a number of cognitive psychologists (whose work I present in chapter 4), Woolf suggests that in the process of remembering we follow a certain path or even obey a charted sequence—a structure. In "A Sketch of the Past," Woolf further supports this construction as she invites us to see the past "as an avenue lying behind" (67). In depicting Lily's remembering, one also recognizes Woolf's insistence on the inherently solitary nature of this exercise. Mental images, Damasio tells us, are "internally generated" (321), and we learned from Edelman that they are made exclusively of "first-person matter." As she remembers, Lily is indeed "perfectly alone."

The most striking feature, however, of this allegorical rendering of recollection lies in the final statement, which presents the unmediated, spontaneous conversion of an aesthetic gesture into memories.[23] For Woolf, the pictorial or verbal medium does not *represent* a memory, it *is* the memory. The painter's blue paint (or the writer's "blue" words) *are* the past. Whereas scientists ponder over the mysterious processes of the brain and mind that bless us with the miraculous experience of seeing the blueness of the sky or hearing the tone produced by a cello, Woolf teases us with the idea that all it takes to convey the particular "feel" or color of the past is a painter's brush and the skills of image making. She tells us that the blue "out there," the painter's blue (and by analogy the writer's words for that blue), can evoke the quale of a personal experience. This blue represents the artistic, aesthetic substance that gives rise to an image of a past impression; the artist's medium is what projects it from the inside out.

This idea may seem odd or extreme, yet it provides a new and crucial insight into the memory images we studied in this chapter. It suggests that certain qualities of the image, such as color, sustain our belief in its truthfulness. Mnemonic images appear to us not as representations of the past: we see them as bits and parts of the past itself, as if the painter's brush, the writer's pen, the rememberer's imagination were able to reconnect with the very blue on the mother's dress, the yellow of that pencil, the sound of that cello. The right shade of blue on the brush applied on a canvas might thus give us more than an analog image, a replica: it might give us access to the very impression, the feeling of the past. With the right tools, we can truly paint our past. Such, I believe, was Woolf's intuition, conveyed in the images that traverse Lily's mind as she paints.

Positioning her rememberer at the easel, Woolf gives us a new insight into what it feels like to remember: one captures, somehow, that shade of blue that made up a corner of the sky on a particular day or that other blue that stood out on a mother's dress. To highlight the epistemological significance of this moment, I want to show, through one example, how it overlaps with the concerns of scientists working on the mind. Consider, for instance, the work of the psychiatrist Seymour S. Kety, who takes stock of the research done on the brain and nervous system in a chapter suggestively titled "A Biologist Examines the Mind and Behavior." His study, now more than a quarter of a century old, gives us a clear sense of the agenda that confronted neuroscientists a generation ago, an agenda that researchers such as Gerald Edelman, Oliver Sacks, or Antonio Damasio have since pursued. The challenge that biologists of the mind must face, Kety establishes, is the "phenomenon of consciousness—the complex of present sensations and the memory of past experiences which we call the mind" (92). Speaking more concretely, he adds that our understanding of the mind and consciousness will be greatly enhanced if scientific research can move from the "threads" of neurological connections to investigating the "patterns" that constitute the mind: "My guess is that in the nervous system we are looking at the threads, while in the mind we perceive the patterns, and that one day we shall discover how the patterns are made of threads." But the interest of the article lies not merely in its substance, but also in its language: a new, and yet for us recognizable, rhetoric is used to convey the urgency of the scientist's central question. In what way, according to this question, "can science account for the qualitative nature of consciousness?" "When we look at the clear sky on a crisp autumn day, a remarkable sequence of physiochemical changes is set in motion," Kety writes, and then gives a number of scientific accounts of this phenomenon. But, he concludes,

> Where, pray, in that sequence is the sensation of blueness? It is neither wavelength, nor nerve impulse, nor spatial arrangement of impulses; it is not necessary to any of these processes, and, though dependent on many of them, is explained or even described by none. It is richer and far more personal. One does not seem to get closer to its nature by increasing the complexity of its material counterpart—it is qualitatively and dimensionally different. As I indicated above, a machine can be built to perform any function that a man can perform in terms of behavior, computation, or discrimination. Shall we ever know, however, what components to add or what complexity of circuitry to introduce in order to make it *feel?* (92)

The early pages of "A Sketch of the Past," together with Woolf's brief allegory on painting and remembering in *To the Lighthouse,* provide us with rich materials and analyses of how "it feels" to remember. In chronicling painstakingly the emergence of her memories, Woolf thus gives us a unique entry-point into the phenomenology of autobiographical recall, a phenomenology of such complexity that it warrants yet another analysis, but from a different, somewhat antagonistic perspective. While this chapter focused on the writer, the next takes the reader's point of view, in order to assess the solidity of the rememberer's constructions.

3 • Reading the Past: Childhood Memories

"A Sketch of the Past" enabled us to follow the path that, from image to scene, led to a first memory. But what if the construction merely looked like a memory, what if it was merely the design that created the impression of a remembered scene? After all, as we saw in the previous chapter, Woolf's memoir obeys a twofold design. It responds to the need, biographical in its essence, to imagine a way of living again from the start, while it also purports to convey the pleasure felt in certain perceptual, figurative patternings. What emerges at the convergence between narrative, perceptual, and aesthetic impulses is not really the "I then" of the child Virginia but truly a writer confident with her style and curious to experiment. Remembering is inextricably intertwined with writing—to the point where the writer is so infatuated with the images she conceives that all that remains is an ecstasy or a rapture. Given all of these elements, how can we trust our rememberer? She may have lured us into a literary journey, to a place where it becomes impossible to draw the measure of what is mimetic and what is creative in a given image. What do we make of her ability to imagine—that is, to embody in language—sensations that she ascribes to her early childhood? With so many questions, we seem to have reached a point where skepticism is unavoidable, especially when it comes to childhood memories.

The arguments on childhood amnesia are so compelling that they can hardly be overlooked. They are of three kinds: the Freudian interpretation speaks of repression; the psycholinguistic hypothesis assumes that a young child's language is not developed enough to constitute memories; while neurological research suggests that the cerebral centers responsible for long-term memory are as yet insufficiently developed.[1] Most of us will have encountered these ideas, yet many instances of presenting or teaching the first pages of "A Sketch of the Past" have convinced me that we spontaneously and often enthusiastically endorse Woolf's memory impressions of early childhood. We are drawn into her picture because it *looks* so much like a memory, which amounts to saying that we respond to her brilliant imaginative work. We might have to concede then that instead of demonstrating the power of memory, "A Sketch of the Past" represents a tribute to imagination.

A survey of my earlier findings invites me to take, however, a more subtle line, where memory and imagination are *not* mutually exclusive. Seeing how closely they work together, I want to explore why a certain type of image lures us into belief in its reality or authenticity. A closer look at the second instance of what Woolf thinks might be her first memory—and this time at her language—might help us understand how images created the impression of mental time-travel. We might understand better then what lured us to believe that she remembers her mother's lap, and beyond even her mother's womb.

> If life has a base that it stands upon, if it is a bowl that one fills and fills and fills—then my bowl without a doubt stands upon this memory. It is of lying asleep, half awake, in bed in the nursery at St Ives. It is of hearing the waves breaking, one, two, one, two, and sending a splash of water over the beach; and then breaking, one, two, one, two, behind a yellow blind. It is of hearing the blind draw its little acorn across the floor as the wind blew the blind out. It is of lying and hearing this splash and seeing this light, and feeling, it is almost impossible that I should be here; of feeling the purest ecstasy I can conceive. (65)

Woolf's "other" first memory reveals amazing grammatical and rhythmical texture, with repetitions built incrementally like an incantation and a closely knit set of descriptions cast in the gerund form ("lying," "hearing," "sending," "breaking," and so on). An unusual grammatical patterning is what leads here to an exceptional experience in autobiographical recall. The insistent use of the gerund—a verbal form devoid of the ascription of person and time—blurs the temporal as well as the subjective articulation of the event that is being described. The images appear to float in a space where time is out of bounds, and the subject to whom these things (lying, hearing, seeing) happen is a mere shadow. Meanwhile, the repetition of words, sounds, and verbal patterns acts like an incantation that produces the final ecstasy. Thus the closing statement: "It is of lying and hearing this splash and seeing this light, and feeling, it is almost impossible that I should be here; of feeling the purest ecstasy I can conceive." The memory scene that Woolf has staged takes her to a place that is outside of any logical map, to an aporia that makes it impossible to say whether the rememberer landed in the past (of the memory) or the present (of her remembering).

Spelling out the two sides of this conundrum brings no resolution. One could assume that the linguistic experiment produces the mental time-travel during which old sensations and perceptions are rehearsed. But one could just as compellingly argue that the bed Woolf sees there and then, namely in her memory, is the familiar place from which our writer, so often bedridden when in a creative fever, fishes for ideas and images. Thus when she speaks of "lying and hearing this splash and seeing this light, and feeling, it is almost impossible that [she] should be here," Woolf might well be referring to the time of her remembering—when, lying in bed (the place from which she typically composed her works), she imagines her past.[2] Woolf herself seems to be aware that memory creates such odd displacements, as is shown in a little experiment that takes her from her desk into the garden. Noticing her amazing success at conjuring up memories, she tries to compare the reality of memory with that of her current impressions and discovers that, when it is at its peak, the rememberer's performance produces an uncanny reversal: images of the past take precedence over the present, and have more "reality" than current perceptions.

> Those moments—in the nursery, on the road to the beach can seem more real than the present moment. This I have just tested. For I got up and crossed the garden. Percy was digging the asparagus bed. Louie was shaking a mat in front of the bedroom door. But I was seeing them through the sight I saw here—the nursery and the road to the beach. At times I can go back to St Ives more completely than I can this morning. I seem to be watching things happen as if I were there. (67)

With the telling phrase "as if I were there," Woolf reveals her belief that she can at times—that is, when her imagination permits such a transport—truly inhabit the past. As these first pages of "A Sketch of the Past" suggest, she is indeed quite aware of what her performance entails: different degrees of success (she comments that "at times [she] can go back to St Ives more completely than . . . this morning") that depend on her ability to "latch onto" the right connection with the past. She is indeed convinced "that strong emotion must leave its trace; and it is only a question of discovering how we can get ourselves again attached to it" (67). If hallucination, in its simplest definition, is the mistaken assumption of an image for a perception, it would seem that at times our rememberer is on the verge of hallucinating her past.[3] Steeped in her writing ("I could spend hours trying to write as it should be written, in order to give the feeling"), she imagines pictures that are more real than her present perceptions. In this way, Woolf invites us to conceive of memory differently, not as a journey into the past, but as a perceptual, literary experience that occurs in the present and, as it were, under the rememberer's pen.

Scene Making

Words, rather than images, are the rememberer's first tools: they determine the patterning of mental images. This discovery tells us something new about the process of symbolization that, as we saw previously, enables us to identify the content of our memories. Woolf's example strongly suggests that the creator of images, the rememberer, relies on a verbal patterning (and not merely on a semantic content) to symbolize perceptual experiences.[4] A structure adumbrates a certain mental patterning that recalls or mirrors what a perceptual experience may have "felt like." In Woolf's own vocabulary, this structure is defined as a scene:

> I find that scene making is my natural way of marking the past. A scene always comes to the top; arranged; representative. This confirms my instinctive notion—it is irrational; it will not stand argument—that we are a sealed vessel afloat upon what it is convenient to call reality; at some moments, without a reason, without an effort, the sealing matter cracks; in floods reality; that is a scene—for they would not survive entire so many ruinous years unless they were made of something permanent; that is proof of their "reality." Is this liability of mine to scene receiving the origin of my writing impulse? (142)

A "scene" is the finished product, the overall construction that emerges from the collage of images; it is the name for the configurations born from the process of association and logical connections.[5] Woolf describes the emergence of memory with a scenario that is not unlike what we know as Proustian memory: she too speaks of the sudden, almost violent irruption of the past into the present. In her description, however, the mnemonic scene is clearly identified with expression, and more specifically, with the act of writing (whereas Proust, as we know, situated the birth of memory in some natural, outside coincidence). Woolf's emphasis on expression leads us back, meanwhile, to Damasio's conception of how memory works.

Memories, he argues, are stored in dispositional forms, while "dispositions are records which are dormant and implicit rather than active and explicit, as images are" (*Feeling,* 160). This means that from a scientist's perspective, memories arise when an implicit, virtual structure becomes representation and, through this process, "explicit." Similarly for Woolf, a scene is the representation of some latent, virtual disposition (she calls it a reality) that until then lay dormant.[6] A subtler point emerges from her description, which suggests that the activation of the scene depends on the rememberer's willingness to engage with the images—on her willingness to follow the "writing impulse." In short, Woolf shows us that "intentionality" is what makes memory possible. She can thus write, upon a particularly successful retrieval, "I am really making it happen" (67). This statement is doubly revealing: it tells us that for Woolf memories are "created" just as for Proust, and it confirms that she too endorses a nonmimetic conception of personal remembrance, thereby anticipating a theory that has gained currency among neuroscientists. Each memory, it is now understood, is a performance and a new creation: as Woolf remembers, she does not try to match an earlier representation, but makes up a scene that feels real just like a memory. The rememberer makes "it" happen, and in Woolf's conception words are both the instrument and the medium of recollection. It is surely worth noting here that while Woolf associates memory with inspiration—with the origin of her "writing impulse"—there is hardly a doubt in her mind that these scenes are "real." How can she tell? From instinct, or, perhaps, phenomenologically: there is something about the feeling that occurs when a scene "floods in" that makes it appear real. She feels this, just in the same way as, when testing her response to memory versus perception by looking out of the window, she feels that "the moments in the nursery . . . can seem more real than the present moment." Behind the rememberer's words lies what looks to us like a compelling belief in the reality of the experience. But the rememberer is not alone in sustaining this belief.

Intersubjective Correlations

Words assume a reader or a listener, in other words, someone at the receiving end, who often may be none other than the rememberer herself. Virginia Woolf, as we know, started her memoirs perhaps at her sister's prompting. However, her conviction that, in her case, remembering and writing are one and the same thing dispels this explanation as superficial: Woolf remembers because she writes. As she writes, meanwhile, she casts an imaginary audience for her memories (even if that audience is just herself, the woman in her late fifties, closing in on her death). These obvious facts invite us to consider a new facet of memory production, namely its social, intersubjective context. This aspect is skillfully described by the French psychologist Jean Guillaumin, who, in his rich phenomenological study *La Genèse de la mémoire*, highlights the verbal dimension of remembrance as he describes the emergence of memory into consciousness. Memory, Guillaumin claims, represents generally a private and incommunicable experience, and it will only accede to consciousness as the subject conceives of it as knowledge that is publishable and shareable with a community. In other words, autobiographical memory comes into existence as a shared experience with a real or imagined audience—as happens when Woolf undertakes to write for herself, for her sister, and possibly for a wider audience. Memories are conceived as images, scenes, or stories told for another—although that "other" may be just oneself.

There is a practical counterpart to this theory: unspoken memories are undetectable and remain invisible. While behavior might occasionally *suggest* the pressing presence of unacknowledged memories, only words can give positive evidence of their presence (and give them a definite shape). Our knowledge of autobiographical memory depends, thus, in a crucial fashion, on linguistic exchange and on the correlation between reports. "Science," Edelman states as he reflects on the challenges faced by scientists working on consciousness, "must couch its descriptions in terms that can be exchanged and understood between any two human observers" (*Bright Air*, 116). Following his train of thought, we can confirm that in the study of personal memory, "intersubjective communication and scientific correlation" are just as interdependent. We can also conclude, with him, that "it is our ability to report and correlate while individually experiencing *qualia* that opens up the possibility of a scientific investigation of consciousness."

This statement entails a startling redefinition of a scientific undertaking, for does it not assume that in the study of memory—of its qualitative aspects—the grounds of objectivity and the grounds of truth have become shifting entities? The science of memory, like that of consciousness, is born in the exchange between different subjects who trade their respective memories. One subject's autobiographical memories are validated, as it were, by the sympathetic observer, who is herself a subject, while the study of memory becomes a matter of reading in other minds (or even just in one's own, as is the case when Woolf analyzes her memories) the forms and contents of a first-person autobiographical narrative. My observation and analysis of the data provided by Woolf seems, then, to fit the modalities of scientific exchange defined by Edelman, as long as we replace his "consciousness" by "memory." What have I done, then, but reported and correlated "while individually experiencing" the kinds of qualia that we associate with memory? In reading, analyzing, correlating Woolf's words, I have created the intersubjective situation that enables the study of the phenomenon of personal remembrance.

But this also means that I have been invited, like every other reader of "A Sketch of the Past," to compare and trade my version, my understanding of autobiographical memories with what I observed in her text. For it is in the very nature of intersubjectivity to assume these two sides: not only does each rememberer reach out for an actual or an imagined audience, but every reader of Woolf's memories will necessarily bring his or her own memories into the picture. The best proof of this fact is to be found in the readers' responses that are elicited from "A Sketch of the Past." Our natural instinct is to take Woolf's memories on trust, against our better knowledge, which would dictate that by all accounts (psychological, psychoanalytical, and neuroscientific) remembering such early events as Woolf describes is impossible. Yet our desire to believe easily takes precedence over our knowledge. Since we, in turn, apprehend the rememberer's memories through our own imagination, we are only too eager to enter a fiction that we would ourselves like to sustain.

I, for one, have found myself lured into this kind of intersubjective exchange when studying Woolf, and have reinvented my own childhood. This is what I wrote, in an earlier draft, some three years ago, and I now adduce this text as concrete proof of the intersubjective process that defines the study of memory:

> I long believed that I had retained a very early memory of myself in a crib, with my mother's arm extending towards me. The image was somewhat nebulous, but all the more comforting in its evocation of an edgeless, cottony warmth—until not long ago I looked again at a long discarded family photo-album. There it was, in black-and-white, the photograph of me in a crib, but without my mother's arm. I had confused a photographic image for a memory, and enriched it with an element of my own fantasy. Writing these pages, I cannot help pondering over my treasured dreams, of the most vivid kind, which I retain as a mystery in the corner of my mind. I had just given birth to my daughter, and fallen into one of those deepest restorative sleeps that come with exhaustion. Fresh from inhaling the baby-smell of her little body, I dreamed an amazingly powerful dream, saturated with sensations. I can summarize it in one vivid image: it seemed I was bathing in warm liquid, feeling an immense, yet not orgasmic pleasure enveloping the lower part of my body. On waking up, I decided that, on the strength of my baby's smell, I had dreamed myself back, as it were, into my warm, wet diapers. I must confess, I cannot quite give up the thought that it might be a memory, although the more rational side of me says it must be a fantasy. The strangest thing is that I feel like turning to Woolf, the absent writer, to say to her: "This is my first memory, this is how far I can go back in my childhood—in memory or in fantasy."

The memory scenes that Woolf constructs in the first pages of "A Sketch of the Past" are so compelling in their phenomenal and structural presentation that we share the fiction and identify with her plight or, rather, with her ecstasies. Because we spontaneously associate with the rememberer, I must have looked for my first memories in the hope perhaps of finding my own rapture. Like Woolf, I must have liked the thought that thanks to memory, one might be able to live life again from the start.

We enter the field of another's consciousness in the same way as a reader "gets into" a text—through words. The rememberer's narrative becomes the object of a crucial exchange: the observer-reader takes the place of the other and reads herself, as it were, into another's mind. This sharing of imagination—this reading—which the rememberer's text demands, provides the epistemological foundation for the scientific analysis of memory contents: it is what enables the necessary work of correlation. Reading needs to be understood, in this case, in a strong sense: as an engagement with a text that aims at retrieving the latter's semantic or symbolic contents. In his rich experience as a thinker devoted to the philosophical exploration of literary works, the Belgian critic Georges Poulet learned to conceive of reading as a transpersonal act that provides access to another mind. In his inspired essay "The Phenomenology of Reading," he argues that reading enables him to share the space of another consciousness. "Through reading, I have lent myself to another," he writes, for the text "awakens in me an image of what was thought or felt there" (282–83). Reading, for Poulet, enables us at times to cross over into another's mind, so that mental objects arise spontaneously from the obscure depths of consciousness, as if we were thinking another's thought or remembering another's memories. Reading becomes, for him, a form of remembering through another.

In Poulet's theory, we have found a convincing explanation for the kinds of epistemological blurrings and confusions that arise in the study of auto-biographical memories. Indeed, we take to another person's memories very much as we take to a work of fiction—with a suspension of disbelief that prepares us to respond naively, candidly to images and representations. In this intersubjective exchange, we correlate impressions to the point of losing ourselves in the thoughts, feelings, and memories of another person. Such "cognitive empathy" lies at the heart of the study of memory: without it, the rememberer's elaborate construction of a memory scene threatens to crumble into mere words. But in lending our belief to the rememberer's text, we confirm our own allegiance to a world in which a scene of the past (provided the images are compelling enough) can be a mental reality. Reading, as Poulet suggested, might chart a passage between minds, but it does not allow us to inhabit another's mind. We have no choice, then, but to base our faith in another's memories on the fact that we too have autobiographical memories.[7] There is thus no neutral, epistemologically pure or safe place from which we can contemplate the scene of others' memories: our experiments are naturally inflected by our own implication in the experience we witness in the rememberer. As Woolf's example suggests, the temptation to fall into the dream of a remembered childhood must unquestionably be the strongest when the rememberer is a convincing writer, one who makes us share the ecstasies of remembering things we thought we had forgotten. It seems hard to resist Woolf's invitation to similarly dream of a readily available past—where remembering is merely a matter of "fit[ing] a plug into the wall and listen[ing] in to the past" (67). She puts at the tip of her pen the memory upon which she can build a life and which makes us, in turn, want to dream: "It is of lying and hearing this splash and seeing this light, and feeling, it is almost impossible that I should be here; of feeling the purest ecstasy I can conceive" (65).

Dreaming Our Childhood

For the French psychoanalyst André Green, dreaming is the analogy that best describes our experience of childhood memories. It tells us that there is no objective, no neutral place from which they can be apprehended. It warns us that such memories are necessarily representations of the past, and not "an unmediated apprehension of the sensible" (40). It also suggests that childhood memories are always retrospective constructions: we are reading the manifest contents of scenes that are not available to consciousness. This is how Green summarizes his conception of remembering as dreaming, in an essay entitled "L'Enfant modèle" ("The Model Child"):

> Just in the same way as the dream-work can only be constructed after the fact, childhood can only be told (narrated) in the past. And this, without a discernible origin. Thus the best use we can make of what we learn about the child is to dream on the subject. (40)

But as he invites us to dream with the rememberer, Green refers us to yet another meaning of dreaming, which is known, in psychoanalytical circles, as countertransference. Countertransference is the place where, the time when, eavesdropping on the rememberer's mind, the analyst, interpreter, or observer brings in his or her own desires. Not only does it identify the observer's implication in the text of another person's memories, it also spells out the fact that this intersubjective exchange is fraught with the observer's own passions for, and investments in, the scene that is depicted.[8] It tells us that our belief in a simple linear construction of memory (our spontaneous adhesion to the rememberer's discourse) is founded on the "dream" or fantasy of some childhood scenes that we similarly treasure. An imagined child speaks in us as we listen to another's memories. Our own childhood memories draw us into the dream that is being recounted, and to that extent, the scene of childhood is a shared fantasy. A scientist would naturally stop short of reaching the kinds of conclusions that Green presented in his article (conclusions borne out, it should be emphasized, from years spent analyzing childhood memories). But the psychoanalyst's invitation to enter the rememberer's dream while relinquishing our desire for a theoretical mastery is provocative and interesting—even though it could hardly gain validation as a scientific method. It has the advantage of placing the subjective aspects of autobiographical memory right at the center of the investigator's concern, rather than shunting them off to the side as mere complications. In endorsing this stance, one naturally forfeits a claim of objectivity, but a psychoanalytical conception such as André Green's provides us with compelling reasons for giving up such a claim. Psychoanalysis reminds us that we all need and want some primal scene, a childhood memory that provides a beginning and an origin for our biographies. It is because we all share this condition and impossibility—as well as the countervailing fantasy that childhood can be remembered—that we so willingly enter Woolf's fiction of a return to the mother's lap or a child's cot. When she suggests that it may be just a matter of fitting the right plug in the wall, and of "listening in to the past," we almost believe her—because we share her desire.[9]

To summarize: a skeptical view shows us that the experiences of early childhood are irretrievable and that a radical break separates the adult from the child. The child's earliest experiences can only be expressed in a language and in representations acquired at a later stage. Woolf's experiment nevertheless shows that we are able to create a language for these memories, a language that expresses the "feel" of vivid sensory, perceptual experiences: her stylistic performance created, after the fact, the lineaments of a dream-childhood. This seeming contradiction takes us back to Green's insightful commentary that memories are "constructed after the fact" *(après coup)*. In invoking Freudian *Nachträglichkeit,* he points to a concept that becomes invaluable as we raise the fundamental question that emerged from this second analysis of Woolf's memories, namely, "Can we still speak of memory when all we share are images born in the present?" Psychoanalytical thought gives us a way of dealing with this paradoxical time-warp—and of calling it memory. In the case of *Nachträglichkeit,* the past is made and thus "occurs" *in the rememberer's present awareness.*[10] As we saw early on with Woolf, we usually think of recall as representing a convergence between past and present (a meeting between "I now" and "I then"), but *Nachträglichkeit* conceives of memory as the activation of a scene in the present, a scene for which no original trace can be found in the past. Our earliest experiences, this tells us, are only available to us as retrospective constructions—that is, as *memories* whose building blocks belong to our present sensibility, awareness, and language.

Because it so richly embodies these aesthetic features of memory, Woolf's "A Sketch of the Past" can tease us with the fiction that if we remember in the right way, we shall be able to live our lives again from the start, from the womb, as it were. The journey into the past she charts here makes us believe, for a moment, that time can be vanquished, that we can dream ourselves out of time. This happens, her text tells us, when the desire to recover, or rather to *create,* pleasure-filled sensory and perceptual experiences and the drive to know the present and to create the future override the need for self-definition. In spite of this seeming regression (or is it not rather *because* of it), "A Sketch of the Past" becomes an exemplary text for our human desire to narrate the self, a desire for a construction that cannot exist without the make-believe of origins. We cannot remember our childhoods, we can only dream them. Yet the fictions of the past that we invent under the guise of childhood memories are the foundations of our life stories.

Beyond its formal and aesthetic features, Woolf's "Sketch of the Past" reveals the existential aspects of personal remembrance. It shows us how profoundly invested we are, as humans, in tracing our personal past back to a compelling origin. We owe to her lucid and unprejudiced analysis of the process of remembrance a clearer, more concrete vision of the epistemological challenges that face us in the study of memory. But Woolf also spells out, in her radical experiment, the unexpected psychological consequences of a journey that is too successful in its displacement of the subject into the past: the rememberer might, quite literally, lose herself in the past—namely in a form of hallucinatory madness, in which the past becomes the present. As the imagined past supplants the present—being more vivid and more "present" than the surrounding world—she lives under the sway of images in what must be a trancelike state, a state of dissociation. There, she endorses a life to be lived purely and exclusively in the realm of images and, even more narrowly, under the autocratic regime of certain signifiers, of words or structures that seem to contain the magic of the past. Losing all references to her present existence, she is totally absorbed in the rehearsal of phantom perceptions. One should not underestimate here the personal, mental risks Woolf took in putting such a premium on her imagination. There is, in the end, more than a hint of madness in a memory experience that is so absorbing as to dissolve the boundaries of the subject and that enables the substitution of imagined, imaged sensations for those that are immediately present.

Fortunately, this hallucinatory state soon spends itself, for such ecstasies as can be found in blots of color, or the rhythm of one-two, one-two are, by definition, fleeting experiences. They can only be sustained in what must be a mystical or poetic trancelike state. Moreover, Woolf knows that if she wants to abide by her autobiographical project, she cannot afford to lose sight of "the person to whom things happened" (65, 69).[11] She soon picks up a more conventional, historical, and documentary thread, leaving behind these moments when the reminiscence is so intense as to dissolve the boundaries between now and then as well as self and other. Thus when we embrace the whole essay, the beginning looks like an odd moment—a moment when the autobiographical narrative seemed ready to stall because of the author's fascination for her earliest recollections. But, resuming her path, she sketches out, in the remaining pages, the draft of an autobiographical account with her person present throughout. Later impressions may not be as strong, but they will be clearly endorsed by a subject. There, Virginia Woolf's account of her memories loses its experimental dimensions and aligns itself more closely with the genre of the memoir. The early commitment to the study of memory vanishes, as she seems increasingly eager to gather facts and stories about her world, so much so that one might almost want to shelve these mnemonic experiments, putting to rest the troubling scientific and existential questions they raise. Yet these experimental first pages of Woolf's autobiographical quest open up a momentous question, one that will haunt us throughout this book—a question whose reverberations are not merely psychological, but also literary and philosophical. This question is not merely what is the measure of reality and of fantasy in the images that we take for our memories. It also asks, more poignantly, why we need the dream of our childhood memories.

4 • George Eliot's Movie-in-the-Brain

In "A Sketch of the Past" Virginia Woolf is confident in her ability to produce, freely and deliberately, images that are memories. Perhaps she betrays a rather naive view. In her fiction, however, she takes a much more sophisticated approach. In *To the Lighthouse,* for example, she creates a scene that seems designed to test our belief in memories: she lures us into experiencing a fictive memory in order to demonstrate how easily we can be fooled into mistaking a storyteller for a rememberer. Some of the images that we review in our mind's eye may very well look like memories, she shows us, but they might be mere fantasy and invention. The philosopher Edmund Husserl claims that our trust in memories derives from our general belief in the existence of the world that we perceive.[1] The representations that Woolf has imagined for us, with their high degree of realism, feed this same desire for an unambiguous reality.[2] As we recognize our mistake and our natural gullibility, however, we will have learned to suspect that a certain type of storytelling leads to the assumption that we hear (or overhear) memories.

Here is, briefly, how Woolf runs this experiment, which is designed to test the ambiguities of scene making. She invites us to follow Lily Briscoe's thoughts while she is painting and thus "collecting impressions," impressions involving, for instance, her friends the Raleys:

> The Raleys, thought Lily Briscoe, squeezing her tube of green paint. She collected her impressions of the Raleys. Their lives appeared to her as a series of scenes; one, on the staircase at dawn. Paul had come and gone to bed early; Minta was late. There was Minta, wreathed, tinted, garish. . . . But what did they say? Lily asked herself, as if by looking she could hear them. Minta went on eating her sandwich, annoyingly, while he spoke something violent, abusing her, in a mutter so as not to wake the children, the two little boys. He was withered, drawn; she flamboyant, careless. For things had worked loose after the first year or so; the marriage had turned out rather badly. (*To the Lighthouse,* 172–73)

This elaborate segment of "stream of consciousness," squarely focused on a scene cast in a remote past, makes us assume, all too naturally, that we are eavesdropping on Lily's silent rehearsal of memories. A scene so vividly described, one that comes to mind so effortlessly and is articulated so fluently, we think, must correspond to an event and translate "real" impressions. It must be a memory. Only a suspicious, skeptical reader will note that Lily never says to herself, "I remember," but just keeps turning images into scenes and, in the words of the text, "collect[ing] impressions." The narrator, meanwhile, deliberately eschews, in her description, a higher order of awareness, in which the mind makes the distinction between "true" and "false" images, or between memory and fantasy. And indeed, when that level of awareness is introduced, it turns out that the rememberer is a fiction maker:

> And this, Lily thought, taking the green paint on her brush, this making up scenes about them, is what we call "knowing" people, "thinking" of them, "being fond" of them! Not a word of it was true, she had made it up: but it was what she knew them by all the same. She went on tunnelling her way into her picture, into the past. (173)

Jolting us out of this scene that was so suggestive of a memory, Woolf denounces our easy belief in emphatic terms, writing, in evocative terms, that Lily Briscoe "had built up a structure of the imagination."

In her biography of Woolf, Hermione Lee writes that the author "masters her memories by structuring them like fictions" (106). The thought experiment we just examined provides us with a more provocative idea: it suggests that autobiographical memories are *generally* structured just like fictions. It also confirms what we learned from a close examination of "A Sketch of the Past," namely that Woolf's ability to create such fictions is truly masterful. Yet while one would then think that her awareness of memory's fictions would make of her a skeptic, wary of inherent confusion between memory and fantasy, this does not happen. The same writer-rememberer who denounces the stratagems of scene making as mere fiction in *To the Lighthouse* embarks candidly on a search for memory impressions at the beginning of "A Sketch of the Past," and confirms her belief, as we saw earlier, that the scenes born from her writing are real. "They would not survive entire so many ruinous years unless they were made of something permanent; that is proof of their 'reality'": in writing these words, Woolf shows her faith in autobiographical recollection. Her example shows how the two attitudes toward memory—the skeptic's and the believer's—can in fact coexist. In fact, this very same contradiction stares us in the face at the end of the passage quoted above: Lily Briscoe can, in the same breath, denounce the mise-en-scène around the Raleys as a fiction, and yet continue "tunnelling her way into her picture, into the past." One may well wonder then whether the past that she produces in her painting will be fictive or remembered.

This same question could be asked about George Eliot's *The Mill on the Floss*, a novel that begins with an experiment that tests our ability to distinguish between memory and fantasy. In the first few pages of her fiction, Eliot projects—on a more ambitious scale than what we saw in *To the Lighthouse*—"a structure of the imagination" that looks like a memory. In painting the first scene of her novel (in the realist, Dutch painting mode that has often been attributed to her), Eliot asks us to consider to what extent remembering resembles dreaming and imagining. More subtly, she makes us wonder how much of what we perceive as reality we owe to our memories.

Beginnings

Our inquiry must begin here with a question that bears on imagination and inspiration. We all know the conventional yet magical beginning of storytelling: "once upon a time." *Once upon a time there was a little girl, Maggie Tulliver, who had a brother called Tom and lived near a mill, deep in the English countryside* . . . But this is not how George Eliot begins her well-known semiautobiographical novel, *The Mill on the Floss,* which tells the story of a girl's failed attempts at emancipating herself from familial, social, and moral bonds to live up to her desires and her powerful intellect. The story is set back in the past by a number of years, by a generation perhaps, which might explain why the author chose to begin differently, by steeping herself in the evocations of a place. In brushing a careful picture of her story's setting, Eliot enables herself (as well as her readers) to step into a world and story of things of the past. Yet in entering into this picture, the storyteller faces a surprise: the scene that springs from under her pen gives off the shimmer of an autobiographical remembrance. Abruptly dismissing this impression, however, the narrator takes her distance from this sentimental scene and proceeds to recount the adventures of Maggie and Tom.

The prologue to *The Mill on the Floss* thus begins auspiciously on the cusp between imagination and memory, so that the novel sustains, throughout, a hesitation, in terms of genre, between autobiography and fiction. Eliot's scenic construction produces a memory, which is then dismissed as an illusory dream. In revealing her skepticism about the nature of the images sprung from her mind, Eliot's narrator brings to the fore a crucial question for any modern novelist: she makes us wonder how much of the writer's experience is embedded in her fiction. This opening does more than just take us into the writer's workshop and to the place where stories begin: she sets the stage for a theoretical reflection on the similarities between memory and fiction writing. This is why this arresting beginning deserves our closest attention. Let us then revisit it: the curtain lifts on a bucolic setting, the description of a mill and of the surrounding waterways—the result of the narrator's musing on images of a past time.[3] The eye dwells on the landscape until it gradually focuses on images of significant objects and of a child—images that lure the narrator into a reflective, mirrorlike structure in which she appears to reexperience a moment of her own past. She envisions herself standing on a bridge, engrossed in the contemplation of the water, and encounters a little girl similarly absorbed. The imagery strongly reinforces the impression of a specular moment: the watery landscape draws the narrator's attention and emotions ("I am in love with moistness," she declares) as if it were a mirror before which the mind peers into the past. A screen that lures her into remembrance, water also separates, insulates one world from another: it produces "a great curtain of sound, shutting one out from the world beyond." The vision arises in this unusual mood of "dreamy deafness"—a shimmering vision where the writing consciousness faces the child at the center of the fiction, a vision where the "I now" (George Eliot) faces little Maggie as if she were her former self.

But while we now seem comfortably embarked on an experience of mental time-travel, Eliot surprises us with an abrupt swerve that creates a revolution in our awareness. Her narrator suddenly turns away from the lure of an autobiographical moment and declares that it was all a dream. A bodily sensation has recalled her to the present, and to her awakened consciousness: "Ah, my arms are really benumbed, I have been pressing my elbows on the arms of my chair and dreaming that I was standing on the bridge of Dorlcote Mill as it looked one February afternoon many years ago." We now understand that in preparing to tell her tale, the storyteller had fallen into a dream—a dream that we, her readers, had shared with her in the guise of a memory. The rupture that Eliot creates in her representation is crucial, meanwhile, for the unfolding of the fiction: it reveals her resistance to the idea that the storyteller's magical phrase—"once upon a time"—has transported her to the wells of memory, along a path of impressions and feelings she endorsed for a moment as her own. At the same time, it enables her to regain the grounds of pure imagination; the writer can move freely into her plot and toward her heroine's tragic death.

Dissociating herself from memory, the author can sever ties between herself and her heroine and gear her tale toward a "poetic truth": exemplifying the waste of female talents, Maggie's young life is violently cut short by a flood, and she meets her death with her brother in a final, forgiving embrace. For the author, the separation from her fictive alter ego is imperative, for how could the "I now" want to write of her own death? On the contrary, she will overcome a difficult girlhood at her heroine's expense. Ironically, the young girl that too closely resembles Mary Ann Evans must die so that the author, George Eliot, can grow into her own literary persona. Eliot's move in her prologue is, then, transparently defensive: seeing that the scene of her imagination has acquired all too personal an inflection, she takes a radical measure and severs the ties that bind her too closely to Maggie. But while the autobiographical inscription can be erased, the emotion this scene triggers cannot. *The Mill on the Floss* remains, nevertheless, in the phrase aptly used by the critic Rosemary Ashton, a text "very strongly felt" (9). We know from George Henry Lewes, Eliot's companion, that the tragic ending caused the writer so much grief that she was shedding hot tears while penning the last pages of her novel. Thus to the end, a certain blurring seems to have occurred in a writer's consciousness between fiction and experience: what should remain a mere fictive construct keeps producing structures of the imagination that give off the feeling of real emotions. Reading the scenes of her own creations, Eliot empathizes. One understands even better why she wants, as much as possible, to steer away from fiction's uncanny and dangerous power of bringing us too close to home.

Here it becomes helpful to consider Eliot's prologue in terms of a personal strategy, and not merely as an experiment: it reminds us that the confusion between dreaming and remembering that she describes is not only ours, but hers as well. This confusion has a name, meanwhile: we call it déjà vu. Déjà vu describes the deceptive feeling of recognition that arises when a perception is wrongly apprehended as a memory. To better understand how writing lends itself to this uncanny feeling, we will now examine, in these first pages of Eliot's novel, the subtle passage that leads from "structures of the imagination" to remembrance.

Structures of the Imagination

Eliot's first narrator, the one who becomes a rememberer, builds through images a mental space that creates the impression of a memory. Behind this simple formulation lies an immensely rich and complex literary strategy that produces this effect. I will try to unpack here the elements of a complex textual architecture that is conducive to remembrance, an architecture in which description leads insensibly and seamlessly to recollection. The translation of image into memory is indeed so smooth that we barely notice the clinching phrase "I remember," which tells us that the image is in fact a memory. "I remember those large dipping willows. . . . I remember the stone bridge," the narrator writes, seizing on a few objects in the picture as mnemonic evidence.

Visual images are the building blocks of George Eliot's construction; put together, they create a picture that is immensely rich, integrating details and further vistas very much like the Dutch painting I evoked before. It is no minor accomplishment to master a topographical description to the point where it looks like a painting, and Eliot has often been admired for this achievement. Memory, we must meanwhile assume, is born from this literary arraignment of *visual* impressions rendered in words. As we know, mnemonic images can be of other types (olfactory or tactile, for example), but since Eliot seems deeply committed here to a literary aesthetics of writing as painting (in the long tradition of *ut pictura poesis*), she is bound to emphasize vision. This effortless, invisible sliding into memory results, meanwhile, from a masterful technique more sophisticated than the metaphor of "painting in words" led us to believe, for Eliot blends into the presentation of images an intricate system of shifting points of view—of focalization—that leads to the crucial encounter where the "I now" seems to meet the "I then." The text offers, as it were, an "avenue" that matches the progress of recollection, an avenue built of moving frames. Her topographical description invites us to follow a perspective and path that we naturally follow when constructing mnemonic scenes. There too, as we shall see in a moment, we rely on the skillful arraignment and interlocking of different images.

However, once we take into account the complex ways in which our gaze—or rather, our imagination—is manipulated into seeing a scene, painting seems too poor a metaphor for the modulations of structure that inform Eliot's description: cinema provides a better analogy. The system of description in these first paragraphs of *The Mill on the Floss* is indeed so astutely set up as to motion us through scenes: the focus keeps changing, we are invited to "zoom in" on certain details, we get close-up views revealing new elements. The writer and critic Michel Butor (himself a brilliant practitioner of literary description) aptly called this kind of descriptive technique *cinéma intime,* aiming for a concept that would capture a form of literary description that strongly conveys an inner vision—where the eye, the mind, seems to roam over an inner picture that is like "an imagined or an authentic memory" (*Répertoire,* 97). The analogy seems all the more relevant when we consider that consciousness is often compared to a "movie-in-the-brain," by

Antonio Damasio, for example, who uses the comparison to reflect on the "curious ability we humans have of constructing . . . mental patterns . . . the temporally and spatially integrated mental images of something-to-be-known" (*Feeling*, 11).[4] What Eliot does so brilliantly here is to motion us—thanks to the topography and the timing of her description—through the "mental patterns" that make us imagine a scene on the river Floss, with the little girl, her barking dog, and the mill's "unresting wheel sending out its diamond jets of water." By the end of the second or third paragraph, she has wrapped us around her little finger, as it were: we have been taken in by her picture—and we think she is remembering.

Butor's evocative metaphor helps us understand how the memory effect is created, but so does, as well, the recent work of psychologists interested in the structures of memory. Ulric Neisser, who is famous for launching a new wave of memory research in the "ecology" of memory, has shown how "visual-spatial schema" intervene in the creation of memories. Eliot's prologue to *The Mill on the Floss* looks like a textbook illustration of a cognitive path that, according to this scientist, determines the "nested structure of autobiographical memory" ("Nested Structure," 71–78). In analyzing the ways in which we provide contexts for mnemonic images, Neisser comes to the conclusion that we organize memories in the same way that we respond to the outer world: we construct a picture of their "reality" with the help of cognitive frames. We construct our memories, he argues, by relying on the same well-rehearsed cognitive schemas that provide us with the spatial (as well as temporal) reference frames of the world we inhabit. The organizing principle of these various frames relies on insertion and expansion or contraction: the nesting enables us to move up or down, from the smaller to the larger unit, or conversely, from a larger picture to a detail. As rememberers, we have learned to move skillfully and seamlessly across these frames, frames that are like the scaffolding for our memories. Eliot's prologue can indeed be described in the terms of Neisser's patterning. The mental picture she draws is expanded, shrunk, or sharpened so as to include specific elements; but while the scene is constructed around shifting perspectives, it gradually focuses on a core image: the river, the mill, the bridge, and finally the figure of a young girl like a past self.[5] The structure has thus produced the kind of alignment suggestive of memory: the "I now" of the narrating, storytelling voice meets on the bridge the figure of a little girl that evokes an "I then."

But like a magician's trick, Eliot's technique can only be understood if we watch her even more closely; let us then look again: "In love with moistness," Eliot's narrator peers into the depths of the Floss, watches the mill—

"the unresting wheel sending out its diamond jets of water"—and then sees a little girl, "watching it too." She, in turn, is "rapt [in the wheel's] movement." In a less attentive reading, one could think that the "I" and the little girl are similarly placed in the picture, but the text in fact only speaks of a shared time, which can be paraphrased thus: "While I was watching the water, she was too, for the same duration." The analogies between these two pictures are so powerful that we blend the two figures into one remembering self: sharing the writer's dream, we imagine—for a moment—a scene in which the narrator recognizes herself in the child's absorption in the water.

"I see it—the past," writes Virginia Woolf, "as an avenue lying behind; a long ribbon of scenes, emotions" ("A Sketch," 67). With her infallible talent for figurative thinking, she offers us an image—that of tunneling into the past—that aptly summarizes Eliot's strategy as well as the cognitive process analyzed by Neisser. Recollection is structured within a linear perspective: a line, a path, a set of receding arches. As the two coordinates of space and time intersect, the subject, caught in the depth of the past, is repositioned in the memory. Thus when she is most deeply absorbed in her autobiographical writing, Woolf proclaims that such an avenue can give direct access to the past, which then loses its pastness to become present, with herself present in the distant event. Following the right perspectival lines and moving seamlessly between frames, the subject can, it seems, transport herself into the past. Woolf describes such perfect, unimpeded remembering in a telling statement: "At times I can go back to St Ives more completely than this morning. I can reach a state where I seem to be watching things happen as if I were there" ("A Sketch," 67).

"Watching things happen as if I were there"! What an apt description for the encounter that Eliot's writing stages between a young girl standing at the edge of the water and the narrator on the bridge. United in the contemplation of the water, the two figures meet fleetingly in Eliot's fiction. The shift of perspective makes us indeed "see" the picture of an observing, remembering figure looking at a remembered self. Eliot's "structure of the imagination" has led us to witness what looks like an encounter between "I now" and "I then"—she has created a memory that makes us assume that the little girl "at the end of the avenue" is the dreaming narrator's alter ego.

In memory studies, there is a technical term for this type of recollection in which an observing self catches a glimpse of former self in the mnemonic scene. Developed in the wake of Freud's study of memory in his article "Screen Memories," the concept is that of "observer memory." Daniel Schacter proposes, in *Searching for Memory,* a simple experiment that helps us grasp what an observer memory consists of. He invites his reader to remember a certain scene with the suggestion that we "ask [ourselves] the following question. Do you see yourself in the scene? Or do you see the scene through your eyes, as if you were there and looking outward, so that you yourself are not an object in the scene?" (21). In the first instance, we are dealing with an observer memory, in the second, with a field memory. An observer memory is already a construction, Schacter argues after Freud, for "our initial perception of an event takes place from a field perspective" (21).[6] This structural distinction between two types of mnemonic scene suggests, then, that the most spontaneous, immediate form of recall (such as an involuntary memory of the kind that interests Proust) leaves the subject of the memory out of the picture, like a blind spot. But as we try to reconstruct the past, we transform it into a picture, a scene where we observe our past self. What we know of observer memories would thus confirm that Eliot's prologue documents a memory in the process of construction.

Here again, the memory is an effect of structure—this time a shift of perspective that, as it were, gives birth to the little girl in the scene. The spontaneous recollection of a field memory representing a landscape from childhood (with the stream carrying the strongest mnemonic investment) has insensibly "morphed" into an observer memory that shows the girl watching, as if mesmerized, the same stream. Thus, Maggie is shown seeing what constitutes the memory: she is perceiving-remembering what could aptly be called the memory of a memory. Indeed, as Freud analyzes the formation of an observer memory, he seizes on this transformation as evidence that a memory has been revised: "Whenever in a memory the subject [herself] appears in this way as an object among other objects this contrast between the acting and the recollecting ego may be taken as evidence that the original impression has been worked over" ("Screen Memories," 321). This type of revision, he adds, is a typical feature of childhood memories: "in these scenes of childhood, whether in fact they prove to be true or falsified, what one sees invariably includes oneself as a child, with a child's shape and clothes" (68). If we accept Freud's hypothesis, we must conclude that the first pages of *The Mill on the Floss* represent a memory of childhood, for which the strongest proof lies in the arresting shift from a field to an observer perspective.

Through this complex patterning of images, George Eliot has created a vista that lures us, her readers, into the fiction of an autobiographical encounter. Her prologue provides us, then, with yet another opportunity for a *rêve à deux*. The mind is trained to build on similarities and tends to assimilate rather than discriminate, so that we naturally focus on the coincidence between the two figures until we distinguish, in the shimmering of the mirror, the familiar construction of a rememberer's encounter with a past self. How appropriate Woolf's words describing her presence in the memory as if she were there. The skeptical narrator will later warn us that this is all a dream and will make us suspicious of such déjà vu. "How easily our perceptions are falsified!" Eliot's wiser voice will tell us. But it should be said, in our defense, that the structural features of her description—the nested images, the focus on a significant detail in the picture, the coincidence between two images of a subject (one in the present, the other in the past)— are typical of autobiographical recollection. The *cinéma intime* on which Eliot relies in these first pages is an art of illusion, specifically designed to make us share the fiction of autobiographical memory. It creates a seamless continuity between the memory voice that tells us that the scenery is drawn from memory (the voice that says, "I remember those large dipping willows . . . I remember the stone bridge") and the scene in which the narrator faces the little girl.

In this way, Eliot forcefully reminds us that in the play of imagination, the odds are stacked very strongly in favor of an autobiographical moment, of a moment in which the subject will find herself, however fleetingly, in the scene. As we just learned, the painting tells a story, however minimal. A story is born from imagination. But *imagination* is too broad, too static a term for what we just saw in Eliot's text. Her text captures the stream of a consciousness; it captures someone's "movie-in-the-brain." Thus the writer's images will insensibly migrate toward an experience, however minimal, of the past. They will tend to come back to the forms of experience. In this, our writer seems to prefigure Antonio Damasio's conclusions concerning the mental patterning, the movie-in-the-brain that he analyzes in *The Feeling of What Happens*: "I would say," he writes, "that consciousness as currently designed, constrains the world of imagination to be first and foremost about the individual, about the individual organism, about the self in the broadest sense of the term" (304).[7] In the first pages of *The Mill on the Floss*, the mental avenue charted by the progression of memory images leads us similarly to the figure of a self, who eventually catches her reflection in the image of a little girl. What was originally cast as a simple musing, narrating voice is now embodied in an individualized figure, endowed with memories and with powerful yet cryptic emotions. The structure of imagination is then shaped so as to reveal the lines of a personal history. The emergence of images in the creative mind testifies to an act of consciousness that ends up serving the needs of autobiography.

Eliot's "structures of the imagination" teach us, meanwhile, that this biographical self is the product of the shifting gaze—of the moving camera—through which the subject ends up watching herself "as if [she] were there." Recollection would be understood, borrowing Freud's words, as the "working over" of an "original impression," of an impression forever lost ("Screen Memories," 321). It would consist in this constructive, imaginative act of making up for the absent origin leading to a point of recognition, where the subject can say to herself, "I seem to be watching things happen as if I were there." The phrase "as if," meanwhile, signifies that recollection occurs in the same epistemological realm as fiction. The most daunting, thought-provoking aspect of Eliot's memory experiment is indeed that it keeps returning us to this awareness of how closely memory making resembles fiction making. We reached this point in our discussion of nested structures, and we see it again when focusing on perspective. The rememberer's encounter with her past self, the specular moment when "I now" meets "I then," is precariously built over an epistemological, or rather a philosophical, abyss that teases us with the thought that perhaps it is all a dream. With her second, skeptical narrator, Eliot turns the mnemonic scene into an experience of déjà vu.

Exit the rememberer, enter then the lucid critic who transforms the former into a dreamer. At the close of the prologue, a new voice intervenes; it belongs to a subject who has endorsed a fully rational perspective. Gone is the dream of an autobiographical memory! The writer disclaims her identity as a rememberer and dismisses the lure of autobiography. Memory has become fantasy, and imagination a deceptive faculty that feeds us with the false belief that the past can be recaptured.

Memory and Fantasy

We have seen that the construction of memory is secured through a scenario that seems realistic and probable—a scenario that follows a predictable sequence of pictures and frames. But clever as it may seem, this structural definition of memory borders on a tautology. Who is to tell that the first image, or the last, for that matter, is not a fiction? The mind has so much practice in moving up and down nested structures that it surely can create realist scenarios quite effortlessly. In many cases, the *cinéma intime*, the movie-in-the-brain, requires a disclaimer, of the kind that Woolf used in *To the Lighthouse*—"Not a word of it was true, she had made it up"—or of the kind we read at the movies—"Any similarity to real events or persons is purely fortuitous." We may indeed need to be reminded of the power of our fantasy.

In arguing that our memories are constructed like clever realist fictions, I have paved the way for the skeptic, who, like Eliot's second narrator, will say, "What if the images I took for a memory were in fact only a dream?" But before we enter more fully into that view, we must grant that the naive position—which takes the realistic sequence of images on trust—is much more natural. The process of construction we witness in Eliot is so habitual (in Neisser's view, it occurs every time we remember autobiographically) that we are only too willing to lend it credence. Reading Eliot's prologue, we say to ourselves that "these must be memories," because the architecture seems so familiar and convincing. Our surprise when we are told that this is the case provides the measure of our innate confidence in a realist scenario. If autobiographical remembering involves the construction of such nested perspectives and if it aims, as we saw with Woolf and Freud, at finding the alignment between a subject in the present and a past self, it is not surprising that the vista Eliot constructed should lure us into the fiction of an auto-biographical encounter. Like a talented moviemaker, she has mastered the technique of realist construction, and as the images gradually fall into a pattern suggestive of a replication, the autobiographical memory that lay dormant at the core of this construction can emerge. Memory, as it were, begins to write itself into the perceptual scene: it seems captured in the very act of writing—of making images and structures, of building this minimal narrative of a specular encounter. Or so it seems—until the unsuspecting reader is woken rather brutally from the easy, comforting sense that a past is to be found just there, at the end of the road.

Eliot chose, then, not to bind imagination so closely to a self: she does not want to turn her fiction into an autobiography. If she acknowledges that these first images are the product of her memory, then how can she prevent her readers from assuming that other images, too, originated in the same fashion? Having struggled so hard to leave behind the young Mary Ann Evans and to fashion herself into the figure of an intellectual and a writer, the author will want to resist memory's enticements and leave behind home and the child that she was. In order to be George Eliot, she must eschew such easy sentimental and nostalgic returns to the past, and free herself from the bonds of memory. Thus, the little girl in *The Mill on the Floss* may well contemplate the watery scene like the narrator, she may well *look* like the figure of an earlier self, but the writer must resist that lure. Dreaming in her armchair, the writer created a girl called Maggie—and not Mary Ann.[8] The artist's overt gesture of dissociation from images as memories foregrounds, meanwhile, the aesthetic dimensions of her undertaking. Her art begins with the free play of images, images she pursues and cultivates because they give her pleasure. In that armchair sits a writer determined to follow her aesthetic sense, a mind at free play, detached from the contingencies of the outer world.

Eliot, nevertheless, cannot prevent the unfolding of another consequence of her experiment—the fact that the free, disinterested rehearsal of images may drift toward remembrance even against her better intentions. Her abrupt recantation (note that her narrator does say, after all, "I remember") proves how compelling the structure has become: almost inevitably, memory gets written into imagination. But it also makes for our surprise: it is our turn to understand that this seductive, compelling construction is in fact no more than a dream or a fantasy. One would have to go very deep into the psychology of reading and into the notion of "suspension of disbelief" (on which our experience of realist representations depends) to embrace the full complexity of our response to this unexpected shift from fiction-as-memory to fiction-as-dream. Suffice it to say here that the ground is pulled from our feet, and so much so that we feel tricked. More than tricked, betrayed perhaps—all the more deeply since Eliot's structure of the imagination comes so close to our common experience of memory. She succeeds, ruthlessly, in jolting us out of our ontological certainty.

What is reality if we cannot trust our imagination to produce real memories? In denouncing the all too easy passage into daydreaming and nostalgia, Eliot's text leads us, ultimately, to reexamine our naive investment in certain types of representations. It alerts us to the risk of confusion between memory and fantasy: she who passes for a rememberer may be, in the end, the supreme maker of fictions. Her subtle manipulation tells us that we need to lose our uncritical belief in the veracity of images. Standing on the edge between fiction and reality, Eliot's narrator gives voice to a crucial and resonant question: what structure of the imagination leads to belief—to a belief in memory? That memory entails belief is attested not only by Husserl, but by scientists as well: "The particular state of consciousness that characterizes the experience of remembering includes the rememberer's belief that the memory is a more or less true replica of the original event, even if only a fragmented and hazy one, as well as the belief that the event is part of his own past," writes the psychologist Endel Tulving (in Schacter, *Searching for Memory*, 17). Neisser himself speaks of confidence: "whether we remember the other levels or not, we are still confident in their existence. That confidence makes construction almost as inevitable in memory as it is unnecessary in perception" ("Nested Structure," 77). What is implied in his words is that we can construct memories only *because* or only *when* we are able to trust the same "instincts" that carry us across perceptions. We can

remember because we have learned that the world hangs together in a certain way, and it is precisely this kind of "hanging together" of the world
that Eliot, as a supreme realist writer, seems to have captured in these pages.

Images, as we saw in the previous chapter, are constructed when we
engage with the world of objects. But in imagination and memory the
objects are absent; they only exist, as Jean-Paul Sartre argues, in the space
of the mind or the psyche (*L'Imagination*, 138). These images of things
that are absent emerge from an inner world—the kind of world we
encounter when we close our eyes, literally or metaphorically, to what lies
in front of us. What makes Eliot's example especially interesting in this
context is an aesthetic commitment to realism. Combined together, her
unerring skill at narrative organization, her relish for certain details, and
the precision of her description convey an uncanny impression of reality.
Most striking perhaps are her narrative skills, which enable her to reproduce or mimic well-established perceptual schemes: they endow the pictures sprung from imagination with a semblance of reality, and they organize what would otherwise be a merely random collection of images in the
form of a *cinéma intime* that recalls a seemingly tangible outer world.[9] This
is why, in reading her, we feel the presence of a perceived world and
respond so easily to the lure of her images. These images, in Eliot's conception, are not different from those that we encounter in our dreams;
however, the fact that they are cast in a familiar pattern, a pattern that corresponds to established cognitive schemes, gives them an air of reality.
Thus Eliot's skills at representing the world have enabled her to reconstruct
a sequence of images "from the inside out." Reading her, we close our eyes
to the outside world and share, on the page, a passage or mental journey
that takes images from the inside to the outside. Indeed, her literary experiment enables us to see more concretely how, in the words of Antonio
Damasio, "images are constructed . . . when we reconstruct objects from
memory, from the inside out as it were" (*Feeling*, 318–19). It also enables
us to reconsider some of the qualities and defining traits of the faculty we
call "memory."

Given her remarkable gift for representation, Eliot helps us see, then, that
"memory effects" are the unexpected by-products of an aesthetic experience. Autobiographical memories can emerge whenever a first-person narrator exercises her mind in the way that Eliot suggests and builds a scene out
of freely associated images. However minimal the story, however simple the
event, what matters is that the narrating voice suddenly finds itself saying,
"I remember" and, for a moment, calls the images of her mental construction her memories. We discover, in these first lines of *The Mill on the Floss*,

how a subject is mesmerized by the spectacle of flowing water, by "vivid grass, the delicate bright-green powder softening the outline of great trunks and branches that gleam from under the purple boughs;" we read of her love of moistness, of her envy for "white ducks that are dipping their heads into the water." Nature, the landscape, the scenery speak to the writer-rememberer in ways that are mysterious and unaccountable. Why should memory alight, at times, on such insubstantial, and ultimately uninteresting, examples? Eliot speaks of a scene on the water; Woolf's favorite memory images are, as I showed in the preceding chapter, "blots of colour" and "waves breaking one-two, one-two." Proust's rememberer celebrates, not only tilleul and madeleine, but "a bubble formed against the side of a water-plant" and the "lingering scent of invisible lilacs."[10] Such are the events that take shape in the rememberer's mind; such are the scenes that the reader is asked to share. One cannot but marvel at the writers' skills: they paint, in words, pictures of the world to which we respond. These writers draw us into their most unaccountable memories. Who would think for a moment that our minds are so willing to dwell on a river, trees, a mill, ducks dipping their heads in water "mindless of the world above," when these vague, insignificant images have nothing to do with us, our selves, our individualities? Form and structure, as I have suggested, can be analyzed and accounted for—but content remains more mysterious. Indeed, Eliot's example forces us to reexamine the issue of content—the content of these mental patterns that we know either as "mere images" or as memories (when we take the required leap of faith).

Memory, according to the model we studied in Eliot, consists in our ability to bind images together, following perceptual schemes; in the impetus of an affect; or in the pursuit of a mood. When we come to the belief that these images of absent objects were known by us in the past, we say, "I remember," casting ourselves as rememberers. But we may decide that we are just imagining, that our "memories" are nothing more than free associations and residues—nothing more than the cobbled-together perceptual fragments of an earlier waking-life. There, we do not say that we remember, because we do not recognize in this picture the template of an earlier analogous impression. Yet even in that situation, as the scientist's theory on images suggests, memory is at work, but *invisibly,* since there is no conscious awareness or recognition of remembering. We do not discern the memories buried among the images.

There is, of course, a major defect in the model that we sketched out on the basis of Eliot's experiment: it is far too conscious, staging over a long duration (that of our reading) what must happen in a brain over a split second—a decision between "I remember" and "I see in my mind's eye." But this does not mean that the various steps that led us to the crucial dividing line between memory and imagination should be discarded. Nor can we discard the sense we get from Eliot's overture to her novel that memory, whether openly acknowledged or not, plays a crucial role in the construction of images that constitute our mental world. The deepest lesson we learned from Eliot's experiment is how tightly intertwined the reality effect and the memory effect are.

5 • Screen Memories

How do we recognize a memory and not confuse it with a fiction? How can we know that a memory is genuine and has been neither dreamed nor fantasized, but corresponds to some real historical event, however personal? Our examination of Eliot's memory experiment leaves us with these resounding questions and with an invitation to resume our analysis of the images involved in the construction of memory—this time in search of "a kernel of truth" amid our awareness of "the tendentious nature of the workings of our memory." I begin with two phrases borrowed from Sigmund Freud that figure at the heart of his questioning of screen memories, phrases chosen because they so aptly epitomize the tension between truth and fiction that this inquiry into personal remembrance reveals. In defining screen memories, Freud opens up a probing investigation into what determines the conviction of truth that we ascribe to mnemonic constructions.[1] It will serve as a departure point for a chapter focused on the truth value of memory.

To turn to psychoanalysis for an examination of this issue may seem like a paradoxical move, for on first appearances, what we owe to Freud is, surely, to have proved the inherent fallibility and the errancies of our remembering. But our debt to Freud's deconstructive approach to memory—an approach that illuminates the imaginary nature of reminiscence— may have led us to overlook the work of careful sifting and logical analysis that enabled the psychoanalytic revolution in our thinking about memory.[2] Before Freud came to the provocative conclusion that personal memories define a psychical reality or an inner, subjective truth regardless of their historical veracity, he applied his scientific, rationalist lens to a large number of so-called personal memories, but perhaps nowhere more probingly than in the essay of 1899 in which he developed the concept of screen memories. Indeed, in his astute commentary on this piece, Jean Guillaumin highlights Freud's search for a method designed to give internal evidence for the reality of a particular memory: "On the basis of this analysis, it would seem that a clinical investigation should provide an assured method for distinguishing between a memory and a pseudomemory, or at least to extract the latter from the former, even if this operation turns out to be difficult" (124). The "clinical investigation," Guillaumin concludes, shows a deep epistemological contradiction that ultimately reveals in Freud "a nostalgic realist." The nostalgic wants to believe that memories, however distorted, are built on the foundation of some true event; the realist knows that the grounds for a distinction between truth and fiction in personal experiences have become so tenuous as to warrant a radical skepticism. The concept of screen memories thus allows Freud to conclude that, however vividly real it may seem to the rememberer, a mnemonic scene is a sort of patchwork that stitches together various pieces of reality but glosses over the true nature of the recollected event. Thus, in tracing the contradictory currents of Freud's "nostalgic realism," we should develop a better eye for what gives memories their sense of reality. Our focal point is a memory recounted in "Screen Memories" by "a man of university education . . . with an interest in psychological questions" who is none other than Freud in disguise.

The Freudian Scene

> I see a rectangular, rather steeply sloping piece of meadow-land, green and thickly grown; in the green there are a great number of yellow flowers—evidently common dandelions. At the top end of the meadow there is a cottage and in front of the cottage door two women are standing chatting busily, a peasant woman with a handkerchief on her head and a children's nurse. Three children are playing in the grass. One of them is myself (between the age of two and three); the two others are my boy cousin, who is a year older than me, and his sister who is almost exactly the same age as I am. We are picking the yellow flowers and each of us is holding a bunch of flowers we have already picked. The little girl has the best bunch; and, as though by mutual agreement, we—the two boys—fall on her and snatch away her flowers. She runs up the meadow in tears and as a consolation the peasant-woman gives her a big piece of black bread. Hardly have we seen this than we throw the flowers away, hurry to the cottage and ask to be given some bread too. And we are in fact given some; the peasant woman cuts the loaf with a long knife. In my memory the bread tastes quite delicious—and at that point the scene breaks off. ("Screen Memories," 311)

The Freudian "scene in the meadow" is the most complex mnemonic structure we have seen so far, and before we can make sense of it, we need a better grasp of how it "hangs together." Virginia Woolf, we recall, teased us with the idea that mnemonic scenes were "representative," "enduring," and somehow "real," but she did not give much thought to their formal features or their organization. A scene, she hinted, organizes into some coherent whole what begins as random images or "impressions." In other words, for her, the scene is above all a structuring device—a device that enables us to "paint the past." It is worth noting, meanwhile, that with these almost interchangeable terms, Woolf confirms her adhesion to a pictorial model, as if memories came to her not as a story but as a vision—as something to be apprehended visually, as something one is meant "to see."

By contrast, Freud's richer example suggests that the mnemonic scene is defined by a narrative impulse that drives us toward an underlying story: here, for example, a tale of children playing, running, crying, and eating, of two boys running after a girl. Indeed, Freud's example invites us to think of the construction of memory as involving more than the mere alignment of images studied by cognitive psychologists. Rememberers do not just "add up" images toward a fuller context, they organize them toward some revelation: thus, for instance, going back to our case studies, a child on her mother's lap, a girl lost in the contemplation of water, a child's summer life in Combray, or boys running to snatch yellow flowers away from a girl. In fact, as has been pointed out by a subtle analyst of literary narratives, Alexander Gelley, scenes are "made to seem coordinate with the referent or the primary object of the fictive representation" (4). In other words, scenes do more than just give a picture of a fictive or, in the case of memory, of a *mental reality:* they embody a subjective intent toward an object. This is how they bring "narrative and perceptual elements together": they organize impressions around an event—an event that, for some obscure or explicit reason, deserves to be represented (156). A mnemonic scene, just like a good story, has a point.

But what we have learned about scenes from our studies of narrative suggests that we need to be aware of another principle, beside narration, that holds the mnemonic scene together, namely an overall affective tonality or mood. In examining the scenic organization of a memory in a text by the nineteenth-century writer William Thackeray, Percy Lubbock emphasizes that the memory effect is beholden to an overall atmosphere or emotion and derives from a scene "steeped in the suffusion of a general tone."

> Though the fullness of memory is directed into a consecutive tale, it is not the narrative, not its order and movement, that chiefly holds either Thackeray's attention or ours who read; the narrative is steeped in the suffusion of the general tone, the sensation of the place and the life that he is recalling.[3]

To get Lubbock's full meaning, we must conceive of Thackeray as another rememberer who shows us the two different currents that shape a mnemonic *scene*, namely the narrative "drive" of the image and a search for a phenomenal quality. These contrasting impulses—toward a narrative, historical conception of memory or toward its phenomenal, perceptual qualities—lead us right to the heart of Freud's investigation, and thus to his screen memory. To get at the principle of construction of a memory, we can follow its topographical organization along the lines we explored with Eliot and Neisser. We will see, in this instance, nested structures, a "zooming in" onto the event, and a defining shift of perspective from a field to an observer memory. But this line of inquiry does not tell us enough; it misses other aspects of the representation such as the variations in focus and the differences in perceptual intensities that are so carefully yet naturally registered in Freud's account. Indeed, when rereading Freud's beautifully scripted and strikingly visual account, I have often felt as if I were in the presence of one of those strips of 8mm film depicting family holidays that we used to watch when I was a child. The image was never quite steady or in focus; the only running commentary consisted in the rumbling sound of the projector, occasionally interspersed with our comments or giggles, so that the scene presented on the screen retained forever a mysterious, elusive quality. This is why, perhaps, the film always seemed too short, and the story never quite seemed to have a point.

As an interpreter or analyst of memories this is precisely where Freud starts, with the sense that the memory recounted by his companion does not make its point, suggesting that something remains hidden and elusive despite the apparent vividness of the recollection. His first guess is that the various impressions converge around an event that, for some obscure reason, cannot be revealed: the true content of the memory is screened off. This phenomenon, whereby one "innocuous" memory-construction serves as a decoy for another imperfectly remembered scene, is what Freud identifies under the name of "screen memories."[4] In the chapter "Childhood Memories and Screen Memories" in *The Psychopathology of Everyday Life*, Freud expands his definition: a screen memory, we learn there, is a mismatch between a memory image that stands out because of its vividness and the scene in which it is inserted. Analysis will reveal that the singular image, whose prominence cannot be justified by the memory's ostensible narrative, belongs in proper to another scene, which the rememberer hides from himself and thus from us.[5]

A striking feature of this personal memory is the deviousness of its presentation, for it turns out that Freud's account of the scene (with its yellow flowers, running children, good-tasting bread) is itself the product of a split voice and of a screening process. Freud is in fact the rememberer, but for the purposes of this scientific investigation, he hides behind the bland mask of "man of university education . . . with an interest in psychological questions" and answers the questions of his alter ego, the real Dr. Freud who analyzes him (309). The analysis will reveal that this scene screens off the memory of a childhood love and of a fantasy of defloration (symbolized in the snatching away of the yellow flowers). Given Freud's characteristic frankness, it would be surprising if the recourse to a split personality had coyness as its cause. It is much more likely that the reason for the dialogic structure is methodological: a clean epistemological break between the scientist and the rememberer can only promote objectivity. In other words, Freud puts himself on the side so as not to hide from us an embarrassing personal fantasy (there are plenty of those in *The Interpretation of Dreams*), but to better see himself. He leaves the field in order to be, truly, the observer. There, his position is not very different from the one I occupy in my family's screening of a home movie: he addresses his audience across the distance that separates him from the childhood scene. Indeed, like any other rememberer, Freud must have felt the split between the "I now" and the "I then," and in splitting his personality, he offers a vivid reminder that we all ultimately view the "film" of our memories through the eyes of a self very different from the subject in the picture.[6]

Yet another reason for Freud's screening strategy might be found in his need to handle two contradictory positions.[7] The "nostalgist" wants to believe that there is some reality to the childhood scene that is recounted; the realist knows that memories are just constructions. If it is to exist at all, Freud's science of memory—his clinical ability to mark the difference between true and false memories—will have to emerge from the dialogue of these alternating voices that, each in turn, examine these mnemonic presentations to decide about their "genuineness" (318). Through this dialogue, Freud can focus on the overlap, however tenuous, between the memories we construct and an external, historical reality. The two investigators appear to press hardest on the nature of the representation—for its realism and phenomenal features. Thus not only do they examine the coherence of the scene very attentively, but they are drawn again and again to wonder whether the vividness of the image can be correlated to its veracity. While the skeptical Freud questions the truth-value of personal memories that nevertheless appear so "strongly felt," another "nostalgic" Freud answers him with a desire to find ways of determining the genuineness of the memory. Indeed, as Eric LaGuardia suggests, "the idea that a recollection *can not* be reduced to an empirical, lived moment is apparently unthinkable" (303). The stakes of this conversation are, then, of crucial significance for our investigation: they bear, ultimately, on the truth status we ascribe to mnemonic constructions.

The Skeptical View

In this subtle shifting dialectic between alternating voices, we first follow the rememberer, who, after just a little prodding from his partner the analyst, is ready to endorse the position of the doubter and worries that memories may be the work of fantasy. He is indeed easily persuaded that the main features of his childhood memory might just answer his dream and fantasy for "the comfortable life" (staying at home and marrying the girl he loves). Freud assents, reassuringly telling him that it is only too natural to confuse memories with the stuff of fiction: "Yes, you projected the two fantasies on to one another and made a childhood memory of them," he tells him, and adds, "I can assure you that people often construct such things unconsciously—almost like works of fiction" (315). The analyst then proposes another idea (toying with and yet not fully endorsing the skeptical view): "It may indeed be questioned whether we have any memories at all *from* our childhood: memories *relating to* our childhood may be all we possess." (Freud expounds this thought in the chapter in *Psychopathology* as he writes: "one is thus forced by various considerations to suspect that in the so-called earliest childhood memories we possess not the genuine memory-trace but a later revision of it, a revision which may have been subjected to the influences of a variety of psychical forces," 68.)

This first move in the dialogue invites us to draw a tentative conclusion, suggesting that we construct our early memories in the same way we create fictions, that is, using fragments of reality to build a scene held together by unavowed, unacknowledged desires. The vividness of certain images merely marks them as screens for other memories that have yet to emerge—or shows that they belong to another scene. Along these lines, the tasty country-bread or the yellow flowers are the products of a wayward imagination: they are either falsely vivid and clear images that have been hallucinated or impressions connected to unconscious desires that correspond to fantasies. In his comment, Freud suggests a direct link between a perceptual intensity and a hallucination or a fantasy:

> The element on which you put most stress in your childhood scene was the fact of the country-made bread tasting so delicious. It seems clear that this

idea, which amounted almost to a hallucination, corresponded to your fantasy of the comfortable life you would have led if you had stayed at home and married this girl. . . .The yellow of the flowers, too, points to the same girl. (315)

In this interpretation, a screen memory provides evidence for the "the tendentious nature of the workings of our memory." The heightened phenomenal presence of certain images (such as the yellow flowers or the delicious bread) is deceptive: far from guaranteeing the memory's veracity, it signals distortions and suggests that the phenomenal features of this scene may have their source outside of reality, in the vagaries of desire.[8] Repression, meanwhile, accounts for both the creation of pseudo-memories that encrypt our fantasies and the confusion between time frames. In short, screen memories remind us of the memory distortions that occur under the sway of instinctual forces and signal the presence of the misremembered or the forgotten.

But in countering the intuition that tells us that a vivid image must be "real," Freud ultimately puts every memory in doubt, suggesting that more often than not, we inhabit, as rememberers, faulty constructions where images fall out of their proper timing and are not windows onto realities, but mirrors that reflect our fantasies. He also dismantles the simple structural view we have defended so far: the constructions that "look like" memories may well be devoid of any secure anchoring in reality, given that they cohere around a hidden core of fantasies, desires, and affects that cannot be accounted for in purely cognitive terms. However, this does not tell the realist or scientist why we believe in such constructions (only the psychoanalyst can say that our world is so profoundly molded by our fantasies and desires that we might as well acknowledge that we live in a hall of mirrors).

At this point, a detour through neuroscientific theories might be helpful. In *Descartes' Error,* Antonio Damasio raises the issue of mental constructions in his discussion of "storing images and forming images in recall," and like us, he ponders over what makes us believe in these constructions (100–104).[9] The most natural explanation, for him, is that we believe in these constructions because of our faulty knowledge of the brain: we assume that it holds permanent pictures of some things—so that, in the end, it might be our stubborn belief in mnemonic traces that makes us naturally trust our memories. The first thing, then, is to dismiss this mimetic model once and for all, which is what Damasio does with real rhetorical zest. "Images are *not* stored as facsimile pictures of things, or events, or words or sentences," he asserts, rejecting, in the space of half a page, all the common, cherished (and more elaborate) metaphors that imply mnemonic traces. Polaroid pictures, audiotapes, cue cards, Teleprompt transparencies, microfilms, hard copies, books—the list of things that memory is *not like* is long, and is clinched with the resounding statement, "[The brain] does not store films of scenes in our lives" (100). Damasio does end, however, with a concession: although we may be aware that memories are "interpretations" or "newly reconstructed versions," we still have the "sensation" that images are present, images that appear to approximate our earlier experiences. This must be the neurologists' way of telling us that, after all, we are all "nostalgic realists," caught in the same contradictory currents of belief and knowledge as Freud. We know that memories are constructions, yet we *like to think* that they are real. Damasio thus articulates, albeit from a different perspective, the two currents of thought at the heart of Freud's internal debate:

> [T]he denial that permanent pictures of anything can exist in the brain must be reconciled with the sensation, which we all share, that we can conjure up, in our mind's eye or ear, approximations of images we previously experienced. That these approximations are not accurate, or are less vivid than the images they are meant to reproduce does not contradict this fact. (100)

Why do we "naively" maintain our subjective view or our *feeling* rather (since this is a quale) that memories truly, mimetically correspond to a past event, when we know for a fact that *(a)* our brain does not store captions of the past, *(b)* recall never faithfully matches the present picture with the past perception, and *(c)* memory images provide us at best with an imperfect and faded picture of the initial perceptions? Like Freud, Damasio argues that the answer to these questions lies in the vividness of certain images. This vividness, he claims, relying on Hume, indicates that we are dealing with a reality that is external rather than internal.[10] One would assume, Damasio reasons further, that because memory images are naturally fainter than perceptions, we would naturally not want to ascribe to them the kind of reality that we ascribe to perceptions. But at the end of this analysis, the paradox remains, as Freud's essay on screen memories shows, and as Damasio suggests in reminding us that all mental images are in the end "constructions of your organism's brain" (97). In matters of memory, it is often the case that what we know theoretically does not match what we feel. Thus, as we remember, we believe (all too easily perhaps) that an internally generated image must have its source in our "photographic" perception of an external reality.

Thus, in questioning the "genuineness" of certain images that are part of a mnemonic scene, Freud helps us see the complications, and the contradictions even, of the phenomenological experience. What has become certain now is that a memory's vividness does not guarantee its reality. But must we then overlook the fact that sometimes memories can seem extremely "real"? We have evidence for this seeming paradox from Woolf's description of a particularly strong reminiscence: she thought for a moment that her childhood nursery was more real than the garden right under her eyes.[11] We now even have Freud's own words in "Screen Memories" to describe this experience: it "amounted almost to a hallucination." These two accounts invite us to pursue the other view—that of the nostalgic realist. Indeed, the small, seemingly innocuous word "almost" is what enables the dialectical reversal that takes us away from the skeptic's position. Since the memory is *almost* like a hallucination (but is not necessarily one), the analyst can now turn his coat inside out, or rather exchange it with the no longer so naive rememberer.[12] Having convinced his rememberer of the constructed and thus fictive nature of mnemonic images, he will now defend their genuineness.

The Naive and Nostalgic View

Thus, shifting his stance, Freud now seizes on these same details—the yellow flowers, the fragrant bread—that led him to the notion of screen memories to assert his own belief in the reality of certain elements of the memory scene:

> I see that I must take up the defence of its genuineness. You are going too far. You have accepted my assertion that every suppressed fantasy of this kind tends to slip away into a childhood scene. But suppose now that this cannot occur unless there is a memory-trace the content of which offers the fantasy a point of contact—comes as it were half way to meet it. (318)

If the flowers and the bread stand out, it is not as signs of displaced desire, but for the sheer intensity of their presence. Shifting discourse, one might say that Freud acknowledges in these images (or rather, in their phenomenal qualities) the mnemonic values that are crucial for the overall mnemonic construction. Let us note, meanwhile, that these distinctive images now belong to two separate maps: one of these maps spells out the subject's desire (his fantasy life), and the other traces, in these few scattered signs, the remnants of private experiences. In this second move, Freud now argues very differently that the rememberer might sometimes encounter a real memory from childhood—in, say, a yellow flower, a white duck, a whiff of lilac, flowers on a dress. But this is where his reasoning becomes truly subtle: such memories, we must understand, are bound to be "genuine" or "real"—because they fit right into the topography of desire, the fantasized memory. Freud's method for "distinguishing between a memory and a pseudomemory" seems to have led him to a paradox: the criteria that establish the genuineness of the memory are epistemologically grounded in the rememberer's fantasy life. The reasoning behind such complexities demands further unpacking.

I first need to qualify my earlier comparison of Freud's meadow scene with a film strip of my childhood, for what his analysis of the perceptual, sensory aspects of the memory now reveals are qualities in the representation—a salience, a vividness—that no camera could capture because they are so clearly projections of the rememberer's mind. Indeed, in focusing on the phenomenal aspects of the scene, the analyst detects in the "over-emphasis on the yellow" and the "exaggerated niceness of the bread" the signs of qualitative differences in the mnemonic presentation—from which he concludes that "the childhood scene seems . . . to have had some of its lines engraved more deeply" (318). Freud's formulation, it should be noted, remains perfectly ambiguous: it does not enable us to establish the origin of the phenomenal traits of the memory. Are they born as the "I now" revisits the scene, as a stylistic feature of the representation? Or, on the contrary, in keeping with a model of memory traces, do these differences in the quality of the presentation attest to the strength of the initial impress—to how a moment or an event was felt by the child (the "I then")? Our choice between these alternatives does not affect, however, the fundamental premise of Freud's thought here, namely that the qualia inscribed in this scene can be taken as evidence of a mnemonic experience. The excessive precision and clarity of the mnemonic picture (Freud uses the word *Überdeutlichkeit*) have become, paradoxically, the hallmark of the memory's authenticity. Indeed, the flowers so yellow and the bread so good as to seem "unreal" provide Freud with the best evidence that a subjective experience is being recalled.[13]

There are yet other aspects of the mnemonic scene that evoke the rememberer's complex involvement in the construction. Once we attend to the vividness and phenomenal qualities that are part of the memory, as Freud does, we understand that a mnemonic construction is much more than a structure of images; it is the careful edifice of a mind drawn to reproduce as *an inner reality* a pleasure connected to missing objects. Far from being the pure product of a cognitive structure, the mnemonic impression derives from, and is sustained by, a perceptual intensity linked to the pleasure promised by these images. Remembering is thus tied up with the pleasure that is given *in* or *by* certain images. In fact, the mnemonic scene offers precisely a way of experiencing both—the fascination for the memory content (for, say, yellow flowers, a smell of lilac, or a watery surface) and the fascination for the act of remembering. The vividness of the perceptual image, which answers a nostalgia for the return of a lived moment, is what lures us into the belief that we are truly, genuinely remembering. This explanation does not, however, fully answer the question of the referent of such mnemonic symbols. On the contrary, it raises a string of questions. Are these—the yellow flowers, the wonderful-tasting bread—genuine childhood memories? Did he, the Freudian rememberer, once, in a past moment, see such a field, green and dotted with yellow dandelions? Did he taste such bread? Has the mind kept a trace? Could it be that these images correspond to the long forgone past, whereas the rest of the memory, fraught with distortions, is revised in the light of more recent experiences?

As we know, for the neuroscientist, the fact that recalled images can be understood as mere mental projections, namely as the effect of neural activity, does not contradict the phenomenal experience, which tells us that these images of the past are somehow "real," where real means that "they are approximations of images previously experienced." On the contrary, the strength of the impression, "almost like a hallucination," might signal that the rememberer's brain has come up with a particularly convincing approximation of a perception. In other words, it becomes conceivable that the vividness of certain images tells us that the scene, however much of it is constructed or "fantasized," contains a residue of a real past. Thus, at the very point in "Screen Memories" where the rememberer becomes skeptical and is ready to interpret this childhood scene entirely in the light of later fantasies and projections, the analyst intervenes to suggest that the vividness of a particular impression identifies the place where the scene touches, tangentially as it were, on a real historical past. "Apart from your own subjective feeling which I am not inclined to underestimate, there is another thing that speaks in favor of the genuineness of your dandelion memory. It contains elements which have not been solved by what you have told me and which do not in fact fit in with the sense required by the fantasy," the analyst explains (318).

The dialectic of Freud's essay is thus resolved by way of a subtle distinction, a careful sifting of the narrative and the perceptual elements of the mnemonic scene, and leads to the conclusion that the "genuine memory" or "the kernel of truth" will appear in the elements that cannot be accounted for in the fantasy. Reality comes back in the recalled scene as what is insignificant and can have no signification.[14] In other words, what is "real" in the memory is whatever remains outside of the analytical story. Thus, for Freud, the truest element in the autobiographical memory stands outside of all narrative, as a phenomenal feature. Meanwhile, the yellow dandelion, the bread that tastes so good—both are invitations, offered by the rememberer's reimagining of the real, to map another world, that of the truly forgotten, which can only emerge in analysis. For among the images of a long-gone past representing our childhood, the only ones to be true are those, vividly present to the point of rapture, that cannot be folded into the structure, those that cannot be incorporated into the cohesive story of the subject's history.

Put in these terms, Freud's account of memory takes on a distinctly uncharacteristic, almost sentimental tonality. It is indeed the sentiment—respected and cultivated in the dialogue with the fictitious rememberer—that the thing that gives lasting pleasure in the recall, regardless of its objective or historical meaning, marks what is genuine, and remains untouched by our ability to construct and make fictions of our memories. The spectacle of this strongly visual and plastic scene must have seemed all the more exceptional and alluring to the author whose memories now take a different form: drawing on a distinction established by Charcot, Freud declares in the *Psychopathology* that he no longer experiences visual memories.[15] There are, then, strong reasons why, in order to fully and accurately remember, the nostalgic Freud, the Freud who holds in his mind a vision of a long-gone past—a precious childhood scene—needs his alter ego, the analyst. He needs both a foil (so that he can stage a debate) and a safeguard (against his nostalgia). That skeptical other will know how to lift the veil to reveal the dreams and fantasies that we take for memories; he will also ensure that the rememberer does not lose a healthy analytical distance. For to be held in the thralls of memory, to experience the full impress of the past without a skeptic's recoil, is to flirt with hysteria.[16] Freud's duplicitous maneuver is not merely rhetorical or pedagogical; it marks the suspicion with which the scientist greets autobiographical memory and a resistance to the sentimental lure of the past. The analyst, unlike the writers whom we examined, wants to deny himself the pleasure of a return. The contrast is striking indeed between the cautious and almost devious stance Freud takes in his presentation of the meadow scene, and the sentimental abandonment to memory represented in Proust's *Recherche*. There the narrator harks for a silence that will enable him, still, to hear himself sobbing in the past (*Swann's Way*, 40).

One might object that such sentimentality opens the road to fiction, but amid such fiction there seem to be, even for the skeptical Freud, a few points that touch upon some authentic, genuine experience. Moreover, given the nature of recollection, an overlap between the rememberer and the fiction writer seems unavoidable. Do they not use, after all, the same tools to construct their scenes? Descriptions, subjective points of view, shifts in perspective, and nuances in tone and representation are all factored into the remembrance. Structural frameworks are thus combined with mnemonic images to endow memories with an air of reality. But one question persists, however, which bears on the relation between a memory and an event. "Now what is there in this occurrence to justify the expenditure of memory which it occasioned me?" Freud wonders in the guise of the rememberer. We still need to ask ourselves, then—not as analysts but as phenomenologists interested in qualitative states—why rememberers can ascribe such vividness to an image that seems, from an objective point of view, so insignificant. Naturally we can only guess, for only the rememberer him- or herself experienced the event revisited in this scene. Nevertheless, though the content of a memory is everyone's own creation, what Freud called "the expenditure" can be felt by everyone—listeners, readers, and students of memory alike.

Mnemonic Values

A memory, we might thus say, borrowing Gelley's definition of a scene, is a "topography in which the subject enacts his fascination and desire" (160). It speaks to us, partly, because of its "expenditure"—because of some mysteriously intense patches of color or sensation that give it a phenomenal presence. In response to this new definition, I want to turn back to George Eliot's rememberer, for, truth to tell, I am fascinated by her claim that in contemplating the mill on the Floss, she fell in love with moistness and became envious of ducks. Why this fascination? Why this desire? By casting another glance at Eliot's prologue, we might see better how cognitive structures and emotion blend in the construction of memory. Relinquishing Freud's psychoanalytical view, I would like to examine another screen memory to give one more twist to my investigation into how a memory "feels."

"If we could observe consciousness we might see a sequence of alternating points of view as remembering progresses, a sequence which is coordinated with shifting concerns, and reactions," writes John A. Robinson in what reads like an invitation to shift our structural analysis to a perspective that involves emotion (240).[17] Indeed, one can revisit Eliot's prologue to observe how "shifting concerns and reactions" form a consistent sequence and help the articulation of the memory. Whereas the scene seems to exist by virtue of an overall mood (that "suffusion of a general tone" described by Lubbock), modulations of affect are also palpably present and nowhere more strikingly than in that cryptic moment when the memory voice says, "How lovely the little river is with its dark, changing wavelets! It seems to me like a living companion while I wander along the bank and listen to its low placid voice, as to the voice of one who is deaf and loving."

> As I look at the full stream, the vivid grass, the delicate bright-green pow-der softening the outline of the great trunks and branches that gleam from under the purple boughs, *I am in love with moistness, and envy the white ducks* that are dipping their heads far into the water here among the withes—unmindful of the awkward appearance they make in the drier world above. (54; emphasis added)

Here, the narrator (and the writer perhaps?) is clearly entranced by her own vision, and yet one cannot help but feel that her "concerns and reactions" are somehow extravagant and clearly in excess of what is represented. Why so much expenditure? Why, for instance, be in love with the moistness or envy the ducks? This must be just a way of speaking—of expressing the fas-cination exerted by these images and reflected in the lingering, and at times nearly static, nature of this scene. For although a "consecutive tale" is unquestionably being told here (a tale that leads to a meeting with the young girl), the perceptual intensities and the pleasure conveyed by certain images are clearly just as important, if not more so. Thus, while this rememberer's "mental time travel" follows a topography of shifting spatial perspectives and frames, it is also determined by affects.[18] The memory scene exists by virtue of intensified perceptual experiences that are grafted onto a structural frame.

With its odd intensities, unexplained vividness, and singular values, Eliot's memory scene holds us, as if spellbound, in the lure of the remem-berer's voice. It is in the nature of the scene to "attract without yielding," and "it offers itself in order to entrap," Alexander Gelley writes in what seems an apt commentary for Eliot's compelling scenic or "cinemato-graphic" abilities (169). It has indeed been our experience throughout, as readers, that certain types of representation produce a "memory effect," as we saw when we studied the first pages of Woolf's "A Sketch of the Past." But with Eliot, the case is different and more subtle. She depends essentially on the mood created by her images, while Woolf "created" the illusion of memory through her pictorial mode as well as, perhaps, through her sheer determination (her confident "I begin—the first memory"). In fact, we are so taken by the mood of Eliot's text, that only the most attentive reader will stop at the strange, irrational idea that her narrator is so infatuated with her white ducks that she would like to be one of them.

What draws us into the mnemonic scene is not the image itself (for what is there to learn from a duck dipping its head in the water?), but rather the mood it conveys. Similarly, it is not the action, which is minimal, but the residual atmosphere of unresolved emotions and enigmatic investments in ordinary objects that hints at a buried "kernel of truth." The presence of mysterious affects, whose true source remains unaccounted for, explains the faintly melancholy impression we get from reading these pages: the mind lingers over certain images as if in search of something that has been lost. Jean Guillaumin suggests that melancholia, with its tonality of enigmatic loss, is one of the defining moods of recollection.[19] This is the mood—the "suffusion of a general tone"—we recognize, and identify with, in the scene George Eliot created. Melancholy is the translation, into the emotional realm, of a structural and cognitive feature that defines the memory, namely the discrepancy between what is shown and what is ultimately told. Indeed, as we learned with Proust, remembering is never complete; there are always more elements to be remembered, always missing parts to a memory. The memory scene always exceeds the images that constitute it; or, putting it differently, there can be no end to the telling, and some things will always be missing. These "ephemeral details" that stand out in the picture—the little river, the white ducks, "the delicate bright-green powder softening the outline of the great trunks and branches that gleam from under the bare purple boughs"—hold us with the mysterious and unresolved charm and significance of an unfinished story.[20]

This is why, beside melancholia, the memory is pervaded by a sense of the uncanny—the emotion we feel when we face a scene that hints at "what is concealed and kept out of sight."[21] We feel it, I think, in the "dreamy deafness" that affects the scene overall, as well as in that "low placid voice . . . of one who is deaf and loving." But this impression of *Unheimlichkeit*— of attraction and of slight anxiety, of at-homeness and simultaneous estrangement—is even more palpable in the closing moment, before the awakening from the memory scene. It is inscribed in the pattern of rapprochement followed by alienation that defines the scene's minimal narrative: the narrator's gaze moves toward a certain point on the river Floss, meets the little girl; a dog is barking, but the girl is too "rapt" to hear it, and then she must go home, and so does the narrator. As we know, this scene is built so as to evoke a convergence between the little girl and the storyteller. But although the narrating voice reinforces the implicit connection between the two figures in a parallel construction ("It is time the little play fellow went in" is echoed by "it is time too for me to leave"), it simultaneously dismantles the lure of the memory scene in sending the child and the rememberer their separate ways. Thus, while the little girl is going home, where "there is a very bright fire to tempt her," the narrator must leave the scene. It is from the contrary motions of "at homeness" and of alienation that an uncanny impression emerges.[22] Indeed, true to the contradictory etymology of *unheimlich* (which Freud analyzed at length in his essay on the uncanny), the rememberer inhabits an in-between, ambivalent space: at home in and yet fundamentally estranged from the moments of childhood. The true home in this scene, with its "bright fire in the left-hand parlour," is forever inaccessible, and while the rememberer can, just like the young child, lose herself in the contemplation of the Floss, there can be no return for her—only the lure of a homecoming afforded by memory and imagination. Here, one might say, the feeling of the uncanny veers toward nostalgia—namely to an acute awareness of the past's inherently irrecoverable nature. Perhaps, as Eliot shows us, our truest, deepest memories always come to us with a sad sense of loss—of something that lies always, uncannily, outside of our reach while seeming so real and so close to home.

Fictions

The architecture of memory, as we just learned, depends only in part on structure and narrative; shifting moods, which determine the phenomenal intensities of certain images, play an equally important role. Thus, the closer we look at the construction of memories, the more it resembles the work of creative writers. Coming from a literary scholar such as I am, this appropriative move will come as no surprise, perhaps. But cognitive psychologists seem to concur; for example, Ulric Neisser's description of mnemonic construction invites a direct comparison with storytelling. Witness the following account of how we build a mnemonic scene with different degrees of elaboration and confidence—and consider, meanwhile, how closely remembering resembles literary strategies.

> Recall is almost always constructive. No matter how well you remember an event, the information available will not specify all the contexts that once gave it meaning or all the molecular actions that were nested inside it. If you care to try, you can build on what remains to reconstruct some of what is missing. How much you make up and how much you are content to omit will depend on your situation at the time of recall and on your intentions.

Detailed and colorful accounts are effective if you want to impress an audience; less elaboration is appropriate when you are testifying in court. (Some
witnesses, especially young children, may not understand the difference
between those two situations.) ("Nested Structure," 78)

With the construction of memory looking so much like narrative development (how much you make up, how much you omit, how much detail, how
much color), it becomes difficult to sustain the idea that memories grow
spontaneously following a natural structural and associative path. Autobiographical memories bear the imprint of an author who shaped them like a
text destined for a particular audience. Rememberers are not just skillful
craftsmen, they are also crafty creators. Proust's narrator acknowledges
this, possibly against his best intentions, when in describing the process of
recollection born from the tilleul and madeleine, he readjusts his vocabulary
from *chercher* to *créer*. Though this narrator never seems to question the
"genuineness" of his memories, he now risks contradicting himself in
emphasizing, this time, the rememberer's active involvement in recollection—so active that he identifies himself as the memories' creator.

As the architects of our past, we erect stone after stone—but imagine all
the while the great arches that sustain the cathedral destined to contain and
celebrate the stubborn survival of our past impressions. *L'édifice immense
du souvenir*, to borrow Proust's metaphor, is the result of a labor of love
(and of self-love, as we shall see in the last chapter of this book). But memories also depend on an act of faith—faith in the fact that the structure of
imagination is not merely a dream or a fantasy. Memories vanish into thin
air when there is no belief (the philosopher's term) or confidence (the cognitive scientist's) to sustain them. The aroma of tilleul, some bright yellow
flowers, a scenery that gives an impression of déjà vu, a few blots of color—
with such minimal cues we build our past in the belief that this perception
reaches back to an experience. The memory prompt does not even have to
be real, as we shall see when we examine, in a moment, the lilac scene in
Proust's *Recherche:* even if merely hallucinated, a mere whiff of lilac can
still provide the occasion for mental travel. One understands, meanwhile,
why the Proustian rememberer puts the highest stakes on involuntary recollection. When they surge up unexpectedly, prompted by an unusual perception, these Proustian memories appear to be all the more real for having
been prompted by an external object and for seeming ready to fly in at the
beckoning of the attentive mind. Indeed, in a flush of enthusiasm and faith,
Proust's rememberer even toys with the concept of metempsychosis in order
to suggest that memories may have an existence independent of our mind.

"Souls," he tells us, are held captive in "some inanimate object," and in hearing their call, the rememberer must eagerly respond so that they can "return to share our life" (*Swann's Way*, 47).

Such epiphanies are rare, however, as even Proust would acknowledge, and most often we end up constructing memory scenes around images that are not as firmly grounded in perception as the aroma of tilleul that brings back Combray or the jolting feeling of an uneven pavement that resuscitates Venice.[23] Sometimes the cue is much more tenuous and the memory much more elusive; sometimes the image is but a screen on which we project our desires. Thus, however reassuring the metaphor of metempsychosis, it cannot entirely forestall the rememberer's natural propensity to spin off memories on the most insubstantial of promptings. "How much similarity must there be between the two moments in order for one to count as a memory for the other? How much of the content of the experience must be reproduced and how accurately? How many portions of the past is the present connected to in a condensed memory, and how is this determined?" Marya Schechtman asks, in a philosophical questioning that invites us to revise a *mimetic* conception of memory (9–10). While we know that structural and quantitative reasoning is misapplied when it comes to understanding what produces the "feel of" or "the belief in" a memory, we may need another reminder, at the end of our qualitative or phenomenological analysis, that the disparity between the cue ("the condensed memory") and the past experience might be much greater than we intuitively, naturally assume. This idea is not new, of course; it is really Freud's, which he develops around the concept of screen memory.

In a curious scene at the end of "Combray," Proust evokes a problematic disparity between a cue and the remembrance it triggers, a disparity suggestive of a screen memory that gives us a chance to sum up what a belief in memory means and entails. The scene reveals the mildly eccentric behavior of a zealous rememberer cursed, it seems, with an impractical addiction to the smell of a lilac (or more broadly perhaps with an addiction to remembrance itself).[24]

> When, on a summer evening, the melodious sky growls like a tawny lion, and everyone is complaining of the storm, it is the memory of the Méséglise way that makes me stand alone in ecstasy, inhaling, through the noise of the falling rain, the lingering scent of invisible lilacs. (*Swann's Way*, 202)

At first glance, we recognize here a foreshortened version of a typical Proustian epiphany—the pinprick of a sensory impression produces a memory.

The lilac's fragrance seems to carry what Walter Benjamin, in his essay on Proust's involuntary memories, so appropriately called the "breath of a pre-history" ("Image," 185). But a closer look reveals complications. First, a hard-and-fast distinction between willful and spontaneous recall all but vanishes. What if, for example, the reminiscence was deliberately induced by the overall mood of a walk under the rain, so that the smell of the flower was merely incidental? Then, how contingent or how overdetermined is the memory, given that even an *invisible* lilac can prompt it? And then other questions arise: namely, where on earth is this lilac truly to be found, in Méséglise (most probably, as long as the people of Combray still plant them) *and* in Paris? Or then, in Méséglise and just in the mind? What if, moreover, the smell of lilac were but a screen for a memory that is more erotically charged and thus harder to come by because repressed?[25]

The vividness of the image (arresting enough to create a moment of ecstasy) initially convinced us that our rememberer was on the scent of another remembrance—but in the absence of empirical evidence, the fragrance may well have been hallucinated. What then of the memory itself? Is it not also a mere illusion or fantasy? Once it loses its anchoring in a perceptual scenario, the memory is indeed (as it always was, of course!) just in the mind: an image whose genuineness can never be guaranteed. The astute reader, with a vested interest in the realism of fiction, might even intervene at this point to convince us that this could not have been a "real" lilac, for our rememberer, known for his allergies, would immediately have started sneezing and wheezing. A similarly inquisitive reader might conceivably board a train for the French countryside to check on the lilacs in Méséglise (if this idea seems foolish, it is what Gérard de Nerval would do, as we shall find out later in this study). While these moves toward the corroboration of an auto-biographical memory may seem absurd, they do show what slippery ground we are on, epistemologically speaking, with this thought experiment.[26] Who is to say, in the end, what is truly remembered or just fantasized? Proust, of course, makes no room in his text for such skeptical questioning. On the contrary, he pushes us repeatedly, with scenes depicting the ecstasies of a rememberer, into believing that memories represent what was truly there in the past. From his perspective, the invisible lilac constitutes an incontrovertible "mental reality": it might be a mere image, but its existence is sustained by the associations formed in memory. Whether such images are purely mental or find their referent in a physical reality no longer matters very much—what matters instead is a belief in their existence, past or present.

Is there anything abnormal in our subject's investment in a scene built on such tenuous ground as the scent of an invisible lilac? Apparently not, Antonio Damasio tells us in *Descartes' Error*. Our experience of the world, he argues, is framed in images, namely in constructions of our brain that are only real to ourselves (97). The world past is made of recalled images "which occur as you conjure up a remembrance of things past," the present made of perceptual images that correspond to "varied sensory modalities," and we also have "images recalled from plans of the future" (these are "images of something that has not yet happened and that may in fact never come to pass," 96–97). Meanwhile, Damasio insists, "the construction is directed entirely from within our brain," and this is true "whether the scenes are a replaying of a real event or an imagined one." Given our brain's natural tendency to spin off—regardless of verification—what Damasio calls "marvelous constructions," there must be nothing abnormal—nothing wrong even—in the confusion between reality and fantasy that we felt in the lilac scene. In not distinguishing clearly between the imagined and the empirical reality of his images, our rememberer is neither mad nor disingenuous; he is simply "imagining." That is, he plays memory's game, summoning images and indulging in "marvelous constructions" that look real to him. As long as he can feel the ecstasy, it does not matter much whether the scene summoned in his "sweet and silent thought process" (to borrow Damasio's phrase) is "a replaying of a real event or an imagined one" (97). If it feels so much like a memory, it must be one.

In probing the limits of the metaphor of memory as construction, we have learned that the play of associations that binds images together into a scene is vested with affects as well as with aesthetic investments. Sustained as it is by a particular love for, or an investment in, the image, the mnemonic scene is inherently dynamic, meaning that our memories are alive to the extent that they are marked by perceptual values and by a recognizable emotional "expenditure." It has been my contention in this chapter, in the wake of Freud's assertion in "Screen Memories," that remembering resembles the making of fiction. Indeed, like fiction, the expansion of memory depends on the suspension of disbelief: "it is not just an image," each rememberer says, "it represents a reality, albeit now absent and past." But, we would still have to assume that while the writer is primarily concerned with drawing her readers into the imagined reality of her construction, the rememberer first responds to the lure of an image and then experiences its "reality" in the memory's architecture. To that extent, the intentions of the writer and those of the rememberer must be different. But there are many places, as I have tried to show, where they blend—for example in their shared endorsement of a nostalgic stance. Indeed, what feeds our belief in the reality of the image is ultimately nostalgia—namely a desire for memory.

6 • Proustian Memory Gardens

At the outer reaches of current thinking on the mind and brain, scientists are confronted with qualitative issues that reopen some of the older questions studied by phenomenologists, questions involving imagination and representation. Oliver Sacks, for instance, prefaces his discussion of reminiscence linked to organic disorders, in *The Man Who Mistook His Wife for a Hat*, with an acknowledgment that his patients' experiences of a "regained" phenomenal universe cannot be understood purely from a neurological perspective, and seems to implicitly defend the value of a qualitative, phenomenological approach. He thus writes:

> We have always two universes of discourse—call them "physical" and "phenomenal" . . .—one dealing with questions of quantitative and formal structure, the other with those qualities that constitute a "world." All of us have our own, distinctive mental worlds, our own inner journeyings and landscapes, and these, for most of us, require no clear neurological "correlate." (*Man Who*, 129)

More recently, in his review "The River of Consciousness," Sacks explains that despite striking advances in brain science and neuro-imagery "something beyond our understanding occurs in the genesis of qualia, the transformation of an objective cerebral computation to a subjective experience" (43). Meanwhile, Christof Koch, a leading researcher in cognitive neuroscience whose work is reviewed by Sacks, similarly acknowledges that the question of the neural, biological underpinnings of our simplest perceptions—say of an orange or a green apple—is far from being resolved. Working with a team of colleagues, he concludes, in an article entitled "Neural Correlates of Consciousness in Humans," that "the directness and vivid quality of conscious experience belies the complexity of the underlying neural mechanisms, which remain incompletely understood" (Rees, Kreiman, and Koch, 261).

The limitations of science when it comes to understanding the phenomenal aspects of memory and perception might account, to some extent, for Sacks's fascination with Proust's work.[1] The attentive reader will indeed find in the *Recherche* among the fullest, richest descriptions we have of a subjective world, and the text is rife with verbal "correlates" for phenomena that belong to consciousness and memory. Proust's imagination brings forth picture after picture of a "distinctive mental world" and relentlessly traces the "inner journeyings and landscapes" that define a human consciousness. But his text reveals more, even, than careful descriptions of phenomenal contents: it provides us with the foundations of a theory that shows how memory creates our sense of reality and helps us construct our very being.

There is no better way of understanding the natural link between memory, reality, and subjectivity that so fascinated Proust than to consider it in the light of forgetting, which represents the true starting point of his *Recherche*.[2] Indeed, in focusing on the "miracle" of involuntary recollection, we have overlooked the existential urgency that marks the Proustian quest and not paid enough attention to the "memory voice" that speaks anxiously of our dependency on memory for our identity.[3] Often enough, however, rather than celebrating the miracles of involuntary memory, Proust's text takes on a graver, more subdued tone, which evokes the anxious knowledge of someone who has understood that to forget is to die. This person can write so compellingly about remembrance because he is haunted by the infinitely complex and ultimately fragile nature of human remembrance. We identified him at the outset of our work: the recumbent rememberer, half awake, half dreaming, who peers into the darkness, straining all his attention toward the retrieval of memory images. We saw the triumphant moments when whole worlds, inner journeyings and landscapes were seemingly reborn from the right cue, the mere prick of a sensation. But there are also moments of failure, when forgetting prevails, and we are reminded of the looming threat of forgetfulness. Sometimes a memory, in spite of a first prompting, cannot be reconstructed, and it is precisely this sort of memory that appears in the final pages of "Combray" through the striking metaphor of a floating island:[4]

> Sometimes the fragment of a landscape thus transported into the present will detach itself in such isolation from all associations that it floats uncertainly in my mind like a flowering Delos, and I am unable to say from what place, from what time—perhaps, quite simply, from what dream—it comes. (*Swann's Way*, 201)

But this is too mild an example; often Proust's tone is more urgent, and the anxiety about forgetting more palpable, as when he compares himself to a solitary night-bird peering into a black night: "I can testify that everything happened in this fashion, I, the strange human being, who while waiting for the time when death delivers him, lives with closed shutters, knows nothing of the world, remains still like an owl and, like the latter, peers dimly into darkness" (*Sodome et Gomorrhe II*, 2:788). Upon encountering this avowal, late in the work, the reader knows that "darkness" describes a mental space to be explored and conquered through writing, where layer upon layer of memories is held in abeyance. In a striking passage, Proust invokes a geological metaphor: a rememberer who digs deeper and deeper into the past until he reaches the "deepest layer of [his] mental soil."

> All these memories, superimposed upon one another, now constituted a single mass, but had not so far coalesced that I could not discern between them—between my oldest memories, my instinctive memories, and those others, inspired more recently by a taste or "perfume," and finally those which were actually the memories of another person from whom I had acquired them at second hand—if not real fissures, real geological faults, at least that veining, that variegation of colouring, which in certain rocks, in certain blocks of marble, points to differences of origin, age, and formation. (*Swann's Way, 203*)

Topographical metaphors abound when it comes to describing the mind—as with Sacks's "distinctive mental worlds" and "inner journeyings and landscapes."[5] But the memory garden I study in this chapter is both a metaphor (a special feature of the mental topography analyzed by Proust) and a real space designed to promote reminiscence. Metaphorically, it represents that part of a mental world where exceptionally vivid and lasting memories have their roots; concretely, it exists as a garden carefully planted with Proustian mnemonic cues. As part of the treatment of memory loss, a number of gardens have been built around specialized residences, in which plants and flowers are specially chosen to evoke childhood memories—very much in the spirit of Proust, as the summary description circulated in the newsletter of the Alzheimer's Association confirms: "The garden's hundreds of plants and herbs are non-toxic, and some plants, such as gardenia and jasmine, were chosen for their distinctive aromas that stimulate the memory" ("Memory Gardens," 2). The visit to the garden can prompt the amnesiac to remember, as one resident of a specialized facility attests in describing her experience of involuntary recollection.

> I think a garden glorifies a house. When I walk out of my house, I feel young, lovely and anxious to see beautiful flowers and green grass. Generally, it lightens my spirit. I feel like dancing. When I was a kid, they always gave me a spot in the garden. We had a big lawn surrounded by

bushes of roses. If I had a house, I would have a garden. (Zeisel and Tyson, 440)

A cue planted in the Alzheimer's treatment garden has resuscitated a memory, and for a while, the patient is safely, happily housed in her childhood, with a spot of garden where roses bloom. Proustian remembrance has given her a "home-scene" to which she can return, as well as the momentary comfort that we draw from continuities of the self. In *The Mill on the Floss*, George Eliot describes the same feeling, but in the richer, more evocative language of a narrator who is in possession of all her mental faculties. The garden that Eliot celebrates has no walls, no obvious therapeutic role; it is just a "piece of nature," but it too is a product of memory and thus creates a feeling of at-homeness in the world:

> The wood I walk in on this mild May day, with the young yellow-brown foliage of the oaks between me and the blue sky, the white star-flowers and blue-eyed speedwell and the ground-ivy at my feet—what grove of tropic palms, what strange ferns or splendid broad-petalled blossoms, could ever thrill such deep and delicate fibers within me as this home-scene? These familiar flowers, these well-remembered bird-notes, this sky with its fitful brightness, these furrowed and grassy fields, each with a sort of personality given to it by the capricious hedgerows—such things as these are the mother tongue of our imagination, the language that is laden with all the subtle inextricable associations the fleeting hours of our childhood left behind them. (94)

With these words, Eliot creates a memory of a memory and represents a physical landscape inscribed with mnemonic images that is part of her own "distinctive mental world." Indeed, each of us, Eliot argues, similarly owns a private garden inscribed with singular moments of being that were experienced in childhood. In our earliest years, we create a first promptbook of the world that will determine, in lasting fashion, our relation to reality. Such moments, she concludes, are forever part of our lives; they are indelible (94). Eliot's notion, it should be noted, seems to converge with Freud's idea that some memory traces stand out more forcefully as "psychical realities."

But equally important for our understanding of remembering, Eliot's sense of memory assumes that these images (the blue-eyed speedwell, the aroma of tilleul, the red and blue flowers on a black background, the yellow flowers, or the smell of bread), because they are more deeply engraved in the mind, would be the most memorable. In other words, what Eliot tells us, implicitly, is that the images of the memory garden are qualitatively different. Long consolidated, these images will be the most easily activated—and remembered.[6] It is on this very assumption that Alzheimer's treatment gardens have been invented: through the happy, seemingly haphazard (but in fact carefully planted) encounter with a strong sensation, the forgetting patient might experience a reminiscence.[7] Indeed, if prompted by the right sensation, the older, deeper memories might reemerge when all else may seem forgotten.

There exists, Schacter suggests, "an exquisite interdependence between encoding and retrieval." According to current theories, it is indeed the affinity between the retrieval cue and the encoded engram that enables the creation of the new entity—the "memory of a memory" (*Searching for Memory*, 62).[8] The memory garden is an experimental, therapeutic space devoted to the cultivation of "appropriate retrieval cues"—cues that will prompt the creation of forgotten memories in the amnesiac's mind. But there is more to this mnemonic experience than just the revival of a mental function that until then seemed lost, and more for the patient than just the sheer pleasure of remembrance. The act of reminiscence provokes an awakening—a moment of consciousness—that reconnects the oblivious patient to a self and to a familiar reality. As Eliot intimates in speaking of a "mother tongue of our imagination," we are cued into reality by memories that lay the foundations of our identity. Inspired by George Eliot and building on this idea, Proust tells us, more provocatively, that "reality takes shape in memory alone."[9]

Encoding and Retrieving the Past: The Proustian View

At the end of "Combray," as he closes the first arc of his disquisition on memory in the *Recherche*, Proust's narrator dreams of, thinks of, and remembers a landscape that is so significant for him as to have determined his very idea of—and his belief in—reality. The discovery of this landscape leads him to the forceful and quite extraordinary assertion that *reality takes shape in memory alone*.[10] This "fragment of landscape," this "piece of nature," this "corner of a garden," and even this "whole landscape"—as this spot is variously called—lies in the center of the Proustian universe, at the crossroads between the "Méséglise way" and the "Guermantes way." Yet in evoking this landscape, the rememberer does more than express his nostalgia: he maps an inner landscape dotted with mental images that serve as cues for further remembrance. There are, meanwhile, literary as well as philosophical-scientific aspects to this reconstitution of a rememberer's private memory-garden. The writing invites us to share the texture of familiar and beloved places, with a precision and richness that seems designed to guarantee the reality of their existence. In this fashion, Proust redefines memory in terms of a qualitative difference of experience—as memorable impressions that define one subject's experience and personal history. As for the philosophical investigation, it starts with the idea that this landscape reflects "the life of the mind," a life rich in "episodes" and "vicissitudes."

"Images," Sartre wrote in his study of imagination, "have an undeniable psychical reality," inviting us to acknowledge that our sense of reality is inseparable from our ability to create images through our perceptions (*L'Imagination,* 138). In this conception, images exist neither in the brain nor in the world outside; rather, they appear in the space between, where we make sense of the world by focusing our mind on its objects. Proust seems to share Sartre's phenomenological view: first, in his insistence that the images found in this memory garden belong properly to the psyche (or as he writes, to "la vie intellectuelle," "la pensée," "le sol mental"); then in showing how the rememberer's sense of reality is shaped or, more powerfully even, determined by the resilience of certain images. Thus, in revisiting the episodes of his life connected to Combray, our author assumes that the images born from his memory provide him with unmediated access (he shows no awareness of their literariness) to past realities. They function for him like transparencies that, seen in the proper light and through the right lens, render a brightly colored, vivid representation of what was: the lighting and the lens are the mental properties of the rememberer, who activates them through a deliberate attentiveness, as his mind explores, as it were, more recesses of his memory garden.[11]

Compared with what we learned about involuntary recollection, a new and more radical definition of memory emerges here. In the early parts of the *Recherche,* we saw how sensations produce images through associations. But in his investigation into memory gardens, Proust grounds his conception of memory in the notion of attention: we respond to the world in a singular and personal way because, in the mental landscape that unfolds in front of us, we latch onto discrete cues of prior encounters, moments, or events.[12] In other words, it is by virtue of an earlier imprint or encoding that the inner garden is kept alive. The question becomes, however, when and how the encoding occurred. Proust tells us that the encoding began in our childhood.

The memory garden, he explains, is first entrusted to the child, "that dreaming child" who, long ago, knew to take an imprint of nature's countenance, an imprint that can now be traced in the narrator's words. This explains why the garden can be revisited mentally again and again, like a Renaissance memory theater, but with the difference that it is a construction of the mind and reveals not so much facts as experiences or "episodes" of the rememberer's life. As the first rememberer, the memorialist-child chose the "ephemeral details" that are "kept alive through the succession of years" and constitute the salient features of this private garden. Fresh to the world and full of wonder, he experienced "the scent of hawthorn, a sound of echoless footsteps on a gravel path, a bubble formed against the side of a water-plant" that define the inner landscape. Given his conception of remembrance as a succession of printings of an initial impression, Proust is indeed compelled to imagine a moment when memories were born, a moment that he describes in this idyllic childhood scene. A child's first wonder provides the foundation for an architecture of remembrance that is so deeply ingrained in the mind as to define its emotional and cognitive topography.[13]

Behind Proust's conviction that the child takes the sharpest and most vivid imprints of the memory garden lies his assumption that there are qualitative differences in the encoding of memories. There is also the intuition, borne out by recent studies, that first-time experiences, which naturally predominate in childhood, are more likely to produce resilient episodic memories.[14] Moreover, Proust's vision adumbrates our current theories involving notions of encoding and retrieval.[15] The memory template—the "engram"—is the creation of the child who took those early snapshots of certain ephemeral details, while the memory itself emerges reactivated and transformed. "The cue combines with the engram to yield a new emergent entity—the recollective experience of the rememberer—that differs from either of its constituents," writes Daniel Schacter, bringing into focus an idea at the heart of Proust's description (70).[16] The act of remembrance, he shows us, involves a new representation of what must have existed only in latent form, as a trace that enables a "visit" through the memory garden to produce memories of memories. To use a photographic metaphor, the child takes snapshots that are not processed until years later, when the images are retrieved because certain features of the landscape prompted the photographer to go back to his lab. The earlier emphasis on the coincidence between encoding and retrieval may have led us to overlook what Proust's text makes very apparent, namely that there is no more than an affinity or interdependence between the first negative and the full picture. Meanwhile, only the fully developed photograph, with its touches of color and specific composition, will bring the picture to life. In other words, it is through the representation—a representation born of remembering—that the picture will be brought to life to reveal a "home-scene."

Reading Proust's disquisition on the memory garden, one is drawn not merely by the urgency of a voice, but by the quality of a description, to believe in the reality of a scene brought to life through traces as minute as "a scent of hawthorn," "a sound of echoless footsteps on a gravel path" or "a bubble formed against the side of a water-plant."

> The flowers which played then among the grass, the water which rippled past in the sunshine, the whole landscape which surrounded the apparition [of these truths] still lingers around the memory of them with its unconscious or unheeding countenance: and, certainly, when they were contemplated at length by that humble passer-by, by that dreaming child—as the face of a king is contemplated by a memorialist buried in the crowd—that piece of nature, that corner of a garden could never suppose that it would be thanks to him that they would be elected to survive in all their most ephemeral details; and yet the scent of hawthorn which flits along the hedge from which, in a little while, the dog-roses will have banished it, a sound of echoless footsteps on a gravel path, a bubble formed against the side of a water-plant by the current of the stream and instantaneously bursting—all these my exaltation of mind has borne along with it and kept alive through the succession of years, while all around them the paths have vanished and those who trod them, and even the memory of those who trod them, are dead. Sometimes the fragment of a landscape thus transported into the present will detach itself in such isolation from all associations that it floats uncertainly in my mind like a flowering Delos, and I am unable to say from what place, from what time—perhaps, quite simply, from what dream—it comes. But it is pre-eminently to the deepest layer of my mental soil, as the firm ground on which I still stand, that I regard the Méséglise and Guermantes ways. It is because I believed in things and in people while I walked along those paths that the things and the people they made known to me are the only ones that I still take seriously and that still bring me joy. Whether it is because the faith which creates has ceased to exist in me, or because reality takes shape in the memory alone, the flowers that people show me nowadays for the first time never seem to me to be true flowers. (200–201)

Proust's meditation provides us with the revelations of a "phenomenal universe" and with the map of his "own, distinctive mental world." The same holds for every one of us; we each respond to specific images that are the privileged signifiers of our world and of our selves. In giving them a name and a habitation, we inscribe the world with our own personal symbols— we create, in other words, *memories of our memories.* Combray-Illiers with its bubble on a pond, the river Floss with its white ducks, or an Alpine slope covered in blueberry bushes: the peculiar, uncanny intensities of certain

images we encounter in our inner journeyings mark them as such symbols—
symbols that designate the sensory intensities and intensities of feelings constitutive of our inner world or consciousness. It must be true then, as Proust
asks us to consider at the end of this passage, that *reality takes shape in
memory alone.*

A naive child, freshly and strongly attuned to the sensory experiences of
the natural world: the central figure of this passage is both a theoretical
fiction and a sentimental dream. In truth, as Proust understood, the child
and its wonder (like Adam and his garden) help us imagine a world afresh,
where impressions are given such primacy that we seem to witness their creation. But the precarious nature of this primal scene of remembrance
becomes only too apparent when we consider how it splits its subject into
multiple entities (as child, memorialist, rememberer, or narrator) and pay
attention to its dizzying display of mirrorings. Indeed, when read more
attentively, what is supposedly a founding moment of the subject's coming
into existence as a rememberer presents us with a confusing sequence of
specular encounters designed to reveal a nature animated and alive with
human features. Ultimately nature seems more constant than this human
subject who keeps appearing and disappearing along the specular chain.
Who could have guessed that the Proustian edifice of memory could be constructed on such fragile foundations?

Amid this rich deployment of human figures, it seems barely surprising
that a piece of nature that is made to carry so many memories should be
endowed with an "unconscious and unheeding countenance": the per-
sonifications that pervade Proust's description merely confirm what we
sensed from the outset, namely that this landscape is the reflection of the
human mind that lingers over it. We treasure perceptual experiences and
sensory intensities and turn them into aesthetic apprehensions, and in this
way, the world we see, smell, hear, and touch becomes our work of art. But
as we "image" or "imagine" this world, Proust tells us, we also reinscribe it
with memories. What we project into this image-making process, what constitutes the "work of art," is determined—to a greater degree than we may
be willing to concede—by earlier experiences. Memories, remembered or
forgotten, acknowledged or repressed, sustain our representations. These
same memories, whether secretly or not, make a world come alive for us.

It is this faith in the quasi-ontological value of memories that impels the
Proustian rememberer to track down the landscape of the past even amid his
dreams: "what I want to see again is . . . that whole landscape whose individuality grips me sometimes at night, in my dreams, with a power that is
almost uncanny, but of which I can discover no trace when I awake"

(202).[17] In Proust's conception, our existence is rooted in memory, in our ability to relate to impressions that connect us to earlier experiences. Past events condition an individual's future experience, and the past is the only true ground for a mental configuration that grows, mostly unconsciously, on its rich and generous soil. Memories spring from a desire that thrives on the repetition of early impressions and affects, and it harks for images that enable a return to our primitive memory-garden. Indeed, when all the real paths have been erased, the rememberer will carry in himself those very paths in the form of mental avenues ("nouveaux chemins," "new paths" is the expression Proust uses to define mental openings leading to truth). A corner of the garden, which, in his words, is "elected to survive in its most ephemeral particularity," attests to the continuities of the mind as well to a singular and unique vision of reality.

In a voice filled with passion and urgency, Proust conveys his confident, optimistic vision of "episodes" so richly and vividly inscribed in our minds that they can reappear after years of forgetting—almost as if stylistic brio or poetic afflatus alone had the power to sustain such strong memories.[18] For how else could this rememberer convince us of his most improbable idea, namely that nature is grateful for being remembered by the child-memorialist, and that it owes its survival across time to this "humble passer-by"—the writer who commemorates it?[19] Not only is the common order of things reversed (ordinarily we think of nature as what remains while human life passes), but the outer world now acquires human features. But this personification brings us closest to Proust's meaning. Human truths, we must thus conclude with him, are to be found when memory inscribes the landscapes that make up our world with a human countenance. Memory enables the projection of human features and meanings onto the world, features and meanings the absence of which would make of this world one flat, continuous, and indifferent surface.[20] This impersonal landscape would appear like a photograph that means nothing to us, one whose picture remains undecipherable and meaningless. Thanks to memory, however, the smallest, most desultory of objects—a burst of color, a flower, a bubble—will speak to us of reality as well as of ourselves.

Forgetting and Remembering

Memories, because they cue us into a personal reality, are vital to our psychic or mental survival. This is true not only for the healthy mind or brain. The very fact that a Proustian conception of memory—which assumes that strong cues provoke the retrieval of long-forgotten experiences—is enlisted in experimental therapies for Alzheimer's patients tells us as much. Clinical observation suggests that with the appropriate prompting, even the impoverished brain of an Alzheimer's patient, gradually extinguished by the plaques and tangles that obstruct synaptic connections, can find a path toward remembrance and awaken from its slumber to enjoy a moment of consciousness. Combined with clinical and psychological accounts of the memory loss associated with the disease, reports on Alzheimer's treatment gardens provide a suggestive picture of how Proust's strategy for recollection might translate into a therapeutic practice.[21] It is my hope that this brief incursion into the universe of the forgetting will do more than strengthen the veracity of Proust's claim about the interdependency between reality and memory. It might show, following Sacks's own acknowledgment, that phenomenological analysis can be just as promising as scientific evaluation in accounting for a mental experience that involves qualia.

Built next to the care facilities that house Alzheimer's patients, these treatment gardens serve several purposes connected with the orienting or stimulating aspects afforded by natural elements. With its unchanging familiar rhythms and patterns of growth, nature anchors us in time; it also offers topographical landmarks to encourage spatial orientation. As a rich terrain of sensory and perceptual stimuli, it invites activity or aesthetic contemplation. While these simple, basic features of nature work for all of us, they acquire an enhanced value given the disorientation, loss of attention, and apathy that Alzheimer's patients increasingly experience. A visit to the garden can stimulate the patient's attention, curiosity, and memory in a situation where every summoning up of mental energy, every new firing of neurons is a small victory over a deadening apathy. A stroll outdoors is bound to provide renewed sensory stimulus: a gentle breeze, a ray of sunshine, the bristling of leaves trigger perceptions and sensations and thus prompt, however fleetingly, a memory. Moreover, provided the landscape feels safe (it cannot be too shady, for instance), it will calm and reassure. For our purposes, however, the most arresting feature of the Alzheimer's treatment garden lies in the creation of a space that invites reminiscence through the display of objects, and more particularly flowers or plants, chosen for their mnemonic values.[22] It is hoped that a visit to the garden, with its carefully planted cues, will ward off the increasing disaffection from reality that is the by-product of memory loss. As an invitation to feel, to see and perhaps even remember, the garden can help awaken the ailing mind to an outside reality.

"A rose blooming at the back door, may bring back deep, otherwise forgotten memories," John Zeisel and Martha Tyson write in their design guidelines for an Alzheimer's garden, seemingly relying on a principle that is properly Proustian. While the memory garden's overall topography is destined to resemble a milieu that is familiar to the patients, its most striking feature is the presence of "symbolic cues" chosen for their familiarity—cues that are deemed to awaken the patient to sensory, perceptual, and cognitive as well as mnemonic experiences (461).[23] Thus, the authors write: "Every social and physical feature of a garden is enhanced when it evokes symbolic or familiar purpose. For example, a bench set alongside a path where lilacs form a grove provides the opportunity to connect to springtime, with past memories of fragrances and with the momentary beauty of the blooms themselves" (455). Proust (although not himself a pathological amnesiac) provides an echo to these words, as well as the hint of an explanation for how these "symbolic cues" might work. It seems to him that the arresting phenomenal power of, say, a bush of lilac lies in its association with deep memories. Here is how he describes the older person's encounter with a primitive, sensory childhood memory:

> When, on a summer evening, the melodious sky growls like a tawny lion, and everyone is complaining of the storm, it is the memory of the Méséglise way that makes me stand alone in ecstasy, inhaling, through the noise of the falling rain, the lingering scent of invisible lilacs.[24]

In the case of Alzheimer's patients, the lilac's aroma owes its efficacy to the very fact that it is old and familiar and thus related to what the authors identify as "deep memories." But what lies behind the notion of deep memories can only be understood if we get a clearer picture of the modalities of forgetting that are specific to this condition. Most broadly understood, amnesia occurs in this disease as an overall and gradual loss in the ability to "make" new memories and to retrieve older memories ("overall" meaning that short- and long-term memory is affected, and, using another categorization, that semantic, procedural, as well as episodic memory are impaired).[25] In keeping with the law of "reversion" or "regression" first established by Théodore Ribot in the 1890s, the illness produces a shift from "unstable" to "stable" memories, so that the rememberer will increasingly only recall what was "stamped" a long time ago and consolidated over time (121).[26]

Deep memories must be understood first as memories that go back a long way, as illustrated in an anecdote recounted by the writer Elizabeth Cohen, who invited her ailing, forgetting father to work on a memory project. "He volunteers memories all the time," she writes. "Most are sharp, focused, detailed. They are also over sixty years old" (214). Her father recalls the "way his 'bubbie' smelled—of schmaltz and lilac perfume," but he cannot remember—his eyes tearing up—his wife's name (214). A name rehearsed a thousand times is washed away, while a much older one is retained—a striking example of what has been called "the differential sparing of very remote memories" (Butters and Cermak, 261). It is to the child that the Alzheimer's patient turns when it comes to remembering—the child who, as we saw in Proust, is the first archivist or "memorialist" of a personal inner world.

But only a more refined description, one that highlights the connections between memory and representation, will offer a fuller sense of why the therapist-gardener's best hope lies in triggering deep memories. As Larry Squire explains, "the neural system in amnesia prevents new learning from being established and also prevents recently formed memories from becoming consolidated. . . . New representations cannot be established because of the unavailability of a critical neural system" (214). Without these new representations, the inner landscape of the amnesiac becomes increasingly antiquated: she must journey further and further into the past to encounter perceptual and sensory intensities.

In the world of the forgetting, then, the past is not yesterday, but that faraway place before the onset of the illness, a place that contained a memory garden that itself contained images of earlier events consolidated over time. The word "deep" invites us to conceive of memory's architecture as two perspectival lines that meet in the time of childhood in the memory garden. Increasingly then, the only way to activate a memory is to think of a cue that evokes a type of raw, yet vivid, perceptual experience that belongs to the origins of consciousness. For the landscape gardener, this means that stimuli must be created whose associations are so basic as to prompt the recall of the earliest of impressions: bright colors, arresting sounds, and, especially, familiar smells.

"Bold flower colors appear to generate the greatest resident interaction," one observer remarks, while another comments, "Some staff would prefer more color in the garden: 'The patients really respond to color'" (Zeisel and Tyson, 488, 462). One study highlights the very positive impact of birds and particularly skylarks on the patients' mood. But it would be wrong to assume that the affective and cognitive resonances that are called forth by such simple phenomenal experiences as seeing a red rose or hearing the warbling of a skylark are due merely to their phenomenal vividness.[27] The value of such stimuli lies in the mnemonic associations they convey—a value that has little to do with a practical or cognitive apprehension of the world but that above all is connected to affects. As Proust himself suggests—in the simple words that describe his own richly cued memory-garden—such images or perceptions stand out because they "communicate directly with [the] heart." They are infused with the kind of primitive, simple affects that are the most enduring features of an inner landscape that is increasingly indistinct and cognitively impoverished.[28]

> The Méséglise way with its lilacs, its hawthorns, its cornflowers, its pop-pies, its apple-trees, the Guermantes way with its river full of tadpoles, its water-lilies and its buttercups, constituted for me for all time the image of the landscape in which I would like to live . . . and the cornflowers, the hawthorns, the apple-trees which I may still happen, when I travel, to encounter in the fields, because they are situated at the same depth, on the level of my past life, communicate directly with my heart. (*Swann's Way*, 201; translation amended)

In naming the major landmarks of his private memory garden and enabling us to visualize them, Proust defines a relation to reality founded on the perceptual map shaped by memories. It is from the same inspiration that he concludes that the flowers he discovers now do not have the degree of reality as those that grew in his memory garden. "The flowers that people show me nowadays for the first time never seem to me to be true flowers," he notes (201). The full meaning of the Proustian theory adumbrated here, a theory that is of crucial importance for understanding the therapeutic value of memory gardens, can only be grasped if we situate it in a current context of scientific reflections.

At stake here is the question of how our brain processes the world, a question that Schacter raises in his chapter "Building Memories: Encoding and Retrieving the Present and the Past." Schacter writes: "Scientists agree that the brain does not operate like a camera or a copying machine. Then what aspects of reality do remain in memory once an episode has been concluded?" (*Searching for Memory*, 40). In identifying elements in the representation that stand out more vividly because stamped more deeply, Proust establishes a qualitative, phenomenal world that clearly shows that the brain does not copy the world with a camera-like device. But Proust also invites us to think further, more counterintuitively as it were, by turning Schacter's notion on its head. What Proust tells us, in effect, is that *we can only experience what has been remembered*—in other words, for him the only "episodes" that we can grasp in our consciousness are our memories. For the rememberer, then, and even more acutely for the person who forgets, the true question is really, "How much memory do we need to create an episode, and inhabit a reality—and not a dream or a fantasy?" In the simple, concrete terms of a therapeutic project, Proust's theory invites us to conceive of situations that enable the activation of "deep memories," which in turn will anchor the forgetting subject in reality.

Drawing on Proust's importance in his own discussion of remembrance, Schacter writes that "all of us share Proust's problem: to understand better who we are, we must somehow generate or find cues that allow us to remember things that might otherwise remain dormant or simply fade away" (65). At this point, we cannot but agree with Schacter's premises: Proustian memory must work for all of us in connecting us to reality: it keeps us alive. But for the Alzheimer's patient, who increasingly inhabits the world of the timeless denizens of Sleeping Beauty's castle, the Proustian principle that says that vivid memories will awaken us to a reality has to be put to work even more actively.[29] Along these lines, therapeutic Alzheimer's gardens are built to, as it were, "administer" carefully calibrated doses of reality and memory to the sleeping, dreaming, hallucinating minds of amnesiac patients. The recipe, meanwhile, is clearly to be found in Proust's books.

"'Old time,' non-toxic plantings, such as lilacs, honeysuckle, and roses provide wonderfully fragrant smells evoking memories of the past," writes a landscape architect, relying on Proustian memory as the therapeutic principle behind memory gardens (Zeisel and Tyson, 485).[30] An empirical study published in a professional journal for nurses and occupational therapists who work with the elderly provides among the most compelling evidence for the efficacy of smell as a mnemonic cue. Thus, in an article published in *Activities, Adaptation, and Aging*, Lynn Erickson and Kathryn Leide use a 1986 National Geographic survey, which quizzed more than a million and a half readers on the subject of odor and memory, to substantiate the fact that "scent can trigger over many decades." They describe the case of a "77-year-old man [who] smelled air brakes and remembered Saturday-morning streetcar rides to downtown Indianapolis, when Grandma would treat him to a chocolate soda at an ice cream parlor" (35). Odor memories, one might say in response to this example, "go deep"; or in a more accurate description, olfactory cues retrieve memories of a remote past—those very memories that the amnesiac Alzheimer's patient is most likely to retain.[31] If the "Proustian phenomenon" lies behind the most striking therapeutic successes in the memory garden, it must be because it best matches the pattern of reversion that characterizes memory loss in Alzheimer's.

A sophisticated study published in *Memory and Cognition* confirms what these nurses learned from experience, namely that odor memories are longest lasting. In their article, evocatively titled "Proust Nose Best: Odors

Are Better Cues of Autobiographical Memory," Simon Chu and John Downes are particularly interested in the phenomenal qualities of odor memory. They demonstrate, for instance, that olfactory cues are connected to a "phenomenologically stronger record" than can be elicited from visual prompts. Relying on research done by Rachel S. Herz, they argue that odor memories are "highly emotional, vivid, specific, rare, and relatively old" (511).[32] They also offer an intriguing explanation for the specific strength and vividness of memories triggered by smell, in relating the qualitative aspect of such memories to the kinds of representation they elicit. Whereas visual or verbal cues can be connected to a wealth of prior images (and thus "automatically induce unrelated and irrelevant detail"), smells, because they exist as peripherally registered elements of a particular episode, will only elicit representations that have been richly encoded and consolidated (512–16). Thus, Chu and Downes conclude that "odors are especially evocative as retrieval cues for the emotional details of autobiographical memory episodes" (514). This rich and compelling study is based, however, on the experience of healthy and articulate subjects (college students and professionals), who can naturally fit into a protocol involving conversations and cognitive testing. I could find no direct, documented testimony in the literature on Alzheimer's gardens confirming that the "nose is best" at creating sensory arousal and remembrance among the forgetting—but only an assumption, drawn from the observation of patients' reactions, that this was the case.

Sensory cues for memory, however, are by no means limited to smell. In *The Forgetting, Alzheimer's*, David Shenk recounts a number of exchanges with patients in the early stages of the illness that provide indirect evidence for how *visual* cues affect amnesiac patients. Here is what Morris Friedell wrote to Shenk:

> I find myself more visually sensitive. Everything seems richer: lines, planes, contrast. It is a wonderful compensation. . . . We [who have Alzheimer's disease] can appreciate clouds, leaves, flowers as we never did before. . . . [A]s the poet Theodore Roethke put it, "In a dark time the eye begins to see." (193)

Shenk accounts for this phenomenal experience in terms of an enrichment of awareness, of "an actual heightening of consciousness" (194); it proves to him that Alzheimer patients live in the "now." Another interpretation arises, however, if we take into consideration Proust's theory on memory and reality. It suggests that the heightened sensitivity to visual cues is really the product of living in the past: it is precisely because the present moment is so badly, so imperfectly encoded by the ailing brain, that the Alzheimer's patients are drawn to a reality that increasingly exists "in memory alone." Put simply, what the amnesiac mind "sees" best and feels most strongly—and thus relates to as a reality—is an image that goes back to earlier imprints and experiences. If the "now" is more present, it is because the "then" has brought it to life. There is indeed a striking resemblance between Friedell's description and the attempts, both by Woolf and by Proust, to convey a child's experience of the world, in all its freshness and novelty. When Laura S. (another one of the "forgetting" quoted by Shenk) looks at a red geranium—a vividly colorful cue—she experiences it as if for the first time:

> It is very clear and real. Look again and it is gone. Look back and it is fresh and new. I am checking this out with a red geranium blossom right now. When I look away, "red" no longer exists except as an abstract term. No blossom image remains. . . . But I can look again. (194)

It is easy to misconstrue what happens here and to consider only the failure of short-term memory, while overlooking the resilience of long-term memory. Gerald Edelman has famously defined consciousness as a "remembered present," and Laura's probing description offers itself as a phenomenal and clinical translation of this conception: it shows her laboring to retain an awareness of a reality that increasingly eludes her because her short-term memory is impaired. Her consciousness of the red geranium depends now on her long-term memory, which presents her with lasting, "consolidated" images.

"Reality takes shape in memory alone." Proust's pronouncement, which we now revisit as a further instantiation of Edelman's theory linking memory and consciousness, gives us the key to the mnemonic scene Laura describes. It tells us that a visual cue has activated a dormant memory, and brought the present to the fore because it is inscribed with past experiences. With the help of "deep memories," she can recognize and label the object (a long time ago a child learned to see and name a flower), she is encouraged to "cue into" its redness, and she becomes aware of the geranium in its vivid reality. If this experience brings such extraordinary pleasure and emotional comfort to Laura, it must be because it provokes an awakening. It takes her out of Sleeping Beauty's castle and into a garden inhabited by her former, healthy self; in that meeting between "I now" and "I then" lies the reassurance of an identity. Laura's repeated assertions—"I notice," "I look," "I check it out," "I look away"—speak of a subjectivity alive in the midst of forgetfulness and able to construct a reality that is, however briefly, "very clear and very real."

To show the heightening of phenomenal awareness that occurs in the earlier stages of the disease, Shenk quotes Morris Friedell's intuition about our ordinary perception of reality: "So many of us go through life like tourists with a camera always between our eyes and the world" (193). His comment is best understood in light of Proust's own perplexed resistance to a flat, merely photographic or cinematographic view of the world that excludes "a certain relation between sensations and memories" (*Le Temps retrouvé*, 3:720). Indeed, like the Proustian rememberer, the forgetting patient inhabits a world that cannot be habitual or mechanical, but only comes into existence in the realm of heightened sensations and memories. Hence the paradox: the patient who is trapped in the Alzheimer's world of memory loss bears more resemblance to Proust and Woolf than to us, ordinary rememberers. There is a crucial difference, however: what among writers is an aesthetic choice becomes, for the patient, part of the crushing predicament created by the disease. There is, increasingly, no recollecting other than such evanescent Proustian moments: because of the gradual encroachment of retrograde amnesia, Alzheimer patients are doomed to live in memory alone. For them the "past ultimately becomes the present," so that the vividness they experience is really that of memory.[33]

Contrary to appearances, then, Laura is most unlike that tourist who keeps pressing the shutter for fear of forgetting or missing a scene. She resembles, rather, Virginia Woolf's painter who captures memories with her blue paintbrush. "Out and out . . . further and further, until at last [she] seem[s] to be on a narrow plank, perfectly alone, over the sea. [Laura] dip[s] into the paint, dips into the past," her brush carrying not blue, but red paint that brings a geranium to life. Appropriately, with Woolf's metaphor the focus falls on the issue of representation—representation that, as Squire noted, is of crucial importance in understanding the memory problem specific to Alzheimer's patients. Photography suggests the regime of reproduction, painting that of representations: forced by her illness to skip the first beat of the mnemonic process, Laura enters a different mode of remembrance, of episodic memories that have been consolidated over time and that she can still paint to herself, with all the pleasure this painting brings. This is why the red geranium becomes such a rich aesthetic experience: its redness is layered with past impressions, its vividness the reflection, perhaps, of Laura's combined past and present emotions, and its wonder that felt by a child.

What must be indeed the "rapture" or "ecstasy"—for someone who inhabits a world of blurred, fading images and is increasingly disconnected from reality—of awakening to a red geranium, to clouds, leaves, flowers! While living in the eye of death, one has arisen to a new morning, "fresh as if issued to children on a beach." Woolf's heightened language not only gives a richer echo to the testimony of the forgetting, but draws our attention to the unusual temporality of such experiences. Research and observation tells us that they take place in a brain, in a mind that is increasingly like that of a child. The Alzheimer's patient inhabits a world that, cognitively and emotionally, resembles the child's (a fact explained by the concept of "retrogenesis" and as such widely documented and explained).[34] If the memory garden feels so good to the patient, and if it seems so filled with wonders, it must be because it exhibits the simple colors and shapes that the wondering child has learned to see and to name in the illustrated storybook. There might come a time indeed when all that the patient sees, in her mind's eye, are the great blots of red, blue, purple, or yellow that possess the vividness of childhood perceptions. There is a time too when the dream takes over, and the dreamer seems locked in her castle, until, perhaps an image of a bright red flower or a whiff of lilac creates a momentary awakening. Or so it would seem.

The Mysteries of Memory

The truth is that however attentively or caringly one scans the amnesiac's face, one will never know for sure (unless she says, "I remember") whether the symbolic cue—the sprig of thyme, the fragrant honeysuckle, the bird's spontaneous trill—has prompted a memory. We thus face a methodological problem that is inextricably bound up with the clinical condition under examination and with the type of remembrance—reminiscence—that is experienced in the memory garden.[35] How do we know whether the patient remembers? What can we know about the content of that memory? While these questions appear to be simple, an attempt to answer them draws us into a new arena, where complex questions of representation and language intervene in (or rather interfere with) our understanding of memory and consciousness. The clinical example brings us right to the heart of a controversy about the place of language in our conception of the mind, but for this very reason it might provide us with a promising starting point.[36]

In their article "Reminiscence and Ageing," psychologists Gillian Cohen and Stephanie Taylor analyze personal remembrance in light of its therapeutic value among the elderly. Their insights help us identify what is also our problem with Alzheimer's patients—a "basic" problem of communication. "Reminiscence," state Cohen and Taylor, has two dimensions, namely "private internal thinking produced by involuntary contextual cues" and "external communication in a social context" (602).[37] This simple, commonsense observation confronts us with an issue that cannot be stressed enough. When it comes to knowing about someone else's memories, we must have their words—words that will bridge the gap between the inner and outer "aspect" of memory. But what happens when language begins to fail, as it inevitably does in Alzheimer's patients? What must we think when, in the image that Pierre Janet uses, there is no "messenger" for the memory that might have passed fleetingly gone through the patient's mind?[38] We look for signs of the minutest kind—a sudden glint in the eye, a clasp of the hand, a rare smile—and think we recognize a memory. Yet it is possible that what we took for signs of her remembering were mere projections, products of a wild dream or fond wish that we might find again, among the tangled threads of that diseased brain (for the duration of that now rare event of neuronal firing that produces a memory), the rememberer we knew. But without her words, we can never be sure.

In her testimony on the relation between language and a memory, Virginia Woolf tells us, "I make it real by putting it into words," emphasizing the correlation—even the identity—between writing and remembering ("A Sketch," 72). Echoing Woolf, the psychologist Daniel Schacter, by describing paintings and photographs of memories in his book *Searching for Memory,* provides another persuasive justification for the fact that memories "need" words. To be understood as memories of memories, these aesthetic representations of recollected events need a title (such as "Memories Weave the Echoes" or "Overlays of Memory II") or the artist's explanation. Indeed, it could be argued that without the words "I remember" or some variation thereof, we would never be able to distinguish between a mere figment of the imagination and a personal memory. We saw this in Eliot's prologue: seamless as it may seem, the passage from imagination to memory is marked with the twice-repeated phrase, "I remember those large dipping willows. . . . I remember the stone bridge."

To be recognizable as such, memories need the stamp of a first-person singular, of someone who is able to say, "*I* remember." When Gerald Edelman states that "phenomenal experience is a first person matter," he speaks as a scientist confronted with subjective phenomenal experiences. He does not, however, consider the full meaning that lies behind the "first person" as a grammarian might. For a linguist, the first person is the key grammatical feature for subjectivity: it is by saying "I" (as in "I remember") that the subject establishes a world, a picture, an event that exists for him or for her.[39] Thus the small, easily ignored word "I" is really an indispensable tool for the rememberer—it stitches the memory together, fashions it around a subjective core. This is why, as we sensed with Proust, the "memory voice" is such an important element in the constitution of autobiographical memories. Not only does this voice, with its sometimes striking rhetorical urgency, convey the rememberer's belief, it also holds the images together. It can be as loud as Proust's, as subtle and complex as Eliot's, or as determinedly confident as Woolf's, or as discrete as the whisper of our own inner voice saying, "I remember." But whatever its tone or articulation, it remains a fundamental element of the mnemonic structure.

As for the *content* of the memory, only a voice rapt in a storytelling mode can convey it to the observer. While it is conceivable that brain imagery (a PET scan, an MRI, or some sort of chemical indicator) could illuminate the neuronal paths of private remembering, it could not show their contents.[40] The presence of "first person matter" would then be registered, but would nevertheless remain formless, devoid of meanings and values. We must then posit a direct correspondence between the mental act of remembering and the "literary" act of stylistic definition, with language expressing the qualitative difference—the qualia—that mark the subject's experiences. Proust speaks of style as "being the qualitative difference there is in the way the world appears to us" and defines the rememberer's vocation in terms of a desire aimed at capturing the singularity and irreducible differences of perception felt by each subject.[41] In his conception, memory images represent stylistic commitments, particular ways of expressing a highly individualized inner world through words.

Thus in Proust's memory garden, trees are not just trees, but oaks or apple trees, and flowers are lilacs, hawthorns, cornflowers, poppies, water lilies, or buttercups. Like Adam in his garden, this rememberer names each object to map out an inner landscape where certain representations are "elected to survive in all their most ephemeral details." In contrast with the elaborate metaphors, synesthetic vibrations, and subtle qualifications that are the usual hallmark of his descriptions, Proust's representations of memory are etched out confidently and precisely. Each symbolic cue is presented with the unusual clarity and specificity that we attribute to an imagist poet, each representation is precisely stamped and endowed with a heightened graphic quality. Moreover, while Proust usually favors a complex syntactic organization designed to render every shading of an idea, in the representation of memories, images are simply aligned as might befit the spontaneous associative process that gives rise to a context. The realism we ascribe to Proust's phenomenological descriptions of memory thus seems to be directly related to a stylistic or aesthetic choice—to an assumption that the word or the name *is* the memory and that the vividness of the recollection (what he calls *la puissance du paysage*) depends on its singular definition *(son individualité)*.

But other stylistic options are available, as we saw in Virginia Woolf, whose realism in representing memory is just as convincing. One can try to "paint the past" so that memory images emerge with a raw immediacy of nascent forms. Thus in her representations of memory, Woolf foregrounds the impression and aims for vividness: the splash of yellow replaces the precisely named buttercup. Phenomenologically speaking, we might understand Woolf as choosing emergent memories, digging "deeper" into the past to find a garden where things have as yet no name. But whether we consider Proust, Woolf, or even Eliot (whose aesthetic is closer to Proust's), the most striking aspect of the relation between memory and language is their collective belief in the power of words. They start with the conviction that words can evoke memories—and that writing constitutes remembering. One could imagine a search for words, in which the self-conscious search for the right vocabulary would overlap with the active search for memory, but this is not the case for these writers. What words cannot say will not exist; memory, in their conception, is not etched out from a background of silence and inexpressibility. An "all or nothing" view follows naturally from a definition of memory as an event or performance, for in the realm of the performative, there is only failure or success.

The view that memories only exist in a vocabulary, grammar, or voice is radical: it forces us to banish the shadow world of half-formed or unconscious reminiscences. In this conception, episodic memories, just like a scripted surface, have no underside—unless we consider the material on which they are inscribed (such as the neurological circuitry that, like a paper, supports the text). As a representation, each memory is made of no more and no less than what the words can say. One can posit the existence of memories that are forgotten (and thus unsaid, unwritten) or misremembered (being invented or fictionalized), but without language we will have no proof of their existence or evidence for their contents. Meanwhile, when a memory has been conveyed in words, some readjustments might be made to the picture, so that it will be stamped more accurately (as when corroboration or further thinking forces one to correct a memory distortion). But overall, the words are still the memory: it would seem odd, if not just pointless, to argue that the flowers on her mother's dress that Woolf remembered were tulips and not anemones, or that the landscape around Combray-Illiers revealed no oaks, but only elms. In other cases, some oddity of behavior might suggest to the observer the presence of acknowledged memories, or perhaps, when listening to the rememberer's story, an attentive party might intuit that the construction is faulty or vastly incomplete. Indeed, sometimes a richer representation might emerge at another person's invitation as happens of course in the formalized exchanges that occur during psychoanalysis. But in all these instances, spoken words will blend with the representation of the memory.

With language so centrally present in reminiscence, how can we know that the speechless woman asleep in the castle really remembers? Does that sudden glint in her eye as a pungent, bittersweet odor of lavender wafts across the air tell us that she remembers the summer afternoons spent gardening, the "murmur of the bees," the "pink flowers," the "gray and silver leaves" and the voices of her children playing? As I reflect on this scene, Nietzsche's probing words in his *Journal* come to mind: "One must revise one's ideas about *memory:* here lies the chief temptation to assume a— 'soul,' which, outside time, reproduces, recognizes, etc.," arousing my suspicion.[42] What if the trust that we place in the therapeutic force of Proustian cues planted in an Alzheimer's garden found its true justification not in any science, but merely in the observer's belief (or fond wish) that some corner of the soul, some place in the inner mental landscape of the forgetting patient has been spared? Naive as it may seem, especially in the harsh light of scientific discoveries about the ailing brain, this view might find some justification—provided we approach it with a less radical conception of the relation between language and consciousness.

As George Steiner points out in *After Babel,* in examining the semiotic model of encoding and decoding, we have inherited two very different philosophies of language: one that assumes that "language is the only verifiable *a priori* framework of cognition" and another that invites us to see in "language . . . a 'third universe' midway between the phenomenal reality of the 'empirical world' and the internalized structures of consciousness" (81). Whereas I have assumed so far that words are the indispensable, in fact the *only* markers of personal remembrance, I want to entertain, for a moment, another possibility that, in conceiving of language as an emanation of "internalized structures of consciousness," invites us to imagine that memories exist outside of language. Scientists, philosophers, and writers seem to support this second view as well, and they raise probing new questions.

They make us wonder, for instance, if language enables us to capture every dimension of the mnemonic experience. Gerald Edelman answers this indirectly when he notes that qualia can "range in intensity and clarity from 'raw feels' to highly refined discriminanda," adding that "the phenomenal scene is accompanied by feelings or emotions, however faint" (*Bright Air*, 114). These observations suggest that autobiographical remembering may involve states of perception, emergent configurations, or affects that no words can translate. Remembering would then sometimes (or perhaps always?) involve "feelings or emotions" so faint that they cannot be captured in the description of the memory, but shadow it, so to speak, with a particular sensory or perceptive modality for which there is no vocabulary. Meanwhile, Antonio Damasio envisages the existence of episodic memories whose contents remain submerged, memories that he thinks are "stored in a dispositional form" and could thus be called "dispositional memories" (*Feeling*, 60–61). His view forces us to discard the blunt "all or nothing" model of remembrance in favor of a subtler picture, one that assumes the existence of virtual memories present as inchoate patterns that are not yet perceived as representations.[43] We can thus experience states of mind that remain outside of our ability to figure them verbally, as Virginia Woolf shows us when, in *To the Lighthouse*, she evokes now and again a *tropisme*—a moment in her protagonist's stream of consciousness that is traversed by an unanchored, unidentified remainder of a thought or impression.[44] From these several perspectives, we are led to conclude that there must be moments when our thoughts are traversed by a memory that we do not identify, a memory that exists in spite of not having been "caught in words." The idea that there exists a residual feeling in our impressions or memories, a certain *je ne sais quoi* that cannot be captured in words and yet inhabits our consciousness, is not altogether surprising: it seems to be part of the very definition of qualia. "The word 'quale,'" A. R. Lacey writes, is "used to express the ineffable psychological something" (397), while Janet Levin states that "there is something in the realm of the qualitative that may be ineffable or irreducibly subjective, namely, the content of these qualitative concepts" (865).[45]

If we endorse this conception, we have to accept that that rare event—the surprise neuronal firing that "expressed" the engram—could have happened in the Alzheimer's patient's brain. Only it could no longer be heard amid the silence. Perhaps the mind holds mysteries that cannot be fully probed by a purely scientific, analytical, or phenomenological method; the miraculous revelation of a red geranium or red rose in an Alzheimer's garden may be one of them. Thus, as we look again at the woman in the garden of Sleeping Beauty's castle, we think that the sudden, fleeting smile on her face means that she remembers. In that smile, perhaps, we place our belief in the ultimate mystery of consciousness—in a theory that the mind, in some parts and in some ways, remains ineffable, unverbalizable. Or perhaps not a theory, a philosophy or a belief, for as Nietzsche appropriately reminds us, the eagerness with which we scan the amnesiac's face bespeaks our belief in the existence of a secret inner garden. This garden houses something like a soul—and that soul may represent no more than the ineffable something or the silent part of our most intimate being.[46]

Yet even as we assume the existence of autobiographical memories outside of language, there remains yet another quandary related to the nature of the mnemonic image and to its representation, where the question becomes, "Is our forgetting patient still capable of constructing a memory?" Memories, after all, are not merely founded on the encounter between "I now" and "I then," but they depend, for their architecture, on the rememberer's present abilities.[47] Here, a brief return to the stylistic options epitomized by Proust and Woolf is helpful. For in making us aware of the presence of a "memory voice," these rememberers add a different, linguistic perspective to the notion of mnemonic representation. Together with them, we must ask whether the memory must be spoken in the language (or from the perspective) of the child that was, or whether it should be coined in the rememberer's current language. Proust, as we learned, presents childhood impressions in the elaborate and precise language of the adult, whereas Woolf chooses a seemingly more immediate path of perceptual images (in evoking, for instance, colors and shapes that only gradually become flowers and acquire a name). While these differences confirm the role of language as an intermediary between the phenomenal quality of the mnemonic image and consciousness, they also highlight another aspect of reminiscence, namely its active, dynamic nature that is currently understood in terms of "recategorization." Recategorization is the concept that underlies Daniel Schacter's description of remembrance as a three-pronged phenomenon involving a cue, a mnemonic trace (or engram), and the memory proper, which we saw earlier.

Modern scientific accounts have gradually dispelled the commonly held mimetic model of memory, with its notion that the mind functions as a storehouse, preserving pictures in the rememberer's mind that can be taken down at will.[48] This means that the notion of "representation" should be understood in a strong sense, not as a synonym for mimesis, but as an *Inszenierung* (an enactment, staging, or dramatization) of the engram. In other words, a reminiscence will have to be a new performance involving new perceptions that correspond to the ever changing mental/neural map that is the mind; it is a unique neurological event that has never happened before in the same way or in the same context. As Oliver Sacks emphasizes, following Edelman, the brain is a constantly evolving structure, involved in an endless process of recategorization:

> Faced with the necessity of survival, for making order, in a teeming and chaotic world—"a booming, buzzing chaos," as William James called it—the brain is highly plastic and adapts itself at each moment. . . . Explorations are never the same, so that the initial category is revised, re-categorized, again and again. Given this incessant recategorization, no perception, no image, no memory, one would expect, would ever be precisely repeated or the same. Yet through its structuring and restructuring, the infant, the growing individual, constructs a self and a world. ("Neurology," 48)

Sacks's view of the mind, with which we started, might thus also help us conclude. This conclusion cannot but remain speculative: if the clinical tale of the patient in the memory garden of the forgetting has a point, it can only be grasped from a phenomenological perspective. The physics of memory escape us; the metaphysics spring from an act of imagination and empathy. The telling of this tale depends on the premise—as all accounts of reminiscence do—that personal remembrance is inherently intersubjective.[49] This analysis may have proved little more than our belief, as empathetic observers, in the mind's resilience and ingenuity in reconstructing itself.

Meanwhile, bearing in mind Sacks's description of recategorization, we would have to concede that if the woman locked up in Sleeping Beauty's castle remembers, it can only be in the forms Virginia Woolf gave to her impressions of childhood: "blobs of color," "sounds indistinguishable from sights," or "curved shapes, showing the light through but not giving a clear outline." If the woman does remember, it will most likely be without even a word or name (such as "redbreast" or "God's bird") for the bird.[50] Indeed, as her cognitive abilities are radically impaired, the recategorization would have to be regressive, primitive. But it would nevertheless remain true that in awakening, however fleetingly, to an outer world she would create a self in her attempt to structure it. Indeed, Proustian moments expressed in such statements as "I inhale the combined aroma of tilleul and madeleine" or "I look at a red geranium blossom" not only epitomize the "directness and vivid quality of experience" and "specific phenomenal content" evoked by Koch. They are also biographical events that warrant an identity and subjectivity through a mnemonic awakening to the outer world.[51] "On any day," writes the Proustian rememberer, "my person feels like an abandoned quarry which believes that everything it contains is undifferentiated and monotonous, but each memory like a Greek sculptor can draw innumerable statues" (1:717). This description of how memories sculpt and shape the self takes on its fullest meaning as we try to imagine, one last time, what the "abandoned quarry" feels like for the listless, dreaming woman trapped in the world of forgetting. Shattered trunks, ruins and rocks without recognizable shape; ghostly faces passing; words that carry no song and have no meaning. What miracle indeed if the right cue could come her way and if the garden could be reborn, even for an instant! Memories sculpt the self, memories write the self, memories constitute the reality that the self inhabits. No writer seems to have understood this better than Proust, and this might explain why paradoxically, his voice speaks so eloquently, albeit indirectly, to the predicament of the forgetting.

7 • A Case of Nostalgia: Gérard de Nerval

The analysis of memory gardens, in their physical embodiment as well as their figurative meanings, reveals a psychological dimension of remembrance that my earlier structural analyses had overlooked—namely a coincidence between memory and the self. It shows as well our extraordinary belief and reliance on memory as a foundation of our psychical well-being. Nostalgia, a disease of memory that came into existence in the late seventeenth century, offers a striking instance of this interdependency.

> Don't you know this feverish disease that grabs us in the coldness of misery, this nostalgia for an unknown country, this anguish due to our curiosity? There is a country that resembles you, everything is beautiful, rich, quiet, and honest. . . .This is where one must live, this is where one must go to die. ("L'Invitation au voyage")

Thus writes Baudelaire in *Le Spleen de Paris* in the mid–nineteenth century, describing a feeling that, by his time, was situated somewhere between a physical (physiological) and metaphysical (mental) condition. In its etymology, *algos* for pain and *nostos* for return, nostalgia is an ailment, and for at least two centuries it had its well-established nosography—a medical definition that could not have been lost on Baudelaire. It spoke of eighteenth-century mercenaries abroad or young girls sent into service dying of *Heimweh,* while others, more fortunate, were dispatched posthaste to their native mountains (away from battlefields or sprawling cities) for fear they might never recover of this lingering disease. A contemporary of Baudelaire, the romantically inclined Balzac still writes to Madame Hanska: "Dear, I suffer homesickness. . . . I come and go without any spirit, without being able to say what I have, and I if I remained this way for two weeks I should die." The nostalgic mind seems to be looking for a place belonging to some inner sentimental geography, but as Kant saw so readily, it is really about time and about a return to beginnings: "what the subject suffering from nostalgia is looking for is less the places of childhood, than childhood itself."[1] Nostalgia has surely become obsolete as a pathology—although, as Jean Starobinski suggests, one might recognize it in a diagnosis of "depressive reactions of social maladjustment" or in theories of "fixation and regression" (102–3). It seems also clear that, as a sentiment, nostalgia has bad press nowadays: it has become synonymous with excessive and unreasonable sentimentality, to the point where nostalgic reminiscing is often greeted with some impatience.[2] What I want to suggest, however, is that nostalgia is a fundamental dimension of human remembrance—as the emotion or feeling that drives us toward the past and sustains our desire for memory. To demonstrate this, I turn my attention to an extraordinary case of nineteenth-century nostalgia to examine the writings and the life of a contemporary of Baudelaire and Balzac—the French romantic writer Gérard de Nerval.

Put together, his writings and his life read like a clinical tale: the tale of a man who seems to have staked his life on remembrance, to the point where one can no longer tell whether the fixation on memory created his madness, or on the contrary, represented the way out of it.[3] In the increasingly troubled drama that was Nerval's life, memory is indeed at the center—alive as a dynamic force turned unpredictably sometimes toward the salvation, sometimes toward the demise of its author. "My life turns in circles," he writes, fearing the threat of loss of inspiration. And indeed living and writing seem to go in a circle for this writer whose themes could only be biographical: as he candidly acknowledges in a preface, "to invent is to remember."[4] The ability to remember becomes then doubly precious for him, a means of psychological as well as literary survival. This is why, in his case, nostalgia is more than a *desire* for memory: remembering is a necessity that takes the form of a personal injunction: "I must remember," Nerval tells himself repeatedly. "Let me put my memories together" *(Recomposons nos souvenirs)* is the phrase from which the whole of "Sylvie," his most successful tale, unravels. It is also the motto that enjoins the writer to make of the search for memory "the prime impulse of consciousness."[5]

The case of Gérard de Nerval helps us see that there is a more profound meaning to nostalgia than we are inclined to grant it—a meaning that speaks of dependency, or even of an addiction to memory. This is a dependency we all share; in Nerval's case, however, the need to remember became excessive, to that pathological point where, as Julia Kristeva suggests, his "memory was without a future" and he could only revisit "archaic psychic experiences" (162, 181). Here then remembrance is so deeply embedded in a psychic and creative economy that it becomes a compulsion—the only way of thinking and imagining that remains available to him when all other attempts at sense-making fail. Nerval died of nostalgia: his life ended when his imagination ran dry and he lost his memory garden, that is, when he could no longer see and imagine in his mind's eye the cherished "home country" of the Valois. For most of us, however, our innate dependency on memory does not lead to a fatal ending—on the contrary, nostalgia, as I will show in connecting it to moods, is a favorable feeling: it enables us to imagine our experience in the image of past happiness; it satisfies a powerful yearning for good memories that all of us experience, at one time or another.

Take for example our, by now, familiar rememberers: Freud, Proust, Eliot, and Woolf. Catching them unawares—that is when they relinquish their analytical and rational stance toward memory—we see their nostalgia, as a powerful yet irrational drive toward revisiting the past. While their fixation on certain memories expresses a search for beauty, meaning, or happiness that the past seems to promise, it also reveals an extraordinary belief in the saving power of remembrance. There is madness, almost, in the excessive credit given to memory images that may be nothing more than literary constructions. But madness lies too in the fixation on images whose significance is so personal, so highly idiosyncratic as to seem totally irrational.[6]

Here is Freud, for example, seemingly the most analytical of rememberers and a man who seems otherwise sharply aware of how we trick our minds to confuse memories and fantasies. Freud, too, has his moments of nostalgia—moments when he seems captivated, against his better judgment, by a constellation of memory images: yellow flowers, the smell of bread, the beautiful woods of his childhood. "I believe now that I was never free from a longing for the beautiful woods near our home," this rememberer acknowledges, bringing his offering to the altar of nostalgia in the guise of his alter ego, the "man with a university education" ("Screen Memories," 312–13). Let us reconsider also Proust's rememberer: we find him standing, as if frozen, at some street corner "alone in ecstasy, inhaling, through the noise of the falling rain, the lingering scent of invisible lilacs" (*Swann's Way*, 202). Such is the spell cast by a whiff of lilac sprung from his memory that he is ready to get drenched under the rain, just to inhale more of that magical "aroma of the past." The same figure of a compulsive rememberer appears in Raoul Ruiz's film on Proustian memory, *Time Regained*. In a scene replayed a few times on the screen, Ruiz shows our rememberer's frozen silhouette, with arms akimbo and one foot higher than the other, trying to recompose the way he stumbled on the memory of a cherished visit to Venice.[7] How unreasonable can nostalgia be? Proust's rememberer jeopardizes his reputation and perhaps his health to recover aesthetic impressions that, to the distant observer, may seem almost meaningless. Yet these memories are important enough to bring a life to a standstill.[8] Finding, or rather creating, a lasting trace of the sensation contained in the lilacs of Combray or the irregular stones of the Piazza San Marco can be, to borrow the words of Virginia Woolf, "what is far more necessary than anything else."

And what of George Eliot's rememberer? She may seem less theatrical in her search for the memory images, but she too seems never free from a longing for a particular spot in the world, the beautiful woods near home. More strangely even, as we saw, she develops, in the first pages of *The Mill on the Floss*, a strange addiction to water and to ducks, writing: "I am in love with moistness, and envy the white ducks that are dipping their heads into the water here among the withes—unmindful of the awkward appearance they make in the drier world above" (54). Surely there is madness in envying ducks—even when one tries, as I naturally did, to read these lines figuratively.[9] A philosophical approach might provide an explanation, however, for the mysteries behind such an image: it will recognize in this scene the characteristic overinvestments in a corner of the memory garden that nostalgia produces. According to the philosopher Vladimir Jankélévich, the symptoms of nostalgia can be found, precisely, in this obscure, unanalyzable drive toward certain emotion-laden images that we have just examined. Jankélévich thus writes in *L'Irréversible et la nostalgie*: "Nostalgia is a geography infused with pathos, a mystical topography whose mere toponymy, because of its evocative power, sets into motion reminiscences as well as imagination" (277). Indeed, Eliot's predilection for watery surfaces and ducks can no more be accounted for objectively than Freud's overinvestment in the color yellow or his love for the smell of fresh bread; in both cases, the representations belong to an economy of affects. It is, in short, a defining feature of the nostalgic imagination that it should ascribe to a particular image or scene values that cannot be assessed objectively or rationally. "Unlike a mathematician . . . what the nostalgic heart sees is a concrete space rendered diverse by sites that are qualitatively heterogeneous," Jankélévich writes (276–77). The water with its ducks, described by Eliot, is such a space: it is inflected with a qualitative difference whose exact source remains indecipherable. Isn't this emotional haze the very thing that the nostalgic rememberer longs for—namely a form of memory that remains inexhaustible, precisely because its true object is nowhere to be found? The unaccountable, unresolved emotion is the hallmark of a map that marks places that exist only in the rememberer's wishful thinking, that is, in her nostalgia.

With Eliot, we hear as well the Proustian voice that, in speaking of the flowers that bloomed in his childhood (lilacs, hawthorns, cornflowers, poppies, or apple trees) remarks: "The flowers that people show me nowadays for the first time never seem to me to be true flowers" (201). It is the particular privilege of a nostalgic imagination (but also its maddening turn) to prefer the past to the present and to find more reality in things remembered than those that can be perceived concretely, in the present. But as the philosophers saw—Sartre when reflecting on imagination and Jankélévich in considering nostalgia—such reminiscing, often bordering on hallucination, can induce a strange mind-set that can lead to a morbid turn away from concrete living. Thus Jankélévich warns us that one should not lose sight of the fact that "the present, even in its dullest and the most discrete manifestation, still surpasses in freshness the most vividly hallucinated past" (253), and Sartre reminds us that only reality can be "always new, always unpredictable" (*L'Imaginaire,* 284). But this is perhaps where Nerval erred: in moving to a place in his mind where the past seems infinitely more desirable, more hospitable than the present.[10]

The Nostalgic Rememberer

Nostalgia is the name given to the desire for memory: it is what fuels our mental time-travel and impels us to imagine the sources of our identity. In other words, it drives us toward a biographical exercise in memory, which is a central part of our personhood. No writer, perhaps, responded to nostalgia more acutely and showed more dedication in pursuing the elusive images of past happiness than Gérard de Nerval. He knew that far from being a gratuitous sentimental indulgence, nostalgic reminiscence might chart the way toward personal salvation; he knew that if memories of past happiness were to acquire enough solidity, he might be able to ward off the present doom. The story "Sylvie," thirty-odd pages to which he gave the evocative subtitle of "Souvenirs du Valois," takes the shape of a nostalgic journey into the past, in which reminiscence is deemed to act as a mood enhancer and an antidote to depression.[11] A first-person narrator tells the story of his increasingly problematic, painful entanglements in love stories that belong to different eras of his life and involve several women, whom he sometimes courts simultaneously. Sylvie, sometimes compared to a sylvan divinity, is one among the rememberer's romantic attachments. But just as these sentimental yearnings draw him, without much logic or reason, to several women whose faces, smiles, or gestures seduce him, so does another form of longing, nostalgia, which impels him to leave an indifferent, superficial Parisian world, for the depths of the countryside and the mythical scenery of the Valois. Because of its complex temporal layerings and the mirrorings between characters (every figure seems to repeat itself, some-times across several doublings), the narrative thread of "Sylvie" is dizzy-ingly complex. Indeed, as Kristeva suggests, the narrative thread is no more than a pretext for a nostalgic deployment of desire: travel is a subterfuge, as is the biographical story of the unnamed narrator, whose life is not unlike Nerval's (172).

For "Sylvie," Nerval invented a narrative organization that is quite unique: it follows the promptings of nostalgic remembrance. The story's events seem to emanate from the places the rememberer visits, in spirit or in person, as, glossing over the present, he focuses on one affectively charged scene after another born from the landscape of the Valois. Richard Sieburth writes, in his introductory note to "Sylvie," that it "is a parable about the raveling and unraveling of fictions, or more precisely, about the kind of ever-shifting palimpsest created by a memory engaged in the simultaneous pressures of recollection and repression, inscription and obliteration" (63).[12] The real theme of his story is indeed a compulsion to remember that verges on the pathological. Whereas I will explore in sections of the next chapter a psychodynamic model of remembrance with notions of "repres-sion" and "obliteration," here I focus on the pressures of recollection, that is, on the patterns of nostalgia that lie at the heart of this exemplary mnemonic text.

A brief incursion into Nerval's biography shows how closely his exis-tence is bound up with the act of nostalgic creation. The more deeply Ner-val moved into his life, the fewer were the opportunities to enjoy the pres-ent; loss, poverty, and illness loomed increasingly, like an ill-fated star, over his creative work. Nerval, "this delicious fool," as he was sometimes called, was by all accounts one of the most talented of the romantic writers. Hav-ing burnt his inheritance early treating his Bohemian friends to fine foods, spectacles, and good company, he lived by his pen, producing page after page of good copy, blending fiction, fragments of his rich readings, and autobiography. He also produced, at the age of eighteen, one of the earliest, and probably best, translations into French (albeit in a romantic vein) of Goethe's masterpiece, *Faust*. But we owe his best works, the stories gathered in *Les Filles du feu* and *Aurélia* as well as the small collection of poems he called *Les Chimères*, to his mature years—the years when he was plagued by depression and manic delusions.[13]

"Sylvie," part of the *Filles du feu*, was hailed immediately as a pure mas-terpiece of French prose. It is work, however, of an errant poet impover-ished and mentally ill, whose only secure home and address were in Passy, at the clinic of Dr. Blanche. As an enlightened practitioner of modern

French psychiatry, Blanche provided Nerval with a room of his own, and the trust that writing might be a salutary activity in the midst of his inner turmoil.[14] There, Nerval wrote much of *Aurélia,* which is a blend of dreams, memories, and hallucinations, but it is in "Sylvie," a more realistic tale, that he tried to recapture scenes of a magical, mythical childhood. It had to become an *autobiographie romancée*—a fiction of the past or life as it had never been. We know from Nerval's contemporaries how desperately he tried to tie together the scattered threads of his life. Afraid of losing his mind, his memories, as well as his livelihood, the author would scribble fragments of his text on stray pieces of paper whenever an idea came to mind: in cafés, in the temporary shelter he found among the downtrodden in the Parisian *Halles,* in coaches when pressed to travel. At a low ebb, but feeling still that a return to familiar places might enable direct inspiration, Nerval begged to be allowed to go back to the sources of his imagination: to the Germany of his early literary career and, above all, to the Valois of his childhood. By then, Nerval's life was in a bind: he desperately needed to produce copy so as to be able to repay his doctor, but intense work led him to breakdowns and devastating periods of insomnia—and more delusions. Soon after finishing "Sylvie," he had to be hospitalized again. A few months later, his body was found hanging on a lamppost on the coldest of January mornings in 1855 in a back street of Paris. To his aunt, who had agreed to look after him after he had begged to be released from Dr. Blanche's clinic, he left a note saying, cryptically: "Ce soir la nuit sera noire et blanche" (Tonight will be white and black). It seems somehow fitting that Nerval's entry into final darkness should be hailed with an image that adumbrates a written page. By that point, to put on paper images that could produce the semblance of a story had become the ultimate wager.

Memory Places

Composed late in Nerval's career and life, in the 1850s, "Sylvie" recounts a double journey into the past and into the landscape of the Ile-de-France, which starts on the platform of the narrator's Parisian present, and moves deeper and deeper into the country of his childhood. The rememberer's travel begins, typically, in a mildly depressing present: life in the "fast set" around the time of the French Restoration seems singularly empty, in spite of the money and the superficial pleasures. This negative mood is conducive to nostalgia, prompting a search for happier places and times. Casting a glance at a newspaper, Nerval's narrator-hero is lured into reminiscence by a two-line announcement: "*Provincial Fête of the Bouquet.*—Tomorrow the archers of Senlis are to return the bouquet to those of Loisy" (108). With the printed words acting as triggers, a first image emerges of "forgotten times, faraway echoes of naive *fêtes* of the past," inviting him to enter into the magic circle of nostalgic reminiscence. In bed, unable to sleep, the rememberer "is revisited by his whole youth" and, determined to catch up with his past, he hastily undertakes a coach journey to the Valois. Time is suspended for the nostalgic traveler—a circumstance marked symbolically by the fact that the hero, not carrying his watch, does not know what time it is. Sitting in the coach, our traveler decides to put together, to "recompose," the memories of his earlier visits to the place of this childhood.[15]

In the course of seven or eight pages, at least four different temporal strands have been established through associative leaps that take the rememberer from one memory to another. There is the present time in Paris, the moment destined to epitomize his childhood when girls and boys dance under the moon. There is the time covered by his hasty excursion into the Valois, followed by some days spent there, and the time (or is it the times?) when he, still in his youth, similarly revisited the same regions. Added to this complex structure, there is a level that should be called "times immemorial," that encompasses all the moments and memories that go back to ancestral traditions: dances, songs, celebrations that would have occurred, similarly, before the narrator's lifetime. Through these different layers, Nerval evokes the density of a past that inhabits a consciousness, a past whose substance seems spatial rather than temporal. While it is nearly impossible to establish temporal markers within the flow of mnemic images, places act like anchoring points for the nostalgic rememberer. Cythère, Le Village, Othys, Châalis, Loisy, Ermenonville, the place-names that serve as headings to chapters, are the landmarks of the hero's journey, a journey down memory lane designed to revive old emotions. Thus Nerval's tale combines mental time-travel and physical journey in the hope that revisiting mnemonic sites or objects will give the rememberer a stronger hold on his autobiographical memories that bear strong emotional associations.

The idea of writing about a sentimental pilgrimage is not new in Nerval's time: in this, the author seems to have imitated other similarly inclined romantic rememberers. Rousseau, Lamartine, and Chateaubriand in France and Wordsworth in England cultivated a topographical imagination with privileged sites for reminiscence. We need only think of "Le Lac" or "Tintern Abbey" to recognize the apparent similarities between Nerval and his fellow romantic writers. There are indeed cultural and historical trends in memory, and with its emphasis on nostalgia "Sylvie" is just a little behind its time—too romantic, perhaps. However, the notion of "romantic memory" has been revived recently in an interesting interdisciplinary context. In a section of *Le Sens de la mémoire* devoted to memory and affect, the brothers Tadié (the neurologist and the expert scholar on Proust) define two forms of recall: "romantic memory" and "imaginative memory." While the former aims at retrieving emotion "through a return to the context to which the feelings were first ascribed," imaginative memory, they explain, "rebuilds, on the basis of a memory-image, a feeling that we believe to have experienced" (177). Nerval, as we saw, relies on both, seemingly giving much weight to romantic memory—on the "an attempt," as the Tadiés put it, "of finding the feelings and sensations through a return to the codes that formerly embodied them" (177). The word "code" is particularly interesting, meanwhile, for it invites us to see differences in remembrance that are not merely historical, but also phenomenological. Thus, a "romantic" rememberer will strive to produce memories through a mimetic process in revisiting a scene or picture that is deemed to prompt a memory of past emotions, whereas another type of rememberer (endowed with more imagination) will create a memory on the basis of an emotional intuition—a sense of déjà vu, for instance, that a certain perception produces. It turns out that in "Sylvie," Nerval explores both types of remembrance, a romantic memory that is essentially topographical and imitative, and imaginative memory founded on buried emotions. He does so in a way that seems to foreshadow current theorizations of divergent mnemonic processes.

Gérard de Nerval's purposeful search for images and scenes that recall happy emotions offers insights into the elaboration of representations that belong to "explicit memory" and are thus more closely associated with a narrative organization than imagination. Explicit memory is our memory for things we remember—a formulation that only begins to make sense if we assume, as some researchers have in recent years, the existence of two memory systems: one, called explicit, which deals with ready-made representations; another, implicit memory that deals with yet-to-be-formed memories.[16] While the implicit system, which is more primitive and is present in early infancy, "automatically records perceptual, imagistic, sensory and affective experiences," the explicit system, which develops during early childhood, "records the output of purposeful, narrative mental activity."[17] In his deliberated search for memories "encoded" in geographic, spatial landmarks (a certain clearing in the woods, a lake, an old room or house), Nerval reminds us, as we learned from our study of mnemonic structures, that such localization and contextualization plays a key role in the emergence of mnemonic scenes. We will see, in the next section of this chapter, how it contributes to the revival of the memory of an emotion.

"We juxtapose," Bergson says, "our states of consciousness in such a way as to grasp them simultaneously: not one inside the other but one next to another; in short we project time into space." Whereas Bergson criticizes this narrative propensity for being too intellectual, in Nerval's case, the impulsion is different: it lies in the creative use of emotion, which inspires an aesthetic pursuit. We can then witness the birth of "an aesthetic space in which, by falling into a composition, moments and places create a work of art, a memorable and admirable unity."[18] A first summing up of Nerval's narrative accomplishments in "Sylvie" in terms of memory seems indeed to call for a comparison with Bergson's ideas, as summarized by George Poulet. Not only does Poulet's description of a Bergsonian model of memory help us understand why space is such an important dimension of memory in "Sylvie," it also provides a compelling explanation for the unusual narrative composition of this mnemonic tale. The creative principle behind "Sylvie," we are to understand, is not merely psycho-logical (as a rational attempt to put order into one's emotions), it is also aesthetic—to the extent that the right art of memory might produce a composition (memories of memories) that elicit admiration. As we know from the utter dismay Nerval felt when critics, hinting at his madness, misunderstood or dismissed his works as mere fantasy, this is a writer who took extraordinary pride in his artistic-mnemonic accomplishments. Among them is his anticipation, decades before, of the Proustian forms of remembrance (how else could Poulet's description have felt so perfectly right for Nerval?). But even more significant, from a historical perspective, is the fact that in showing in "Sylvie" two forms of remembrance—one "romantic," the other "imaginative"—Nerval also sets up the foundations for a distinction whose significance I hope to make increasingly clear in this book, a distinction between an interiorized and an exteriorized mode of recollection. Describing its visibility in Baudelaire, Sylviane Agacinski refers this separation to "a classical gesture" (for indeed, it is already present in Kant in the difference he remarks between *Gechächtnis* and *Erinnerung*): it consists in the separation between "a memory of the mind that synthesizes, suspends, interiorizes, and an exterior remembrance that has the material exactitude of archives" (86). Baudelaire and Nerval, whose lives overlapped, inhabited indeed the same historical configuration or "paradigm" of philosophical convictions about memory (it can still be traced very clearly in Proust): it opposes experience to history. While most of the next chapter is devoted to the subjective form of recollection, I want to address here, in response to Nerval's quest for mnemonic sites, the older form of remembrance that tries to objectify memory through exterior, material prompts.

Revisiting the Past: The Memory of an Emotion

One scene stands out in "Sylvie" for the rich satisfactions it offers the rememberer: a bride, an abundance of food, even a maternal presence. Visiting the village of "Othys" accompanied by Sylvie, the hero goes to her house, a "sanctuary of faithful memories," to find there an abundance of milk, bread, sugar, berries, and flowers (chapter 6, 120–24). They dress up in the wedding costumes, Sylvie in her aunt's dress and Gérard in the clothes of her defunct uncle. At the sight of this young couple, the aunt breaks into tears, overwhelmed with memories. Only when she begins to sing old songs from her wedding, with the young people "repeat[ing] together those unsophisticated rhythmic lines, with their traditional pauses and assonances," does this moment find a happier resolution (124). The songs—part of a collective, folk memory—preserve what a personal memory invested in objects cannot recapture, namely things as they were of old. Back in the old decor, the rememberer feels above all the discrepancy between now and then— between a lost and absent "real" scene and the mimicry that now replaces it: a false marriage, where old accessories are invoked, to hide the fact that time has passed.

The wedding scene is proof of the failure of romantic memory: miming the past does not satisfy the rememberer's yearning; on the contrary, replaying the old scene only increases the sense of loss and the discrepancy between "I now" and "I then." The experiment of the "literalist" who hopes to capture past emotions by going back to the place and reviving the old gestures ultimately fails. Instead of the expected happiness, he experiences a more acute sense of loss, and of emotional deprivation. The harsh lesson that this naive belief produces is made clear in Nerval's text. Finding the objects that inhabit our past and representing them (however careful the mise-en-scène) is not sufficient to re-create the emotion. On the contrary, when the past is revisited and represented to excess, it loses its emotional aura. The objects singled out for their sentimental evocations were just a lure, marking what is lost and what has changed. For indeed, as the philosopher Sylviane Agacinski suggests in discussing modernity and transience, we feel the passing of time not only "in some interior and subjective memory," but that feeling is "conditioned as well by our relation to objects and to places" (68). While objects and places change, so does our relation—our emotion—toward them. Summarizing a disappointment and disaffection felt by both the hero and the heroine of this scene, Sylvie's says pointedly "ça ne dure pas"—it doesn't last. The passage of time cannot be redeemed by the protagonists' attempt to rehearse an earlier wedding scene: wearing eighteenth-century clothes that are out of fashion, the protagonists fail to experience memory's redeeming features. Instead, they are made to feel the jarring discrepancy of time we call an anachronism.

A second visit to the same "sanctuary of memories" increases the sense of an irrecoverable past. Returning to the same house, the hero comes to the painful realization that the visible features of that idyllic past are gone: modern items have replaced the old objects marked with sentimental associations. Even Sylvie, who seems happily settled into a modern way of life, has changed. She has relinquished the old art of lace making in favor of the craft of making gloves (on a machine that is called, revealingly, *une mécanique*); she sings modern opera airs embellished with sophisticated trills instead of the old ballads, and she has updated her room to reflect the current style:

> Her room was decorated simply, but the furniture was modern. The old pier-glass, on which was painted an idyllic shepherd boy offering a bird's nest to a shepherdess in blue and pink, had been replaced by a mirror in a gilded frame. The four-poster draped chastely in old, flowered chintz had been replaced by a walnut bunk bed with a draw-curtain; at the window there were canaries in the cage where the warblers used to be. I hastened to leave the room, finding nothing to remind me of the past. (133–34)[19]

Bemoaning the loss of such objects, Nerval learns the harsh lesson that greets all romantic rememberers: their attempts to concretize past emotions by revisiting the original scene are doomed to fail. The past cannot be found again at the end of a coach journey to the Valois. The rememberer discovers at every juncture, and to his dismay, that the landmarks of earlier, happier emotions have vanished. The forest where of old he danced under the moon with his beloved Adrienne is now a site for tourism—the place one visits to see where Jean-Jacques Rousseau used to meditate. The houses the rememberer visited are still there, but their inhabitants have moved or changed almost beyond recognition; even the quaint furniture is gone, replaced by modern amenities. People change, or they die: Sylvie's familiar presence and voice inspire regret, but cannot bring back the earlier mood of happiness. It is in vain that the hero tries to reexperience the memory of emotions that were felt earlier in the same spot. Now freed from its material props, the hero's nostalgia can only feed on air. The last pages of "Sylvie" resonate with the quintessential nostalgic question: *Ubi sunt?* (132).[20]

The story recounted by Nerval could be used to illustrate a change in sensibility: it would speak then of the "acceleration of history and a new fragmentation of time," which are both, according to Agacinski, part of a new era marked by nostalgia and the pursuit of images (68–69). But in a discussion devoted to memory, mood, and emotion, the focus must shift to the rememberer's private fate. Will his nostalgia save him from despair? As he revisits the Valois one more time—in a last attempt to revive the past through a sentimental pilgrimage—the hero discovers the landscape emptied of all childhood associations and fit for a guidebook. In this scenery that has lost its aura, all happiness is gone as well, leaving the rememberer with an irredeemable nostalgia.

> Sometimes I feel a need to behold again these places of my solitude and reverie. There I sadly discover within myself the ephemeral traces of a time when naturalness was an affectation. . . . The ponds, excavated at such great expense, are filled with useless, stagnant water that the swan disdains. Long gone is the time when the Condé hunt used to pass through there. . . . To reach Ermenonville, there is no longer any direct route to be found. Sometimes I go via Creil and Senlis, sometimes via Dommartin. (146–47; translation amended)

The flattening out of memory shown in this picture results from too many returns, too many rehearsals of the same memory. Seen from a current perspective, the mnemonic progression Nerval charts in "Sylvie" vividly illustrates the transformation of episodic memory into factual, semantic memory. Indeed, as the scene of the rememberer's early visits turns into a mere spectacle, it is the very nature of the remembering that changes: mental time-travel no longer leads to the "sort of reliving of something that happened in the past" that defines episodic memory. It summons up familiar images now voided of their emotional salience—mere facts on flattened map. The process is one of gradual depletion: closing the circle, the rememberer is brought back to a mood of regret, conducive to more nostalgia, and wonders if his adventures were but a dream.[21] The nostalgia and emotional restlessness that the rememberer experiences speak of a modern sense of time that is haunted by its passage. "Modernity," Agacinski writes, "marks an experience of passages *(passage)* and of transience *(passager)*, of movement and the ephemeral, of fluctuation and mortality" (19). The story Nerval recounts in "Sylvie" is the prefiguration of a nostalgic longing that is still with us, as a telling anecdote will show.

A Modern Case of Nostalgia

Fetishism defines an attitude of mind where one says, "I know, of course, that. . . , but I believe nevertheless . . ." In this sentimental age, we seem to have filled our world with mnemonic objects designed to cue us into remembrance and to help us imagine that time can stand still. I would be very excited, I think, if one day, after so many moves, I came upon the colored pencil that I used in my school days. I know of course that even if I were to find the very same one I used for my drawings in first grade, the yellow pencil could not bring back the carefree happiness I felt when drawing my first suns and tulips. But I still believe that if I could find again the old tint, smell, and feel of object, I would reexperience the mood of one of those childhood days. Most of us, I trust, treasure some such object—objects that we think or hope will magically evoke a moment long gone.

For its last issue of the twentieth century, *Smithsonian* magazine chose to present, under the title "The Colors of Childhood," an article describing the Americans' fondness for Crayolas. Its ostensible subject was the emotional attachment elicited by this prosaic coloring instrument, connected to school days and childhood. Crayolas are a familiar sight, touch, and smell to many Americans, who grew up in a world colored by the evocative names affixed to each tint. "Crayola crayons take us all back with their fondly remembered look, scent and feel on paper," says the lead of this article devoted to the objects of a nostalgia—to memory props for a culture intent on cultivating a sentimental attachment to childhood ("Colors," Py-Lieberman, 32). Thus when the manufacturers, Binney and Smith, decided some time ago to withdraw some eight colors to replace them with more fashionable tints, there was an uproar—one that included picketers at the headquarters—protesting this decision. There were similar protestations when the manufacturers renamed some colors "when sensitivity required a new name" and *indian red* became *chestnut, night blue* replaced *Prussian blue, flesh* was renamed *peach*. But it was not only the color that was fondly remembered: the very recognizable smell of Crayolas played its part as well in the nostalgia. According to Py-Lieberman's article, a study on scent recognition conducted at Yale ranks crayons as "number 18 out of the 20 most recognizable scents to American adults" (34). This article was striking enough to elicit a vivid response from readers, as was shown in the reminiscence-filled letters published in a subsequent issue. In one such letter, parents recount the story of their young daughter uttering the fond wish that traffic lights should no longer be red, orange, and green; taking her poetic inspiration from the labels of her Crayolas, she wishes they were "pink, periwinkle and thistle."[22]

Behind this article's apparent simplicity lies a set of issues involving memory: questions about the limits of nostalgia, about an unnatural or fetishistic fondness for certain objects that carry our memories, and even further, a responsiveness to certain words or names that evoke past emotions. But this anecdote offers above all compelling evidence that autobiographical remembering bears not merely on the structures of cognition, but just as importantly on the management of our moods and emotion. Indeed, sentimental and irrational as these stories about Crayola may seem, they introduce a crucial notion for our understanding of autobiographical memory. They suggest that the occasion of our mental travel into the past as rememberers may be nothing more than a faint desire or regret for things of the past. Thus, the feel of a Crayola, the emotions associated with its name (pink, periwinkle, or thistle), seem, in a deep and subliminal way, to reassure Americans that a certain happy, idealized childhood past is still fully available to them. They hold forcefully and emotionally onto such objects because they like to be surrounded with the emotional comfort they evoke. The example highlights, meanwhile, the general features of a pervasive, but most often invisible, nostalgia that makes us value, often without our awareness, objects that carry happy associations.

With this anecdote, we are in a better position to understand, for instance, Proust's idealization of the past: if his sense of reality is grounded in the scenery of his childhood, it is because it evokes more powerful emotional associations than the streets of Paris. Similarly, if the nursery seems at times more real to Woolf than the garden, it is because she was able to invest its representation with emotions. A similar mechanism opposing the flatness of the everyday present to the past's emotional richness—a similar nostalgia—can be detected in the letter that the fond parents sent to the *Smithsonian* telling of a little girl's petitioning for nicer colors for traffic lights. Sitting in the car, waiting for a light to change (in a scene that surely epitomizes modern life), the child pronounces the magical words "pink, periwinkle and thistle." Suddenly, for the passengers in the car, a new world opens inside everyday boredom and banality, a world that has the features of a long-gone childhood perceived through the veils of emotion and nostalgia. I may be making far too much out of a simple story, but my point is precisely this: most of us indulge in nostalgic memories like Nerval, and one does not have to be Proust to experience a Proustian moment . . .

Memories are not merely a reflection of what we *know*: they speak for what we *feel*. Remembering is more than a structural process involving the construction of scenes; it is a dynamic phenomenon determined and inflected by strong affective currents that shape our existence. Emotions give memory images their salience and significance—and not only in the extreme cases of traumatic memory. Indeed, as this story shows, the urge toward autobiographical recall can occur in the most banal of circumstances, as we spontaneously draw on the past to color our present experience. Here too, memories enter our consciousness at their own behest, but with the surprise gift of a happy emotion. A sip of tilleul, a surprise glimpse of a brightly colored crayon, and we are flooded with a wealth of images as if reliving a past moment.

With this description we encounter what is Nerval's signal, groundbreaking contribution to our understanding of remembering: involuntary memory as the art of dipping into the past by hopping from cue to cue. Proust, himself a keen reader of Nerval, noticed it right away, declaring that his forerunner's narrative genius lay in his ability to render the unexpected, abrupt leaps our minds take between present and past.[23] The nineteenth-century writer thus deftly mimics a mode of mental functioning that is so much a part of us that we rarely pay attention to it. He shows a subject living in time, a subject whose very consciousness and life story result from the double-stranded narrative born from an incessant shuttling between perception and memory. Virginia Woolf herself had a word for this: she called it tunneling into the past. Proust, similarly, evokes an existence lived on stilts, in which we tread dizzyingly over the depth of the past. But neither of them attempts what Nerval achieved perhaps not even consciously, but just from trying to tell a fictionalized story of his most significant adventures and experiences—a totally natural (or should we say naturalized) representation of our multilayered consciousness as an "ever-shifting palimpsest."[24]

We dip into the past all the time, moving seamlessly between the two planes of the present and of the past, the warp and the woof of our biographical narratives. This is what "Sylvie" represents so vividly. A mere glance at a newspaper, where the printed words speak of a familiar place, and the hero is transported to the Valois of his childhood. Waking up from his dream, he mistakes the outline of old buildings with the convent where he met his first beloved (118). The smell of hay evokes an emotion-filled landscape, made of woods and hawthorn, that belonged to his past (128). These moments are the templates for the Proustian *tasse de tilleul* or, as we have seen, for the moment in the car with the child who says the magic words "pink, periwinkle and thistle." While the unexpected, involuntary irruption of a memory in the present is, of course, a common experience, it may well take a writer to show us the full complexity of the mental construction that can emerge from involuntary recall. Proust was reading Nerval at the very time he began working on his own magnum opus, to which he then thought of giving the title "Intermittences of the Heart."[25] Whereas the work's final title highlights, with the word *recherche*, the cognitive dimensions of his project, the older, working title focuses on memory's other dimension, namely its affective underpinnings. It acknowledges that the primary impulse behind the rememberer's journey into the past is emotional: it springs from a "heart"—a physical organ as well as the traditional locus of our feelings—which thus becomes the source of our story, that is, of the motions of our consciousness.[26]

The force exerted by emotions is the dynamic principle that sustains the construction of memory. What are these Proustian "intermittences of the heart," if not changing, shifting moods that arise with perceptions or memories, moods that are most strongly felt when perceptions are tightly interconnected with memories? Psychologists and cognitive scientists have established, under the name of "mood congruence," a correlation between memories and moods and have shown that a depressed person typically tends to retrieve sad and impoverished memories.[27] A recurrent pattern of sad memories is, in fact, a symptom of depression, suggesting that the same brain chemistry that produces depression inhibits the normal process of spontaneous reminiscence in which pleasant and less pleasant memories mingle freely. In the *Emotional Brain,* the neuroscientist Joseph LeDoux attributes this fact to the existence of a double system of storage for our memories: what we explicitly remember is bound up with what we do not know we remember (and is thus forgotten) and yet represents a lingering emotional residue or mood. By the same token, a mood—which cannot be fully controlled by our consciousness or will—can determine what we explicitly remember. A certain perception or state of mind might carry a memory in its wake unbeknownst so that we find ourselves "in the throes of an emotional state that exists for reasons [we] do not quite understand" (203). Haven't we all, at times, experienced some of these affects without a cause—a passing mood whose origin eludes us? Current research suggests that it is determined by forgotten, unconscious memories.

With this first foray into the links between emotion and recall, we are finally able to cast Nerval's romantic quest for happy memories in a somewhat different light: not as a pathetic attempt to revive past images and impressions in the face of an unbearable present, but rather as a noble and worthy attempt at mood management. As I hinted above, the correlation between mood and recall goes two ways: while our memories are affected by our moods, the reverse happens as well, for in "managing" our memories in a certain way, we can modify our emotions. The cultivation of happy memories might work as a mood enhancer. It is hard to imagine how a scientific protocol could demonstrate this; however, we have Proust's rich phenomenological description. Just consider what the encounter with a *tasse de tilleul* on a drab, depressing day did for his rememberer, or what happiness the fond parents get from being reminded by their child, even if only subliminally, of a happier childhood moment. The uplifting psychological effect induced by happy memories suggests that the nostalgia that impels us to cultivate such reminiscence may well carry a crucial existential value. To recreate a positive emotion in memory seems, then, the most natural psychological reflex. Casting a glance over our shoulder, we recognize the outline of a pleasurable scene, which our imagination will fill with images and representations. The impulse is emotional, rather than intellectual, and the outcome is the creation of a powerfully evocative landscape of the kind Nerval imagined in "Sylvie."

Nerval's sylvan tale still touches us, as has been proven by generation after generation of readers, because it strikes the chords of a deep, collective nostalgia.[28] Writing, in *Les Lieux de mémoire,* on the attraction that woods have long held (an attraction recently revived thanks to a new "ecological" sensibility) in the French imagination, the historian Andrée Corvol suggests that "woods, because they eschew the norms of time, are to us like lands of freedom. This is why they alone can carry certain symbolic functions that long haunt our memories" (2766). Written from a contemporary sociological perspective, which assumes (as Agacinski does philosophically) that our nostalgia expresses a need to escape from a modern experience of time, these words read like an indirect commentary on "Sylvie" and help explain the appeal that this singularly crafted narrative has held for generations of readers. Nerval's nostalgic writing transports us into the wooded landscape of Valois as if it were still there, unchanged, just outside of the ever-noisy, ever-busy metropolis. His tale casts its spell on us, its readers, in helping us imagine a landscape where our collective nostalgia can find a cause, a local habitation, and even a name. Indeed, Nerval's text fills with rich hues the sylvan landscape merely outlined by Freud, and gives concrete meaning to George Eliot's idea that such woods provide a "home-scene" and "the mother tongue of our imagination" (*Mill,* 94). Even the sharpest of analytical minds can still, in a hidden and barely acknowledged corner, treasure the thought, or rather the *feel,* of the best bread, the most vivid of yellow flowers, the woods near home. These objects have as much reality for Freud as did "the tufts of white upon the tips of grass" and "the strawberries floating in milk" of Nerval's Valois ("Sylvie," 110 [translation amended], 121). They are unimpeachable signs of a happier past, born under the sway of nostalgia. The memory of an emotion gave Freud the impulse to believe, for a moment, in the objective value of a memory: it gave to a multilayered construction, which integrated fragments from different eras of the rememberer's life, the appearance of a reality. Indeed, the stronger the image's appeal, the more we want it to be real and true. Meanwhile, the credit we give to the pictures drawn from imagination gives the measure of our nostalgia—of our psychological dependency on happy memories.

But one does not have to be an aesthete, a devotee of high art like Proust or Nerval (or an intellectual like Freud) to experience the pathos of nostalgia. When prisoners convicted in drug-related cases were asked how they whiled away their time in their prison cells, they told the psychologist that much of their time was spent daydreaming about the places where they used to "do drugs." Remembering these places, enables them, it seems, to experience artificially the pleasurable sensations they had known when under the influence of drugs.[29] Here too, as was the case for Nerval, nostalgic remembering provides the means of psychic survival. One can hardly imagine a greater contrast than that between a prison cell in Arizona and Proust's cork-lined room in Paris or Freud's rooms on Berggasse, but Nerval wandered the streets and slept in shelters. He, however, dreamed of woods and flower girls, not of street corners, seedy rooms, and dealers, and his pleasure was not chemically induced. Meanwhile, for the writer and the prisoner alike, nostalgia seems more like a gift than a curse—a gift of memory and imagination that enables us to re-create, in our minds, the idea of pleasure or happiness.

8 • Textures of the Past

A memory image exists by virtue of an emotion. If it were just a flat picture, devoid of emotional vibration, this image would probably not have been retained. Or if it had impressed us for a moment as a memory, it would almost as soon have been relegated to our memory for facts, and lost its auto-biographical dimension. Experiences thus flattened out remain with us, of course: they are the elements that we recite when asked to provide a bio-graphical statement. But they do not belong to the rich and complex text that constitutes our private autobiographies: the singular and intimate stories of our lives are made of events that express our moods, feelings, and affections. A yellow pencil, a bubble next to a water plant, red and purple blots of color on a dress, the blue-eyed speedwell in a wood in May, the smell of fresh bread are things that exist, still, by virtue of the affective reverberations they hold for each rememberer. How then are affective resonances embedded and rendered in the text that constitutes our memory? This question, which may seem at first exclusively literary, has been broached by scientists—and it is to the scientists that I now turn in order to understand more fully the complex relationship between memory and emotion.

Neuroscientists suggest that memories owe their liveliness, their salience, to the emotional charge they acquire outside of the subject's conscious awareness, when the subject first encountered an event that triggered a com-bination of bodily sensations. A subsequent encounter with a similar stimu-lus will reactivate these sensations through a mechanism of conditioning, and typically give rise to an explicit memory similarly inflected with an emo-tional charge. However, it is through atypical situations that neuroscientists elaborated this model. Their research centers on a mysterious paradox: how, in the midst of what seems to be profound amnesia, can one explain the existence of isolated islands of memory, islands where memory func-tions, but outside of conscious awareness? They came to the conclusion that a double process is at work as we remember. One function determines what we explicitly remember, and the other what is remembered only implicitly, without our conscious knowing. Explicit memory is conscious, conceptual, and identified in images and representations; implicit memory is unconscious, perceptual, and inchoate. While explicit memory feeds into the knowledge we have of an event, implicit memory registers and retains its emotional impact. It is held now that a special area of the brain, the amygdala, houses the most primitive of these two structures.

Our memories come to life, the neuroscientist Joseph LeDoux argues in *The Emotional Brain,* because they are configured, in part, by the implicit system: "without the emotional arousal elicited through the implicit system, the conscious memory would be emotionally flat" (201). His research shows that different parts of the brain are involved in the affective and conceptual aspects of memory, albeit with some overlaps.[1] In experiences that produce extremes of emotion (in traumatic situations) or in certain pathologies (where one of the systems has become dysfunctional) they can be dissociated. Then, only the most resilient of the systems, which produces implicit memories, remains fully operative. This explains why subjects who seem totally amnesiac can be prompted to remember skills or factual contents, at the subliminal level that is the domain of implicit memory. But this recent research also shows that our spontaneous, involuntary autobiographical memories are shaped by unconscious somatic processes connected to strong affects.

Among psychologists as well, the study in recent years of the complex interplay between remembering and forgetting in the case of trauma (whether physical or emotional) has led to the creation of a new categorization, one that distinguishes between explicit and implicit memories. Great attention has been paid, for example, to the emotional context of memory retrieval, or to the qualitative differences that mark the representation of certain memories, such as their persistence, their intrusiveness, their illogical construction. It would seem that the memory of an emotional experience takes on a different shape from that which defines an ordinary event. Thus, in *Searching for Memory* Daniel Schacter pointedly remarks that the painter Cheryl Warrick, who almost died in a fire that destroyed her apartment, represents this experience in "images [that] are hazy and illogical but penetrating in their emotional force" (180). The artist's answer to trauma is to try to recapture "perceptual memories of shapes, forms and objects." On the basis of his research, Schacter assumes the "existence of a subterranean world of nonconscious memory and perception normally concealed from the conscious mind." With these metaphors, the psychologist bears witness, just like the neuroscientist, to the fact that memories encode information that lies outside of the well-established paths of representations. When the memories of our emotions, which we cast consciously as scenes or images, are crossed with unconscious emotional memories, they truly come to life: we begin to remember what had been forgotten.

This dynamic conception will preside over the new stage of our investigation into the "subterranean" aspects of Nerval's reminiscences. Marcel Proust, his insightful and sympathetic interpreter, will act as our guide. For while the narrative content of a memory is easy to detect, analyzing the emotional aspects of remembrance requires refined critical instruments.[2] Scientists tell us that the emotion that arises during recollection is palpable, measurable: it takes either good clinical skills (reading the pulse, listening to heartbeats or to breathing) or fine recording instruments designed to measure, for example, the droplets of perspiration on the skin.[3] In ordinary life, however, we do not rely on such instruments—all the more so when we examine a text. Where is the emotional pulse or breathing that brings to life a memory to be found in "Sylvie"? Proust's answer to this question, in his beautifully crafted early essay on Nerval, is textual: he examines the verbal devices that vivify a memory, through an interpretative method that deciphers signs embedded in the representation—signs that symbolize affects.

Memory, Imagination, and Reminiscence

The closing moment of Nerval's tale suggests that the rememberer is himself keenly aware of the overriding sentimental tenor of his narrative—he needs reassurance that he will be understood, and that someone will see what is at stake in this nostalgic journey. Hence his discrete plea to his readers' sympathy: "Such are the chimeras that bewitch and lead astray in the morning of life," he writes. "My attempt to record them has been somewhat haphazard, but many a heart will understand me" (146; translation amended). Nerval thus addresses his *captio benevolentia* to an empathetic reader, one willing to validate his confusing mnemonic. Marcel Proust answered him eagerly, with an interpretation of "Sylvie" that seized on the tale's intimate emotional tonalities, eschewing the nationalist writers' view of this text as an advertisement for a collective nostalgia.[4] For Proust, only tendentious vision could extract from Nerval's text the equivalent of calendar pictures of a "good old France": to him, it was clear that the author spoke of "a Valois [that] exists as much in his heart as on a map." With this, the critic proceeds to decipher in "Sylvie" images that are highly idiosyncratic, but invite entry into a very personal emotional universe. It was clear to Proust that Nerval had taken substantial risks in writing "Sylvie"—and that madness might lie in wait for a rememberer so deeply obsessed with and affected by the images he summons up:

> With Gérard de Nerval, an emerging, not yet declared madness is nothing but a kind of excessive subjectivism, a subjectivism that gives more significance to what is attached to a dream, a memory, to the personal quality of a sensation, than to what this sensation holds commonly for all of us and is perceptible by all of us, namely to reality. ("Gérard de Nerval," 182–83)

As one could have predicted, knowing his own interests, Proust is drawn to the manifestations of imaginative memory. Little is said about real journeys; what matters to him is the figure of a rememberer who lies in bed, in a state between dreaming and sleeping, recollecting the "most striking pictures" that make up his youth. Proust thus invites us to focus on scenes such as this one:

> I painted in my mind the picture of a castle of the time of Henri IV, with its slate-roofed, pointed towers and its reddish façade quoined in yellow stone, and nearby a great open greensward surrounded by elm and linden trees, their foliage pierced through by the fiery rays of the setting sun. On the greensward a number of girls were dancing in a circle and singing old songs taught them by their mothers, the words in such a pure, natural French that the hearer was acutely conscious of being in old Valois, where the heart of France has been beating for more than a thousand years. I was the only boy in that circle, having been brought along by Sylvie, a little girl from a neighboring village who was my dearest companion. ("Sylvie," 109; translation amended)

This is merely the first of a succession of four mnemonic pictures (or *tableaux* as Proust calls them) that involve a mode of representation saturated with mnemonic signs ("je me représentais" is the phrase Nerval actually uses). Shapes, colors, textures are specified, with hardly any detail left to chance or impression—as it were essential to render, in this instance, as many dimensions of this memory picture as possible, while keeping them tightly in the frame of a tableau. Indeed, in spite of its inner animation, the picture seems arrested, as if it said—in the demonstrative gesture of deixis— "there it is": "there is the castle, the setting sun, the dancing and singing girls." This imaginative, imagistic exercise in reminiscence is so productive, meanwhile, that it spawns more pictures, more memories.

Thus, another three tableaux emerge from this first image, as the rememberer drifts deeper into a mood of reminiscence: he kisses Adrienne, the most beautiful of the girls; Adrienne sings as dusk falls imperceptibly on their circle—and in the end, she vanishes. These new images reveal a subtle change of tonality—a blurring of the lines, which is the verbal equivalent of a draftsman's shading or stumping. We thus discover a meadow under the moonlight, the girl's pure voice emerging from the falling dusk, "her golden hair glistening under the pale rays of the moon." The subtle and persistent modulations of color and sound create a scene that is suffused with an overall haziness, and with harmonics like a vibrato. It is in such harmonics—the product of a particular style—that Proust "reads" the emotional aspects of Nerval's sentimental journey and helps us see a shift in the representation of memory images, from denotation to connotation, toward the creation of an emotional memory.[5] Going back to the distinction that scientists make, we witness in Nerval's text the effects of an implicit memory system, namely textual traces of perceptual, imagistic, sensory, and affective experiences.

In such moments, the narrative of "Sylvie" almost seems to come to a halt, as if the rememberer were mesmerized by the image born on his page. The mechanism or rather the form taken by remembrance is very different from what we saw in the previous chapter, and is best described by the notion of reminiscence. "Reminiscence," Webster's dictionary proposes, is the "improvement of the memory for an experience despite the lapse of time since that experience." This unconventional definition is the fitting counterpart to Nerval's style in these examples—a compulsion toward the precision, the phenomenal enhancement of the images. Like Proust's bubbles near a water plant or Freud's yellow flowers, then, Nerval's "greensward surrounded by elm and linden trees" is the magical token of a long-forgotten emotion. But Nerval's highly stylized writing enables us to observe more closely how a mysterious verbal alchemy "produces" signs that seem attuned to the workings of implicit memory. This subtle strategy explains why, in spite of its seemingly banal romantic features, the tableau seems so vivid, intense, and alive—and so true to memory. "Reminiscence," Jankélévich writes, "aims at augmenting the concentration of our being, at increasing the ontic fullness, density, and weight of a becoming that is perforated with non-being" (216). These words ring especially true in Nerval's case, for whom imaginative memory seems to offer a better road into the past: a detached, free-floating act of imagination gives birth, unexpectedly, to signs that are invested with emotions. Whereas romantic memory, because it is essentially mimetic, fails to create the emotion, imaginative memory, which draws on more primitive perceptual affects, fills the representation with subjective, emotional contents.

"Beyond the freshness . . . beyond the evocation of the past" there is something "inexpressible" or "indefinable, which communicates to us an immeasurable disturbance *(un trouble infini),*" Proust writes evocatively, pointing at the darker emotional undertow and vague anguish that permeates certain representations in "Sylvie." It is here, in this compounded effect between a spell *(un enchantement)* and subtle emotional disturbances *(un trouble)* and in "pleasure compounded with anxiety," that Proust recognizes the signs of true madness in Nerval (189–90). In his appraisal of Nerval, Raymond Jean notices, similarly, the ominous signs of negative emotions, but he chooses to focus on Nerval's accomplishments as a supreme mnemonist:

> Before Nerval the past, the world of recollections was only seized objectively, through the voluntary, quasi-mechanical exercise of memory (by the "great" Romantics, for example): with him, it became the object of immediate subjective knowledge, of a knowledge that cannot be separated from an anguish, a sense of the uncanny *(un trouble),* and which is born from a deep exploration into the depth of time. (*Nerval par lui-même,* 133)

Who is to tell whether Nerval was really the literary inventor of this interiorized, highly subjective memory that Jean ascribes to him? While such a claim is hard to prove, what seems to be the case is that in "Sylvie," Gérard de Nerval found a way of blending—in one creative gesture—the conceptual, representational aspect of a memory and its perceptual, sensitive dimension. To state this in the scientific language of LeDoux's description, Nerval created, through the texture of his writing, a point of convergence between the explicit and the implicit systems, between the memory of an emotion and an emotional memory. For the neuroscientist, this blending of the two systems occurs in "working memory and its creation of immediate conscious experience" (201). With Nerval, this convergence seems to happen in the act of writing as memories emerge on the pages of "Sylvie," memories telling us that, in certain circumstances, one can relive something that happened in the past. Nerval's style is such that it enables the integration of the explicit and the implicit memory systems that produces "pregnant" memories.

The Colors of the Past: Emotional Memory

Can we be even more specific? What is it, in the lines printed on a page (or in the strong Proustian memory that springs to mind), that brings a memory to life? Here, an older taxonomy of memory, developed by the nineteenth-century thinker Maine de Biran, might come in good stead. In an essay devoted to thinking and habit presented to the French Institute in 1803 (*Influence de l'habitude sur la faculté de penser*), de Biran defined three types of memory: "mechanical," "representative," and "sensitive."[6] While the first of these categories corresponds to what is now called procedural memory, the others announce the distinction between the explicit and the implicit systems.[7] Thus, while a representative memory is produced through the recall of a sign "accompanied" or "immediately followed by the clear appearance of a well circumscribed idea," a sensitive memory involves "an affective modification, a feeling or even a fantastic image . . . which cannot be brought back to a sense image" (319, 156). The interest of this theory, for us, is its focus on communication—that is, on semiotic and, ultimately, linguistic issues. For de Biran, signs, in whatever form (whether as instinctive gestures or as elaborated, artificial codes, such as words), establish a correspondence with impressions and represent our medium of communication between the exterior world and our inner mental universe. While sensitive memories are beyond the reach of our thinking and cannot be conceptualized, they can, however, be traced in certain words, which act almost like talismans. Indeed, for de Biran there exist certain words that seem to bring forth a certain *je ne sais quoi,* which is not an idea, but an affect.[8] Such words, he suggests, are endowed with a floating signification and sometimes even with an unusual "excitatory power."

In his interpretation of "Sylvie," Proust hints at the existence of such "sensitive signs" in his focus on color. He thus relates the inexpressible dimension of memory to an atmosphere that is uniquely colored—it is "bluish and purplish," which in turn endows his images with "the character of nostalgia, the color of dream" (192). Moving subtly between the literal and figurative dimensions of such coloring, Proust further remarks on Nerval's reliance on delicate coloring to produces quasi-musical reverberations: "the true color given to every item [in the description] moves one like a harmony." Nerval's first reminiscences seem almost saturated with colors; thus, for example, the "picture of a castle of the time of Henri IV, with its slate-roofed, pointed towers and its *reddish* façade quoined in *yellow* stone, and nearby a great open *green*sward *(une grande place verte)* surrounded by elm and linden trees, their foliage pierced through by the *fiery* rays of the setting sun" (109) and "my remembrance of Adrienne, a flower of the night born in the *pale* moonlight, a *pink* and *golden* ghost gliding over *green* grass bathed in *white* vapours" (111).

Painting the past demands an uncanny talent for choosing the right colors. We had our first intimation of this idea with Virginia Woolf, who expressed her thoughts on the stylistics of memory through the figure of Lily Briscoe: "as she dipped into the blue paint, she dipped into the past there."[9] Nerval gives us a more precise idea of the aesthetic principles involved in the creation of memories and their phenomenal presence. In them, the rememberer seems to have encoded the intense presence of the past, the emotional intensity of its return, as well as the vivacity of a first impression.

· If color is instrumental in reminiscence, as Nerval's mnemonic experiments suggest, then we may have to revise our earlier interpretation of the collective nostalgia that surrounds Crayolas. This nostalgia for crayons may be motivated by more than a desire to hold onto an object that *belonged to* the past: in addition, the object takes its value from the fact that it *speaks of* the past (symbolically, that is). The sight of a colored pencil (even in imagination) holds the promise that an old impression can be revived, however fleetingly, extending for a moment the promise of a new beginning and of a world awash in strong sensations. This world, "fresh as if issued to children on a beach," in Woolf's words, is what the nostalgic mind is driven to.[10] *Pristine* is the word that best summarizes it. Indeed, of the five letters published by *Smithsonian* magazine, two dwelt on the "pristine" quality of Crayolas—as if writers had found in this banal object a symbol for their nostalgia and the promise of a world drawn in the fresh colors of a new beginning.

Vividness, however, is not always the trademark of Nerval's colors. More often, as Proust saw, his memory images are bathed in more subtle, attenuated tints, as if the primary colors were perceived through a haze. The writer must have known instinctively that in attenuating or veiling the intensity of presence of chosen mnemonic signs he would reinforce their uncanny appeal. These modulations into the tints of *bleuâtre, rougeâtre, blanchâtre* evoke the "depth of the past." They, unlike the almost hallucinatory vividness of other mnemonic representations, speak of the *memory* of the impression. This is why the scenes of "Sylvie" affect us with the uncanny ghostliness of a world that can be reached only through our nostalgic dreaming.

The Melody of Experience

As this change of register in the presentation of memories suggests, Nerval relies, for his mnemonic effects, on more than mere denotation: his rememberer is also drawn toward the singular connotations of certain words, reminding us of Jankélévich's idea that nostalgia combines topographical features with toponymy. The map of our nostalgia contains more than just places, it resounds with names that reverberate with emotions. Could it be, perhaps, that our deepest, least accessible emotional memories are encrypted in the music of language? Could it be, then, that we respond as much to the voice of the past as to its images?

Proust suggests as much, in drawing our attention to a series of proper nouns whose emotional resonances seems so strong that they can literally make us shiver: "one shivers *(on frissonne),*" Proust writes, "on reading the name 'Pontarmé' in a railway schedule." Names, Proust explains, are what fuel memory: "Châalis, Pontarmé, like islands in the Ile-de-France, are what exalts, to the point of ecstasy, the thought that we could, by a sunny winter morning, go to see for ourselves these dream-countries where Nerval used to walk."[11] "Sylvie" is for him like a vast echoing chamber, inhabited by nouns that reverberate with inchoate, quasi-physical emotional memories. Place-names in particular, Proust suggests, are a way of "plugging in" and "listening in to the past." Hence the insistent, magical presence of *Loisy, Othys, Châalis, Ermenonville, Mortefontaine,* and other such words in Nerval's text: they cue the rememberer's mind into further reminiscence when the mnemonic signs or prompts of the outer world have all but disappeared.[12]

To that extent, memory becomes in "Sylvie" a mind game, which is indeed what a recent account of mnemonic processes by the cognitive scientist Douglas Hofstader suggests. In an article entitled "Analogy as the Core of Cognition," Hofstader examines how we map our world through "analogical" or associative structures and provides one example of such a cognitive pattern in analyzing a memory that emerged surprisingly from a game of acronyms.[13] The scientist becomes a rememberer in his free time: while playing randomly with his letters, he creates a new cluster that, miraculously and unexpectedly, transports him back to earlier days spent in Denmark. Hofstader had clearly forgotten the "very detailed personal memory" born surreptitiously from this verbal game. How is it then, he wonders, that the image of a missed romantic encounter on a pier in Denmark springs to mind as he sits at his desk while trying to solve a word game? Unraveling the path that led from a present experience to a past event, he concludes that the recollection was prompted by the similarities between sounds or phonemes, and that the solution to the riddle is, in essence, musical. An involuntary memory is born from the phonemic quality of an invented word that, because of its resemblance to a Danish place-name, insensibly fueled the nostalgia conducive to the creation of an emotional memory. The word "nostalgia" is mine, for indeed Hofstader's description (a rough version of "stream of consciousness") does not allow for much emotion or romantic longing:

> That time I spent an hour or two hoping that my old friend Robert, whom I hadn't seen in two years but who was supposed to arrive from Germany by train sometime during that summer day in the little Danish fishing village of Frederikssund (which in a series of letters he and I had mutually picked out on maps, and in which I had just arrived early that morning after driving all night from Stockholm) might spot me as I lurked way out at the furthest tip of the very long pier, rather than merely bumping into me at random as we both walked around exploring the stores and streets and parks of this unknown hamlet. (131)

It is nevertheless clear that the idle play of a bored scientist at his desk is the cause behind a mental phenomenon that is Nervalian and Proustian in spirit: it tells us that memories can be born from a mere sound from which a representation, a mental picture, can emerge. Proust himself thought that Nerval's secret tool for recall is to be found somewhere *in* the words or even *between* the words, along an associative or analogical chain.[14] Hofstader's foray into the nostalgic rememberer's world appears to confirm his theory: the haphazard configuration of letters that makes up a word sometimes resounds with a melody of its own, a melody that is perhaps the most profound, most accounted for impulse behind a mnemonic trip. The surprise emergence of a proper name has produced a memory, and with it a combination of feelings that can be detected, but barely, from the cognitive scientist's description. Read in light of our recent encounter with Nerval, Hofstader's prose nevertheless offers suggestive intimations of the nostalgia that marks a fated, irrecoverable moment; it also evokes, albeit discreetly, whiffs of romantic longing for an encounter that could still happen, were it not that it could only be "in memory." That this encounter with an involuntary, long-forgotten memory should produce such an indistinct medley of emotion is not surprising: Hofstader's account brings us closer than any of the literary descriptions we have examined to the raw, unprocessed "feel" that defines an emotional memory.

Language is necessarily two-sided for the rememberer: it represents images of the past, while also producing the unavowed affective resonances embedded in the images. Words resonate with private emotional associations, and like Proust's magnetic paper clips, they draw in their trail hitherto unknown images, emotions, and memories—as if activating the "dispositions" that, according to Damasio, lie in wait in our minds.[15] While scientists have identified this double aspect of memory in distinguishing between the explicit and the implicit systems, Nerval's writing helps us to see how the two systems might converge in the act of recall. The "scenery" and the "melody" are the two sides of the poetic language that we analyzed in "Sylvie." Nerval's evocative prose suggests that our most powerful memories are sustained by an underlying preverbal emotion that emerges at the juncture between image and sound.[16] It might be useful, heuristically, to differentiate between the memory of an emotion (produced by the explicit system and "imagistic") and an emotional memory (created by the implicit system and "melodic"). What this distinction helps us see is that rememberers cultivate a poetic relation to language in trying to bring about a coincidence between a representation and affect. They invoke words that enable a toponymic mapping of consciousness, a toponymy without which our world, just like our memories, would be simply flat. Behind a poetic word— a word used musically—a memory lies in wait.

Absence

We use words to invoke what is absent, as I intimated early on by quoting the poet Mallarmé, who argues that thus in speaking the word "flower," I will bring it "into" memory and lift it "out of the forgetting where my voice relegates other contours."[17] This discussion of nostalgia would indeed be incomplete if we did not ultimately acknowledge that the fullness ascribed to our memories is the product of a desire—a desire that overlooks the fact that memory is part of a structure of infinite regress. Not only does memory make objects present in absentia, memory becomes a way of dealing with absence by representing what was absent in the first place. The Valois that Nerval draws in his mind and then even revisits can never live up to its remembered, dreamed-up beauty. When Eliot invites us to revisit the woods of our childhood, she maintains the same dream and the same fiction of an idyllic past, a past that can only exist in imagination. Mallarmé tells us that the flower sprung from memory will remain missing from every bouquet. As for Proust, he declares, in an often quoted phrase, "les vrais paradis sont les paradis perdus"—the paradises we remember are always already lost (*Le Temps retrouvé*, 3:706).

Memory is about loss and absence: while we always know, intellectually, conceptually, that this is true, it takes a nostalgic writer to make us understand the emotional, psychological reverberations of this fact. What this nostalgic subject experiences, and testifies to, is how the fullest forms of our happiness (what Proust called his *paradis* and Woolf her "raptures" and "ecstasies") can only be known to us after the fact and belatedly, that is, in our memory. Thus Proust's famous statement brings us back to Woolf's provocative celebration of the beauty of the past: "the past is beautiful because one never realizes an emotion at the time," giving it a different inflection. Proust emphasizes the loss, while Woolf dwells on the retrieval of an image that embodies the combined attractions of a satisfying aesthetic and emotional experience. It is because such aesthetic paradises can only exist in memory that nostalgia exerts its irresistible seduction on both these nostalgic rememberers: the fact that no present can live up to such idealizations renders the past immensely attractive. In the scattered notes of his journal, Gérard de Nerval writes boldly "supériorité du passé sur le présent" ("superiority of the past over the present"), words that have an unreasonable, if not perhaps mad, ring to them.[18] When nostalgia becomes one's life philosophy, one incurs a double doom: not only can the present never live up to our desire ("things" are never as good as they were), but one also lives with ghosts. Showing some detectable impatience with the deep nostalgic streak in *A la Recherche du temps perdu,* Gaëtan Picon concludes that this work is built on Proust's deep-seated conviction of "the incurable imperfection that lies at the heart of the present" (143).

But we have known from the outset that nostalgia is unreasonable: it feeds on the belief that a return to the past is possible, when we know that time moves forward. It wants, stubbornly and unreasonably, to capture an emotion that was never there in the first place. Our thinkers are well aware of this. In his study of nostalgia, Jankélévich points out that, paradoxically, "one doesn't need to have been happy to experience nostalgia." Reflecting on childhood in *The Interpretation of Dreams,* Freud ponders over the same contradiction and ascribes the illusions that mark our nostalgia to the repression of sexuality. He develops this thought gradually: "We think highly of the happiness of childhood, because it is innocent of sexual desires," he writes in the first edition (in 1900), by way of identifying the cause of our nostalgia in a longing for presexual times. Then he returns to this subject in 1911, with the knowledge that these presexual times never existed: "Closer study too has given us ground for feeling some doubt in regard to the happiness of childhood as it has been constructed by adults in retrospect" (*Interpretation of Dreams,* 163–64). Thus, we must conclude that the happiness of childhood is a retrospective construction that we owe to our nostalgia.

The famous *scène du baiser*—the bedtime kiss—in the first volume of

Proust's work provides a vivid illustration of this statement, and, from the perspective of memory as absence, it is well worth a closer examination.[19] Coming shortly after the episode of the madeleine and tilleul, it represents "Marcel's" first memory, born from the nostalgic mood set by the initial moment of reminiscing. But "first" is too weak a word: *inaugural, originary,* or *primordial* might be better suited to describe what is not only the first of a series of other autobiographical memories, but also a psychological landmark in the protagonist's experience.[20] A child's desire for his mother's kiss announces here all other subsequent desires and becomes the founding moment of all subsequent nostalgia—a nostalgia all the more poignant for abiding by the principle that "one doesn't need to have been happy to experience nostalgia." Indeed, as an attentive reading shows, the much-longed-for, long-awaited, and thematically crucial motherly kiss never "happens" in this scene. It is wished for, eagerly awaited, but also paradoxically deferred to times past and now remembered, when the nightly kiss must surely have been a reality.

The scene is well known by readers of Proust: one night, because of a "grown-up" evening (Swann, the neighbor, is visiting them), little Marcel is sent to bed early, missing his chance to receive the precious "viaticum" of his mother's kiss, but with the memory of earlier kisses. Obsessed by a single desire—a desire to feel "the sensation of her cheek against [his] lips"— he breaks all rules, posting himself in the staircase in the hope of surreptitiously getting his reward.

The child's demand is met with the surprisingly permissive gesture of the father: the mother can spend the night with her child. A bed is prepared for her, and a birthday gift (George Sand's novel *François le Champi*) is opened in advance, in the hope that a bedtime story will divert the boy, who is now unaccountably upset. Yet the kiss remains missing, forgotten in the emotional turmoil created by the father's unexpected licensing gesture. This famous Proustian scene, the source of all later nostalgia, presents us in fact with an absent kiss, a kiss that is always already lost. Meanwhile, the child cries, and his sobs are still heard by the rememberer, who holds his own vigil:

Of late I have been increasingly able to catch, if I listen attentively the sobs ... which broke out only when I found myself alone with my mother. In reality their echo has never ceased; and it is only because life is now growing more and more quiet around me that I hear them anew, like those convent bells which have been so effectively drowned during the day by the noises of the street that one would suppose them to have stopped, until they ring out again through the silent evening air. (*Swann's Way*, 40)

"Never again will such moments be possible for me," the narrator had exclaimed by way of prefacing a vivid description of nostalgia. For what else but nostalgia could account for, on second thought, this mind-boggling fascination with an unhappy childhood memory. The rememberer keeps fantasizing about this maternal kiss that no other kiss can surpass, so that throughout *A la Recherche du temps perdu* this missing kiss—which is either always past, as a memory, or anticipated on the basis of earlier memories (as a desire)—will epitomize the perfection of happiness. Yet it only truly exists as a memory—under the impulsion of nostalgia and as a retrospective construction. "Imaginative memory," the Tadiés write, "reconstructs, on the basis of an image, an emotion that we think we have experienced" (178). A detour through the original text, which speaks of belief, helps us understand how a nostalgic memory overlaps with what is really a desire, as Proust shows in describing his young rememberer's surprising skill at representing the kiss that will never have happened:

> And so I promised myself that . . . I would put beforehand into this kiss, which was bound to be so brief and furtive, everything that my own efforts could muster, would carefully choose in advance the exact spot on her cheek where I would imprint it, and would so prepare my thoughts as to be able, thanks to these mental preliminaries, to consecrate the whole of the minute Mamma would grant me to the sensation of her cheek against my lips, as a painter who can have his subject for short sittings only prepares his palette, and from what he remembers and from the rough notes does in advance everything he possibly can do in the sitter's absence. (29)

Nostalgia—the expression of our desire for memory—is what drives the subject forward, helping him shape his desire. The missing, remembered kiss is what inspires our rememberer to imagine more such kisses; it embodies a concrete promise for a future happiness. This is how nostalgia can, paradoxically, enhance our moods. Dwelling on happy memories, re-creating those absent paradises that lure Proust into his own memory work, gives us a chance to reimagine, against a backdrop of everyday drabness, boredom, or confusion, different and happier configurations for our actions or our desires. For even in memory, paradises are still paradises.

This investigation into nostalgia enables us to see a new meaning in Woolf's aphorism, "the past is beautiful because one never realizes an emotion at the time": it becomes an invitation to imagine beauty in the present under the pretence of remembering (*Diary*, March 18, 1925). The raptures and ecstasies Woolf creates in writing about happy childhood memories really belong to her present, suggesting that we shape our present mood through idealized retrospective fictions. Nerval could not have been so wrong, then, in gambling his future on nostalgia—even if he was to lose it, ultimately, to an intensity of reminiscence conducive to madness. Indeed, what a close study of the *scène du baiser* reveals is that nostalgia is Janus-faced: it shows a smile on one side and tears on the other. When the sense of loss, the awareness of what is missing takes over, then the creative power of memory fades away and the rememberer contemplates absence.

Nerval captures this hesitancy or oscillation between presence and absence beautifully in an analogy applied to a memory of Adrienne. Paradoxically, it is the very absence of an original that renders her memory so vividly, so dazzlingly present:

> The image of that face of hers, forgotten for many years, suddenly became and remained singularly clear in my mind; it was as if a pencil-drawing blurred by time had become a painting, like one of those old sketches by master painters once admired in a museum, which one recalls later upon seeing elsewhere the dazzling masterpiece it foreshadowed. (111)

The word "dazzling" (*éblouissant* in the original) comes across here as the fittest counterpart to the term *flat*. Here truly is a case where a memory is *not* flat, but on the contrary so enlivened as to carry the force of an original imprint or impression. Casting his net into the pool of memories, this rememberer sees a figure that miraculously no longer emerges as a pale, faded copy, but with the clarity and vividness of the original work. Thus nostalgia opens up an avenue in "Sylvie" toward an ever-receding image of luminous beauty, known only through her ghostly presence: "Adrienne, a flower of the night born in the pale moonlight, a pink and golden ghost gliding over green grass bathed in white vapours." Through the mysterious alchemy of his words, the poet has imagined the absent.

It is because emotion and recollection are deeply interconnected that "forgotten" memories can make their way to the surface of consciousness. However, we now know, thanks to Nerval, that memory is not really the counterpart to a "lost" emotion—it is, rather, the emotion itself. What this means, among other things, is that just as new emotions kept being produced during the writing of "Sylvie," so did new memories. I propose to test this idea by examining again, this time from the perspective of implicit memory, the wedding scene in Nerval's tale. My hypothesis is that the "sanctuary of faithful memories" holds more than just the memory of an emotion. I am suggesting that this scene contains a lost, buried, or forgotten emotion, an emotion that belongs to the domain of implicit memory.

Remembering the Forgotten: The Power of Emotional Memory

How can a close encounter with a literary style and practice enhance our knowledge of what scientists tells us? This question, which arises with my claim that the process of writing can produce implicit memories, is important enough to warrant a brief digression into the history of my research. As a zealous reader of Nerval, I had long held that the wedding scene in "Sylvie" carried a secret, because of the exceptionally palpable emotional intensity that marked these pages—an intensity that seemed out of proportion with their narrative content. An overlay of pictorial references in this scene—an eighteenth-century portrait on the wall and a famous engraving by Greuze with a country bride as its focal point—further wetted my curiosity and took me to a fine-arts library. The comparison showed something that the text does not make clear, namely a striking similarity between the two pictures, as if they might correspond to one single referent buried or encrypted within the scene. With these results in hand, the terrain seemed ripe to try to combine a literary with a psychological approach and to develop the following hypothesis: what, from the perspective of representation, figures in this mnemonic scene as a blind spot can be defined in terms of memory as part of the implicit system. In other words, in writing this scene, the author has created a reminiscence invisible to himself.

But what does this tell us about the uses of memory in chapter 6 of "Sylvie"? As we know, this episode overtly recalls emblematic images of childhood happiness: an abundance of milk, strawberries, cherries, gooseberries, flowers; a fire in the hearth; staging a mock wedding with a girl he fancied. She as the bride, he as the groom, they don the clothes of another time. Critics have pointed out that Nerval wrote, over time, several versions of this marriage scene, but none comes as close as this scene to unveiling the fantasy that shaped it.[21] The representation is unusually vested with feelings (desire, chagrin, disappointment, happiness, melancholia—one moment after another is strongly connoted through emotions), and it is unusually detailed. Its main focus is the description of the bride. In the picture on the wall, she appears as "an alluring, mischievous, tall and slender [young woman] in an open-bodiced dress adorned with a ladder of horizontal ribbons, and teasing with pursed lips a bird perched on her finger." In her reincarnation as Sylvie, she "looked like Greuze's *Accordée de village*" (123). The feminine figure is given prominence in this wedding snapshot in a fashion suggesting that it holds a private significance for the rememberer: such wealth of details, such attention paid to particularities!

That she resembled a figure in an eighteenth-century painting or engraving is all Nerval ever knew of his mother, who, having followed her husband, an army doctor, to Silesia, died of fever in Germany when Gérard was two. "I never saw my mother," he wrote. "Her portraits have been lost or stolen; I only know that she resembled a woman of an earlier time, by Prud'hon or Fragonard, called 'Modesty.'"[22] A comparison between the figure of the bride in Greuze's painting with eighteenth-century engravings on the theme of modesty reveals a striking similarity, suggesting that one archetypal shape or figure haunts the pages of "Sylvie." Dimly and yet perceptibly, the picture of the *Accordée de village* slides over into another picture: the lost portrait of a mother who died too early for her child to remember. Sylvie in her wedding clothes is fashioned on the model of Nerval's mother. What emerges here on the page and becomes a representation is an autobiographical subtext and the memory of something long forgotten, namely the features of a mother last seen by Nerval when he was a very young child. The pictorial, fictional images of "Sylvie," many of them engraved more deeply with symbolic particularities and affects, commemorate the absent mother, who now appears, albeit in a disguised fashion, on the page. But *appearance* is perhaps not the right word here; *presence* might be more appropriate.

Writing similarly, in "A Sketch of the Past," about her own mother "who died too early," Woolf provides a revealing analysis of the influence she exerted. Woolf's words are so resonant, in fact, that they offer an implicit justification for the notion that the mother is a "presence" in Nerval's text:

> She was one of those invisible presences who after all play so important a part in every life . . . all those magnets that attract us this way to be like that . . . have never been analysed. Yet it is by such invisible presences that the subject of this memoir is tugged this way and that every day of his life; it is they that keep him in position. . . . I see myself as a fish in a stream; deflected; held in place; but cannot describe the stream. (80)[23]

We must rely on metaphors to describe the mind or the psyche; thus Woolf's figure of a stream gives us further insight into the dynamics of implicit memory. Indeed, as we have learned in this section, remembering subjects are not merely architects who have a vested interest in building representations of the past: affects drive them, insensibly as it were, toward certain images. In Woolf's image, rememberers ride an emotional current, which mysteriously and unbeknownst to them keeps them on a certain course, yet sways them in certain directions. The maternal complex—as this textual and psychological configuration could be called—born on this revealing page of Nerval's text provides a vivid example of an emerging autobiographical memory.[24] Placed as it is under the sign of an unconscious affect, the wedding scene is endowed with emotions that lie, as it were, beyond memory's ken.[25]

Just like daydreaming or dreaming, thus, writing can be conducive to the emergence of buried memories. Here, Nerval's literary experimentation with nostalgic memory appears to bear out, as we shall see shortly, Daniel Schacter's suggestion that as early as in the nineteenth century, experimental conditions were available that enabled the study of implicit memory. Unbeknownst to Nerval (or if it was known, we have no evidence), a memory emerged on the page, supporting my idea that writing matches the dynamic process that gives birth to memories. The page is like the tablet where the mind lays down, or rather *creates*, memories.[26]

My hypothesis that writing can be conducive to the expression of forgotten memories—that it mediates the passage from the implicit to the explicit memory system—lacked a more objective support until I came upon Daniel Schacter's attempt to chart a genealogy for current investigations into implicit memory. Thus in "Implicit Memory: History and Current Status," Schacter makes interesting connections between modern discoveries about the unconscious aspects of remembrance and nineteenth-century practices of crystal ball gazing and automatic writing.

> Although modern practitioners might be reluctant to admit it, a good case can be made that nineteenth-century psychical researchers were the first to document implicit memory phenomena on the basis of controlled empirical observation. Two major "implicit memory tests" were used: crystal ball gazing and automatic writing. . . . Although the purpose of these procedures was to document phenomena such as telepathy and clairvoyance, several investigators reported that fragmentary representations of past experiences, devoid of any familiarity or autobiographical reference, frequently appeared during crystal gazing and automatic writing. (321)

This defense of the epistemological value of automatic writing and crystal gazing broadens the scope of the gedankenexperiment that, throughout history, have helped us enhance our grasp of human remembrance. It tells us that a systematic exploration of the irrational, emotion-driven creations of our imagination can be part of a science of memory. It also invites us to conceive of automatic writing and crystal gazing as compelling analogies for the rememberer's intense transcribing and scanning activity that produces reminiscence. A protocol of exploration that so deliberately eschews the normal frameworks of cognition or rationality may seem all the more relevant for a discussion of a rememberer such as Nerval, who seems naturally driven toward emotionally charged memories. One could indeed argue that like the crystal gazers and practitioners of automatic writing who followed him, Nerval produced the "fragmentary representations of past experiences" by giving free rein to his visionary imagination. He showed that writing can do more than document the emotional life that makes up our autobiographies; it can, at times, *give birth to* memories. Lost in the shadow of forgetting, there lies a perceptual and affective event or experience that will come to life when touched—if only tangentially—by a representation. To be accurate, one would have to describe this barely discernable image as "virtual," for by definition it cannot be a fully fledged memory but the ghost of one. Indeed, were it not for writing's uncanny ability to give shape to subliminal images, that memory would be truly forgotten.

"Sylvie" is the product of neither crystal gazing nor automatic writing; however, Nerval approached writing within a tradition that later influenced the circles of psychical research Schacter describes. His fascination with German romanticism led him to cultivate dreamlike states and an inspirational mode of writing, while the strongly subjective and introspective drift that marks his best works (*Les Chimères, Aurélia* and *Filles du feu*) led to his rediscovery by the surrealists. What the surrealists saw in Nerval, namely his ability to dwell in the domain of subconscious poetic creation, is also what may have led him toward private symbols that encrypt his emotions. This is how, in writing "Sylvie," Nerval came across an image that evokes, however dimly, the mother he never really knew. We have no reason to assume that the author "intended" to commemorate his mother in chapter 6 of "Sylvie." But we know that in constructing what he called a "sanctuary of faithful memories," this rememberer ended up enshrining a forgotten maternal memory in the texture of his prose.

That this maternal image should be a mere adumbration (perhaps the product of the kinds of stories that a child is told about a dead relative—that she looked like this or that picture, for example) should not puzzle us. It is well known that over time no memory can remain pure.[27] Autobiographical memories are most often built incrementally, through the addition of elements that we gather along the way, from hearsay, from pictures, and even from the manner in which we are prompted to recall. Each new recollection tampers with a first, "genuine" memory: we all know, for example, how photographs seem conducive to, and yet interfere with, autobiographical recollection.[28] We should not be puzzled either by the fact that Nerval's mnemonic images are not exact replicas of each other. The image is but a pale copy of the original—and not, as the familiar phrase goes, because of a "memory distortion." For how could there be a distortion in the absence of a source image? The image summoned up in the text is a feeble imitation, because an emotional memory is by definition an unformed representation. It is thus only tentatively and fleetingly or tangentially that it approximates the initial perception. For a child of two, the maternal face is probably just a blur of affects, perceptual and sensual intensities; it is not yet a portrait with distinguishable features. Scientifically speaking, memory at such an early age can only be located in the more primitive implicit system. Moreover, it would be totally erroneous to look for a resemblance in a portrait that, as Maine de Biran taught us, could provide no more than a "sensitive sign," namely a "fantastic image," which "expresses an affective modification" (156).

To get a better grasp of the surreptitious emergence of an emotional memory on the writer's page, we must return to modern scientific conceptions. As we saw, in ordinary circumstances memories emerge in our consciousness through the coincidence between the explicit and implicit "current." However, the case of "Sylvie" is not so ordinary insofar as the writer sedulously pursues two forms of remembrance: romantic as well as imaginative memories. It is thus *while* the writer tries to capture memories of certain emotions, by creating scenes and scenarios for his nostalgia, that he encounters, coincidentally, an emotional memory. In *The Emotional Brain,* LeDoux writes: "There is a place . . . where explicit memories of emotional experiences and implicit memorial memories meet—in working memory and in its creation of immediate conscious experience" (201). The emotional resonance—the intensity of this scene in "Sylvie"—is a reflection of that event: the birth of an autobiographical memory on the page. What we witness in Nerval's writing is thus truly memory at work, that is, a moment when the conjunction between the implicit and the explicit system gives shape to a long-forgotten personal experience. The assumption that pregnant memories are necessarily sustained by unconscious, implicit mental "dispositions" as well as by unacknowledged emotional currents has immediate consequences for our analysis of mnemonic representations. Proust may well have been right: it is "entre les mots," or as we might say, in a place *beyond words,* that the most powerful emotions are elicited. As shown by our discussion of Nerval's "Sylvie" and even more so by our encounter with Douglas Hofstader's description of a memory, affect is the most elusive and hardest element to describe in a mnemonic scene. There are times when, analyzing a memory's emotional contents, I have myself felt like a crystal gazer searching for images amid the diffracted patterns created by words. Thus, for example, although the path leading from pictures of a wedding scene to the embodiment of maternal loss may have seemed compelling from a researcher's point of view, there is no way I could ever ascertain the truth of this discovery. What remains true, however, even from the perspective of rigorous neuroscientific explanation, is that the subliminal presence of a forgotten memory could help us account for the unusual mood and the emotional aura that pervade the wedding scene in "Sylvie."[29]

But these last remarks invite a comment on method. As my reader may have felt throughout this chapter (and perhaps most strongly in my discussion of the wedding scene), this examination of memory's emotional underpinnings has entailed a reluctance to elicit narrative contents from the scenes I examined. With this topic, I have indeed put myself in the same position as someone who must articulate the feelings that can be elicited from a certain musical piece: I have had to find words for what lies outside of narrative, namely the emotional configurations that sustain remembrance. This restricted agenda has meant, however, that I have had to read Nerval's text against the grain, overlooking the overriding story that emerged from his memories. Indeed, unlike a poet, who does not need a narrative frame and limits himself to playing with words, the writer of fiction will naturally want to gather images and words toward a story, a story that makes sense of the pattern of emotionally laden images born from a creative imagination. Meanwhile, as creators of fictions, Woolf, Nerval, and even Proust enjoy a freedom usually denied to other rememberers: the freedom to explore to the utmost the intimations about the nature of human experience that are inscribed in mnemonic scenes. This is how they help us see better some of the underlying narrative principles that shape personal remembrance. Thus Nerval, whose "Sylvie" reveals the strong and sometimes overriding current that seems to shape our reminiscing, tells us that the primary impulse behind our remembering lies in a desire to go back to our beginnings—a nostalgia for origins.

Our autobiographical remembering must necessarily rely on the make-believe of a beginning, on a "first memory" (to quote Woolf) or a "primal scene" (of the kind we saw with Proust)—thus the need for a narrative structure would create the memory. But the reverse may be true as well: the deep-seated memory of the maternal bond may determine the structure of our nostalgia. In its most radical form, reminiscence drives us toward a pre-oedipal universe, to the dream of a dyadic bond that holds mother and child together. These experiments in nostalgic memory thus unveil the ultimate fantasy behind all autobiography: the desire to start from scratch, remaking one's life, as it were, from the mother's womb.[30]

The nostalgic subject dreams that the mental journey into the past will lead to a country where his or her mother can be found again. Thus, in his essay "The Uncanny," Freud writes: "There is a joke saying that 'Love is home-sickness'; and whenever a man dreams of a place or country and says to himself, while he is still dreaming: 'this place is familiar to me, I've been here before,' we may interpret the place as being his mother's genitals or her body" (245). I used to think of this passage, I must confess, as one of the wilder speculative moments of psychoanalytic writing, until I reread it in the light of my inquiry into nostalgia, and with Proust, Nerval, and Woolf in mind. It now strikes me as being truly prescient: it shows how in the mind of the dreaming-writing nostalgic rememberer what first appears as a mere innocent image—the country of the past, the place that was home—is welded into an emotional scenario whose strongest current is the desire to return to maternal origins. Thus the places that Nerval revisits in "Sylvie" and the encounters that say, "I have been here before" ultimately point toward the absent maternal figure. That her image should barely emerge is not surprising: nostalgic memory is such that it can at best circumscribe, and approximate, the shape of a lost, an absent, object. The shaping force, meanwhile, is what scientists have called an emotional or an implicit memory. As for the psychoanalyst, he would call it the unconscious.

9 • The Rememberer's Task

In 1915, at the invitation of the Berliner Goethesbunde and against the backdrop of the First World War, Freud wrote a short essay on the subject of transience. It begins with his personal recollection of a walk taken in a beautiful, flower-filled summer landscape in the company of an unidentified literary author and of the latter's surprising response to such natural beauty. Instead of growing lyrical, looking for words and images to translate his aesthetic experience, the poet falls silent and Freud is puzzled. How could the man perceive such beauty and find no pleasure in it? The frailty of all things, Freud reflects, elicits two kinds of responses: the painful despair shown by this writer for whom "everything that he would otherwise have loved and admired lost its value . . . because it was destined to vanish," or a defiant impulse, which says "such beauty must, in some way, survive, it can be saved from the forces of destruction" (225).[1] While the latter attitude, Freud comments, is not fully realistic, it is revealing of a human desire to endow objects with lasting value despite life's evanescent and transient quality. Our instinct to remember and commemorate—in this instance, to mark "a thing of beauty" through our words and thoughts—is life affirming, a way of resisting time and mortality. Aesthetic experiences are within our grasp, inspiring our poetic imagination, as long as we are in the mood for them, for "even a flower that blooms for only one night will impress us with its splendor" (226). The cause for his interlocutor's refusal or incapacity to commemorate, Freud concludes, must be psychological. The poet is tongue-tied perhaps because of his excessive attachment to things of beauty—anticipating his own death, he mourns for the transience that affects all life. His imagination failing, locked up in silence, he inhabits the gray and dulled universe of depression in which the flowers have lost their color, the woods are just a clump of indifferent trees, and the savor of life is gone.[2]

As we learned earlier with Eliot and Proust, the memory garden is our subjective creation; our imagination, desire, and affections determine the salience, significance, and beauty we ascribe to chosen elements of the surrounding world. As the culmination of these different aesthetic and psychological impulses, autobiographical memory becomes our bulwark against the forces of destruction and mortality. Freud's essay on transience thus revisits, in the guise of a psychological exploration, the dilemma the rememberer faces, who can endorse, as we have seen repeatedly, either of two possible stances: that of the skeptic, or that of the idealist. Depending, then, on which mood takes the upper hand—melancholia or an inspired, imaginative responsiveness to the objects surrounding us—memory will be felt in its failures, or on the contrary, as a triumph over loss and the corrosive forces of time. We cultivate memories as a response to mortality and as part of our survival, Freud shows us in this essay.

But "cultivating" is perhaps too weak a term when we consider the word Freud chooses to describe the rememberer's gesture of commemoration. Indeed, as if echoing the writers we have studied, he evokes a dynamic process, using a verb, *entrücken,* that means "transport" (the noun form *Entrückung* means "rapture" and "ecstasy"). Remembrance becomes then a subjective motion or "emotion" that, in lifting us out of our immanent condition, helps us make sense of our existence and of ourselves. Unless we are incapacitated (memory-sick like one of the forgetting) or depressed (caught up in sadness and existential anguish like Freud's silent poet), we will naturally want to endorse our task as rememberers, and make beauty as well as sense out of the world surrounding us. Indeed, the poet's silence can best be understood when contrasted with that of our writers-rememberers. Proust's enthusiastic response to the promptings of involuntary memory, Woolf's ecstasies of remembrance, and Nerval's painstaking reconstruction of the imaginary woods of his childhood represent reactions to transience and loss of a kind that is temporarily unavailable to Freud's grief-struck and rationalizing poet. The essay on transience is built around the implicit assumption that creative writers are naturally entrusted with a commemorative mission. Indeed, as we shall see later, remembrance expressed and imparted to others amounts to an intersubjective gesture: it represents a gift of a sometimes hard-earned intimate knowledge that is open to humanity at large.

Situated as it is at the intersection between psychology, aesthetics, and an existential questioning, Freud's essay on transience helps us widen the scope of our enquiry into the nature of personal remembrance. It invites us to see that the scenes of the past that rememberers create do more than merely mark an aesthetic experience, for their meaning is ultimately existential: they are life-affirming responses to our mortal condition. The first inspiration behind them is nevertheless aesthetic; it springs from an acknowledgment of beauty. "A thing of beauty is a joy for ever," the poet Keats writes, so that "on every morrow" we are "wreathing a flowery bond to bind us to the earth" ("Endymion"). Indeed, as rememberers we resemble the romantic poets in our eagerness to acknowledge our ties to nature through our imagination and through the poetry of words. In emphasizing the overlap between remembrance and creation I do not mean, however, to romanticize personal memory or to diminish its scope; on the contrary, literary remembrance is of crucial significance because it shows us why the creation of memories plays so vital a part in the human condition.

In this chapter, I intend to reexamine personal remembrance from the new perspective that Freud delineated for us—a perspective that puts memory at the crossroads between a quest for the meaning of existence and our affect-laden and aesthetically vested response to our world. Virginia Woolf was involved in a lifetime search for ways of forestalling death and "the forces of destruction." This is why her project in writing and remembering will naturally take center stage. However, for a better elucidation of her conception of remembrance, I will also draw, in this chapter, on Lou Andreas-Salomé's work on narcissism and memory. In "Narzissmus als Doppelrichtung" ("The Dual Orientation of Narcissism"), we will find a theoretical counterpart, inspired by psychoanalysis and philosophy, to Woolf's own philosophico-literary investigations into the meaning of remembrance. At the center of both these authors' vision we can indeed identify two singular and original axioms: first that memory is a creative act (or *Dichtung*, as Salomé tells us) and second that personal remembrance, when pushed to its ultimate limits, transcends the individual's particular situation to reveal the underlying forms (in Salomé) or patterns (in Woolf) of human existence.[3] This chapter aims at demonstrating the validity of these two propositions.

An Existential View of Remembrance

In an extraordinary passage of her diary written on February 27, 1926, Virginia Woolf records what she might have described, in her own words, as a "moment of being" and accomplishes precisely what Freud's poet found himself incapable of doing. Against transience, as it were, she writes of an aesthetic experience that connects her to the surrounding world. The object is not a flower this time, but a moon and sky above Russell Square that "impress" her with their "splendor," or rather with their "beauty":

> I enjoy almost everything. Yet I have some restless searcher in me. Why is there not a discovery in life? Something one can lay hands on & say "This is it?" . . . What is it? And shall I die before I find it? Then (as I was walk-

ing through Russell Sqre last night) I see the mountains in the sky: the great clouds; & the moon which is risen over Persia; I have a great & astonishing sense of something there, which is "it"—It is not exactly beauty that I mean. It is that the thing is in itself enough: satisfactory; achieved. A sense of my own strangeness, walking on the earth is there too: the infinite oddity of the human position; trotting along Russell Sqre with the moon up there, & those mountain clouds. Who am I, what am I, & so on: these questions are always floating about in me.

The interest of this passage is not merely literary (an analogous description might be found in *Mrs Dalloway* perhaps, or *The Waves*) but also psychological and above all, philosophical. In its contemplation of a human subject caught *sub specie aeternitatis* and in its emphasis on "the oddity of the human position" it is indeed reminiscent of another similarly inclined writer, Blaise Pascal.[4] The aesthetic moment is surrounded by, or rather embedded in, a reflection on the sentiment and the meaning of existence. In acknowledging the "restless searcher in [her]," Woolf clearly implies more than a literary or broadly aesthetic impulse: she shows us, in effect, that the rememberer's gesture must be understood in the framework of an existential quest involving the self and the world. A woman alone trotting in the London streets, as Woolf describes herself, experiences an aesthetic epiphany that invites her to reconsider her subjectivity ("Who am I, what am I") and the meaning of the world (described through the shifting terms of "everything," "something there," "the earth").

"Beauty" is the place where, for Woolf, philosophy begins: her thoughts, we can tell, are inspired by a moment of intense aesthetic perception. But while her thinking is clearly philosophical in its scope and tenor, it remains tentative, as is revealed by her difficulty in naming the terms of her experience. This "rootedness" in an artistic practice might explain why Woolf never achieves the philosophical clarity that would enable her to spell out fully the nature of this revelation. Even though "beauty" may not necessarily be the right word, as she tells us, it nevertheless helps her account for the urge she feels to commemorate impressions culled on an evening passing through Russell Square, an urge that is part of her enjoyment of "life."[5] The impression remembered and registered is felt to be a sign toward other wonders; this is how it inspires broader reflections about her existence. Indeed, just as for Proust the salience of certain impressions and the corresponding commemorative impulse is connected to some deeper truth and mystery, for Woolf, there is something in the images she presents and remembers that exceeds their "beauty" (as she herself knows in expressing her doubts: "it is not exactly beauty that I mean").[6] Indeed, for both Proust and Woolf, an acute aesthetic responsiveness to the surrounding world becomes the foundation for a relentless search for "reality" or "truth" whose instrument is memory.[7] In other words, for her, writing-remembering is to be understood, in the same way as for Proust, as a "search for lost time"—where "time" takes on an existential meaning.

What "time" can mean existentially speaking can best be understood, perhaps, if we envisage, albeit briefly, Woolf's own conception of time. From this perspective, the most significant aspect of the passage under examination lies, obviously, in the choice of tense: the present and not the past of narration, as if to insist that the existential revelation springs from the act of writing itself, and does not precede it. "As I write and thus remember, I am," Woolf shows us through this disquisition, and the subjectivity that she claims for herself exists by virtue of that encounter (however difficult the naming of it) with "something there, which is 'it.' " (Were we to translate Woolf's "existential moment" for which she cannot find the proper words into an orthodox philosophical vocabulary, we might be inclined to say that her "investigation is of the meaning of Being.")[8]

When Woolf analyzes her philosophical adventure in Russell Square and under the moonlight, she has already made the major intellectual discovery—a discovery that explains the mysteries of a temporality that is not connected to chronology, but rather with the feeling of existence (or putting it differently, what *her* existing means). Thus, on March 18, 1925, she intuited that memory indeed represents the emotional *presence* of things past: "The past is beautiful because one never realizes an emotion at the time," she notes (March 18, 1925, *Diary,* vol. 3). Read too quickly, this axiom could easily be overlooked or misunderstood as an invitation to nostalgia or even, as the empty gesture of an aesthete expressing her world-weariness. But the conflation of beauty, time, and emotion gives it a place at the heart of these reflections on the role of memory in our "being-in-the-world." In connecting the rememberer's instinct to give salience to certain impressions with a life-enhancing emotional state, this brief notation reveals a mental impulse that can only be ascribed to the rememberer—an impulse that is crucial to our understanding of memory's existential value. The author asserts here, in effect, that the world only comes alive to us in its mnemonic traces, as belated impression or affect (this is why, as she knows, the word "beauty" is partly a misnomer).

Freud, as is well known, tried himself to conceptualize an experience of temporality in which experiences only come to their full meaning retroactively, and for this he invented the notion of *Nachträglichkeit.*[9] Like Woolf, he thought that we apprehend the world, both cognitively and emotionally, through a temporal delay or a time warp defined as "deferred action." But whereas for him, the retroactive aspect of memory was a crucial psychological discovery, for Woolf it has an existential, intensely felt dimension. It speaks of being alive to the outer world or just "conscious" (as Gerard Edelman argues in defining consciousness as a remembered present).[10] Indeed, the rising moon around Russell Square remained invisible until she, our exemplary writer-rememberer, saw it, as it were, under her pen. What "the past is beautiful because one never realizes an emotion at the time" tells us, in other words, is that we exist, in this vast world, thanks to our episodic, autobiographical memory: memory breathes life into our surroundings, but naturally always in the form of a delayed response.[11] Were we to be deprived of such moments of inspiration, were we to be totally amnesiac or just emotionally distraught and tongue-tied in the fashion we discovered in Freud's anonymous writer, the world would lose all animation for us and we, in turn, would lose not merely our "enjoyment" but no doubt our very soul or "being." For if, as the existentialist philosophers tell us, we exist through our dependency on and interaction with "things" in the world, it would have to be true that when the world becomes dead for us because of our failing memory, not only all beauty but life itself is extinguished for us. At the same time, our very identity is threatened. Indeed, as Woolf intuits in this passage, her own human position is tied up with the existence of the "moon" and "mountain clouds" greeted through her words. Each image brings her closer to "who" or "what" she is—even if only fleetingly.

The feeling of existence Woolf ascribes to her experience of Russell Square under the moonlight cannot be separated from the commemorative act that consists, in her case, in writing. This is how we end up discovering, in Woolf's diary, fragmentary elements of an existential philosophy that Woolf will put into practice in her fiction. But what interests me most, in this chapter, is to draw—from Woolf's poetics of memory—a lesson about remembrance that transcends the narrow confines of a personal, solipsistic experience of her lifetime. Through her own epiphanies, the writer helps us see how memory is instrumental to our "being in the world." Indeed, as rememberers we are all, just like writers, involved in stitching our present together with the mostly invisible thread of memory—unless we suffer from amnesia or the kind of writer's block we briefly envisaged through Freud's experience with the reluctant, tongue-tied *Dichter*. But only writers, perhaps, have the time to dwell long enough in the realm of remembrance to fully grasp and express the "moments of being" that memory produces.

Unlike us, ordinary and practical mortals, writers as rememberers are, by definition, contemplative and thus eager to put such experiences under a magnifying glass, as Virginia Woolf did, for example, in designing one of her most radical projects around one "epiphany." The diary shows that she thought she could devote a book to commemorating this minute yet momentous human event that seemed to have encapsulated for her a particularly significant "moment of being": a woman's encounter with a flower. On November 23, 1926, she writes: "I am now & then haunted by some semi mystic very profound life of a woman, which shall all be told on one occasion; & time shall be utterly obliterated; future shall somehow blossom out of the past. One incident—say the fall of a flower might contain it." In March 1927 she adds, describing the conception of this new book: "For some weeks, since finishing To the Lighthouse I have thought myself virgin, passive, blank of ideas. I toyed vaguely with some thoughts of a flower whose petals fall; of time all telescoped into one lucid channel through wh. my heroine was to pass at will."[12]

The story line may seem thin, but the project is cast in such a way that it will redefine time in existential terms, as a single individual's "lived" experience, caught between past and future. It is also designed to address, around one much magnified exemplary encounter, a subject's "relationship with a thing" in the world. It should, in other words, pose the type of questions that puzzled Woolf in the Russell Square experience, namely "who am I, what am I?" and similarly express her intuition of "an astonishing sense of something there, which is 'it.'" But we cannot overlook the aesthetic underpinnings of a project that she herself described as a "very serious, mystical poetical work." Woolf was untrained in academic philosophy. Had she read the *Critique of Judgment,* she would have known that for Kant, a flower (a wild tulip in fact) could constitute, precisely, the prime example of "the purposiveness without purpose of the beautiful object."[13] She did not need Kant to conceive of that "greatest book," a work commemorating an aesthetic revelation that would make of an autobiographical memory the foundation of an existential revelation.[14]

In light of our earlier investigations into Woolf's poetics of memory, we could emphasize, once more, her interest in capturing the qualitative nature of a subject's experience, and imagine a work essentially about qualia— about the qualitative, phenomenal, or "felt" properties of mental states experienced by this woman.[15] But the descriptions we just examined, although scant, make it clear that the project is of an even broader scope, bearing, as it does, on a "moment of being" blown out of proportion to the dimensions of a book. But the fact remains that Woolf never wrote this experimental work, whose challenges must have become apparent to her soon enough. The technical difficulties of writing a book around the memory of a flower must have seemed immense, and then, how to ensure that such a minimal experience would say enough about subjectivity, about "the infinite oddity of the human position"? The diary shows that the "story" of the woman and her flower became part of a book tentatively titled *The Moths* (for at some point, moths were added to the initial scene) that eventually became *The Waves*. In the final form, the flower has all but disappeared, and the solitary woman (now writing at her desk) has a very marginal presence.[16] The truly radical work remained indeed unwritten, and it took more than a decade for Woolf to come up with the concept, the "moment of being," that might have helped her place the event of a woman's encounter with a flower in its proper philosophical scope.

Thus, in "A Sketch of the Past," the "incident of the flower" reemerges, but this time in an avowed autobiographical frame ("it was *my* experience," she tells us this time), in conjunction with a theory (which Woolf modestly calls a digression). How to describe, she wonders, what she, "in [her] shorthand" calls "non-being"—especially since "every day includes much more non-being than being"? In surveying the previous day, Woolf finds that "separate moments of being are embedded in many more moments of non-being" or, figuratively, "in a kind of nondescript cotton wool," and she concludes from this that "a great part of every day is not lived consciously" (70). Yet the full, ontological meaning of her "moments of being" only becomes clear when she turns toward the more distant past, and revisits her biography in charting a number of intense, punctual encounters that came to her like shocks.

"Something happened so violently that I have remembered it all my life," she writes and then proceeds to present three moments of being. Two are clearly unpleasant: finding out about aggression during a fight with her brother and experiencing the horror of a suicide, as she recalls the event on passing a certain tree (72). As for the pleasant experience, which involves a sense of organic, natural wholeness and seems to have an immediate meaning, it focuses on a flower:

> The second instance was also in the garden at St Ives. I was looking at the flower bed by the front door; "That is the whole," I said. I was looking at a plant with a spread of leaves, and it seemed suddenly plain that the flower itself was part of the earth; that a ring enclosed what was the flower; that that was the real flower; part earth; part flower. It was a thought I put away as being likely to be very useful to me later. (71)

In what can only be a retrospective projection on part of the writer (for how could a child have such foresight and imagine the work to come?), Woolf remembers "seeing," in a moment defined as "being," a flower whose presence seems to epitomize both her presence in the world and her consciousness of the world.[17] It is by elaborating on such impressions, she claims on the next page, that she finds a pattern and a meaning in the world. Her ability to respond to such strong impressions (or "shocks," as she calls them) *through language* endows the event with reality. She thus writes, "I make it real by putting it into words." Words also enable her to break away from a solipsistic framework; such experiences speak to "all human beings" and express a truth that transcends the initially personal and singular frame:

> From this I reach what I might call a philosophy; at any rate it is a constant idea of mine; that behind the cotton wool is hidden a pattern; that we—I mean *all human beings*—are connected with this; that the whole world is a work of art. *Hamlet* or a Beethoven quartet is the truth about this vast mass we call the world. (72; emphasis added)

Woolf's philosophy thus depends on an aesthetic, mnemonic, and verbal performance that enables her to retrieve the moments of her "being" from a welter of other unrecorded, unnoticed impressions. In creating the right scenes, the writer gives an aesthetic unity and meaning to what was initially just a shock, and dealing with such shocks seems to be her vocation, as she explains:

> And so I go on to suppose that the shock-receiving capacity is what makes me a writer. I hazard the explanation that a shock is at once, in my case, followed by the desire to explain it. I feel that I have had a blow; but it is not, as I thought as a child, simply a blow from an enemy hidden behind the cotton wool of daily life; it is or will become a revelation of some order; it is a token of some real thing behind appearances; and I make it real by putting it into words. (72)

"A token of some real thing behind appearances": this is undoubtedly Woolf's key phrase when it comes to grasping the existential dimension of her aesthetic practice founded in memory. It highlights the visionary, exemplary place of a rememberer who is able to spell out the signs that connect us to the meaning of existence. This is how, in remembering moments of being, the writer not only situates her own self with regards to the outer world, but also reaches some broader, more universal "truth about this vast mass we call the world."

This need for a wider vision is adumbrated in a revealing diary entry that mentions Proust—and, implicitly, the need to outgrow her nostalgia for a child's view:

So the days pass, & I ask myself whether one is not hypnotised, as a child by a silver globe, by life; & whether this is living. It's very quick, bright, exciting. But superficial perhaps. I should like to take the globe in my hands & feel it quietly, round, smooth, heavy. & so hold it, day after day. I will read Proust I think. I will go backwards & forwards. (November 28, 1928, *Diary*, vol. 3)

What Proust's work might provide, it would appear, is a recipe for unity as well as ways of apprehending a totality—expressed figuratively in that appropriative gesture of seizing, feeling life like a globe in its roundness, smoothness, and solidity (or earlier, in the 1926 entry as "something one can lay hands on"). However, the very fact that in Woolf's mind, the gesture exists essentially as a desire ("I should like to . . .") is very telling: it is precisely because "life" is not smooth, but bumpy, fragmentary, and at times aggressively violent that one wishes for a simple, harmonious unity. Between the lines of this brief, allusive diary entry, one detects, then, a questioning that will take Woolf away from the temptations of Proustian memory toward a richer, more encompassing conception of remembrance. Indeed, once the founding gesture of this existential philosophy has been established—as the need to create the scene, through her words, that "put[s] the severed parts together" and tells her "who she is"—it becomes necessary to envisage the negative as well as the pleasurable shocks of existence. While it remains true that as a consummate rememberer, the artist will want to capture a world awash in pleasurable sensations and rich in "ecstasies" and "raptures," she is also called upon to answer, through the language of literature, a number of shocks and impressions for which "beauty" would be a misnomer. Woolf puts "her terrific capacity . . . for feeling with intensity" and her "shock-receiving capacity" at the service of an awareness that includes painful as well as ecstatic memories.

The rememberer's task goes beyond the recording of beautiful, perfect moments: it involves dealing with disjunctive moments—moments when the world makes itself known to the subject in its full ugliness (here, of course, just as the word "beauty" was problematic for Woolf, so is my use of "ugliness" to describe harsh and violent encounters with reality). Indeed, "A Sketch of the Past" reveals only a few moments of aesthetic stasis: these are clearly outnumbered by unpleasant impressions, some of them conceived of as inherently traumatic. In short, though Woolf may well have been tempted to devote most of her energy to recollecting raptures and ecstasies, she is quite aware that our experience of the world cannot be summed up in the apprehension of beauty; she is herself too intimately acquainted with a harsher world beyond the memory garden to stay within its confines. Whereas her idea for a book on a flower reminds us how tempting it might be to sometimes "forget" or, as we now commonly say, to "repress" unpleasant memories, most of her other fiction deals with traumatic events.[18] Clearly, Woolf strives to give memory the richest of existential meanings: it needs to encompass the painful as well as the happy moments of our being. This is where "mental time-travel" becomes an inner journey that takes the rememberer through "hell" as well as "paradise." I have in fact borrowed the words "hell" and "paradise" from "Narzissmus als Doppelrichtung" (1921), the essay in which Salomé redefines narcissism in its two dimensions, as an ego-preserving complex and as biographical impulse dependent on memory. It is indeed at this point, when Woolf articulates an imperative to remember that reaches beyond mere aesthetic responsiveness to involve a need for historical accuracy (which says, "Life is not only beautiful"), that her thinking rejoins the underlying thoughts of Lou Andreas-Salomé's essay on narcissism.

Expanding Personal Memory

There are indeed surprising overlaps between Salomé's essay and Woolf's literary practice as a writer and rememberer, so many that a presentation of the philosopher's text provides us with what amounts to an elucidation, in the form of a theory, of Woolf's insights into personal remembrance. The difficulty of Salomé's essay forces me, however, to proceed in a somewhat unusual fashion: rather than taking my reader directly to her text, I will start with an overview of her ideas, often in paraphrasing her terms. Later in this chapter, I will tackle specific aspects of her discussion with a greater number of direct references.[19]

For Salomé then, memory is the recording instrument of the life experiences that accrue to the subject, experiences that provide the foundations of a powerfully intimate biography of strong impressions.[20] She argues that it is only through remembering the high and low points of our lives (the "bliss and the bale," as Henry James might have said, or the "shocks" and "ecstasies," as Woolf writes) that we can begin to make sense of the forces that bear upon us, shaping us as human beings. Central to Salomé's thought is the idea that our existence unfolds as a series of impressions that mark the encounter between our inner emotional lives and the structures or "patterns" imposed by the outer world.[21] The pursuit of private memory, provided it is intense enough, will enable us to trace the most meaningful, that is, *most affecting* among such impressions. Remembrance, in Salomé's conception, represents the coincidence between an inner experience and an outer incident; in endowing the event with meaning, memory gives it a place in our biography.[22] Thus, in finding the words to describe the ways in which the outer world impresses itself on our psyche, we have the necessary elements not only for self-knowledge (a knowledge demanded by our narcissism) but also for defining our place in the world. Salomé's emphasis on the role of language in the making of impressions has its counterpart in Woolf's intuitions about remembrance in "A Sketch of the Past" and about the need to put the shocks of existence "into words." But the connection between language and memory is important for another reason besides the obvious need to represent or articulate the past in such a way that it can become part of a narrative: language, because it is turned toward others, enables a witnessing that opens up Narcissus's experience toward other human beings. Thus, as the architect of memory constructs her scenes and "puts the severed parts together," she articulates a pattern that is immanent to the world of human experience but that nevertheless transcends the individual to reach toward "all human beings."

In slipping insensibly into the language of Woolf, I want to acknowledge the commonality of vision and purpose that impels both authors to assert that, however solipsistic or "narcissistic" it may seem, the act of private remembrance will produce in certain writers a revelation that is destined to transcend the personal and individual to speak toward a broader humanity. Woolf's writings on memory thus reveal an intersubjective concern that is distinct from her practical and theoretical interests in her own biography or the art of memoir writing. She argues that the search for personal impressions must lead to a vaster historical awareness revealed in the "patterns" that render individual experience transmissible. The art the writer projects into the representation of autobiographical memory and the language she reaches for are designed to make sense collectively and for humanity at large. This is why, at the end of her defense of writing-remembering, Woolf moves from the first-person singular to a collective plural: "*we* are the words." While her narcissistic impulse gives her an opportunity to save herself or her "ego" through her memory work, it can also be a gift to others— the gift of her "philosophy."[23] Thus her insistence that "all human beings" are connected to the hidden pattern that art reveals, and thus her artistic and existential credo: "we are the words; we are the music; we are the thing itself. And I see this when I have shock." How can private memory take a path that leads to a level of generalization? The question that Woolf sketches out—how to build a bridge between private memory and a broader history—is echoed or perhaps even answered by a central statement of Lou Andreas-Salomé's essay: "In truth our narcissism is nothing else than the still obscure knowledge, rooted in our affective life, that posits *the ultimate in subjectivity as resulting from our objective existence.*"[24] For the philosopher too, the impulse that draws the writer to peer repeatedly into the mirror of her past is a gift to the world at large because it enables us to discern the underlying "objective" patterns of human existence. In writer-rememberers, narcissism, which produces the work of art, is necessarily shared knowledge and thus endows a personal quest with a pedagogical significance. "I live for myself *and* so that the others can see what it means to live," is the principle behind the narcissus complex as understood by Salomé and experienced by Woolf.

Painting herself through a ceaseless revisiting of impressions (and we must remember here that painting is her best analogy for remembrance), Woolf painstakingly traces "the pattern hid behind the cotton wool" in such a way that her literary vocation, though driven by her self-absorption, cannot be exhausted by it:

> This conception affects me every day. I prove this, now, by spending the morning writing, when I might be walking, running a shop, or learning to do something that will be useful if war comes. *I feel that by writing I am doing what is far more necessary than anything else.* ("A Sketch," 73; emphasis added)

Woolf searched to the end of her life for a language that would be a fitting medium for her most intimate emotions and perceptions, and yet would speak of universal forms of experience. Her desire to transcend the merely personal aspects of memory becomes most apparent when, speaking of the "invisible presences" that influence her (the "subject of this memoir," as she calls herself), she unexpectedly broadens the scope of her analysis to envisage larger sociohistorical currents:

> Consider what immense forces society brings to play on each of us, how that society changes from decade to decade; and also from class to class; well, if we cannot analyse these invisible presences, we know very little of the subject of this memoir; and again how futile life-writing becomes. (80)

The memoirist's task is to define the influences or structures that inform a life, as "life-writing" (Woolf's word for biography) aims then at identifying and tracing the forces that bear on historical subjects. "A real life has no crisis; hence nothing to tighten. . . . It must lack centre. *I* must amble on. All the same, I can *weave* a very thick pattern one of these days, out of that pattern of detail," she writes in her diary (November 1, 1940, *Diary*, vol. 5; emphasis added). Written at a time when she was working on "A Sketch of the Past," these elliptical remarks echo her thoughts on "moments of being"; literature must provide a way to recompose the loose centerless entity that is "real life" into a patterned shape.

Woolf's "philosophy" takes on a fuller, clearer meaning in light of Salomé's more overt claim for the ethical meaning of personal remembrance. The latter's central tenet, which is articulated around a redefinition of narcissism as a positive, ego-sustaining complex, is that autobiographical remembrance is intimately bound up with the duty we owe to ourselves, as human beings, to know ourselves and to know our place in the world. However personal or intimate their writing, *Dichters,* in Salomé's conception, unveil for us the fuller meaning of human existence, for in probing into their memories, they cannot but encounter the broader, overall patterns of experience. These memories bear the traces of a composite experience of the world, an experience that involves not only knowledge but deep affects as well, born from powerful impressions or "shocks." Autobiographical remembrance not only gives us the ability to chronicle and sustain an impression; but it also repeats, as a form, "what once happened" and in this way reveals a history of humanity viewed from the subject's perspective. For Salomé too, the search for the "still obscure knowledge rooted in affective life" is driven by a need to represent what is inherently literary. In other words, in his quest for self-knowledge, Narcissus could only be a writer and rememberer.

Autobiographical Memory Revisited

It becomes increasingly clear, as we make our way through the "Dual Orientation of Narcissism," that Lou Andreas-Salomé confronts us with a model of memory different from our earlier structural vision. As one would expect from an author deeply vested in psychoanalysis and in "the unconscious life of the emotions," the most striking reorientation occurs around the importance ascribed to affects.[25] Moving away from a simple linear model organized in a narrative form, Salomé conceives of biography as made of crucial moments or encounters that are the nodal points of a subject's life. (Here too, interestingly, her vision intersects with Woolf's redefinition of experience in terms of intensities of affect and "moments of being.") Remembrance may indeed involve the "transports" celebrated by Proust and Nerval, or the "Entrückung" that interested Freud, but the idea of "mental time travel" becomes a misnomer when, as is the case in Salomé's theory, memory is reconceptualized in front of Narcissus's mirror or in the writer's blank page in narrating punctual, emotionally charged encounters with early impressions. Personal remembrance then presents a specular structure that compels rememberers to peer again and again into the mirror of their past, not so much in nostalgia as in an act of self-love and self-preservation. Narcissism is the name Salomé gives to the compulsive, fated need to create autobiographical moments, even at the risk of encountering a defaced image of the self—an image that is so alien to the present self as to prevent recognition or identification.

In this fashion, "The Dual Orientation of Narcissism" moves the paradigm of memory forward, to a place where it becomes openly literary and textual, along the lines sketched out by Paul de Man in his often quoted essay "Autobiography as Defacement." Like de Man, but many years before him, Salomé conceives of literary creation in terms of "a possible convergence of aesthetics and history" (67). Thus, the fundamental drive behind the artist's work lies, for her, in the need to revisit the historical "events" that constitute his or her experience and belong to a personal biography.[26] Like de Man, also, Salomé highlights the autobiographical impulse that sustains the work of creation; like him, she acknowledges the presence of scattered, punctual "autobiographical moments" that are the work's aesthetic as well as historical landmarks. "The autobiographical moment," writes de Man, "happens as an alignment between the two subjects involved in the process of reading in which they determine each other by mutual reflexive substitution" (70). In substituting "memory" for "autobiographical moment," we encounter what is, in a nutshell, Salomé's own argument, which she presents, however, through many detours. She indeed never reaches the clarity of exposition that we owe to the literary theorist, and partly because of an issue of method and discretion. A psychoanalyst and not a professional reader, Salomé derives most of her insights from a source or "case study" that she owed to her intimacy with a poet, namely Rainer Maria Rilke. However, the only, but truly significant, acknowledgment of Rilke's presence in her essay is to be found in a footnote that, revealingly, quotes his poem "Narziss."

It is from her conversations with Rilke, no doubt, that Salomé learned that "it seems as if creators are fated to experience again equally the paradise of childhood as well as its hell" (219). Biographies and letters tell us indeed that the poet was deeply in Salomé's confidence, for a number of crucial years when, struggling with depression and writer's block, he fought hard with these inner demons in the hope of a turning point that would unleash his creative powers.[27] (It is a teasing thought that the poet who inspired Salomé to write on narcissism may well have been the same anonymous writer around whom Freud developed his reflections on transience.)[28] They envisaged, for a time, that psychoanalysis might be helpful, but Salomé advised against it (although she had analyzed Rilke's dreams) for fear that therapy would destroy his creativity. Rilke agreed, but gave her, meanwhile, an unparalleled opportunity to watch him forge his works in the smithy of his soul. It is through Rilke that Salomé learned about the intertwining of narcissism, writing, and remembrance and understood the compulsion to repeat earlier experiences that keeps the writer chained to a desk or bed, sometimes to the point of almost unbearable pain.[29]

The creator, the *Dichter* she calls him, is driven, compelled, or even, in her words, "fated" by his narcissism to revisit the past in its happy as well as unhappy aspects. This coming face to face is rarely innocuous, however, since it may involve a return to earlier traumas, forcing Narcissus to contemplate, at times, what turn out to be life-threatening images.[30] From the stanzas of Rilke's poem quoted by Salomé in a footnote, we learn about the risk of defacement that affects Narcissus as he peers into the water. Two lines, in particular, evoke the mortal threat inherent in the dual act of self-love and self-contemplation: he who plunges too deep risks losing himself when the image in the mirror dissolves into boundlessness and formlessness, that is when it abuts on pure drives and unprocessed, raw affects.[31] In invoking Rilke's poem, Salomé identifies a crucial wager behind Narcissus's gesture of self-contemplation, the necessity to assume the rememberer's fate in all its potentially threatening dimensions without, however, losing oneself completely in the reflection of the past.[32]

In drawing our attention to modes of personal remembrance that involve deep, unprocessed affects, Salomé demands that we consider the place of the body in reminiscence. Here, her thought is probably at its most intricate, but amid her densely meshed argument, the metaphor of a kernel and the shell, which she borrows from Rilke's poem, is enlightening, in part because it corresponds to a model of subjectivity developed in Freud's ego psychology, a model that distinguishes between a surface that provides "a perceptual and protective envelope" and an "intrapsychical reality" figured as core or kernel. Narcissism drives the rememberer to an inner, psychical reality that reconfigures the boundaries of subjectivity.[33] When contemplating his image, Narcissus says: "Nothing binds us enough / Yielding matter at my core, kernel of weakness / That cannot contain its flesh."[34] Salomé echoes this with her own thought: "One would like to say," she writes, "that artistic creation to some extent removes the shell from the body, revealing the fertile kernel that then germinates in all directions in the work" (217). What this metaphor describes is a changed relation between the inner and the outer world, where the lifting of repression makes room for a bodily, sensual, and thus also sexual experience. The mnemonic image retrieved in the creative gesture of Narcissus thus bear the trace of affects that reach back to primitive bodily experiences as well as to an economy of pleasure (the French translation of Salomé's text aptly speaks of *jouissance*). Whereas we have focused so far on the subject's effort to testify to moments of being culled from punctual impressions produced by the outer world, Salomé urges us to pay attention to the inner forces, the drives and compulsions that pattern our biographies. In this way, Salomé's reconceptualization of memory in terms of affect invites us, in due psychoanalytic fashion, to acknowledge the inherently regressive nature of private remembrance. Through this new perspective, we can discern the elements of a broad narrative configuration that drives and shapes our private remembering, a configuration so deeply buried in our psyche, so much forgotten that most of us remain unaware of its pressing presence. According to Salomé, it takes a writer (and a narcissistic one for that matter) to chart a biography that takes into account the deepest strands of our lives—those strands that are enmeshed in our bodily, sensual selves.

Body Memory

As we learned with Salomé, the narcissistic poet is naturally driven toward an intimate kernel of bodily affects; moving deeper into remembrance, he or she reaches back toward a sensual body and a core of early sensory intensities that have little place in ordinary, practical remembering. We had intimations of this regressive path through Woolf's experiment, in "A Sketch of the Past," with emerging memories that drove her toward purely sensual and somatic images and toward a maternal body. Even in Nerval and Proust, a number of memories stand out that reveal a nostalgia for the maternal world and imply primal fantasies related to the mother. Indeed, the "nodal point" of the mnemonic construction in the wedding scene in "Sylvie" as well as the scene of the kiss in *A la Recherche* is the mother—as object of the gaze, in one case, and as source of sensual, erotic satisfaction in the other. In Nerval, the memory traces a desire to marry the mother and in Proust, a desire to sleep with her: in both cases, the representation "yields" a thinly veiled sexual/sensual fantasy that seems to belong to the "core" of the rememberer's psychic life. From these converging patterns, we must then assume that the originating point of the rememberer's biography lies in a preoedipal experience of fusion with the maternal body.

Meanwhile, in anchoring their biographies in somatic and sensory experiences that belong to early psychical configurations, these rememberers tell of a memory structure that overlaps, uncannily, with the developmental narrative that we owe to psychoanalysis. This narrative, which tells of an insurmountable nostalgia for the mother's body as the source of sensual intensities, is summarized in evocative terms—terms that resonate with our inquiry—by Adam Phillips, in *The Beast in the Nursery*. "It is now a commonplace assumption that something essential is lost, or at least attenuated, in the process of growing up," Phillips writes, adding that "bodily appetites, and therefore imagination" are "the hero and heroine of this story" (138–39). Building on Freud's work as well as, secondarily, on Melanie Klein and Winnicott, Phillips shows that "growing up is a process of disillusionment," which takes us further and further away from the immediacy of sensual bodily pleasures (xiv). This psychoanalytical account enables us to better understand the narrative strand leading to the "kernel" that Salomé posits at the heart of the rememberer's narcissistic quest: it evokes an insurmountable nostalgia (shared by most of us, ordinary rememberers, but usually repressed) for the earliest childhood impressions and for the type of "passionate relationships" of a time before the Oedipus complex. Phillips makes this point emphatically:

> But what was radically puzzling originally about Freud's work was the implication that . . . after childhood there was nowhere to go, and that the disillusionments of the Oedipus complex were an acknowledgment of this. You couldn't marry your mother or father, but the erotic life that evolved in the crucible of those first passionate relationships was an irresistible ideal. It could never be dispensed with, only (hopefully) displaced or deferred. And even before such Oedipal crises dawn, the infant and young child is immersed in the best of all possible worlds. (133)

As we learned from our authors, the rememberer consistently, as if naturally, harks back to the early moments of a childhood that seemed to offer "best of all possible worlds."[35] Proust's rememberer, for instance, keeps reinventing—in his desire for Albertine, in the various landscapes he visits, and even in the pillow that greets his dreams in the first pages of *A la Recherche*—the round, warm, maternal cheek/breast of his infancy. In Nerval's "Sylvie," the aesthetic intensities summoned up in moments of reminiscence are intertwined with an erotic desire that harks back to the maternal figure.[36] *Perdue à jamais,* "lost forever," she is the deepest source of the nostalgia. But for a most striking example of how the maternal body is the source and origin of all later beauty and will haunt the rememberer's imagination forever, it is worth citing again, from "A Sketch of the Past," a revealing moment of mnemonic regression:

> I should make a picture that was globular: semi-transparent. I should make a picture of curved petals: of shells; of things that were semi-transparent; I should make curved shapes, showing the light through, but not giving a clear outline. Everything would be large and dim; and what was seen would at the same time be heard; sounds would come through this petal or leaf—sounds indistinguishable from sights. (66)

Woolf's text provides us with a vivid example of a writing/remembering driven toward the "kernel of bodily affects" that Salomé uncovered in her study of narcissism. Indeed, in its insistence that full autobiographical remembrance returns us to the body and to the earliest moments of childhood, Salomé's model of narcissistic remembrance helps us understand the narrative drive and configuration of the biographical exercise in which rememberers are relentlessly involved. "Something essential" has been "lost" or "attenuated," and it is the nostalgic rememberer's singular vocation to want to track it beyond the realm of the possible, in a place where it can only be fantasized and rendered in vivid images. Thus it is the *fantasy* or *fiction* of a return to the maternal body that provides the point of origin of a memory work.

In this new context, defined by Salomé's theory about the somatic underpinnings to our deepest memories, we also need to pay closer attention to what Proust called *la mémoire du corps*, "body memory."[37] In a few places of his *Recherche*, he describes memories that are summoned up internally, by a bodily state, thus hinting at the possibility that the most profound strands of our personal memory overlap with a somatic topography—a map whose landmarks are sites of pleasure and of pain. Our bodies appear to retain traces of our pain (almost like stigmata) as well as of our pleasures, and might at times give way to somato-sensory images that are the deepest, most resilient thread of our biographies.[38]

In the *Recherche*, Proust appears to draw such a bodily map, when he ascribes to the heart the painful recollection of the hero's grandmother (this heart was already, in the scene of the kiss, the organ that most strongly registered the child's anxiety), or keeps reinscribing on the cheek memories of sensual intensities felt by the Proustian body.[39] The demonstration culminates in the long episode of mourning for the beloved Albertine, in which the body revives, with a shock, what the mind has long forgotten.[40] Again and again, to use Jeanette Winterson's apt phrase in her novel *Written on the Body*, the disconsolate lover relives the past as "the physical memory blunders through the doors the mind has tried to seal" (130). More broadly, the notion that body memory provides the foundation for the rememberer's biography is announced at the very outset of Proust's book. The subject in search of a self in the first pages is gradually brought back to consciousness by parts of his body, by "ribs," "knees," and "shoulder-blades" that anchor him in space and time. The body, he insists, is the "guardian of the past":

> My body, the side upon which I was lying, faithful guardians of a past which my mind should never have forgotten, brought back before my eyes the glimmering flame of the night-light in its urn-shaped bowl of Bohemian glass that hung by chains from the ceiling, and the chimney-piece of Siena marble in my bedroom at Combray, in my parents' house. (6)

Such brief sketches of body memories are scattered throughout the *Recherche,* even though Proust fails, in the end, to revise this theory in light of this major finding about memory's bodily underpinnings.[41] The value of Salomé's theory of memory, meanwhile, is that it helps us discern the intimate connection between bodily states and remembrance in the broadest terms, namely as what underwrites the structure of remembrance and gives the architecture of memory its primary impulse. The point here is indeed not to push further into the territory of psychoanalysis to focus on the underlying, latent contents of memory, but to show, rather, the momentous impact that the notion of memory as affect will have on our understanding of how personal memories are constructed. These examples suggest, on the one hand, the powerful presence of early somato-sensory images in autobiographical memory, while hinting, on the other hand, that personal remembrances reaches back, narratively speaking, into the subject's prehistory. Indeed, the mnemonic scenes that the rememberer designs or creates are not merely determined by external encounters with "this vast mass we call the world"; they are also responses to or, rather, repetitions of the early pleasures of the flesh. If there is one striking lesson to be learned from Salomé's interest in the affective underpinnings of personal remembrance, it lies here: in this insistence that the aesthetic production that we call memory results, in part, from such embodied images and scenes as we surveyed in Woolf, Nerval, and Proust.

Writers as Rememberers

In recasting her definition of remembrance in terms of affects and, moreover, toward a time before language, Salomé cannot avoid the issue of representation or, as she puts it in her lexicon, of symbolization; for if the core of our biography involves bodily drives, as she suggests, a translation must by necessity occur, which will enable the verbal presentation of memories that would otherwise remain unformed and inchoate. Salomé's reasoning on this matter provides us with a compelling explanation for the central place held by writers in the articulation of experiences that belong to our private biographies. There is something in the nature of private memory itself, she argues, that imposes on the rememberer a literary task of expression and representation. Or, putting it differently, it takes a narcissistically driven writer—a Rilke or a Woolf, for example—to answer the high claims made for memory as affect.

Writing about Rilke in her essay "Mein Dank an Freud," Salomé identifies the main sources of the writer's vocation as a rememberer: "The poet lays hold of his sense experiences out of primitive impressions in which world and man are for him undifferentiated reality, and it is this that he *realizes* in his work" (302). In "The Dual Orientation of Narcissism," she develops this idea along two directions: she highlights, on the one hand, the poet's ability to speak of the body and then ascribes to him, on the other, the ability to find words as well as figures for experiences that usually lie outside the confines of representation. Literary authors, she argues, have mastered a form of remembrance—*Erinnerung*—that enables the return of "primitive impressions" and makes it possible to "keep something of the intimacy of libidinal behavior."[42] There are, she writes, "aspects of living experience that remain hidden from ego psychology as the stars are hidden from daylight . . . only a return into the dark night of these dreams will enable us to reach the full dimensions of our present existence." The need to reach for memories outside of the confines of ordinary awareness explains why Salomé explicitly compares remembering to dreaming, and argues that Narcissus's images are gathered from the same place as dreams are found. In steeping themselves in a universe of newly emerging and unbounded representations and symbols, these narcissistic rememberers can then reexperience an earlier mode of existence, in which a unity of sensibility was possible, thus reaching for a time when object and subject were indistinguishable and the outer and the inner world seemed like one world. Thus her definition of poetic creation as memory: "*Dichtung*," she writes, "is the extension of what the child experienced and of the life the adult must sacrifice for the sake of practical existence. Poetry is perfected remembrance."

As for the writer's sacrifice—his or her entry into a solipsistic world, his enduring and often painful commitment to remembering—it is a response to narcissism, a narcissism that demands a gesture of abstraction from the world for the sake of the self and entails a fascination with introspection. The narcissistically driven writer thus reaches a disengagement from practical existence that is unattainable under ordinary circumstances. Remembering, as defined by Salomé, becomes a vocation and a task that suffers few compromises. Most of us, she argues, could not afford to live under the sway of memory and affect; most of us, ordinary mortals, cannot while away our time dreaming or remembering a long-lost past.[43] But like young children who want to hear the same story again and again, Salomé argues, creative writers find their pleasure in the rehearsal of memory that is realized in the work of art, and can potentially be repeated forever. Practical individuals, meanwhile, are too involved in a *Daseinspraxis* (a concrete existential condition) to indulge in reminiscence. "In the name of their adaptation to a world of action and praxis," Salomé writes, "they are compelled to forget."

The distinction Salomé draws is very stark, and one might want to adduce that, surely, there might be, among us ordinary mortals, some who share the narcissist's traits without being writers. What about the nostalgic types or the Proustian characters, who like to reminisce and cull intimations of the past? Such inclinations alone would not suffice to change us into the rememberers that Salomé has in mind. A good number of us, she notes, probably like to recollect our beginnings and share a nostalgia for childhood, but only writers have the necessary psychical and verbal resources to do so in a truly significant and exemplary fashion. They alone are able to imagine symbols for experiences that occur at the limit of representation. They have "words even for what doesn't have a name, but only a kind of words that will emphasize the ineffable, which makes them use words as if they were entities" (197). Moreover, as practiced dreamers, they are naturally gifted with an imagination in which "the most complicated combinations can be endowed with the astonishing force of a form, of a convincing creation." Among writers, the creative impulse is indeed intimately bound up with an interest in form—a form through which affects can be both delimited and objectified.[44] The need for form is what steers the poet away from a regression into the realm of pure libido or raw affects, just as it moves him away from the "autism" that threatens any rememberer who becomes too absorbed in the repetition of the past. Form, according to Salomé, is the artist's indispensable safeguard against the threat of psychical disintegration: it protects against the pitfalls of regression on the one hand, while overcoming repression on the other.

Form (and here Salomé seems to echo Woolf's notion of a pattern) is also what contains the free, untutored growth that arises when the protective shell that separates us from a "bodily kernel" has been removed. Unlike children or psychotics, Salomé explains, writers are capable of inventing linguistic structures of universal symbolic value; they find words that stand for a private, intimate experience and yet at the same time act as anchoring points situating us in a world of objective realities. This gift for figuration is what enables writers to stretch the boundaries of remembrance and to bring memories to life with their emotional, existential coloring. In Salomé's conception, the rememberer's words or "symbols" are indeed dynamic (and not referential) entities: they capture the affective currents of our psychic life, but they do not represent a world that exists "out there." This point is worth emphasizing, for it helps us understand why Woolf could imagine writing a whole book on a flower. It is precisely because the flower she remembers bears no resemblance whatsoever to a "real" flower (such as the one on my desk this morning) that "painting" it—in a way that would speak of *her* life and would adumbrate at the same time a "truth about this vast mass we call the world"—might have demanded thousands of lines. Rememberers use words as symbols to conjure up a feeling of being-in-the-world, not as a way of designating concrete, material objects. As writers, they become the master creators of symbolic figures for psychical and inherently subjective realities that have no objective, referential correlatives, but figures that define human *experience*.

In the end, Lou Andreas-Salomé's reconceptualization of personal remembrance around narcissism provides us with two fundamental notions: it postulates a deep connection between an aesthetic practice founded on memory and a subject's personal fate, and it argues that the writer-rememberer's quest is of universal existential significance. The concept of repetition, which is central to her discussion, helps us bring together these two different strands. Here then is her thesis, in summary form: narcissism binds the subject to a place (the rememberer's desk, bed, or her page) where pleasure and pain, although felt as distinct emotions, are subsumed under the need for a repetition of subjective experiences—a repetition that occurs in a sublimated aesthetic form. The creative writer's vocation and her task lie in this exceptional ability to bind intimate experiences into a form of propitious repetition: "Sie binden ihre Erlebenissweise an die Wiederholbarkeit." On the writer's page, memories acquire a lasting presence, as the subjective experience becomes repeatable *ad libidem*—not literally, but aesthetically and mentally, as an image. Art thus substitutes one kind of repetition—namely aesthetic representation as form and symbol—for another symptomatic and potentially nefarious form. Art derives its existential value from the forms it can give to experience. Because these forms are, by definition, what an aesthetic practice communicates, the rememberer's private world opens up to us ("gives us to see") scenes that testify, in an exemplary fashion, for our inscriptions, as subjects, in a reality (or to use, Woolf's formulation, in a "truth about this vast thing we call the world"). Remembrance of the kind practiced by *Dichters* is then an ethical act, because it shows a more authentic relation to existence than that which is granted to ordinary individuals, for whom memory is essentially a practical tool. The ethical, for Salomé, is to be found not in the rules and principles that the objective, external world has imposed on us: it emerges from the kernel of a subjectivity that holds the traces of our earlier libidinal, affective relation to the world. The specular path taken by Narcissus is of general, universal significance, because it speaks of an exceptional knowledge of what human existence entails. Indeed, the writer attests to "nothing else than the still obscure knowledge, rooted in our affective life, which posits *the ultimate in subjectivity as resulting from our objective existence.*" Since Lou Andreas-Salomé's ungainly philosophical vocabulary translates uneasily into our contemporary idiom, let me reach in conclusion for another formulation, with a more familiar ring to it. What singles out the work of the writer-rememberer is the possibility that it will yield to us, its readers, insights into forms of experience and modes of existence that can only occur once we accept that aesthetics and history cannot be separated. As we saw with Woolf, a recollected event as intimate as the discovery of a "moon up there" and "mountain clouds" over Russell Square may be part of a "discovery in life" and may speak, however obscurely still, of a human experience of universal significance—in this case, an experience of "being in the world." If we accept this, then we will have to acknowledge that history (albeit history of a certain kind, private and intimate) sometimes gets written in front of Narcissus's mirror. An anecdote might confirm this point.

In late January 1939, Sigmund Freud visited Virginia Woolf and brought her a narcissus. A few months later, on April 18, inspired perhaps by Freud's gesture, she began working on her memoir, that is, on the pages later collected under the title "A Sketch of the Past." She makes no claims for her project, beyond the practical, professional point that the incursion into autobiography might provide a comfortable counterpart to the arid discipline of biography (she is working, at the time, on a book on Roger Fry). But what is a mere change in genre for the author can mean something else for the woman: the shift to the memoir shows that Woolf is getting ready to "experience again equally the paradise of childhood as well as its hell" and, in so doing, is taking care of herself.[45] There is no way of knowing what whimsical thought or perhaps deep understanding lies behind Freud's striking gesture. However, coming from the author who gave the concept of narcissism its fame, the gift could surely not have been free of symbolic overtones. I read behind this mysterious gesture an invitation to pursue a different analysis of memory in Virginia Woolf—one, namely, that develops the kind of psychoanalytical and existential approach to Narcissus advocated by Sigmund Freud's friend, Lou Andreas-Salomé.

10 • Virginia Woolf's Life-Writing

"Our memory is like a diary that writes itself as we live," Jean Delay suggests in *Les Maladies de la Mémoire,* underlining, in a scriptural metaphor, the natural and profound link that exists between living and remembering (73). As we live, he tells us in substance, we write the diary of our memories. However, Virginia Woolf's conception of "life-writing" reverses this proposition: it shows that a certain form of writing-remembering is what keeps her alive, as "the person to whom things happen" ("A Sketch," 65–69). In this way, Woolf endows the exercise of "biography" with a new urgency, teaching us to weigh differently the notions of remembering, writing, and living. Whereas Delay conceives of remembering and "life-writing" as a natural, effortless process, remembrance for Woolf is not so easily folded into living: it is not a given, but a matter of art and necessity. The book of life does not write itself; it needs the rememberer's, the creator's active engagement. This is why writing, for Woolf, is a vital undertaking, in which her passion for a biographical literature that reflects experience becomes the precious instrument of her unfolding consciousness, of her emotional well-being, and ultimately, of her will to live. Her life depends for its continuation on the biographical impulse that lets her imagine a future in laying to rest what are, sometimes, overwhelming emotions.

Woolf devoted her life to filling out the pages of the existential diary Delay describes. She does so in the most immediate fashion, keeping a journal from the late 1920s to the weeks preceding her death. Her need to address the vicissitudes of her life seep into her fiction as well: "I wonder, parenthetically, whether I deal openly in autobiography and call it fiction," she writes in her diary on January 14, 1920. Jotted down at the outset of her literary career (at the time, she had only published *The Voyage Out*), this casual remark takes on prophetic or programmatic overtones, defining a form of fiction that will always be autobiographical. It is mostly as an author of fiction that Woolf works her way through her past—perhaps, as Lou Andreas-Salomé believed, because only creative writers can truly remember. The literary work meets a need for the narrative articulation of experiences that cannot be fulfilled elsewhere.[1] Writing, in other words, produces remembrance: the long maturation that led to the creation of *Jacob's Room, Mrs Dalloway, To the Lighthouse, The Waves, The Years, Between the Acts* reflects the interval that separates a personal event—often, for Woolf, a violent impression—from its recollection.[2] Woolf's literary mnemonics enable a "working through" that resembles a psychoanalytic process, in its emphasis on forgetting, in the way it converts resistant impressions or traumatic moments into conscious images, and in its temporality that is analogous, as we saw, to Freud's *Nachträglichkeit*.

Because life-writing has become a global existential condition, which so tightly ties Woolf's psychic and physical survival to her creative abilities as a rememberer, an abyss opens up whenever the pages of that lifesaving "diary" threaten to be blank (which happens when a new book is finished or when Woolf is too busy or too sick to write). Among the last pages of Woolf's diaries, written just before her suicide, there is one that spells out a looming disaster in telling us about a radical failure of memory: "Why was I depressed? I cannot remember."[3] Once the rememberer is past assiduously recollecting the sources of a dark mood and when strong affects seem to have no cause—because one cannot remember—imagination is left void; there is no clearing leading one back to the past, no way out of the emotional darkness. Woolf died, it seemed, when she saw that her mental time-travel was coming to an end.

In this chapter, I examine Woolf's literary project as "architexture"—as a mnemonic construction and a textual, rhetorical structure. What interests me above all is to define the forms of remembrance that constitute an autobiographical narrative. Woolf's life, I propose, writes itself through a mnemonic process—through *techniques of recollection* that, taken together, enable her to shape the events that were experienced as "shocks" into life experiences or, in her expression, as "moments of being." An autobiography, Louis Althusser suggests, represents a narrative of affects, of "emotional experiences" that "mark" us for life.[4] Woolf's autobiographical project invites us to emphasize the direct connection between experiences ("shocks") and the constitution of a person or personality (to the extent that shocks become our singular, life-defining adventure). Her life and work give a sometimes beautiful, sometimes dramatic shape to what is, for most of us, a natural process—namely the stitching together of mnemonic images that provides us with a sense of our existence. In her radical experiment in writing-remembering, there is no life, no living outside of those small, momentary acts of self-definition made of "autobiographical memories." Indeed, as part of her particular philosophy, Woolf wants us to consider that the "moments of being" that such memories define are what gives human existence its measure, its shape, and, ultimately, its meaning.

Writing about autobiographical remembrance in a psychoanalytic vein, Adam Phillips notes that "memory is never redemptive in Freud, it is merely constitutive, necessary for (psychic) survival" ("Childhood Again," 152). Woolf's solution to life's quandaries and her "psychic survival" takes the form of a literary adventure whose conditions are narrative as well as rhetorical. Under the pressure of remembrance, her task is to find a story and develop the appropriate figures and tropes with which to tell it. "I make it real by putting into words," she proudly proclaims, putting full weight on the symbolic transformation that she achieves through writing ("A Sketch," 72).[5] Contrary to Freud's belief, there may be some redemption in store for the rememberer: first, as Woolf intuited, in the fact that memory "realizes" the emotional experiences constitutive of autobiography (and in so doing lifts us out of what might be a nightmare or dream); second, through the saving power of art. I focus, in this chapter, on the second of these redemptive traits of memory, for my aim is not to "psychoanalyze" the author but to elucidate further the aesthetic process that gives remembrance its full efficacy—as a process that keeps a subject alive.

Memory Troubles

Woolf faced no greater shock in her life than her mother's premature death.[6] In these circumstances, it is no surprise that she should articulate her project of remembrance, which she calls "life-writing," around this momentous event. Noting that her mother represents "one of those invisible presences who after all play so important a part in every life," she insists that biographies that do not analyze the powerful hidden forces—which, like "magnets," influence a life—are flawed. They fail to do justice to the subject's life in occluding or erasing from the mirror those very presences that hold her in place. Her mother may be dead, but remembering her is a condition for the proper unfolding of Woolf's autobiographical project.

> It is by such invisible presences that the "subject of this memoir" is tugged this way and that everyday of his life; it is they that keep him in position. Consider what immense forces society brings to play upon each of us. . . ; well, if we cannot analyse these invisible presences, we know very little of the subject of the memoir; and again how futile life-writing becomes. I see myself as a fish; deflected: held in place; but cannot describe the stream. ("A Sketch," 80)

With these comments, Woolf defines a project in biography or life-writing destined to deal, in the first place, with maternal loss. Coming from the writer who wrote, "we think back through our mothers," this move seems entirely justified from the point of view of a literary poetics. But a psychological justification is equally compelling: as we know from Freud, with the mother's absence comes the first impulse to effect that "symbolic transformation" which language (as well as memory) enables. The motivation behind the *fort/da* game that Freud's grandson plays in his crib lies in the need to recall the maternal presence.[7] If, in Woolf's life-writing, the recollection of the mother's disappearance and the need to re-present her are so fundamental, it is because, as Woolf perceived, this maternal loss constitutes the *Urtrauma* and thus the point of origin and strongest force behind all remembering. But how can we make sense of her claim that marking this invisible presence is a necessary condition of autobiography?

I find the clearest justification for this claim in Thomas Cottle's "bio-autography" *When the Music Stopped.*[8]

> I think it is fair to say that much of my self is constituted of (by?) the self of my mother. Martin Heidegger was right, I believe: we don't *have* relationships as much as we *are* relationships. People literally live within us not only in the form of our recollections and memories, but also as the stuff of our selves, and our souls. For years I have scoffed at the notion that my mother, in the words of some, would always "be there for me." (xii)

The forceful argument Cottle develops from Heidegger ("we *are* relationships") helps us understand the mother's crucial placement in Woolf's autobiographical discourse: Woolf's relation to her mother is part of her very identity. Moreover, as Woolf herself hints in the figure of a stream ("I see myself as a fish; deflected: held in place; but cannot describe the stream"), the maternal presence is a vital element of a dynamic principle (the stream of life) that keeps her afloat.

There is no better place to understand Woolf's claim for life-writing as a therapy and as a way of anchoring the self amid the various currents of life than to examine how she creates memories of her mother, in a project that extends across many years of her life. Woolf leads us to believe that the passage from shock to writing-remembering is immediate: "And so I go on to suppose that the shock-receiving capacity is what makes me a writer. I hazard the explanation that a shock is *at once* in my case followed by a desire to explain it" (72; emphasis added). But an examination of her diaries, her fiction, and her autobiography shows that, on the contrary, when it comes to dealing with maternal loss, the transfer can take ages: a long shadow seems to have fallen between what may have been her "desire" to remember her mother and her ability to do so.[9] For a long stretch of her life, Woolf is haunted by the figure of her mother in what is a form of *false remembrance*—the kind of remembrance that was diagnosed by both Sigmund Freud and Pierre Janet.[10]

She tells us as much in "A Sketch of the Past," when she writes: "Until I was in the forties . . . the presence of my mother obsessed me" and offers further proof in her reflections on *To the Lighthouse* one page later: "I suppose that I did for myself what psycho-analysts do for their patients. I expressed some very long felt and deeply felt emotion. And in expressing it I explained it and then laid it to rest" (80). When, in the intervening paragraphs, Woolf speaks of the defect of other biographies that never "analysed . . . the invisible presences who after all play so important a part in every life" and again, of the need "to analyse these invisible presences," it must have been in full awareness that she was competing with another school and other techniques of recollection—namely those professed by psychoanalysts.[11] But how can a literary practice rival that of psychoanalysis? And further, how can an examination of Woolf's writings about her mother help us understand the singular efficacy of writing as a mnemonic cure? By following Woolf's progress as a rememberer, we will gain a better grasp of the redemptive power of life-writing. In learning to remember, Woolf learns to make her way through life, carefully swerving around that "terrifying edge" that Hermione Lee sees hovering around her.[12]

Meanwhile, it is only if we assume the existence of forms of personal remembrance that *fail* to deal with loss that we can study how Woolf schools herself into remembrance, to the point where she can indeed claim that she "expressed some very long felt and deeply felt emotion. And in expressing it . . . explained it and then laid it to rest." Her own awareness that she needed a creative breakthrough, namely *To the Lighthouse,* suggests as much: the burst of creative inspiration that cured her of her reminiscences becomes, in her elated language, a celebration of writing:

> Then one day walking round Tavistock Square, I made up . . . *To the Lighthouse;* in a great, apparently involuntary rush. One thing burst into another. Blowing bubbles out of a pipe gives the feeling of the rapid crowd of ideas and scenes which blew out of my mind, so that my lips seemed syllabling of their own accord as I walked. (81)

The rememberer is suddenly blessed with the scenes and the words that express what she defined as a "very long felt and deeply felt emotion."

Thirty years after her mother's death, she finds a voice that enables her to tell the story of the loss she endured as a child. She remembers feeling nothing at the time, or feeling at odds with the situation. Thus, she explains in her diary:

> I was 13, & could fill a whole page & more with my impressions of that day, many of them ill received by me, & hidden from the grown ups, but very memorable on that account: how I laughed for instance, behind the hand that was meant to hide my tears; & through the fingers saw the nurses sobbing. (May 5, 1924, *Diary*, vol. 2)

This earlier memory, jotted now in the diary, reveals a child in a state of shock and unable to suppress the inappropriate laughter suggestive of hysteria—of a fatal dissociation between her knowledge and her feelings. This account indeed suggests that Woolf in 1924 "suffers," as the famous phrase goes, "from reminiscences." As do Freud's hysterical patients, she experiences the return of recurrent, intrusive images that cannot be integrated into a narrative or "metabolized."[13] Thus again and again, and for years afterward, she takes note of the event—the loss of her mother when she was thirteen—yet stops short of expressing her sentiments. "My mother died when I was thirteen," are the few, too scarce words that appear at regular intervals in her letters, uttered as if mechanically. In "A Sketch of the Past," the memorable, momentous cipher thirteen occurs three times over the space of three pages, gaining force (but not meaning) by virtue of mere repetition. We saw how strongly Woolf believes in her shock-receiving capacity, and she is increasingly confident of her ability to retaliate in words: "as one gets older one has a greater power through reason to provide an explanation; and that this explanation blunts the sledge-hammer force of the blow" ("A Sketch," 72). However, neither reason alone (which dictates the words "my mother died when I was thirteen") nor raw emotion (which haunts her with hallucinatory visions of her mother) suffice: only a representation that joins knowledge and affect could help Woolf properly remember and "work through" the pain of loss.

This search for proper remembrance—for "life-writing"—occupies her almost to the end of her life. Indeed, as she explains in a quizzical formulation, she is still looking for maternal memories in "A Sketch of the Past": "In certain favourable moods, memories —what one has forgotten—come to the top."[14] One such mood led, as we saw, toward the construction of Woolf's earliest childhood memories; another, the sudden "rush" of inspiration when walking around Tavistock Square, toward *To the Lighthouse*, the work that became, as we shall see, a masterpiece of mnemonic architecture—a mausoleum that put the maternal ghost to rest. But implicit in Woolf's idea that "certain moods" condition memory is the idea of failed remembrance, an idea that I want to pursue through two different examples of how memory might fail, not just through lack of affect but also, at times, through being *overwhelmed* by affect.

In a melancholy diary entry in September 1934, Woolf begins by registering dryly Roger Fry's death, focusing on a mood of disaffection that is best described, perhaps, in Proust's vocabulary as *une sécheresse de l'âme* (a dryness of the soul).

> Roger died on Sunday. I was walking with Clive on the terrace when Nessa came out. We sat on the seat there for a time. On Monday we went up with Nessa. . . . Women cry, L. says: but I don't know why I cry—mostly with Nessa. And I'm too stupid to write anything. My head all stiff. I think the poverty of life now is what comes to me, a thin blackish veil over everything. Hot weather. A wind blowing. The substance gone out of everything. I don't think this is exaggerated. It'll come back I suppose. . . . And I can't write to Helen, but I must now shut this & try.
>
> Maupassant, on writers—(true I think).
>
> "En lui aucun sentiment simple n'existe plus. Tout ce qu'il voit, ses joies, ses plaisirs, ses souffrances, ses désespoirs, deviennent instantané-ment des sujets d'observation . . . Il analyse malgré tout, malgré lui, sans fin, les coeurs, les visages, les gestes, les intonations."
>
> I remember turning aside at mother's bed, when she had died, & Stella took us in, to laugh, secretly, at the nurse crying. She's pretending, I said: aged 13. & was afraid I was not feeling enough. So now.
>
> The writer's temperament.
>
> Sur l'eau 116
>
> "ne jamais souffrir, penser, aimer, sentir comme tout le monde, bon-nement, franchement, simplement, sans s'analyser soi-meme après chaque joie et après chaque sanglot."[15]

Woolf writes here from a country of the mind where melancholia runs so deep that it casts a pall even over her writing. But she knows the cause of that sterility, and identifies it as intellectual detachment: like her fellow writer Maupassant, she is trapped in the mirror of self-analysis. Her inability to deal with Fry's death is a reminder of what happened when she lost her mother; then, too, she could not "feel enough." Much of the poignancy of this entry lies in its terseness—in the two words, for example, that compare behaviors: "so now." Now as then, Woolf responds to the shock of a sudden, premature death in dismay, chiding herself for a lack of feeling that locks her in a world where "the substance [has] gone out of everything"—

where representations are mere shadows without life. As we saw, affective dissociation, an unusual dryness, a tendency to be just factual is the main tenor of Woolf's overt autobiographical discourse on her mother's premature death.[16] She rightly acknowledges in her long diary entry that this discrepancy between an affect and its representation stands in the way of remembering. In her disaffected state, the rememberer does not deal with the event, but merely contemplates it as though from a distance or, worse yet, watches herself reeling under its blow without being able to feel it "frankly, really, simply."[17]

At the opposite end of the spectrum, Woolf's writings dwell on images that are like nodal points of sheer affect. Not surprisingly, given her investment in remembering as painting, words representing colors are among them: they are the aesthetic correlatives of the emotions associated with the maternal sphere; they symbolize these powerful, unarticulated emotions.[18] Thus the "red and purple flowers on a black background" of "A Sketch of the Past" are related explicitly to her mother's disappearance: "How immense must be the force of life which turns a baby, who can just distinguish a great blot of blue and purple, into a child who thirteen years later can feel all that I felt on May 5th 1895—now exactly to a day, forty-four years ago—when my mother died," Woolf notes (74). The perception of color (a manifestation of "the force of life") is the counterpart, or rather the subjective response to shock; it provides a translation for the intensities of affect. In her fiction, Woolf relies similarly on color to convey, in an almost formulaic fashion, the pain associated with certain representations.

In *The Waves*, Bernard, as the writer's alter ego, evokes the interminability of mourning and the impossibility of recollection in the persistence of violent, nonintegrated sensations. Looking at paintings, he sees them as emblems of pain, but several times removed from himself: "Madonnas and pillars, arches and orange trees . . . but acquainted with grief . . . there they hung and I gazed at them" (220). The effect is subtle but cumulative; thus a painting by Titian punctuated by vivid colors elicits a comment blending vision, voice, and physical sensation around the (for Woolf) heavily connoted word "gizzard": "That crimson must have burnt in Titian's gizzard . . . the ruffled crimson against the green linings . . . the orange behind the black, pricked ears of olive trees. Arrows of sensation strike from my spine, but without order" (129).[19] Recalling, if only subliminally, the vividly colored blots of "A Sketch," these colors are reminders of impressions inscribed with pathos. Indeed, "A Sketch of the Past" reveals that Woolf connects her mother's disappearance to phenomenal changes in her vision. Casting a new aura onto her world, death effects a symbolic transformation in the guise of an intensification of colors: "My mother's death unveiled and intensified, made me suddenly develop perceptions, as if burning glass had been laid over what was shaded and dormant," she writes (93). The pain of loss translates into a new perceptual mode, where objects appear to "glare" at the rememberer ("as if something were becoming visible without any effort," Woolf writes) with an intensity suggestive of hallucination.[20]

Thus Bernard's words upon contemplating a representation of the Virgin seem to encrypt a statement about mourning and remembering: "Behold the blue Madonna streaked with tears. We have no ceremonies, only private dirges and no conclusion, only violent sensations each separate" (129). His analysis evokes a form of remembrance outside of ordinary conventions and discourses and an inability to build a scene that would bring the sensations together. Instead, the rememberers (the "we" representing the writer and her double) affix their grief to a symbolic representation, a blue Madonna, who resembles Virginia Woolf's mother. "She was a mixture of the Madonna and a woman of the world," Woolf writes in "A Sketch of the Past"; and reinforces this connection in her diary when she quotes the words of an acquaintance (removing the quotation marks as if to endorse this statement as her own): "I remember your mother—the most beautiful Madonna & at the same time the most complete woman of the world" (May 4, 1928, Diary, vol. 3). What Woolf shows us through the detour of her fiction, but cannot articulate, is a universe of pain in which loss is expressed in a phenomenal world of exaggerated perceptions and in objects vested with cryptic symbolic and mnemonic meanings. One cannot help but wonder whether this is not, in a sense, the way toward madness, with its hallucinations and psychosis.

Examining this text closely and thoughtfully for its mnemonic traces or the "private dirge" that Bernard announces, I have had to ask myself whether my analysis is, like the figure in the carpet in James's famous story, just an effect of my own gaze and thus a mere illusion.[21] I have no certainties, for there is no voice telling us, "I remember." There are, meanwhile, traces of a working through or a symbolic transformation. The problem with this transformation is that it is incomplete; it is not a scene or a construction, but an evocation of a transformed phenomenal reality that corresponds to raw, unbounded affects. While this cryptic subtext of private symbol may well have represented, for Woolf, a compromise formation—a compromise formation she *could* and *did* live by in the wake of her shock— it comes very close to the threatening dissolution of all form that Rilke's Narcissus saw looming in his mirror.[22]

In *Les Maladies de la mémoire,* Jean Delay relies on a clinical distinction that separates three modes of recollection—sensory-kinetic, social, and autistic. The latter, he writes, involves our deep emotions and "comprises the countless memories that do not exist as representations, but as pure affect" (17). In normal life, autistic memory occurs in our sleep: dreams spring from a resurgence of affects, a resurgence that in turn may lead to a representation of a memory that, until then, was inaccessible (19). However, during our waking life, autistic memory speaks in a language that is nonlogical, radically subjective, and deeply asocial; its language, in other words, can verge on delirium.[23] In this model, Woolf's remembering in *The Waves* would have to be labeled "autistic" because it falls so much outside of the social grammar and the narrative conventions of remembrance. In investing so much in private symbols, the writer has reached the limits of communication, arriving at a place where her memories will perhaps cease to mean because they can no longer be validated. When the memory is so deeply encrypted, there is no one to tell. "No one to tell": the grammatical ambiguity of this phrase reflects a double erasure—of the subject of the memoir, who is ultimately overshadowed or even "written off" by these powerful but impenetrable signs, and of her audience, who will not hear the secret dirge sung in this text. Skirting around psychosis in this fashion, the rememberer may well have risked her life for her art. Reflecting on Woolf's autobiography, Shari Benstock writes that "the mother's removal from temporal and spatial existence . . . provides the central trauma of Woolf's narrative, an absence over which scar-tissue knots this narrative and refuses to let the story unwind itself over the years" (26). Benstock may well have been right: when it comes to dealing with her mother's death, Woolf finds that the grammar of remembrance eludes her—there are only "violent sensations each separate." As we know, however, a breakthrough will occur with *To the Lighthouse*, through a new mode of remembrance that will enable an overwhelming emotional experience to be integrated into a narrative.

To the Lighthouse: A New Architexture

To the Lighthouse focuses, in its very architecture, on the mother's disappearance: Mrs. Ramsay dies mysteriously in "Time Passes," the section conceived like a hiatus between the first and the third part of the text. Lily Briscoe, meanwhile, who is present throughout the narrative, takes on the role of a witness, rememberer, and mourner: the task of painting the maternity scene—the child on the mother's lap—that will commemorate the invisible presence is ultimately hers to take up. Many years before "A Sketch of the Past," painting is already figured as the rememberer's best ally, providing Woolf with a screen as well as a framework for her emotions. Briscoe's aesthetic quest for the right picture thus overlaps with the rememberer's apprenticeship in remembrance. At such a remove, the writer can stage, as in (a) play, the emotion that was missing earlier and speak it in the borrowed voice of the painter-rememberer Lily Briscoe. The cry that erupts in the midst of Woolf's text is that of a child—perhaps that child who, at the time of her mother's death, could only laugh hysterically. But whereas a child has only a limited grammar and rhetoric in which to express her pain, Virginia Woolf, who is working toward what is perhaps her masterpiece, has all her art to represent that memory:

> "Mrs. Ramsay! Mrs Ramsay!" she cried, feeling the old horror come back—to want and want and not to have. Could she inflict that still? And then, quietly, as if she refrained, that too became part of ordinary experience, was on level with the chair, with the table. Mrs. Ramsay—it was part of the perfect goodness to Lily—sat there quite simply, in the chair, flicked her needles to and fro, knitted her reddish-brown stocking, cast her shadow on the step. There she sat. (186)

Recollecting her past through the detour of her art, Woolf "sees" a picture of the mother. In the homeliest of settings, with its chairs and tables, a woman is sitting, knitting—but if her presence is felt, it is, ultimately, because of Briscoe's childlike and anguished cry. Memory's "architexture" combines the naive realism of a van Gogh portrait (depicting, for instance, Augustine Roulin, the postman's wife), and the cry of the artist longing for a maternal presence. The autobiographical memory is born figuratively, in an act of imagined creation—painting—that encompasses Woolf's own aesthetic impulse to give shape, autobiographically, to an emotional experience.

Briscoe's apprenticeship as a painter—which takes her from an abstract, formalist mode toward an art that is expressive, visionary, and ultimately figurative—overlaps with the rememberer's progress: she has learned, for example, that structures alone will not bring a memory to life and that they must be inflected by affective, sensory, and sensual elements.[24] Meanwhile, what initially appeared in the novel as an "odd-shaped triangular shadow" on Briscoe's canvas has now acquired the recognizable features of the deceased Mrs. Ramsay; what used to be a mere form has been turned into a mnemonic sign. "There she sat." As a ghost, a hallucination, a vision, Mrs. Ramsay is dead and can only come alive in a space that lies beyond the realistic frame of Woolf's novel. She exists as an image, or rather as a *memory*—as what St. Augustine calls "the present of things past."[25]

In his comments on autobiography, Adam Phillips suggests that "the experiences of childhood . . . are at once our privileged and elusive referents" ("Childhood Again," 153). This scene in *To the Lighthouse* represents an "elusive referent" of childhood in two ways: psychologically, in making visible the reference point of Woolf's autobiography, and philosophically, in creating the illusion of reference through a representation. In the deictic phrase "there she was" and the surrounding description, what has been absent is made present. It is language, ultimately, that lures us into believing this real presence. There is more to this scene than just an allegory of remembrance: the scene is marked by a performative gesture that "produces" a childhood experience. In other words, we must acknowledge in the power of that interjected voice the rhetorical force constitutive of remembrance. "Mrs. Ramsay! Mrs Ramsay!" Lily's cry is so shrill, so piercing that it traverses the screen of the fiction, returning us to the real and thus to a referent.[26] Commenting on this passage in *Woolf and the Language of Madness*, Daniel Ferrer emphasizes the paradox of a representation that abuts a space outside of fiction, existing alongside a referent that memory tries to recapture: "The representation of the hallucination inside Virginia Woolf's fiction does not have the effect of inserting one real into another. . . . Instead, however fleetingly, it brings to the surface, within the space of representation, the real" (64).

As readers of this powerful scene, we witness the birth of an autobiographical memory, a birth that is brought about by a rhetorical twist in Woolf's writing. Briscoe's outcry not only gives a face to the absent and names the loss, it also has the rhetorical power, as a prosopopoeia, to render the absent present. Prosopopoeia is commonly defined as an appeal "by which an imaginary person is represented as speaking or acting"—that is, as a figure that addresses another person fictively, in an intersubjective gesture. The rememberer has thus found the appropriate rhetorical figure not only to represent the affect that had so far remained missing, but also to create that intersubjective space where she is not reenacting her pain but telling and "addressing" it to someone.[27]

What Pierre Janet found, in studying hysterical patients, is that these amnesiac patients find it extremely difficult to recollect a visual image of the face of the person they lost, particularly the mother. He thus tells us about his most famous patient, Irène, who was brought to him because she could not remember her mother's death: "This picture was shaped gradually; for a while already Irène had been able to see her mother's shadow, her bearing, and even her dress, but she was unable to see her face" ("L'Amnésie," 19). Bre, another of Janet's patients, who lost her husband, similarly could not recall her husband's features (24).[28] In this context, Woolf's recourse to the figure that, the etymology says, creates *(poien)* a face *(prosopon)*, becomes all the more meaningful. Casting her words in the trope that is designed to bring faces to life, Woolf took the greatest of chances and succeeded in creating a face-to-face encounter, an autobiographical mirroring that, as we know from Salomé, founds remembrance and does so, moreover, through a creative, aesthetic gift. What Woolf "finds" in the mirror of her writing is no longer her mother (which was the case when she remembered obsessively and in the mode of hallucinatory reminiscence), but herself as a remembering subject shaped by her mother's "invisible presence." In other words, the prosopopoeia, in addressing the mother, becomes a way of comforting the self. This is why Woolf can ultimately write, "I did *for myself* what psychoanalysts do for their patients."

True to our earlier discoveries, Woolf's fiction reminds us of the crucial role of language in autobiographical remembrance: a linguistic turn is what enables the repositioning of the subject in regard to an event and transforms it into a lived experience. Writing about the power of language, Paul de Man invites us to see how deeply we depend on signifiers for a sense of reality. We have seen with Woolf how a certain rhetorical figure— prosopopoeia—cuts across the fiction to bring forth a subjective reality. We might thus say, with Paul de Man, that "the phenomenal and sensory properties of the signifier have to serve as the guarantors for the certain existence of the signified and, ultimately, of the referent" ("Hypogram and Inscription," 48).[29] For Woolf, these signifiers, organized grammatically and rhetorically, are the guarantors of personal memory. De Man's philosophical stance usefully reminds us, meanwhile, that words are all we have when it comes to naming the world or articulating our pain. What is true of writing applies to memory as well: remembering involves a wager. We try out words in the hope that they will do their work—the work of naming, however fleetingly, a referent. In writing this page of *To the Lighthouse,* Woolf took this risk of naming. She gambled that a certain signifier would enable remembrance, and in my reading of this passage, it indeed does.

In rearticulating the event through a new personal grammar—not merely as "it happened" but rather as a demand to witness, to "see what happened"—Woolf suggests a way out of a traumatic state, for then the rememberer can truly say, as she does in "A Sketch of the Past," "I seem to be watching things *as if* I were there." Memory truly acts as the mirror—a diffracting mirror that reveals, around each mnemonic encounter, the person who, in the very act of looking at the created scene, emerges as a subject.

Fiction, meanwhile (to which the phrase *as if* refers) provides the mode of emancipation from sheer repetition. The philosopher and psychoanalyst Monique Schneider provides a compelling model for this process. She explains that in placing a traumatic event in a narrative context, the remem-berer who tells her story summons up, or rather crafts, a scene that involves the past self, but now places her in a different position, in a different light. When recalled in an hallucinatory form (as fantasy) or reactivated in a transferential situation (as repetition), the traumatic scene still holds the subject at the center, as its victim—as an object upon whom an agent has come to act. In writing-narrating the scene, the rememberer moves out of the nominative or accusative position into the dative, the grammatical form of attribution: "See, it was done to me," the rememberer is now saying, replacing the former "I was hurt" or "Something hit me" with a rhetorically more powerful description.[30] "It happened to me," says Woolf as in her writing she produces the desired "coincidence, around an event, of inner experience and outer incident" that defines an autobiographical memory.[31] For indeed, only the external, narrating "I" can take it upon herself to say what happened in the incident; at the same time, however, she can, as the remembering figure that stands apart from the event, speak of the inner experience, of how "it felt." Whatever changes, distortions, or defacements naturally occur, the two figures—the rememberer outside and the subject inside the memory—are held together by the continuity of affect, for what happened to the child still reverberates in the adult who, in creating this continuity, saves an earlier self from erasure or destruction.[32]

Remembering the lost maternal figure entails finding her a place ("there," on the stairs) as well as a time (the past marked by the past tense "she was"). But through her literary performance, the writer has also found a way of uttering at last the cry of suffering that had remained strangled in her throat—in her "gizzard." The prosopopoeia creates a temporary irruption in the web of a story that now belongs to the past, but its full significance depends upon its being placed within this broader narrative context. Play-ing, as it were, with Briscoe her double, Woolf was able to cross over into her own past, transferring her own emotions onto the page in the mode of fiction.[33] It would seem, then, that by representing her predicament, rather than enacting it, Woolf is able to break out of the paralyzing frame of rem-iniscence where she lives among ghostly presences, to start recollecting her life. She must be cured, the Freudian analyst would say, *because* she is now remembering—rather than just repeating or hallucinating—the trauma. In other words, the rememberer's creative, aesthetic project creates the autobiographical memory. By creating a space for an emotional outcry and letting the poignancy of such a cry reverberate through her narrative, Woolf is not simply writing her life; she is writing *for* her life.

Intermittences of the Heart

There is something satisfying in the idea that the pain of loss can be captured and put to rest through the efficacious remembering Woolf practices in *To the Lighthouse*. However, if the acknowledgment of strong presences and influences is a condition of life-writing, then remembrance cannot cease. Such is the power of maternal influence on the child that it will have to be remembered forever: Woolf writes about her mother until the very end of her literary career, as we know from studying "A Sketch of the Past." The astounding pages of Woolf's autobiographical text present, one after another, scenes that depict her mother. "I see her at the end of the table. . . . I see her knitting on the hall step. . . . I see her stretching her arms out to Mrs. Williams. . . . I see her writing at the table. . . . And there is my last sight of her; she was dying; I came to kiss her" ("A Sketch," 84). On that same page, the mother's dying is recounted twice. Although I have read this page many times, only today (why?) do I read it with emotion, my eyes tearing up, because of what is, really, its punctum. The detail that pricks me, that I find poignant, is what Barthes in *Camera Lucida* (his aesthetics of photography) calls by this name.

But before I consider my own "intermittences of the heart" and try to understand how Woolf's personal memories could affect me, a different person, I need a fuller, more global grasp of how she patterns her remembrance toward an emotional revelation. For indeed, it is not as if she could be done, once and for all, with remembering her mother; autobiography is not to be understood as revelation, but rather, as Phillips writes, as "repetition that formalizes the continuity, however disguised, between childhood and adulthood" ("Childhood Again," 153). Woolf repeats her remembering across genres: some scenes in "A Sketch of the Past" were already represented in *To the Lighthouse*. What then if autobiography where an incremental process, like a series of themes with variations, discrepancies that keep unfolding in a connective, narrative chain that can be stretched for as long as is needed—as the memory of a memory of a memory of . . . and so on? There is a problem with assuming an endless rehearsal of memories—a problem that leads Woolf to ponder the question of memory's diminishing returns. If dealing with the past means "putting it to rest" (that is, forgetting it), won't her memories of her mother become increasingly faded? "Why," she writes, "should my vision of her and my feeling for her become so much dimmer and weaker?" ("A Sketch," 81). What if she had now lost both feeling and the memory? It is a daunting thought that one may have remembered to the point of exhaustion—and truly buried the dead.[34]

"A Sketch of the Past" offers vivid proof that this is *not* how memory works: it shows, with scene after scene of maternal remembrance, that the core of the mnemonic construction is potentially inexhaustible, because remembrance bears on emotion and not cognition. It is not a matter of "explaining away" the past, but of keeping it alive. Thus at the very moment Woolf's analytical self worries about memory's fading, her creative, imaginative side is at work constructing another scene of maternal presence. "Certainly there she was," she resumes, relying on an emphatic deictic construction, in a gesture that can be traced back to some of her earliest literary projects, such as the 1908 "Reminiscences":

> But now and again, on more occasions than I can number, in bed at night, or in the street, or as I come into the room, *there she is;* beautiful, emphatic, with her familiar phrase and laugh; closer than any of the living are, lighting our lives as with a burning torch, infinitely noble and delightful to her children. (40)

Thirty years or so later, in "A Sketch of the Past," Woolf writes similarly:

> Certainly there she was in the very centre of that great Cathedral space which was childhood; there she was from the very first. My first memory is of her lap; the scratch of some beads on her dress comes back to me as I pressed my cheek against it. Then I see her . . . her voice is still faintly in my ears. (81)

Now, if autobiographical memory were only about narrating and explaining away, there would be no need for a repetition of a scene that is already scripted in *To the Lighthouse* and represented in the first pages of "A Sketch" (as the rememberer moves from blots of color to flowers and then to being on her mother's lap). From the depths of forgetting, the image emerges, as if from a dream, of a child or infant's cheek pressed against the maternal breast, marking a time of physical proximity and sensuous feeling. This new version of maternal remembrance is testimony to Woolf's idea that memory's true aim is emotion. Very interestingly also, its structure, which corresponds to a field memory, contradicts what we thought we had learned about the shifting form of remembrance, where an initial field memory vanishes, supplanted by observer memory.[35] The observer memory was created there, in 1927 or so, as Woolf was working on *To the Lighthouse;* twelve years later, in "A Sketch" she is able to represent what it "felt like" to be in such close, loving proximity with her mother. At the end of her apprenticeship, Woolf casts a memory in which her own figure is not visible in the mirror, but a memory nonetheless suffused with feeling and bodily affects.[36] With its physical, sensual register, this may be the most Proustian of Woolf's memories: a pure sensory impression—*a cheek against a maternal breast*—evokes a moment suspended in time; a long-forgotten memory has come to the top. We do not know what triggered this involuntary memory, but it stands out, clearly, because of that very same "vitality" that is the trademark of Proustian remembrance and that is very aptly summarized in Andreas Huyssen's description in *Twilight Memories:*

> Paradoxically, is it not the case that each and every memory inevitably depends on both distance and forgetting, the very things that undermine its desired stability and reliability and are at the same time essential to the vitality of memory itself? (250)

This rhetorical question, which focuses on the paradox that founds both Proustian memory and "memory as what one has forgotten" in Woolf, invites us to resume earlier discussions of forgetting, to reconsider the question of "the vitality of memory" from a psychological perspective—namely as a coincidence between thought and affect. Here, we must turn to Proust, since he is more inclined than Woolf to buttress his descriptions of "vital" memories with broader, theoretical insights.

One such coincidence is presented in a section of *A la Recherche du temps perdu* subtitled "Intermittences of the Heart," which shows the rememberer suddenly and miraculously recovering from a period of failed remembrance following the death of his grandmother.[37] Given the strong presence of this maternal figure throughout his life, how could the Proustian hero forget such a momentous event? The narrator's answer to this question is almost Freudian: not all memories are equally present in the mind; some are repressed, shelved away until a later encounter.[38] Such temporal discrepancies or "anachronisms" are frequent, he writes, and "prevent . . . the coincidence between facts and feelings from happening" (*Cities of the Plain,* 756; translation amended). However, when the coincidence occurs, the effect is overwhelming, as shown in the intense, unexpected grief the rememberer suddenly experiences as he "recaptures the living reality [of his grandmother] in a complete memory and involuntary recollection."

Disruption of my entire being. On the first night, as I was suffering from cardiac fatigue, I bent down slowly and cautiously to take off my boots, trying to master my pain. But scarcely had I touched the topmost button than my chest swelled, filled with an unknown, a divine *presence,* I was shaken with sobs, tears streamed from my eyes . . . I had just perceived, in my memory . . . the tender, preoccupied, disappointed face of my grand-mother . . . of my real grandmother, of whom, for the first time since the afternoon of her stroke in the Champ-Elysées, I now recaptured the living reality in *a complete and involuntary recollection.* (783; emphasis added)

The involuntary memory described in this passage occupies a singular posi-tion in Proust's *Recherche.*[39] Present in his notebooks long before he started working toward his madeleine and tilleul, the moment when the vivid mem-ory of this maternal presence "comes to the top" is the very first instance of the psychological phenomenon—*la mémoire involontaire*—that so fasci-nated Proust that he built his work around it.[40] But, unlike the other, better-known examples, this instance makes it very clear that the highest forms of remembrance are, for him as for Woolf, not merely aesthetic but deeply emotional experiences. It also shows that the function of remembrance in his *Recherche* cannot be confined within a "blind, senseless, frenzied quest for happiness."[41] Although it demands an engagement with painful events, such remembrance is preferable to amnesia. Proust thus argues insistently in the voice of his newly redeemed rememberer: "Never should I be able to eradicate from my memory that contraction of her face, that anguish of her heart, or rather of mine"; "I was determined not merely to suffer, but to respect the original form of my suffering." For Proust then, as for Woolf, "the preserve of memory" includes the shocks of existence—those vivid rec-ollections that hurt:

> I clung to this pain, cruel as it was, with all my strength, for I realised that it was the effect of the memory I had had of my grandmother, the proof that *this memory was indeed present within me.* I felt that I did not really remember her except through her pain, and I longed for the nails that riv-eted her to my consciousness to be driven yet deeper. (786; emphasis added)

The grief that accompanies the "complete and involuntary recollection" is the fitting, natural emotion (one very long in the making) that turns the event into an experience or, as Proust calls it, "a real moment of life."

> As for the state of forgetfulness of my grandmother in which I had been living until that moment, I could not even think of clinging to it to find

some truth; since in itself it had nothing but a negation, a weakening of the faculty of thought incapable of recreating a *real moment of life* and obliged to substitute for it conventional and neutral images. (787; emphasis added)

To sum up then, the first of Proust's involuntary memories shows the rememberer striving, in the name of biographical accuracy, for the kind of coincidence between thought and affect that Woolf herself demanded—for a form of remembrance that makes us human because it shows us as neither immune nor indifferent to loss.

It is only when Proust, in assessing the meaning of his first discovery, hits upon the idea that the body is the locus of remembrance that a significant difference emerges between his sense of the past and Woolf's more abstract and intellectualized conception of remembrance. Whereas she sees in memory the visionary effect of writing, Proust traces it back to the body:

For with the perturbations of memory are linked the intermittences of the heart. It is, no doubt, the existence of our body, which we may compare to a vase enclosing our spiritual nature, that induces us to suppose that all our inner wealth, our past joys, all our sorrows, are perpetually in our possession. Perhaps it is equally inexact to suppose that they escape or return. In any case if they remain within us, for most of the time it is in an unknown region where they are of no use to us, and where even the most ordinary are crowded out by memories of a different kind, which preclude any simultaneous occurrence of them in our consciousness. But if the context of sensations in which they are preserved is recaptured, they acquire in turn the same power of expelling everything that is incompatible with them, of installing alone in us the self that originally lived them. (784)

In this first tentative description of how Proustian memory works—namely as a moment of vivid consciousness triggered by sensory stimuli—we have no trouble recognizing the template of later instances of involuntary recollection, which are all rooted in a physical impression.[42] From the start then, introspection alone could not produce the kind of mnemonic events that his rememberer needs in order to escape from the regime of "conventional and neutral images" and to reconnect to a living past. Proust and Woolf thus share a similar conviction that only a certain form of remembrance can produce autobiography. In speaking of sensations that alone can instill "in us the self that originally lived them," Proust tells us, in essence, that the upsurge of an involuntary memory is the only mode of access we have to a past self. In short, as our "true" stories, our "real" stories, depend on involuntary recollection, so does the summoning up of a "self" that can last and survive the injuries of time.[43]

We learned early, when we first inquired into Proustian memory, about the foundational value of personal memory in the constitution of a subjectivity. But this examination of the original impulsion behind Proust's project in light of Woolf's own theory of memory invites us to draw a more complicated and subtle picture than we had initially thought. True remembrance is not motivated solely by a hedonistic instinct where cups of tilleul produce happy memories of childhood. It begins, rather, with a sense of personal loss, which is doubtless strongest when the lost object happens to be the mother. Proust knew this as much as Woolf did. But the fact remains that Proust chose not to display overtly in his fiction the true genealogy of involuntary remembrance. To start his *Recherche* with a heartache connected to maternal absence may have felt like a weak move for someone of his literary ambition (and it might have slanted his text too much toward the autobiographical). But it is nonetheless true that at times, the voice of Proust's rememberer takes on the same emotional inflections as does Woolf's—the inflections of that child who has learned to say "gone" or *fort*.

> I knew that I might wait hour after hour, that she would never again be at my side. I had only just discovered this because I had only just, on feeling her for the first time alive, real, making my heart swell to breaking point, on finding her at last, learned that I had lost her for ever. Lost for ever [. . .]. (785)

It is a teasing thought that the foundational block of that masterful "cathedral" that was to become *A la Recherche du temps perdu* is a scene of remembrance in which "she," the mother-grandmother, is found "at last." My emphases in the previous quotations from Proust's text are meant to show how closely Proust matches Woolf in his effort to define a form of memory that renders the absent "present"—but here, the absent is not any object (a flower, a bubble, a lilac in bloom) but the prime referent of memories: the mother.[44]

Punctum

Literary critics agree that Barthes wrote his essay on photography, *Camera Lucida,* under the influence of Proust, and particularly the episode we just studied.[45] But unlike his model, the twentieth-century critic shows no qualms in articulating an aesthetics of memory around a biographical, sentimental attachment to his mother. If Barthes's essay seems so relevant to this inquiry, it is, however, not merely because of a convergence in themes. *Camera Lucida* presents an aesthetics of remembrance that is centrally concerned with autobiography and provides a rich echo to, as well as an enlightening commentary on, "life-writing." What makes a memory autobiographical? What brings it to life? The very questions that are raised by Woolf and Proust are answered by Barthes's treatise in the guise of a reflection on photography, which leads to a very specific answer: punctum. This recondite Latin term refers to a detail embedded in the picture that marks or symbolizes the intimate, subjective poignancy of an emotional experience.

Thus, memory and emotion converge, for example, in the picture that Barthes lovingly describes—but does not reproduce—of the Winter Garden. (This is the picture in which Barthes found "the truth of the face that [he] loved" [67], that of his mother—showing in this very formulation his debt to Proust's own "intermittences of the heart.") What Proust learned about memory—namely how to seek a subjective reality—Barthes applies to photography. But in this process he also travels the same route as Woolf—toward an embodiment of the maternal presence—which is shown in another picture, again not reproduced in the book. He thus writes: "contemplating a photograph in which she is hugging me, a child, against her, I can waken in myself the rumpled softness of her crêpe de Chine and the perfume of her rice powder" (65). The print contains the child who feels his mother's presence through touch and smell—just as Woolf's words, recalling the beads on her mother's dress and her voice, convey her mother's presence in a sensory, and not merely visual, form. When he speaks of these chosen photographs (the ones he says he loves), Barthes writes, "I saw only the referent, the desired object, the beloved body" (7). Coming from a critic known for his sophisticated semiotic analyses and his passion for texts and signifiers, this remark, which makes of photography so transparent a medium that it expresses "the real," has puzzled more than one critic or philosopher.[46] But to us, it may not seem so surprising: Barthes greets particular photographs with the same exclamation that our rememberers use with certain memories: "There she is"—*la voici*—as if indeed a representation could produce a presence or that most elusive of referents: a childhood experience. Indeed, as Beryl Schlossman so clearly shows in her analysis of punctum, Barthes establishes a mode of representation that creates the lure of reference: "Gazing at the image or the photograph, the subject suddenly encounters the referent. This face-to-face meeting produces the *punctum* when the referent suddenly and unpredictably reaches out to the viewer through a fragment or detail" (155). But Barthes himself is aware of this yearning for a referent: like the rememberers we have studied, he inhabits the phenomenological space of a suspension of disbelief, where a representation (a photograph) "carries the referent with itself" (5). He thus argues that "in the Photograph the power of authentication exceeds the power of representation" (89). In an aesthetics of memory, our belief in a picture's reality must indeed supplant our logical, rational knowledge of what it shows. How else indeed could the contemplation of a print produce a tactile or olfactive sensation such as Barthes describes: "the rumpled softness of her crêpe de Chine and the perfume of her rice powder"?

We may well know, rationally, that the figure in a photograph is produced by a combination of optics and chemistry transferred onto a material surface, and yet discard, in our phenomenological experience, what we know about the medium to indulge in the "reality effect" it produces. I, for one, have spent hours and days pondering the nature of words or signifiers that produce the memory effect described as Proustian or as autobiographical memory. But caught unawares one morning when studying Woolf, I forgot everything I knew about representation to indulge in an emotional experience, a sentimental moment, that marks my life. Against all intellectual odds, it seems indeed possible to feel the punctum of a certain representation and to experience it as an autobiographical moment, when one feels alive with an invisible presence, even if this feeling is that of pain:

> And there is my last sight of her; she was dying; I came to kiss her and as I crept out of the room she said: "Hold yourself straight, my little Goat." What a jumble of things I can remember, if I let my mind run, about my mother: but they are all of her in company; of her surrounded; of her generalized; dispersed, omnipresent, of her as the creator of what crowded, merry worlds which spun so gaily in the centre of my childhood. ("A Sketch," 84)

I can still tell, several days later, what words, what image touched me with that punctum which is the mark of what Proust would have called a "true memory" or a "complete and involuntary recollection." But would my reader care? This question seems irrelevant, but it is nevertheless one that Barthes had to face when he built his revolutionary aesthetics around an acknowledgment similar to mine—namely that some representations touch us against our better knowledge. Attuned as he is to the phenomenological and critical discourses of his time, Barthes knows where to reach for a formulation: lavishing emotion over what is a mere picture to account for his mistake. It is perhaps to ward off criticism about his naive belief in reference that he invokes in his essay a notion borrowed from Julia Kristeva, that of a *vérité folle*—of a mad truth in which affect becomes "a guarantee of Being." He also speaks of photography as "a temporal hallucination" (115). What better phrase might there be to describe an autobiographical memory that makes present what was absent? Some pages later, he provides us with a philosophical and grammatical explanation for this process, by way of a commentary on the deictic construction *la voici*. "There she is" is a turn of phrase (in Richard Howard's translation) leads him to argue that a photograph "accomplishes the unheard-of identification of reality" ("that-has-been") with truth ("there-she-is!") (113). What these words tell us is that the photograph seems to create a moment of reference, through a rhetoric that can make the past (of the aorist "has been") present ("she *is*" says the spectator of the image).

Punctum could thus be described as the photographic effect that occurs in remembrance—through an aesthetic process that Barthes identifies in pointing out the existence of photographs that appear to bear, in their "sensitive points," the impress of a certain inner, subjective reality. These pictures, like certain memories, can capture an impression in the fashion described by Lou Andreas-Salomé, namely as a "moment of coincidence, around an event, of inner experience and outer incident." As symbolic transformations of personal experiences, they are endowed with an irreducibly personal or subjective dimension. What is felt there, in the photograph, is at once so ineffable and intimately personal that, according to Barthes, it cannot be objectified: "I cannot reproduce the Winter Garden Photograph. It exists only for me. For you, it would be nothing but an indifferent picture" (73).[47] But it can be conveyed, as we know, through the rememberer's words: because the photograph alone fails to declare its punctum, Barthes is involved by default, image after image, in a literary exercise that demands that he describe the detail in the picture that pricks or wounds him. His words, like the photograph or rather *in lieu of* it, will "reproduce endlessly what happened only once," namely the impression (4).[48] Barthes's aesthetics in *Camera Lucida* is indeed inconceivable without his recourse to writing as an instantiation or "translation" of the mnemonic experience brought forth by "the Photograph." As rememberers, Proust, Woolf, and Eliot are similarly beholden to words, not merely in their representational function, but for their punctum—for their ability to create, symbolically, moments of "authentication" that enable "the superposition of reality and past" that brings a memory to life (76).

"A photograph's *punctum* is that accident which pricks me (but also bruises me, is poignant to me)," claims Barthes (26–27). Woolf's moments of being are a counterpart to Barthes's "accidents which prick me," while her "shocks," "blows," or (closer even to *punctum*'s etymology) what makes a "dint" found a mnemonic aesthetics that closely resembles his. In the same way that Barthes opposes to punctum a form of "civilized" or intellectualized representation of the past (which he calls *studium*), Woolf strives to write images and language that break away from the inventory or enumeration of facts typical of conventional biography. Dismissing right at the beginning of "A Sketch" "the enormous number of things [she] can remember," she wants to look for memories she can love because they evoke a referent (64). Indeed, ordinary recollection, like a banal photograph, encourages forgetting by voiding impressions of their spontaneous emotive content. When it comes to such affects, "reproducing life as a connected chains of events" (in Freud's definition of recollection, "Screen Memories," 303) may not be good enough, for how could the intensities of certain experiences be rendered in what is merely a narrative chain? Neither Woolf nor Barthes believes in memory as narration; both set out in search of a form of remembrance that reorganizes biography around intensely subjective aesthetic encounters that correspond to emotional experiences.

Barthes assesses the autobiographical value of photography by comparing it to traditional "anamnesis"—a simple life summary—in order to express his preference for a form that enables him to witness his own history and is grounded, as Woolf would say, in "the person to whom things happen": "No anamnesis could ever make me glimpse this time starting from myself . . . whereas contemplating a photograph in which she is hugging me, a child against her, I can waken in myself" (65). The photographic effect he describes as punctum thus becomes, unexpectedly and miraculously, constitutive of subjectivity in producing the kind of aesthetic awakening we witnessed among our rememberers. Picking up on Sartre's discussion of newspaper photographs that "say nothing to [him]," he describes his own search for a telling picture in revealing terms: "in this glum desert, suddenly a specific photograph reaches me; it *animates me,* and I animate it" (20).

If *Camera Lucida* can be studied as a narrative describing the search of a soul (of that *anima*) in an age of technological reproduction, then the encounter with the punctum represents a miraculous coming to life of a self across time—a meeting between then and now involving the "I." This is what I take Barthes to mean in one of the more obscure moments of his difficult essay. The image, he tells us, does more than transport the past into the present; it also substitutes one self for another: "The photograph is the advent of myself as another: a cunning dissociation of consciousness from identity" *(une dissociation retorse de la conscience d'identité)*. The key phrase is "advent of myself": an autobiographical subject is born in the split of personality that occurs around the punctum—as the image that makes the past present. But Barthes's translator makes short shrift of another important word, "retorse" (which he translates as "cunning"), a word denoting artifice, and particularly cunning verbal artifice. If indeed the photograph produces a consciousness of identity—a fleeting autobiographical moment or presence—it is thanks to a visual trick (the equivalent of a rhetorical trope in literature).

This reminder of the constructed and crafted nature of mnemonic representations invites us to contemplate Barthes's project in the broader context of aesthetic discussions. It also helps us focus on the paradox that lies at the heart of personal remembrance—a paradox that says that the "reality effect" of a memory depends, ironically, on a moment of aesthetic suspension and even fiction. Writing philosophically, Colin McCabe attributes the power of the punctum's persuasion to negation: "The *punctum* indicates that moment at which the referent touches the subject, destroying the world of objects, and the moment of comprehension disclosing the drives that make the world comprehensible" (74). Memories can suspend our perception of the world around us: Barthes says as much when he explains that when looking at some photographs, he finds that the world around him (and the photograph itself) vanishes, replaced by the presence of the image. While we know of similar "temporal hallucinations" in Woolf and Nerval, Proust's psychological description of this experience is worth bearing in mind too. Here is his version, from "Intermittences of the Heart," of the negation that enables remembrance: "If the context of sensations in which [our past joys, all our sorrows] are preserved is recaptured, they acquire in turn *the same power of expelling everything that is incompatible with them*, of installing alone in us the self that originally lived them" (784; emphasis mine). The aesthetic miracle (or should we just call it a trick?) we witness here is one whereby an outer reality is suspended in favor of recaptured sensations—sensations that MacCabe labels as "the drives that make the world comprehensible." But comprehensible is too bland, too intellectual a word. These sensations, as we know, are what make the world alive for the subject who in turn arises from this creative act, as when Woolf writes, "I make it real by putting into words" ("A Sketch," 72). The work of aesthetic negation becomes a condition for the creation of subjectivity, for then indeed, as MacCabe tells us, "the referent touches the subject."

Thus a detour through Barthes's theories helps us see more clearly how autobiography depends on art. An autobiographical memory, like the Photograph, exists by virtue of an aesthetic negation or rhetorical trick, whereby one kind of reality (objective, historical, "realist" even) is dismissed in favor of an aesthetically constructed reality that is entirely subjective. This new subjective reality, grounded in personal memory, depends, as we know, on a seeming paradox, in which imagination (the ability to create and respond to images) takes precedence over perception. A world of images renders the rememberer oblivious to the world around her and draws her relentlessly—if she happens to have the life and the talent of a Virginia Woolf—to the world of art. In his discussion of *Camera Lucida,* Jean-Michel Rabaté quotes Sartre on negation: "Reality is never beautiful. Beauty is a value which can only apply to imaginary productions and which implies a complete annihilation *(néantisation)* of the world in its essential structure."[49] Sartre's words allow us to understand, in its full depth and sentimentality, the axiom that may well have presided over Woolf's life-writing: "the past is beautiful because one never realizes an emotion at the time." In revisiting her project in light of what Proust and Barthes thought about memory, we have learned to give full philosophical weight to her words. We understand then that the verb "realizes" celebrates an aesthetic accomplishment. It speaks of consciousness—to the extent that personal remembrance is the instrument of consciousness; it also evokes a singular creative act that enables us to witness and even to share (as I have been reminded in my experience of punctum through someone else's emotional experience). Memories are indeed the most amazing of human constructions, telling us, in Yeats's words, "of what is past, or passing, or to come." Our examination of Woolf's strategies for life-writing shows us, meanwhile, that autobiographical remembrance can only be born from a solitary and singular apprenticeship, for indeed, as the poet says, for the soul there is no "singing school."

The Color of the Past: A Postscript

Autobiographical memory, we have seen, involves our cognitive, emotional, imaginative, and aesthetic abilities. If there is one thing this book will have achieved, it is to show the infinite complexity of memory. It will have "denaturalized" this most common and natural of human acts that we call remembering. Beyond the daring tasks of construction, imagination, and stylization involved in remembrance lie two even greater challenges, which we revisit at the end of this book in discovering the story of yet another rememberer. One of these challenges bears on the nature of autobiography and seems almost insurmountable, for it has to do with the nature of time itself. While autobiography is a precondition of our human identity, it implies, as Jean Starobinski points out, a double difference: a difference in time (between now and then) and, connected to it, a difference in identity (between "*I* now" and "*I* then").[1] Rememberers have to overcome these differences in order to create the "recapitulative knowledge" born from the accumulation of experiences. The other impediment is psychological: it springs from a contradictory human need, which demands that we be able both to remember and to forget. Caught between these contrary currents, human memory is necessarily imperfect—it is frail, fallible, and often unreliable. In summing up the second of these paradoxes, Vladimir Jankélévich highlights the vital function of remembrance: "memory (though always precarious and contested by oblivion) and oblivion (though always capable of remembrance) are correlated and inseparable even in their antagonism—together they give shape to our human destiny" (217).

True to this necessary predicament, the rememberers who are featured in this book have undertaken the challenging task of remembering in a mode that brings them closest to the paradoxical nature of human memory. As writers and as human subjects intent on leaving traces of their most meaningful experiences, they rely on acts of imaginative and verbal creation to evoke memories of the forgotten—in the hope that writing will lead to the experience of new, fresh, and vivid memory. What this truly means, meanwhile, is that their literary texts present us with exercises or experiments in remembrance (Benjamin hinted at this problem when he wrote that "*A la*

Recherche du temps perdu may be regarded as an attempt to produce experience synthetically," "On Some Motifs," 157).

Yet how does literary memory overlap with autobiographical memory as we know it in the outside, practical world? As we have learned, in the universe of fiction and thought experiments, memories take the shape of wonderfully expressive and engaging constructions or scenes. Does this remain true once we leave the world of fiction? Experts in the field, such as Mieke Bal (a cultural critic) or David Pillemer (a psychologist) tell us that memory is typically "awkward" or "messy." There may be reasons, however, for this messiness, as these remaining pages show in addressing the relevance of literary memory for our understanding of history and in suggesting that the messiness of human remembrance may ultimately be a redeeming feature—that is, as long as we accept that in our modern times, history is no longer impersonal but made of singular experiences.

How does the singularity of an experience endow it with a collective meaning? This is a question that Lou Andreas-Salomé raises in "The Dual Orientation of Narcissism." In the last lines of her essay, she uses figures to sum up her thoughts and suggests that we create not merely images but in fact the very colors of our past. What she means by colors can best be understood if we return to her theory on memory and to a crucial distinction she makes between *Gedächtnis*, on the one hand, and *Erinnerung*, on the other. Drawing most probably on Hegel, Salomé articulates her conception of remembrance in comparing *Gedächtnis* (recollection), a form of remembering that is abstracted from images and resembles thought, to *Erinnerung* (reminiscence), in which memory maintains "its sensory shape and recalls its inner meaning." She establishes the superiority of the latter.[2] *Erinnerung* gives a different inflection to remembrance: it renders impressions as "they felt," in a singular fashion that veers away from the beaten track of conventional descriptions or impoverished feelings.

Recollection works against the interests of remembrance, she tells us in a resounding statement: "Extreme precision, the triumph of perfect recollection, stands in inverse proportion to the clarity of reminiscence, reminiscence that brings into existence the associations that shape our impressions and comes to consciousness only by, so to speak, skirting around our life: we *possess* recollection, but we *are* memory" (214). To strengthen her case, she resorts to a well-known analogy. Recollection, she argues, is like cinema, and it has the same disadvantages: "cinema as the actualization of the past has a deadly impact on memory: it disorganizes, it breaks down what was a fundamental totality." Discussing the nature of the "aura" surrounding works of art, Walter Benjamin develops a similar argument some years later and suggests that the camera works against the aura and is thus the enemy of spontaneous, involuntary recollection. He writes that technical reproduction stands in the way of "the associations which, at home in the *mémoire involontaire*, tend to cluster around the object of a perception" and that "the perpetual readiness of volitional, discursive memory, encouraged by the technique of mechanical reproduction, reduces the scope for the play of the imagination" ("On Some Motifs," 186).

Put next to Salomé's conception of *Erinnerung*, Benjamin's commentary on memory usefully foregrounds the need for imagination in memory, as the mental faculty that brings to life the complex associations that define an impression or a perception. Indeed, as we saw in examining George Eliot's experiment in remembering, the images that give shape to our inner experiences lie on the other side of our rational, analytical faculty: they emerge from acts of creative imagination; they are born as fictions. Such memories give form to experiences that no camera will ever capture, and the imaginative, verbal act that enables reminiscence is radically at odds with the mimetic, exclusively visual reproduction of images that we commonly owe to photography or cinema.

This is why, in Salomé's argument, writers are such good rememberers— because they remember creatively and aesthetically, knowing fully that memory has little in common with mere mimetic reproduction. As *Erinnerung*, memory can never be copied: it is born each time at the cusp of the present, as a spontaneous, unmediated correspondence between inner impressions and a concrete existence. In this fashion, Salomé adumbrates what is really a revolution in our conception of memory and time—a revolution that situates memory in the present (Freud signaled it with his concept of deferred action, and scientific thought follows suit in conceiving of memory as recategorization). As the performative enactment of the past within the living present, remembering can become the ultimate existential act: it gives shape to what Woolf called "moments of being." Salomé's formulation of the relation between memory and subjective existence is less radical; she conceives that remembering and living run on a parallel course *(am Leben entlang)*. Instead of reproducing and mirroring a past life, writing gives intimations of an existence fully lived. At the convergence between inner and outer impressions, writing gives birth to an autobiographical self held in place by vaster historical and natural forces.[3]

The case study I want to adduce to connect literary memory to natural memory involves a modern rememberer equipped with pen and paper, but wishing he had a camera. It shows that once we accept Salomé's argument that personal memory and historical truth are interdependent, we will find that subjective memory and historical knowledge often coexist uneasily—in that messy or awkward fashion I hinted at earlier. This fact is vividly illustrated by a one-page news story (published under the rubric "Lives" in the *New York Times Magazine* in early 2001) and told by David Tereshchuk, a British journalist and documentary filmmaker. While it embraces the recapitulative knowledge characteristic of autobiography, its theme is memory. The author recalls how he found himself, as a yet unseasoned journalist, caught in the maelstrom of a historical event. He witnessed how, on that ill-fated day in Derry that came to be known as Bloody Sunday, British troops shot randomly at a protest march, killing fourteen people. His account first takes him back to his vivid recollection of the event, it then shows him at the witness stand, the position he occupied during the inquiry launched by Prime Minister Blair to address the "Catholic community's lasting sense of outrage."

Tereshchuk remembers that the sudden, brutal firing took him by complete surprise: he huddles behind an improvised barricade, holding onto his notepad, and acutely aware of his need for a camera.

> Wanting to do *something* of use, I scribbled notes: the time according to my cracked watch, the fractured sobbing of a woman nearby, the number of shots I could count—a near impossible task since they overlapped. One recollection is stronger than any other—a soldier in a red beret, down on one knee, leveling his self-loading rifle toward me and shooting. (66)

A soldier in a red beret leveling his gun and shooting: this is, in Tereshchuk's account, the single strongest picture that emerges from this terrifying and confusing experience. It is the one that he holds onto, certain "of the truth of the evidence," when questioned by an army lawyer a few weeks later. Twenty-nine years later his "most vivid memory" is still there when the inquiry is reopened and he is questioned again.

A soldier in a red beret—an image, a color. One way of making sense of this memory is to consider it in the context of trauma. "I was 23 and scared witless," the journalist writes. We know that memories born from fear, if they are recalled explicitly, will most often "have a strong sensory, and particularly visual component" (Pillemer, 22). A neuroscientist, such as LeDoux, for instance, might explain that the memory image described by Tereshchuk exemplifies the type of coincidence that brings autobiographical memories to life—a coincidence between the explicit and the implicit systems. The narrative representations characteristic of purposeful recollection intersect with perceptual, sensory, and affect-laden impressions. It is in the overlap between the image and perceptual intensities that the memory of a red beret comes to life as a palpable element of consciousness. But other explanations can be brought in as well, invoking what we have learned about the focus on detail or the importance of color in the mental imagery that defines personal memory.

Thus, the beret becomes part of the mnemonic scene not only because it embodies the violence of the impression. It is there as the kind of detail that contributes to the reality effect of the mnemonic representation—because it feeds the rememberer's belief that the event could not have been imagined. With its vivid, lasting presence in the scene, the beret has become the "guarantor" or "underwriter" of the reality of the experience depicted in the memory. In the insistent presence of such irrelevant details and in the unexpected expenditure that they warrant, we find confirmation of the inherently dynamic nature of remembrance. Narrative and structural elements are combined with figures or symbols that express intensities of affects so that Tereshchuk's memory becomes a force field of signs and private meanings. These emerge, with their singular qualitative traits—as qualia—from the depths of a private history of perceptions, impressions, and affects. Were it not for such subjective coloring, the picture would have seemed flat and would have been lost to oblivion.

Scientists tell us indeed that if a mnemonic scene does not tap into the world of subliminal, somatic affects, it soon loses its status as a personal memory, to be washed away in the never-ending movie-in-the-brain that constitutes our consciousness or to become a mere fact, embedded in the mass of practical information that helps us run our lives. How different this is from our vivid memories, of those memories that are the landmarks of our private, subjective experiences! The red beret exists by virtue of the affective reverberations it encapsulates for this rememberer: the act of remembering summons up an autobiographical self—a self that is constituted right there and then in such a mnemonic sign. As Salomé tells us, *Erinnerung*, with its sensory shape and inner meaning, is what defines us. This is how the red beret has become the emblem of this subjective coloring of the past.

What we learned from Virginia Woolf will help us understand, meanwhile, that there is also an existential significance to this coloring. The best rememberer, Woolf argues several times, is a painter, and we saw how significant colors become in Woolf's representations of her experiences. In "A Sketch of the Past," the scene of the child on the mother's lap—seeing the red and purple blots of color—evokes the birth of a self. Emerging from her writing and remembering, these blots of red, purple, and blue connect the rememberer to the origins of sentience and thus of her being. For Tereshchuk, too, the red is doubly significant, as the crucial image of an emotion-filled scene and as the sign invested with an existential, quasi-onto-logical significance. In seeing, feeling the colors of her past, Woolf experi-ences the continuities of her existence. They help her say to herself, "*I was there*," "*I felt it*." The same is true for the journalist who witnessed the bloody massacre.

To sum up, the colors we give to our memories, whether literally or metaphorically (we have other ways, as rememberers, of stamping our memory images with personal affects), mark our subjective involvement in the past, at the convergence between memory and subjectivity. As the seem-ingly irrelevant but fully expressive detail that sticks out from the picture, the red beret endows the rememberer's snapshot of the past with punctum while offering palpable evidence of the affective impact that a scene had on him. The impact is renewed, the subject brought to awareness, each time the memory is revisited. Each time, it speaks of a subject who, from being a mere bundle of perceptions and affects, emerges into consciousness. What the rememberer shares through his most vivid memory lies much beyond mere information: it is the sense of his own mortality—and of his own sur-vival.

Our memories for events are, by nature, designed to render how an event "felt to us"; they are meant to help our survival, and thus they can only be subjective. Yet history is partly built around them: what Tereshchuk saw, together with many others, on that June day in 1972 might already be part of a textbook of Irish history, part of a collective memory. But the question remains, what effect will personal memory, with its subjective traits, have on collective pursuit of historical objectivity? Mieke Bal answers in a for-mulation that almost amounts to a paradox: "memory is a function of sub-jectivity," she writes. "Cultural memory is collective, yet, by definition, sub-jective" (180). In spite of our need for historical objectivity, we rely on memory pictures created by rememberers that are colored, or tainted even, by individual perceptions, which are then woven into the very fabric of his-tory. What Bal concludes from this is that "these subjective features of memory infuse it with something beyond academic historicism, something as awkward and compromised as feeling" (181). Feeling, an indispensable element of human remembrance, compromises the accuracy of our memo-ries. There is perhaps no better place to understand this than in Freud's thinking about screen memories. What if the red beret were but a cover for other more meaningful, but repressed impressions? For the psychoanalyst, the paradox of the vivid presence of a detail has its source in a temporal con-fusion. A later affect is superimposed on an earlier image, leading to such questions as "When was the red added to the picture?" or "What other impression combined with this event gave the beret this more vivid red feature?" or "What activated this particular image?" The last among these questions may be answered by recalling that a multilayered history of prior sensations and perceptions "wired" together in the rememberer's brain can produce that one image and color of soldier in a red beret. As for the rememberer, meanwhile, he will have convinced himself of the reality of that picture. As Tereshchuk writes, in 1978 when he made another deposition, "the investigators . . . asked a simple question—one [he] had never been asked before—about my most vivid memory, the soldier firing toward me. "What was on his head?" Without a moment's pause, I recalled his red beret."

In the rememberer's mind, the colored image has acquired a "psychical reality," as Freud would say. But a psychical reality has no anchoring in historical time; instead, it floats in the rememberer's mind as a secure, carefully built construction of what the world must be like—or rather, taking into account the interval that separates impression from perception, *of what it must have been like*. From such a perspective, the color of the past truly signifies a private reality so deeply ingrained in the rememberer's psyche that it holds true regardless of its historical veracity and reality. The reformulation, by Laplanche and Pontalis, of what Freud means by "psychical reality"—"something that would have all the consistency of the real without, however, being verifiable in external experiences. It would belong to a category which might on first approach be designated as structural"—sounds like a warning bell. What if the memory in question were not true after all?

The question comes down to comparing the image on the celluloid strip with the one that our rememberer holds to be genuine. When Tereshchuk was confronted with documentary evidence—a series of photographs—he found out that the soldier he had seen was wearing a helmet. Going against his better instincts as a serious journalist, the rememberer had somehow become an "unreliable witness." He confesses to being deeply shaken when seeing his error, writing: "My life's effort to extract hard truth from messy surroundings has been severely humbled by the messiness of my brain." Yet when he closes his eyes, he still sees the red beret. David Pillemer declares at the outset of *Vivid Memories, Momentous Events* that personal memory is often "idiosyncratic, emotion-laden and messy" (4). Given Tereshchuk's dismay when he learns that his seemingly secure memory failed him, it is hard to tell whether the psychologist's authoritative statement might be enough to reassure him that in other circumstances he might have been an excellent witness.

How indeed could he not be aware of the awkwardness that arises when the veracity of a memory is put to the test in a collective, a public, context. The notion of the image's psychical reality may fare well in the privacy of a psychotherapist's office, but will surely become troublesome in a courtroom and a situation that demands factual accuracy. In private, the rememberer can easily say to himself or herself, "Perhaps I am not remembering exactly—but I like to think that this is how it was." Thus Woolf too might have convinced herself, even against her better rational judgment, that she had kept a precise memory of a dress her mother wore on that day in the train to St. Ives when she was a very young child. When it comes to our private memories, we can indulge in such aesthetic gestures and adorn our images with the colors of our liking, just for pleasure. "I know—but nevertheless I believe . . ." is the phrase that defines fetishism. We may well turn certain personal memories into a fetish or a talisman—but who is to worry? Whoever said that autobiography is an accurate science?

In the public sphere, however, the "tendentious nature of the workings of memory"—in Freud's weighty pronouncement—becomes a problem. Having remarked that personal memory is naturally messy, Pillemer concedes that "in a court of law, accuracy of even minute details can have profound consequences, and a blanket assumption of memory accuracy or authenticity would be ill-advised" (59). In the eyes of the law or of "academic historicism," getting the color wrong can have tremendous consequences: it can invalidate once and for all the rememberer's testimony. Whatever explanation might be given for the mistake—and surely the most convincing one would say that remembrance always is a construction—in the eyes of the law, in the gaze of history, our rememberer is in error, as the pictures prove.

The truth is that when it comes to the most meaningful of our memories—those that constitute the nodal points of our autobiographies—we tend to make up our own photographs, which we end up coloring by hand, as it were, adding a measure of fantasy here, a special emphasis there, and sometimes even rearticulating them around a symbolic knot. For Tereshchuk, it had to be that the soldier leveling his gun would be without a helmet—it made him less machinelike, more human. It spoke of human aggression against another human, in a way that the more realistic, and in the end, *true* picture cannot express. And one can speculate even further: the red *had* to be there to underline a face-to-face encounter with a death-dealing human being. Such rhetorical emphasis, one might say, became indispensable in the cognitive and emotional work of building the scene: the color makes the present meaningful, and the picture sticks despite its errors—rather *because of* them. What this means is that the error of perception is part of the memory construction. Given the life-threatening, extreme nature of the experience, accuracy of perception will naturally, necessarily be overridden by a need to enlist the mental faculty of remembrance in the service of survival. Recollection always entails the reordering of the event into a sense-making narrative. But when, as is the case here, it is destined to provide a way out of the trauma, it is more likely than ever that the details of the scene will be flawed and inaccurate. The picture must be retouched to serve the rememberer's immediate needs; in order to divest the event of its violence, the rememberer must be able, for instance, to encase it in a known structure. He can, for example, re-create it in its mythical or archetypal proportions. Cain strikes Abel. In the illustrated Bible I used to read, Abel had a huge red spot on his forehead. In Tereshchuk's rendering of this story, the blood has splattered on Cain's face. There had to have been no helmet: the two of them, young, eager, were just brothers—until one of them went to war on the other.

But this is sheer speculation, of course, for who can really tell what lies behind a private symbol? Only the rememberer, as we know, holds the key to the secret contained in the colored blot in the picture. Nonetheless, moments of overinterpretation are a likely occurrence for anyone who with empathy listens to a rememberer. Indeed, as I made clear in the early chapters of this book, autobiographical memory is an intersubjective phenomenon: this is why it so easily lends itself to overreading and to such countertransference. I have naturally—as we all do when we read or listen to another person's memories—projected my own knowledge and my own sensibility into the picture that is evoked by the rememberer. Yet beyond my imaginative empathy, I can find two external, intellectual reasons that have led me to this specific interpretation.

The first is theoretical: if memory, as I have argued, is not an empirical fact but a textual creation, then it should be possible to reconstitute the architecture or the "pattern," as Woolf might have said, that sustains it. It is when the event meets a structure that the perception becomes a memory. What is it in the rememberer's construction of the event that demands that the red beret be so imperatively real and present? This question led me to the text of another rememberer who had been similarly shocked and surprised, providing me with a second, this time textual element in my search for structure.

"Week after week passed," Virginia Woolf writes in "A Sketch of the Past," "and nothing made any dint upon me. Then, for no reason that I know about, there was a sudden violent shock; something happened so violently that I have remembered it all my life" (71). Woolf tells, as one of these shocks, of fighting with her brother and suddenly realizing the cruelty of it all. "Why hurt another person?" she found herself thinking all of a sudden. "Why fire at another person? Why try to hurt me?" Tereshchuk's story is filled with the same questions, questions that he cannot articulate, but which stare at him, and at us, in the vividness of that red beret. The pain of discovering human aggression in a face-to-face encounter with her brother marked Woolf indelibly. Tereshchuk symbolizes a similar affect in making the beret red. For while personal memories are singularly, qualitatively different, this singularity does not exclude a commonality of experience. The surprise juxtaposition of these two personal memories hints at a structure—a structure that speaks of human violence so powerfully as to demand words, a narrative, a form of explanation that will "blunt the sledge-hammer force of the blow" (72). Words, a narrative, an explanation: as our rememberer searches for them, he or she will inevitably, and however unconsciously, rewrite the moment. Indeed, what is represented is never the event in itself, but a rememberer's attempt to reorganize the event as a meaningful structure—that is, as an explicit memory.

Thus while our recollections are built like fictions, these fictions are naturally overdetermined. So many layers of private impressions and experiences are woven into the redness of the beret that its significance could never be fully fathomed: the mythical construction I unraveled is just one possible reading, one way of accounting for the nodal points in autobiographical memory. Our private memories are stories, stories that we hold for cherished or necessary truths. Or, to take a less radical stance, they are compromise formations, where the rememberer finds a middle way, a middle voice between perception and emotion. The subjective element is indelibly woven into the tale—a tale that cannot tell of the event, but only, by definition, of what over time, often through many revisions, became its memory. But the question ultimately remains: where is the real truth about the event to be found, in the photographic shot, or in the picture that the rememberer has held for so long in his mind?

This is, perhaps, too unwieldy a question, but if we consider it as two distinct issues, we may be able to take steps toward an answer. We can ask ourselves, first: what is, ultimately, the referent of memory? Then, in a second step, we can try to figure out the limits and limitations of autobiographical memory, in the wake of Tereshchuk's claim that he feels "severely humbled by the essential messiness of [his] brain." Whatever we conclude about the referent of memory will have to take into account that a blend of currents, cognitive and affective, lies at the root of the elaborate constructions that constitute our memories. The representations we have of our experiences are thus naturally colored by a subjective aesthetic and an expressive element. In stitching together a memory scene, we create the verbal conditions that give memories their reality. We create, through verbal and rhetorical means, an impression or effect that produces the belief that these words refer to some "real" occurrence.

This interweaving explains the importance of the rhetorical figure of prosopopoeia in our study of the performative, verbal underpinnings of autobiographical memory. Our autobiographical memories, we concluded, are the reflections of our dream that words be true. They exist, these autobiographical memories, because of our recourse to language as a medium of our relation to the world and because of our belief in the signifiers we use to symbolize certain felt realities. When Woolf, after a particularly successful stretch of writing that leads to the discovery of memories, exclaims, "I make it happen," she intuitively expresses more than her personal triumph as a rememberer, she reveals how deeply responsible we are, as creatures of language, in creating our past. Our memories "come right" when the words are right, namely when they give us the illusion (or answer our desire) that the signifier should guarantee the "existence of the signified, and ultimately of the referent." We must indeed acknowledge, slipping into Paul de Man's words, that the "phenomenal and sensory properties of the signifier" are what enables us to create signs by which we commemorate our impressions. If there is any referential value to be given to autobiographical memory, it is only within such localized memory-performances where the rememberer is able to color the past, verbally and expressively, with the right affect.

But if collective memory can only arise from the gathered threads of rememberers' tales, we are bound to recognize that history is not only *studium*, but that it has, as well, its *punctum*. For ultimately, the referent of memory is not the world (not a history unfolding outside) but the subject himself or herself, summoned into existence in the scattered blots of color and symbolic knots that bring memories to life. However powerful our need for perfect memories, we cannot do away with the "messy" and "awkward" subjective and emotional element that makes up what Woolf called "the truth about this vast mass that we call the world."

As for what we make of this essential messiness of our brains, there are two different responses. Psychologists and cognitive scientists seem to agree that our memory for events is generally pretty accurate; it does a good job in reproducing the main elements of a situation, even though there might be distortions in the margins and errors in the details. Thus William Brewer, a scientific authority in matters of autobiographical memory, writes:

The qualitative analysis of autobiographical recall found few overt recall errors and thus supports a partly reconstructive view of autobiographical memory . . . which suggests that recent personal memories are reasonably accurate copies of the individual's original phenomenal experiences.[4]

Given what we just learned, we can give up altogether a more skeptical view, which suggests that perhaps "a large store of memory falls into the category of screen memories" (Freud, *Psychopathology*, 65). What if most of our remembering were a displaced response to reality, and, in the strongest sense, a construction of our minds? Could it be that we are all, collectively and individually, dreaming, fantasizing, or even hallucinating different histories? Eliot and Proust both tease us with the thought that remembering is all too close to dreaming for us not to be lured at times into a world of fantasized memories. Literary minds and psychoanalysts are not alone in deconstructing our easy, confident certainties about what makes up the real world. In discussing amnesia, Oliver Sacks draws on research based on the electrophysiological properties of the brain in waking and dreaming to show how our brains process perception (*Anthropologist*, 57 n. 7). It would seem, Sacks argues, that our waking consciousness functions with exactly the same mechanism as our dreams: it has to meet a ceaseless interplay of image and feeling. The only difference arises when, in an awakened state, we register a sensory input. Then, we move out of a state of "fantasy, hallucination or dream" to respond to the constraints imposed by an external reality.

If indeed most of our mental life is spent dealing with a dream world—if the line that separates a hallucination from a perception is so fine—then rememberers' ability to come up with creditable, organized pictures of their sensory encounters with reality looks like a remarkable feat. We are licensed to dream and to hallucinate, and yet we try, as hard as we can, to awaken to the reality that faces us. In light of our precarious anchoring in reality, Tereshchuk's ability to build a creditable autobiographical memory of a moment that must have been saturated with sensory inputs and sheer terror, strikes me as remarkable. Why blame himself so hard for allowing a stray red beret to make its way into the picture? In the light of all we know, "making sense of the vast mass that we call the world" is cognitively, affectively, and ethically the most challenging of tasks. It is the task that Tereshchuk endorses in adverse circumstances. As he constructs the memory that connects him to a historical event, he shows, in the very failings of his memory, his humanity. In reading Proust, Woolf, Eliot, and Nerval as the exemplary architects and painters of memory images, this book celebrates the elusive complexity and immense richness of autobiographical remembrance. It also documents our ceaseless efforts and accomplishments, as human beings, in mapping out a world that is inflected with existential values. In saying or in writing, "I remember," whether out loud, or on the page, or in the innermost reaches of our minds, we are involved in a linguistic sense-making activity that defines the very conditions of our existence. For in the end, it would seem that our brains—unless they are seriously impaired by an ailment or an injury—are far less messy than the world is. The marvelous constructions of autobiographical memories we studied in this book are a tribute to this triumph—the triumph of mind over matter.

Notes

1. In *Les Maladies de la Mémoire,* Jean Delay thus asserts that "the psychoanalytical school has rethought psychiatry in light of amnesia" (77). Throughout this book, translations from French and German are my own, unless the bibliographic reference corresponds to a translated text.

In order to preserve the clarity and fluidity of my argument, I have chosen for this introduction to reference only the citations that are not discussed elsewhere in this book. Elsewhere, because the critical literature on the literary authors I discuss is immense, I have only cited the works that are directly pertinent to my subject and omitted dozens of books and articles that were consulted in preparation for this book. This means that the bibliography presented at the end is far from exhaustive: it only lists the materials cited in the text or the notes.

2. In Daniel Schacter's definition, episodic memory "allows us to explicitly recall the personal incidents that uniquely define our lives" (*Searching for Memory,* 17). In *Memory from Mind to Molecules,* Larry Squire and Eric Kandel specify that "episodic memory, unlike semantic memory, stores spatial and temporal landmarks that identify the particular time and place when an event occurred" (106). For a detailed discussion, see Martin A. Conway, "Identifying Autobiographical Memory," in *Autobiographical Memory,* as well as David Pillemer, *Momentous Events, Vivid Memories,* 49–51.

3. Looming in the background of his description are the quarrels with formalists and functionalists—and a dismissal of theories arguing that mental processes can be modeled through algorithms and can be simulated through sophisticated computer programs. John Searle provides a useful summary of these controversies in *The Mystery of Consciousness.*

4. As is acknowledged by Gerald Edelman, who writes in *Bright Air, Brilliant Fire* that "science cannot describe individual or historical experience adequately" (163).

5. My thinking of autobiographical memory owes much to three essays by Walter Benjamin: "On Some Motifs in Baudelaire," "The Image of Proust," and "The Work of Art in the Age of Mechanical Reproduction."

6. For a recent survey of this trend, see Bruce Weber's article "It's All about Me, Especially the Ugly Parts," who in sketching out an "amateur literary history" suggests that for the last thirty-five years literature has taken a "direction that has rarely been traveled in the past . . . defined by its most solipsistic elements" (*New York*

Times, January 18, 2004, 12). One must assume that the current success and visibility of personal memoirs and autobiographical confessions in the literary field is part of a more global cultural transformation.

7. Marguerite Holloway reports on Herz's research in "The Ascent of Scent."

8. Esther Salaman, "A Collection of Moments"; and Ernest G. Schactel, "On Memory and Childhood Amnesia."

9. See Stephen S. Hall, "Our Memories, Our Selves," 32.

10. See Sacks's preface to *The Man Who Mistook His Wife for a Hat,* vii–x.

11. I am quoting from an article by Jeet Heer entitled "Haunted," D1.

12. "Pattern" is the word that Woolf uses, as if she were anticipating later psychoanalytic discourse in laying out an existential philosophy founded on memory in "A Sketch of the Past."

13. Among the studies that define the background of my own enquiry are the groundbreaking book *Testimony: Crises in Witnessing in Literature, Psychoanalysis, and History,* by Shoshana Felman and Dori Laub; Cathy Caruth, *Unclaimed Experience: Trauma, Narrative and History* and the volume of essays she edited, *Trauma: Explorations in Memory;* Lawrence L. Langer, *Holocaust Testimonies: The Ruins of Memory;* Andreas Huyssen, *Twilight Memories: Marking Time in a Culture of Amnesia;* two remarkable collections of essays, *Holocaust Remembrance: The Shape of Memory,* ed. by Geoffrey H. Hartman and *Acts of Memory: Cultural Recall in the Present,* ed. by Mieke Bal, Jonathan Crewe, and Leo Spitzer; Eric Santner's *Stranded Objects: Mourning, Memory, and Film in Postwar Germany;* as well as Avishai Margalit's *The Ethics of Memory.*

14. See Annette Wieviorka, "On Testimony," 30.

15. However, several scholars, working in different quarters, have put into question our certainties about trauma and truth—most notably, Allan Young in his examination of PTSD from an anthropological perspective in *The Harmony of Illusions;* Ruth Leys, who examines the contradiction-filled history of the concept of trauma in *Trauma: A Genealogy;* and Frederick Crews, whose book *The Memory Wars: Freud in Dispute* takes the form of a systematic attack on "recovered memory therapy."

16. In "The Man with Two Heads," Elena Lappin lays out in detail the elements of this case, and the result of her research in Switzerland, where Bruno Dösseker (alias Binjamin Wilkomirski) grew up as the adopted child of a well-to-do Zurich doctor.

17. Felman herself discusses the pedagogical aspects of this seminar, but in its first presentation (*Testimony,* 47–56).

18. Felman discusses, in relation to the poem "Todesfuge" by Paul Celan, the tensions between testimony and the aestheticization of "art performance" (*Testimony,* 31–35). The seminal questions about the relation between art and barbarity were raised by Theodor Adorno and George Steiner. For recent studies that focus on questions of history and aesthetics, see in particular Ernst von Alphen, *Caught by History;* and Marianne Hirsch, *Family Frames.*

19. For a brilliant discussion of loss and absence in the terms I have outlined

here, see Richard Stamelman, *Lost Beyond Telling*, in particular the chapter "The Representation of Loss." Georges Poulet discusses the difference between Proustian memory and Mallarmé's conception in emphasizing the negativity that marks the latter's work: "To remember [for Mallarmé] is to look once again into absence and emptiness" (*Interior Distance*, 250–51).

20. I also draw my inspiration from Antonio Damasio, who writes in *The Feeling of What Happens: Body and Emotion in the Making of Consciousness*, "T.S. Eliot might as well have been thinking of the process I described [i.e. consciousness] when he wrote, in the *Four Quartets*, of 'music heard so deeply that it is not heard at all,' and when he said 'you are the music while the music lasts'" (172).

21. For a scientific view of how memory defines the future, see Damasio's discussion of images in *Descartes' Error*, 96–98; for a clinical view, see his discussion of "David" in *Feeling*, 113–21. For a philosophical view, see Gilles Deleuze's presentation of Bergson's conception of duration *(durée)* in the chapter "Memory as Virtual Coexistence" in *Bergsonism*. In his chapter on Proust in *Etudes sur le temps humain*, George Poulet richly develops the argument that Proustian remembrance is turned toward the future.

Chapter 1

1. From *Remembrance of Things Past: Volume 1*, by Marcel Proust, translated by C. K. Scott Moncrieff and Terrence Kilmartin, copyright © 1981 by Random House, Inc., and Chatto & Windus. Used by permission of Random House, Inc. The most up-to-date (but unwieldy) edition of Proust in French is the new 1987 Pléiade edition; I have relied on it as a source of scholarly materials. Otherwise all direct citations from the French refer to the three-volume edition published by Laffont (Bouquins). Whenever the title of a volume is in English, I am referring to the Moncrieff-Kilmartin translation.

2. Involuntary memories have featured in French literature at least since Rousseau, Chateaubriand, Nerval, and Baudelaire, but we owe the concept to Proust.

3. Damasio defines involuntary memories in terms of submerged contents (*Feeling*, 227). Richard Weiner, introducing his survey of different forms of pathological amnesia, intimates that the formulation "a forgotten memory" raises complex issues: "Is the memory forever lost or is it merely beyond retrieval?" (577). Because he is keen on demonstrating the striking aspects of a certain type of memory retrieval, Proust does not dwell on this ambiguity. It leads, however, to crucial questions: are there things we do not remember because we did not register or encode them? or does our brain contain traces or "engrams" that we are unable to activate? These questions lie much beyond the scope of this study, but the epistemological complexity underlying this formulation should not be overlooked.

4. Next to Linton, there are a number of psychologists who, starting with

William Bartlett, published groundbreaking work in this new field of memory research, most prominently Endel Tulving, William Brewer, Ulric Neisser, and, pursuing her own original method, Esther Salaman.

5. Thought experiments are "controlled exercises of the imagination in which test cases are envisaged with a view to establishing their conceptual coherence or their compatibility with some proposed theory," says the *Oxford Companion to Philosophy*, ed. by Ted Honderich. David Gooding suggests that such experiments "are powerful because they appeal to lived experience of a world which their narratives reflect, selectively, back at us" (*Routledge Encyclopedia of Philosophy*, ed. by Edward Craig). In *Bright Air, Brilliant Fire* Gerald Edelman stipulates that gedankenexperiments represent a scientifically valid way of testing and analyzing consciousness, but "any properties postulated must be completely consistent with presently known scientific observations from whatever field of inquiry and, above all, with those of brain science" (113).

6. In *Le Temps retrouvé*, Proust himself compares his method to that of scientist, emphasizing his reliance on induction: "Impression is for the writer what experiments are for the scientist, with the difference that for the scientist intelligence comes first, while for the writer it comes after" (*Recherche*, 3:713). In "What Is Science?" J. M. Ziman argues, however, that "science arrives at Truth by logical inferences from empirical observations" (4). He suggests, moreover, that induction (Proust's method) is favored by "most serious philosophers" and represents a leading influence on the work of practical scientists.

7. For a discussion of Proust's "tentative and aborted experiences," see Samuel Beckett, *Proust*, 23–25.

8. In this respect, the study of memory is no different from other kinds of sciences, such as "astronomy or geology, where we can only observe the consequences of events and circumstances over which we have no control" (Ziman, 4).

9. From a letter to Antoine Bibesco, dated November 1912, quoted by Paul Vernière in "Proust et les deux mémoires," 945–46.

10. The best and richest discussion of such associations from a literary and philosophical perspective is to be found in Christie McDonald's *The Proustian Fabric: Associations of Memory*.

11. In *Le Sens de la mémoire* Jean-Yves Tadié and Marc Tadié write, "Proust understood that he could not construct his novel on involuntary memory alone, which is too rare and too aleatory; it had to be nested in voluntary memory" (207). Paul Vernière takes a different direction in emphasizing that the distinction between these two forms of memory is not as steadfast as Proust makes it; he acknowledges, meanwhile, that involuntary memory provides the author with a valuable moment of illumination, with a discovery that is not merely intellectual but one that in fact "poeticizes" memory (938, 948–49). The distinction between voluntary and involuntary memory is discussed below.

12. Penfield's work, done jointly with P. Perrot, was published under the title "The Brain's Record of Visual and Auditory Experience," creating a stir when it came out in 1963. It is often referred to in the literature on episodic memory. This is how Sacks describes the experiment: "Penfield was not only able to locate the origin

of [reminiscences] in the temporal lobes, but was able to *evoke* the 'elaborate mental state,' or the extremely precise and detailed 'experiential hallucinations' of such seizures by gentle electrical stimulation of the seizure-prone points of the cerebral cortex, as this was exposed, at surgery, in fully conscious patients" (*Man Who*, 137). Penfield's findings turned out to be more problematic than he or Sacks had initially envisaged. It seems that the stimulation created, in most cases, what were in fact false memories (Schacter, *Searching for Memory*, 77–78).

13. For a rich and thoughtful presentation of the variety of terms used to define personal remembrance and the nuances among them, see David B. Pillemer's *Momentous Events, Vivid Memories*, 49–52.

14. Around a hundred neurotransmitters are involved. The most important ones are well known: dopamime, serotonin, acetylcholine, norepinephrine, and glutamate. In *Science and Structure in Proust's A la Recherche du temps perdu*, Nicola Luckhurst discusses the chemical analogy (56–57), emphasizing that the metaphor "involuntary memory-chemistry" stands out "amongst the overwhelming prolific scientific metaphors" of this work. Luckhurst's book, which appeared when this chapter was already well under way, provides an illuminating commentary on a number of issues I discuss: she argues as I do that "Proust is at once a scientist and a poet" (31).

15. Psychological studies on autobiographical memory and olfaction in psychology appear to have found confirmation in recent neurobiological work on memory and emotion. Odors have an unrivaled ability to "reach" the emotional parts of the brain (the amygdala, in particular), and thus to prompt vivid, emotion-laden mnemonic images. I thank my students at Boston University, Caitlin Bonney and Shane Smith, for their research on this subject. I develop the theme of odor memory in chapter 6, "Proustian Memory Gardens."

16. Proust also discusses sensory promptings that arise within the body, as I show briefly below, as well as in chapters 9 and 10.

17. See in particular the work of Israel Rosenfield, *The Strange, Familiar, and Forgotten*, and of Antonio Damasio, *Descartes's Error* and *The Feeling of What Happens*. In their research on consciousness and memory, Sacks, Edelman, Rosenfield, and Damasio have each in their own way questioned the traditional boundaries between body and mind, enlisting neurology, physiology, and biology to study aspects of the human psyche.

18. Edelman provides a scientific definition of memory that emphasizes its dynamic and performative aspects: "a physiological basis for memory—synaptic change—is often mistakenly equated with memory itself in an attempt to simplify matters. To clarify the issue, let us agree that, whatever form it takes, memory is the ability to *repeat a performance*. The kind of performance depends on the structure of the system in which memory is manifest, for memory is a system property" (*Bright Air*, 102; emphasis added).

19. Thus in *The Mystery of Consciousness*, John Searle summarizes Rosenfield's view in the following way: "When I form an image of some event in my childhood for example, I don't go into an archive and find a preexisting image, I have to consciously form an image" (184). Edelman insists that "above all, biological memory

is not a replica or trace that is coded to represent its object" (*Bright Air*, 238). For Damasios' comments on this subject, see chapter 5, "Screen Memories."

20. In studying autobiographical memory, William Brewer comes to similar conclusions: very soon, an autobiographical memory becomes a fact, albeit a personal fact. In his groundbreaking essay "What Is Autobiographical Memory," he thus establishes a detailed classification of memories related to the self on a scale in which memories become increasingly less subjective. They end up shifting from the category of episodic memory to that of semantic memories (in Rubin, *Autobiographical Memory*, 26).

21. If there is a Bergsonian dimension to Proust's treatment of memory, it lies in this broad distinction between mechanical, habit-driven memory and a creative, dynamic form of recall that brings up new images in the rememberer's consciousness. The seminal texts on this subject are *Essai sur les données immédiates de la conscience (Time and Free Will)* and *Matière et mémoire (Matter and Memory)*. For Proust just as for Bergson, habit, which turns emotions into mere reflexes and generally dulls our sensibility to impressions, is memory's worst enemy. Proustian memories are typically born in the midst of a mechanical, habitual action.

22. I borrow this evocative formulation from Oliver Sacks's study of the "Lost Mariner" in *The Man Who Mistook His Wife for a Hat*, 29.

23. "Sleep is a natural state of unconsciousness," Damasio writes as he investigates body-states as states of consciousness. As we shall see, his presentation of consciousness (particularly *Feeling* 250–54) overlaps, in a striking fashion, with Proust's phenomenological description.

24. The technical term for such sensations is *proprioceptive*, a term often used by phenomenologists, (Merleau-Ponty and Sartre among others), which has been revived in a psychoanalytical context (see, for instance, Kaja Silverman, *Threshold of the Visible World*). Antonio Damasio, meanwhile, uses the term *somato-sensory* to define, similarly, our awareness of inner, sometimes visceral, bodily states.

25. In his essay "On Practice," Montaigne analyzes his physical and mental sensations after a fall from his horse, when he finds himself "with no more movement or sensation than a log" and has "no idea where [he] was coming from nor where [he] was going to" (421–22). In the second chapter of his *Rêveries d'un promeneur solitaire*, Rousseau analyzes his sensations after falling under a carriage. He "did not remember anything" and "had not the least idea of what had happened to [him]" (*Reveries of a Solitary*, 48). These texts representing "awakenings" are classics of French literature, and Proust must have known them. We have no evidence that he had them in mind when composing this scene, except perhaps for the phrase "sentiment de l'existence," which is to be found in Rousseau (see below, n. 26).

26. This phrase appears in Rousseau's "Cinquième promenade," whose first few pages can be read, in a phenomenological vein, as an exploration of the relation between bodily sensation, perception, and consciousness.

27. In transient global amnesia as described by Damasio, "a person is suddenly deprived of the records that have been recently added to the autobiographical memory" and is "thus deprived of both personal historical provenance and personal

future but retains core consciousness for the events and objects in the here and now" (*Feeling*, 203). The distinction between a primitive, minimal form of consciousness ("core consciousness") and extended consciousness (which corresponds to what philosophers commonly call consciousness and is specifically human) lies at the center of *The Feeling of What Happens*. In discussing this case of mild transient global amnesia, Damasio is able to offer a vivid illustration of the passage from one to the other: while she experiences global amnesia, this patient still retains core consciousness.

28. The style of their remarks is naturally different: hers are concrete and practical as befits a situation that is fraught with anxiety: what if she does not remember who she is? Proust's rememberer, by contrast, clearly enjoys this moment of uncertainty filled with imaginative possibilities, and seems to luxuriate in his creative work of recollection: for him, the answers to these questions are at hand—not so, however, for Damasio's patient.

29. A striking neurological case of amnesia discussed by Schacter in *Searching for Memory* seems to confirm the long-held idea (since Plato) that writing and remembering can be interchangeable. Schacter presents the story of Neil, who became amnesiac as a result of a treatment for a brain tumor, as an example of the complexities surrounding the question of mnemonic retrieval (66). Neil, it turned out, could only remember past events in writing. Because he could no longer read and could also not remember what he had written, his personal memories had to be read out to him, and sometimes even needed to be identified for him as such (64–69).

30. Sacks makes this point (*Man Who*, 124). David Hume develops his well-known thesis on the connection between memory and identity in part 4, section 6, "Of Personal Identity," in book 1 of his *Treatise of Human Nature* and concludes: "As memory alone acquaints us with the continuance and extent of this succession of perceptions, 'tis to be considered upon that account chiefly, as the source of personal identity."

31. Under the title *Le réveil dans la chambre obscure* ("Waking up in a dark room"), Jean-Yves Tadié's "genetic" edition of Proust's text (published in the Pléiade collection) presents the many drafts that led up to the extraordinary first sentence of his novel. The present-perfect tense used in the final version establishes, once and for all, the time of the novel as a seamless continuity between the hero's adventures in time and the narrator's project writing on times past.

32. Damasio argues that autobiographical memories form a "backdrop for our minds" and wonders whether their constant activation is not "an intolerable burden for neurons." The metaphor I use is inspired by his suggestion that the heart is similarly "sentenced for life to . . . repeated contractions" (*Feeling*, 224).

33. Quoted by Sacks in the chapter "Reminiscence" in *The Man Who Mistook His Wife for a Hat*, 148.

34. Jean-Yves and Marc Tadié discuss this point in *Le Sens de la mémoire*, suggesting that scientists prefer to speak of emotional memory, or sometimes more pointedly of *mémoire sensitive*, which "floods us with the sensation felt in the past

before or even without the memory image's coming into consciousness" (177). This latter definition overlaps with what I have called, relying partly on Sacks's work and partly on literary discussions, "Proustian memory."

35. Thus, Damasio argues, from the perspective of neuroscience, that memories are different for each of us because they arise within certain dispositions made of earlier sedimented and reclassified perceptions (*Feeling*, 223).

36. Edelman discusses qualia as a feature of higher consciousness, defining them as "the qualitative, phenomenal or 'felt' properties of our mental states" (*Bright Air*, 114–16). I develop the subject of memory and of *qualia* in the chapter "Painting the Past: Virginia Woolf's Memory Images."

37. These examples refer to a widely used categorization of memory, into semantic, procedural, and episodic memory. Semantic memory enables us to retain facts (it corresponds to our "general knowledge of the world"), procedural memory corresponds to skills, and episodic memory (of which Proustian memory is a subset) "allows us to recollect specific incidents from our pasts." See Daniel Schacter's summary definition in *Searching for Memory*, 135–36.

38. I am well aware that with this assertion I pick up the terms of a rich scientific debate (whose underpinnings are ultimately philosophical) on the nature of the brain and the mind. Sacks merely hints at it in the postscript to "Reminiscence," in speaking of the limitations of a cybernetic model. Gerald Edelman discounts the Turing machine as a valid model for the brain (*Bright Air*, 60, 220–23). In *The Mystery of Consciousness*, John Searle analyzes the debate around materialist or reductionist models versus phenomenological ones (predicated on "qualia") that unfolded in the *New York Review of Books* between 1995 and 1997. He discusses the Turing machine on pp. 10–12.

39. "To carry out referral, a formal representation must become an intentional one. In human beings, this requires a consciousness and a self—a biologically based personal awareness, a first person," writes Edelman, *Bright Air*, 238.

40. Sacks discusses the history of clinical tales and their value for a "neurology of identity" in the preface to *The Man Who Mistook His Wife for a Hat*.

41. I discuss in chapter 9, "The Rememberer's Task," a significant example of painful memory in Proust's *Recherche*.

42. Mrs. O'C., who is elderly and somewhat deaf, suffers from temporal seizures during which she hears "old Irish songs." Sacks quotes her own evocative description of Proustian memories: "I know I'm an old woman with a stroke in an old people's home, but I feel I'm a child in Ireland again—I feel my mother's arms, I see her, I hear her voice singing" (*Man Who*, 137).

43. To be absolutely clear in my definition of Proustian memory, I must specify here that I reserve this term for vivid, emotion-laden recollections that constitute so-called happy memories. As this book unfolds, however, the issue of unhappy or traumatic memories will be envisaged as well. Proustian memories and traumatic memories show many similar phenomenal features, but the emotional aspects of traumatic recollection are very complex and require separate study, which I develop in connection with Virginia Woolf in the last two chapters of this book.

44. The telling word, in Proust's description, is "lost" *(perdu)*: the past was "lost

forever," until it was miraculously recovered through the power of involuntary memory. In a similar vein, Sacks comments on Mrs. O'C.: "she recaptured a crucial sense of her forgotten, lost childhood" (*Man Who*, 143).

45. These reflections on memory's aesthetic dimensions are deeply informed by the conception of aesthetic experience that Peter de Bolla develops in *Art Matters*.

46. He develops this argument in section 3 (on poetry) of his lectures on aesthetics. See Hegel, *Vorlesungen über die Aesthetik*, 431–35 in particular.

47. In chapter 9, "The Rememberer's Task," I discuss Lou Andreas-Salomé's article on the subject of memory, "Narzissmus als Doppelrichtung" ("The Dual Orientation of Narcissism"). As a philosopher and psychoanalyst, she points out that very little room is made for personal memory in a practically oriented existence. In "On Some Motifs in Baudelaire," 157–58, Benjamin also shows that Proustian memory is the product of a *vita contemplativa*.

Chapter 2

1. I want to consider beginnings and thus the emergence of Woolf's first memories. My analysis bears essentially on "A Sketch of the Past," 67–69.

2. The idea that imagination and memory involve the seeing of internal pictures is already present in Plato. There are some important landmarks in the history of this philosophical debate: in British empiricism, Locke and Hume (see Sutton, in particular 193–95); in the modern era, Henri Bergson, *Matière et Mémoire* (1900) and Jean-Paul Sartre *L'Imagination* and *L'Imaginaire*. I discuss some of the recent work on memory and image by cognitive psychologists in the coming chapters.

3. Arguably however, one could also consider the material aspects of writing: thus, the pen and the paper, for example, or the page. These define the most immediate physical space where writing and remembering emerge.

4. In *Descartes's Error*, 280 n. 3, Antonio Damasio writes that "the value accorded to images is a recent development, part of the cognitive revolution that followed the long night of stimulus-response behaviorism" and singles out the work of Roger Shepard and Stephen Kosslyn. Presenting the different trends in the contemporary work of cognitive scientists in *Dreaming by the Book*, Elaine Scarry makes the distinction between "pictorialists" (who believe in mental images) and "descriptionists" (who believe no such images exist in the mind). She sides, as I do, with those who believe in images, namely with the pictorialists (258–59 n. 6).

5. As he examines Descartes's conception of "animal spirits," John Sutton explores the epistemological difficulties that arise from the fact that we must try "to picture the unseen." He thus begins this section of his book, suggestively titled "Ontologies of the Invisible," with the question, "why should we believe in what we cannot see?" (119–21).

6. Damasio develops the question "Will We Ever Experience the Consciousness of Another" in pages 305–9 of *The Feeling of What Happens* and concludes: "The mind and its consciousness are first and foremost private phenomena, much as they offer many public signs of their existence to the interested observer" (308).

7. Damasio can help us clarify this distinction: "When I use the term *image*, I always mean *mental* image. A synonym for images is *mental pattern*. I do not use the word image to refer to the pattern of neural activities that can be found, with current neuroscience methods, in activated sensory cortices" (*Feeling*, 317). I follow his definition, where images are "mental patterns built with the tokens of each of the sensory modalities—visual, auditory, olfactory, gustatory, and somatosensory" (318).

8. As I show in chapter 6, "Proustian Memory-Gardens," Proust is similarly intent on exploring mental life and consciousness, as his many explicit declarations about *la vie intellectuelle* or *la vie de l'esprit* confirm.

9. Scenes have come to represent an important concept in the sciences as well. Thus Edelman sees in an animal's ability to categorize and bind unconnected parts of the world into a *scene* the basis for primary consciousness. For him scenes are "a spatiotemporally ordered set of categorizations of familiar and nonfamiliar events, *some with and some without necessary physical or causal connections to others in the same scene*" (118). The Tadiés note that a "particularly salient event 'engrams' everything that surrounds it, including details that would otherwise have been forgotten, just as the fall of a bomb will dig around its impacting point a crater that is larger than the bomb itself" (118). Neisser writes similarly, but relying on the concept of "nested structures," about our ability to glide, mentally, from "molar units" to larger, extended contexts (75). Thus for him, too, images are placed within the larger frame of a scene.

10. Hermione Lee shows in *Virginia Woolf* that the author returned many times in her fiction to the same kinds of memory images, "like a painter making repeated versions of the same subject." She gives examples from *Jacob's Room*, from *The Waves* and its drafts, as well as *To the Lighthouse*. But Woolf "makes sure that her deepest memory is disguised or displaced: 'This shall be Childhood: but it must not be *my* childhood,' as she says of *The Waves*" (23–25).

11. Note how our rememberer imposes fine sensory discriminations on what is one of her first memories, a memory that, as I show, seems otherwise made of such primitive components as light and darkness, and the most primitive of rhythms. Could it be then that the little acorn, just like the anemones on her mother's dress, is truly the product of a retrospective construction or projection around what was initially an ill-defined, inchoate image?

12. Not only does Woolf present two memories that could each be the first, she also presents the same memories several times in her text.

13. This process is best seen in the first memory, where colorful blots are only gradually labeled as anemones.

14. I owe this idea to Joanna Spiro's very insightful discussion of self and estrangement in Woolf's text (20–29).

15. For Woolf's theory concerning "moments of being," see "A Sketch of the Past," 70, from which I borrow the image of cotton wool.

16. I am citing Jean Guillaumin here, who shows how the Henris' work relates to Freud's own questionings on the construction of memory (*La Genèse du souvenir*, 122).

17. See, for example the passages I quote in chapter 1.

18. Jean-Paul Sartre's early work *L'Imagination* provides us with one of the best discussions of a phenomenological conception of the image. Sartre presents, in this book, a detailed historical critique of the role played by images in philosophical theories of consciousness, and demonstrates that phenomenology created a decisive epistemological break when Edmund Husserl determined that these images had to be seen as distinct from the subject's mind. Devoid of sensory contents *(contenus sensibles)*, they occupy a transitional space, and can no longer be said to inhabit the mind as a mental content *(un contenu psychique)*. They exist at the boundary between the inner and outer worlds (between consciousness as such and the object apprehended by consciousness) and their reality and substance is inherently "psychical."

To use a more current psychological formulation, images are a *mental* phenomenon. Sartre summarizes this finding with a resounding phrase, which he offers as the new definition of the image in phenomenology: "l'image est une réalité psychique certaine"—which can be paraphrased as "an image is undoubtedly a mental reality" or "an image constitutes an incontrovertible psychical reality" (158).

19. Thus, Sartre claims, "we could very well assimilate the perception of a picture *as image* to the intellectual apprehension of a psychic (mental) content" (*L'Imagination*, 149).

20. Gerald Edelman devotes his book *The Remembered Present* to discussion of this loop, from a perspective that is biological and neurological as well as philosophical.

21. The connection between mental images and images in literature is thus often made—in terms of literary construction, of fiction or of storytelling. In *Evolution de la mémoire et de la notion du temps*, Pierre Janet writes that "memory is a literary construction that occurred slowly through a gradual perfecting" (242). In *L'Imagination*, Jean-Paul Sartre notes that for the phenomenologist, "the 'exemplary' *donnée*" is often a pure fiction, created in imagination (141). Damasio writes that "the imagetic representation of sequences of brain events" constitutes a form of "wordless story telling," and he adds that "the entire construction of knowledge, from simple to complex, from nonverbal imagetic to verbal literary, depends on the ability to map what happens over time." This process, which amounts to consciousness and "registers what happens in the form of brain maps," is compared to "telling stories" (*Feeling*, 189).

22. This is, for Woolf, a characteristic image for the mind: repeatedly in her writing, especially in her diaries, the mental space is likened to an unfathomable and at times dangerous medium that threatens to submerge the subject. Not here, however, where the image of the sea is devoid of affective connotations. But it might have led, by association, to the next image: that of the color blue.

23. Proust, similarly, seeks to establish a relation between his aesthetic practice and the phenomenon of memory. But his model is less straightforward. In the long section on memory in *Le Temps retrouvé*, his narrator claims that *metaphors*, which enable "the miracle of analogy," can trace a reality that fuses present and past sensations into a "remembered present," creating an enhanced, "truer" reality (*Recherche*, 3:720).

Chapter 3

1. Freud sets up the puzzling nature of this question in vivid terms in *The Psychopathology of Everyday Life*. As this formulation reveals, it is deeply embedded in his theorization of repression: "We forget how high the intellectual achievements and how complicated the emotional impulse of which a child of some four years is capable, and we ought to be positively astonished that the memory of later years has as a rule preserved so little of these mental processes" (66). Jean-Yves and Marc Tadié propose these three divergent accounts of childhood amnesia in a summary in *Le Sens de la Mémoire* (37). David Pillemer presents an excellent overview as well as an analysis, from a psychological perspective, of this issue in *Momentous Events, Vivid Memories* (see in particular p. 20 as well as pp. 108–15). In "Childhood Amnesia: An Empirical Demonstration," the psychologists Scott E. Wetzler and John A. Sweeney present a wealth of data destined to support what "has been a confusing array of anecdotal evidence and ingenious theoretical suppositions" (199). Among neuroscientists, Joseph LeDoux invokes the insufficient development of the hippocampus, while George McKee and Larry Squire consider the insufficient maturation of neurocortical structures.

2. The phenomenological aspects of illness and its relation to imagination and creation are the heart of Woolf's essay "On Being Ill" (see my article "Speculating Carnally"). Hermione Lee's chapter in *Virginia Woolf* entitled "Madness" offers, together with Woolf's own diaries, what is to my mind the best account of Woolf's illness.

3. Here I follow Sartre's definition in *L'Imaginaire*, 287.

4. I pursue this issue in chapter 8, "Textures of the Past" as well as chapter 10, "Virginia Woolf's Life Writing."

5. Woolf explicitly refers to such memory scenes on pp. 71 and 79 of "A Sketch of the Past." Meanwhile, Ian Hacking makes a compelling case, in *Rewriting the Soul*, for conceiving of autobiographical memories as scenes (see in particular pp. 251–55).

6. In a broader perspective (such as Damasio's), which does not focus exclusively on autobiographical recollection, memories do not necessarily have the narrative, episodic qualities that we are studying. They can be a feature of behavior, and can thus be activated as movement, motor action, and emotion.

7. In *Being and Nothingness (L'Etre et le néant)*, Jean-Paul Sartre considers, briefly, the situation of empathy where affect, and not memories, is transferred from one subject to another. Referring to James Baldwin's psychological theories, he writes: "this author has indeed established that we can experience certain emotions in our affects, without feeling them concretely" (379). From a psychoanalytic perspective, one could also invoke the Freudian notion of identification. Meanwhile, Edelman's approach, with which we started, does not consider affective elements and focuses exclusively on epistemological issues.

8. Countertransference defines the affective dimensions, unconscious feelings and desire, that link the analyst to the analysand. Moving out of a "purely objective" epistemological frame, I consider here that the analyst is to the reader what the

analysand is to the rememberer. The notion of countertransference is richly defined by J. Laplanche and J.-B. Pontalis in *The Language of Psychoanalysis.*

9. "Instead of remembering here a scene and there a sound, I shall fit a plug into the wall; and listen in to the past. I shall turn up August 1890. I feel strong emotion must leave its trace" ("A Sketch," 67).

10. Laplanche and Pontalis remind us that *Nachträglichkeit* (deferred action) represents a central concept of Freud's thought and provide a lucid and rich survey of this notion. In "Freud and the Uses of Forgetting," Adam Phillips comments on this concept in the following way: "Meaning is made, according to Freud, in the revision consequent upon deferral. The status, or the state, of what is forgotten is, in his account, indeterminate, so memory is a way of inventing the past" (34).

11. In her mystical moments, Woolf appears to think for a moment that "things we have felt with great intensity have an existence independent of our minds," thereby repeating Proust's compelling creed in *A la Recherche du temps perdu* that with memory we can overcome death. (But unlike Proust, she makes no attempt to build a consistent philosophy or metaphysics of memory; in her case, the moment of transcendence is brought back to a psychological state of "rapture" or an "ecstasy.")

Chapter 4

1. As is shown by Jean Guillaumin (9), Husserl's conception of memory relies on the concept of *Urdoxa* or *Urglaube,* developed in *Phänomenologie des Inneren Zeitbewusstseins.* Thus, in his discussion of memory the phenomenologist invokes a central philosophical premise: that of our strong, unalloyed, and "originary" belief in the reality of experience. In this conception, our belief in the reality of memory is sustained by our other belief in the reality of our experience in the world. Guillaumin writes: "[Memory] involves a particular form of complex belief, which is founded on a more general characteristic of consciousness: 'originary belief,' 'pure belief in the strongest sense' in the reality of experience. In the experience of remembering, the assertion of reality is posited in the past" (9).

2. The common assumption is that memories "depict" for us what are past events. This is why, no doubt, we so easily think of memory in terms of likeness, or of some mimetic reproduction. Discussing the origins of memory as image, and as the image of something, Richard Sorabji provides in *Aristotle on Memory* a truly enlightening commentary on the issue of mimesis and memory (2–8).

3. The memory experiment I consider in this section corresponds to the first chapter of Eliot's novel, "Outside Dorlcote Mill," 53–55.

4. "Movies are the closest external representation of the prevailing storytelling that goes on in our minds. What goes on within each shot, the different framing of a subject . . . what goes on in the transition shots achieved by editing, and what goes on in the narrative constructed by a particular juxtaposition of shots is comparable in some respects to what is going on in the mind" (Damasio, *Feeling,* 188).

5. In *Dreaming by the Book,* Elaine Scarry argues that verbal, literary images come to life or "acquire vivacity" when they match perceptual schemes—"imaginary

vivacity comes about by reproducing the deep structures of perception" (9)—and shows how "the verbal arts constantly engage us in moving pictures" (35). I argue similarly that it is by following a recognizable perceptual structure that Eliot's description invites us to "move into" a memory picture. I develop this structural approach more fully in the next chapter.

6. In fact, Freud himself owes his awareness of this distinction to earlier research. In 1886, in a survey involving more than a hundred cases where subjects were asked to recount childhood memories, Victor and Catherine Henri discovered that we typically "see" memories of ourselves from two possible perspectives: in one perspective, the past self is embedded in the memory; in the other, it takes shape from an observer's position, from the vantage point of the one who looks in onto the scene (see Guillaumin, 125).

7. The claims that Damasio makes for consciousness and individuality correspond to the Tadiés' similar conviction that memory and personality are related: "The way in which we perceive our sensations cannot be dissociated from our personality. . . . Couldn't we go so far as to say that only the sensations kept in our memory are constitutive of our personality, because they marked and fashioned our brain?" (310); "Our memories must adhere to the conception we have of ourselves in the present and toward the future" (329).

8. Each of our rememberers occupies a different place and symbolic stance: in Eliot, the daydreamer's armchair; in Proust, the dreamer's bed. In "A Sketch of the Past," Woolf places her rememberer at her desk—as she did with the figure of the "lady-writer" in *The Waves* (see pp. 12 and 224, for example).

9. This is also Scarry's argument in *Dreaming by the Book*. She studies the realism of such writers as Hardy, Emily Brontë, Huysmans, Proust, and Homer, as instances of perceptual mimesis (see in particular 6, 9, 23, 34–35), and argues that writers provide their readers with instructions for forming mental images: "literature consists of a steady stream of erased imperatives" (35).

10. "A Sketch of the Past" 79, 64, and 66; *Swann's Way*, 200, 202. "The novelist is the memorialist of what appear to be the most ordinary perceptions" (Tadié and Tadié, 109).

Chapter 5

1. This chapter focuses especially on the 1899 essay "Screen Memories." But I refer as well to the chapter "Childhood Memories and Screen Memories," in *The Psychopathology of Everyday Life* (1901), from which I cite the phrase on the tendentiousness of memory, 62. As is rightly pointed out by Edward Joseph, Freud's essay "Construction in Analysis" (1937) *SE,* vol. 13, provides a pendant to Freud's earlier theorization of screen memories. It is there that the phrases "kernel of truth" and "the conviction of the truth of the construction" can be found (269, 266). Joseph (himself a psychoanalyst) also notes that "papers on 'the sense of conviction' are rare" (569).

2. Ned Lukacher's *Primal Scenes: Literature, Philosophy, and Psychoanalysis*

develops this question extensively. He shows that "the notions of memory, the event, and the subject have [lost] their constructive form and become nothing" (13).

3. Gelley, 157, quotes from Percy Lubbock's groundbreaking study in narratology, *The Craft of Fiction.*

4. In *La Relation d'inconnu,* Guy Rosolato provides the following summary definition of a screen memory: "It is an ordinary-looking memory whose apparent banality helps to hide something" (198). For further discussions of screen memories that center on the truth/fiction debate, see, besides Joseph, Phyllis Greenacre, "A Contribution to the Study of Screen Memories"; Eugene Mahon and Delia Battin-Mahon, "The Fate of Screen Memories in Psychoanalysis"; and Michael Good, "Screen Reconstructions."

5. The definition emerges from Freud's analysis of one of his own memories: "When I began in my forty-third year to direct my interest to what was left of my memory of my own childhood there came to my mind a scene which had for a long while back (from the remotest past, as it seemed to me) come into consciousness from time to time, and which I had good evidence for assigning to a date before the end of my third year" (*Psychopathology,* 70). The memory Freud describes shows him crying, as a young child, in front of a wardrobe. Self-analysis will reveal that this seemingly insignificant episode is as a "cover up" for a truly significant event in his childhood: the birth of a sibling. Freud's own childhood memory is thus enlisted to illustrate the concept of screen memory.

6. It could be argued that analogous discrepancies or "disidentifications" are often produced through writing. For instance, two separate personae are involved in the conflicted interpretation of the opening scene of *The Mill the Floss* and are implicitly involved in a dialogue: the "I now" (known as the author George Eliot) and the "I then" whose experiences are recounted, a younger Mary Ann Evans.

7. In "Childhood in Autobiography," Eric LaGuardia rightly remarks on the epistemological confusion that might arise from Freud's rhetorical choice: "The rhetorical strategy of 'Screen Memories' has a strange correlation with the theory it propounds. In talking to himself in this self-fulfilling manner Freud engages in a game of pre-determined meanings raising the very issue of the fictional vs. the genuine to which the essay is addressed" (301). In this reading, Freud's strategy fails to produce one coherent solution or meaning to the issue since it reproduces the very divisions that it tries to surmount.

8. Here is how Guillaumin defines the relation between memory and desire in Freud's conception: "The secret of memory is a kind of myth, in the strong sense of the term, that is, a fictionalized elaboration of the past, woven with affect and fantasies, whose essentially subjective value is established in function of the subject's present needs and desires. In short, [Freud is now] certain that to remember is not so much to remember the past as it was as to be moved about it and to experience it in the way that our desires have outlined it" (134).

9. I have interpreted Freud's conception of screen memories phenomenologically, which is what enables me to relate it to Damasio's work. It should be noted, however, that there is a limit to this comparison, since a psychoanalytic understanding of screen memory will necessarily assume that a powerful psychological mecha-

nism—repression—plays an essential role in the ways in which we "manage" and acknowledge mental images.

10. "The images that we reconstitute in recall occur side by side with images formed upon stimulation from the exterior. The images reconstituted from the brain's interior are less vivid than those prompted by the exterior. They are 'faint,' as Hume put it, in comparison with the 'lively' images generated by stimuli from outside the brain" (Damasio, *Descartes' Error*, 108). For a rich and lucid discussion of images that bridges the gap between a literary and a scientific conception of the image, see "What Is an Image?" in W. J. T. Mitchell, *Iconology*, in particular 9–14 and 17.

11. See "A Sketch of the Past," 67 and my discussion in chapter 1.

12. In "Construction in Analysis," Freud returns to the issue of hallucination as a way of identifying memory. He thus writes: "These recollections might have been described as hallucinations *if a belief in their actual presence had been added to their clearness*" (*SE*, 23:266; emphasis added). The discussion that ensues makes it clear that at this later point, Freud is ready to "deconstruct" the difference between memory and hallucination. But his earlier essay on screen memories makes it clear already that hallucinatory vividness is not a good factor when it comes to discriminating genuine from false memories.

13. Roland Barthes's discussion of photography in *Camera Lucida* provides us with a useful analogy through his concept of punctum—as the arresting detail that brings a photograph to life for the viewer. Though an element that is to be found in the picture, the punctum is essentially (and initially at least, until it is described to another) visible to one subject alone, to whom it speaks of a singular quality—phenomenal as well as emotional—that the photograph elicits. The small, evocative detail, Barthes argues, is what brings us closest to the reality of what the photograph represents. In fact, as Jacques Derrida has argued in "Les Morts de Roland Barthes," it is present not as part of a code of signifiers, but on the contrary as the "referent" of the picture (272). Similarly, in the meadow scene, the yellow flower or the bread suggests to Freud the existence of a referent. The analogy can be stretched even further when we consider what Derrida argues about subjectivity and the punctum, namely that it has a "dative or accusative function whereby it addresses *me* or is destined *to me*." The mnemonic representation that we are studying in Freud guarantees both a reality and a subject through the phenomenally more present details or punctum inscribed in the scene.

14. Analyzing memory, Freud comes to conclusions that are strikingly similar to those of Roland Barthes in his examination of realist writing. Barthes argues that it is the meaningless detail that is the true index of reality or produces "the effect of reality" (see "L'Effet de réel"). In *Momentous Events, Vivid Memories*, David Pillemer notes that "memories of apparently trivial details can fulfill important psychological functions, which are distinct from the deliberate transmission of central messages" (62). Among these functions there is, then, a phenomenological anchoring in a sense of reality. I pursue this subject in the next chapter.

15. Freud endorses Charcot's distinction between two types of rememberers: the *visuels* and the *auditifs/moteurs*. One can speculate that in his professional capacity,

Freud, given his involvement in the "talking cure," would have been "hearing" more than "seeing" memories. Meanwhile, the strikingly plastic dimensions of the meadow scene are almost a giveaway: "In my own case," Freud writes, "the earliest childhood memories are the only ones of a visual character: they are regular scenes worked out in plastic form, comparable only to representations on the stage" (*Psychopathology*, 68).

16. "Hysterics," as is well known, "suffer mainly from reminiscences." The hysterical subject presented by Freud and Breuer in *Studies on Hysteria* lives and suffers out of a need to revisit the past. See p. 7, for example.

17. John Robinson's conception of memory thus relies implicitly on intentionality, as did Alexander Gelley's model of the scene that I discussed above. Like consciousness, it is directed toward an object, and for him memory is not merely a function, but an act that is determined by its object.

18. Robinson can thus conclude that "memory perspective could be interpreted as a metaphoric mapping of spatial relations onto various mnemonic qualities and objectives" (240). The word *affects,* which I use, emphasizes the psychological underpinnings of what Robinson describes, a little too blandly, as "mnemonic qualities and objectives."

19. In his discussion of nostalgia, Vladimir Jankélévich evokes in a similar vein "the unappeasable foreboding *(inquiétude)*" that characterizes the desire for a return into the country of the past. "What makes the illness incurable," he writes, "is the irreversibility of time" (298).

20. Proust, in a passage of "Combray" that I will discuss at length in the next chapter, evokes details of a remembered landscape that have "a charm, a significance that is for [the rememberer] alone" (*Swann's Way*, 202).

21. Freud, "The Uncanny," *SE* 17:223.

22. Yet here again, in giving prominence to the image of the fire, Eliot dwells on a perceptual intensity, hinting at its particular "mnemonic value." This fire, it should be noted, marks the passage between the memory and the beginning of the fiction proper, with "Mr and Mrs Tulliver . . . talking . . . as they sat by the bright fire in the left-hand parlour" (55).

23. In his essay "On Being Bored," Adam Phillips writes about events that might change "the shapes of a life" and reflects on the contingent nature of the Proustian moment: "We are drawn, in fact, to ask a brash question: a *madeleine* or an analyst? An analysis can at least be arranged. But it cannot, alas, organize epiphanies, or guarantee those processes of transformation—those articulations—that return the future to us through the past" (*On Kissing,* 77).

24. The Proustian rememberer reveals his addiction to memory in *Contre Sainte Beuve,* when he confesses that he has often been spotted by his friends in the typical remembering stance: frozen, as if spellbound, midway in one of his walks because an object, a perception was beckoning him (60). In "Proust et les deux mémoires," the critic Paul Vernière suggests that Proust's preference for a certain type of reminiscence (frequently synesthetic, and relying on an unnatural intensification of the senses of smell and touch) may be due to his medical condition and the particular drugs he was taking (948). This is an intriguing point, and it could be argued that

the rememberer's addiction to the smell of lilac is connected to intense sensory perceptions (whether natural or drug-induced) that he experienced earlier. Recent studies of emotional memory show a link between memory and addiction. Thus, reporting on recent research, Denise Grady writes in "The Hardest Habit to Break: Memories of the High" that "the intensity of a moment [such as the "high" that occurs with drugs] helps burn emotional memories into the brain circuit" and that "a sight or smell can trigger brain circuits altered by drug abuse and spur a relapse" (9).

25. A psychoanalytic approach would want us to "dig out" the childhood memory hidden behind the whiff of lilac. For that, we need to return to the cabinet in "Combray" that smells of "oris-root" and is the site of the hero's initiation into solitary pleasures (33). An earlier version of this scene, in *Contre Sainte Beuve*, describes a cabinet that could be locked, but whose open window "left room to a young lilac that had pushed . . . its fragrant head into the opening" (69). Reading Proust psychoanalytically reveals then that the Parisian lilac covers an earlier, repressed childhood memory.

26. In case my reader feels that my analysis is not valid, since I seem to be dealing with a scene of fiction as if it were a "real" psychological event, I should add that here I interpret Proust's text very much in the phenomenological vein, using it for a gedankenexperiment. "It does not matter much," Sartre writes about this method, "whether the individual fact that supports the essence is real and imaginary" (*L'Imagination,* 141). Even as pure fiction, the "exemplary" element contains the essence from the very fact that this fiction was conceivable *(du fait même qu'elle ait pu être imaginée).* As a fiction conceived by a remembering, imagining mind, this Proustian scene provides, on par with all the others I examine in this book, a valid terrain for an investigation into the "true conditions" of human remembrance.

Chapter 6

1. In his 1979 article anthologized in the section "Encoding and Retrieval" of *Human Memory: A Reader,* Endel Tulving remarks that psychological research has focused, in a disproportionate fashion, on encoding rather than retrieval and notes that "activation of latent memory traces has received little attention" (204). Proust's influence could then be ascribed as well to the dearth of psychological studies in the field that he charted with his theory of involuntary memory.

2. On the importance of forgetting in Proust, Antoine Compagnon writes, "Proustian memory comprises, presupposes forgetting; it comes after forgetting, draws from forgetting; it does not preserve, it resuscitates . . . and the book follows this pattern, 'a book is like a large cemetery, where on most of the tombs, one can no longer read the erased names'" (3864).

3. In his chapter "Building Memories" (in *Searching for Memory*), which is heavily indebted to Proust, Daniel Schacter makes a more precise point, which is of seminal importance for this discussion: "Because our understanding of ourselves is so dependent on what we can remember of the past, it is troubling to realize that successful recall depends heavily on the availability of appropriate retrieval cues" (63).

4. In his description of autobiographical memory in *The Feeling of What Happens,* Antonio Damasio envisages cases where "certain contents of autobiographical memory remain submerged," and are yet revealed as partial reconstructions or as motivating forces behind the retrieval of other seemingly unrelated memories (227). With the image of Delos, Proust similarly evokes the theoretical possibility of a partially reconstructed memory. Daniel Schacter points out, meanwhile, in *Searching for Memory,* that the search for memory associations depends on the conviction that a context is available (114–18). With this example, Proust provides us with further evidence for the weight given to belief in matters of remembrance: a perceptual detail that "feels like" a memory, but whose context remains "submerged," creates a belief in the existence of a "forgotten memory."

5. Proust's geological image has its counterpart in Freud, who compares himself to an archaeologist sifting through successive layers to uncover a buried city. In a letter to Fliess, for instance, he speaks of his discovery of the primal scene in terms of archaeology as if "Schliemann had again uncovered the city of Troy that was thought to be imaginary" (December 21, 1899). In 1892, in *Diseases of Memory,* Théodore Ribot warned his reader that this metaphor might be misleading, and suggested that "it would be puerile to suppose that recollections are arranged in the brain in the form of layers in order of age, after the fashion of geological strata" (128). In Ribot's conception, which adumbrates the current notion of consolidation, the qualitative differences among memories are determined by their degree of stability.

6. For a detailed scientific study predicated upon the notion of qualitative differences in the encoding of memories, see Endel Tulving, "Relation between Encoding Specificity and Levels of Processing," in *Human Memory,* 201–22. My analysis in this chapter owes much to Tulving's theory, which neuroscientists seem to have endorsed as well, that "it makes sense now to think about forgetting, too, in terms of the relation between the properties of the memory trace and the characteristics of the (functional) retrieval cue" (217).

7. "A reminiscence is a personal memory of a distant past" (Cohen and Taylor, 602).

8. What is implied by the phrase "memory of a memory" is best introduced in Emerson's observation that "most remembering is only the memory of memories, & not a new & primary remembrance" (quoted by Shenk, 55). As Shenk comments, "the act of remembering itself generates new memories," and this idea remains central to this chapter.

9. *The Mill on the Floss* is a seminal text for Proust. Thus, in the first notes toward the magnum opus (which first led to *Contre Sainte Beuve*), Proust jots down a brief reference to the beginning of *The Mill on the Floss.* As Edward Bizub demonstrates (50–52), Eliot's novel remains present at many levels, literary and philosophical, in Proust's *Recherche.* This direct influence explains why, in the Méséglise and Guermantes passage, Proust's recapitulation of the principles of memory, with its emphasis on associations, reads like a pastiche of Eliot.

10. The discussion focuses on pp. 200–202 of *Swann's Way* (pp. 164–66 of *Du Côté de chez Swann*).

11. Tadié discusses the formation of memories under the rubric "Attention et concentration" of *Le Sens de la mémoire,* coincidentally adducing this passage of Proust as an example (108–10).

12. In showing us that we organize reality with what amounts to a map encrypted with mnemonic images, Proust shows uncanny prescience. Thus Daniel Schacter writes that "memory is part of the brain's attempt to impose order on the environment" (*Searching for Memory,* 52). In "Memory and the Unconscious," Robert Pollack argues that "as we focus our attention, we unconsciously sift our store of memories and bring to consciousness some, but not all, of the memories associated with that perception" (61).

13. Here Proust's theory seems to intersect with that developed by Freud around screen memories. Pollack discusses qualitative differences in memory traces in the introductory part of "Memory and the Unconscious" (61).

14. In *Diseases of Memory: An Essay in Positive Psychology,* Ribot argues that the acquisitions made in infancy are the most stable: "the impressions are received in virgin element" and are likely to be reinforced through "continual acquisitions" (129–30). Another argument is invoked by Jansari and Parkin, based on the idea that "first time events" (which are bound to occur most often in the early years of life) leave particularly vivid and thus more resilient memories (85, 88). The fact that in the early years, the affective, emotional aspects of remembrance dominate over the higher, cognitively more elaborate forms might also account for the greater resilience of childhood memories. Current research on the localization of memory has confirmed Ribot's earlier intuition that differences in storage explain the persistence of emotional faculties (120).

15. For an overview of psychological research, see the section "Encoding and Retrieval," in Tulving, *Human Memory;* and Schacter, "Building Memories," in *Searching for Memory.* The "encoding specificity principle" as defined by Tulving tells us that "the likelihood of later recalling [an] event depends on the extent to which a retrieval cue reinstates or matches the original encoding. Explicit remembering always depends on the similarity of affinity between encoding and retrieval processes" (quoted by Schacter, 60).

16. With the notion of engrams, the idea of memory traces is not abandoned altogether but becomes more refined. Engrams are mobile constructions that change over time, as new experiences are successively registered in the brain, and thus resemble Damasio's "dispositional forms." Schacter defines engrams (a term invented by the German biologist Richard Semon in 1909) as "transient or enduring changes in our brains that result from encoding an experience" (58). The Tadiés similarly point out the topicality of Semon's concept, which "emphasized that the engram was not an immutable and definitive trace, but that the acquisition of new memories modifies older ones and that the recall of a particular memory consists in a new creation of the remembered perception" (61–62). Butters and Cermak invoke the notion of engram in their study of amnesia, pointing out that recently acquired engrams are less resistant to forgetting (256).

17. I read the passage at the end of Combray as Proust's reworking of the *données* he found in Eliot's thought experiment at the outset of *The Mill on the Floss.*

Here too, the relation between imagination, reality, and memory is explored through the conceit of a child and an older rememberer who revisit a familiar landscape. But Proust's text presents us with Eliot's vision turned upside down. While she gives us the skeptical view—that memories are just like dreams—Proust uses this example to assert his belief in memory as what grounds us in reality.

18. Bowie discusses Proust's "time voice" at the beginning of his chapter on time in *Proust among the Stars:* "Inside [the narrator's] accustomed voice, there is a time voice—urgent, serious, elevated, expansive, and given to sudden bursts of semi-philosophical speculation—whose sound is fashioned, as telephone voices are, by a sense of occasion and a need to impress" (30). Bowie's term provides a useful shorthand identifying the voice that speaks of memory in a similar tone.

19. There exists no French word for the English term *rememberer.* To describe the remembering child, Proust invokes the idea of a "mémorialiste," who commemorates the events of the subject's inner life as if they were on par with a king's progress.

20. For a discussion of intensities in the representation that bring reality to life, see Bowie's discussion of Schopenhauer's *The World as Will and Representation* (*Lacan,* 197–98). For Schopenhauer, art is what "rescues" and "elucidates" the visible world. Proust's "aesthetization" of memory and the way it is enlisted to create "sensuous discriminations" may have been influenced by Schopenhauer's theories.

21. My main sources for a definition of the Alzheimer's treatment gardens is a chapter by John Zeisel and Martha M. Tyson that discusses findings and guidelines developed around five case studies of such gardens. For a description of the "American Landscape Society of America Alzheimer's Garden Project" see http:www.abc news.go.come/sections/us/DailyNews/alzheimer's000709.html (accessed August 25, 2003); another presentation can be found at http:www.centerofdesign.org/pmg/fea tures.html (accessed August 25, 2003). Most examples of Alzheimer's memories are taken from David Shenk's book *The Forgetting.* I borrow from Shenk the evocative term *the forgetting* to describe Alzheimer's patients.

22. The chapter on Alzheimer's treatment gardens reveals that in every instance, a deliberate effort is made to reconstruct an environment that would have been familiar to the residents in their earlier years and within a certain geographic community. Thus plants and flowers are carefully chosen to match those the patients would have known in their youth, as are the "stage-props" that are placed in these gardens, such as fountains, gazebos, and tool sheds.

23. "Symbolic places," Zeisel and Tyson write, "have a distinct and familiar character reflecting culture, climate, geography, and context of the area where the facility is located. Such places are particularly important to evoke deep memories of those with memory impairment and cognitive loss" (449).

24. This example of Proustian memory is discussed as well in chapter 5, "Screen Memories."

25. My main references for the analysis of how Alzheimer's disease affects episodic memory are Larry Squire, *Memory and Brain;* M.-Marsel Mesulam, "Aging, Alzheimer's Disease, and Dementia: Clinical and Neurological Perspectives"; and Nelson Butters and Lair S. Cermak, "A Case Study of the Forgetting of

Autobiographical Knowledge Implications for the Study of Retrograde Amnesia"; as well as Jonathan Franzen, "My Father's Brain."

26. "The progressive destruction of memory follows a logical order—a law. *It advances progressively from the unstable to the stable*," Ribot explains (21). With his notion of "stable memories" Ribot intuited what is now understood in biological terms as "consolidation." Larry Squire thus writes that "from a neurobiological perspective, this idea implies that post-learning events could influence the fate of memory by actually remodeling the neural circuitry that underlies the original representation . . . some aspects of memory for the original event are forgotten, while those that remain are strengthened" (205).

27. Starting in the intermediate stages of the illness, "attentional deficits interfere with the ability to maintain a coherent stream of thought and to sequence goal-directed activities" (Mesulam, 465). But the loss of attention is more global than Mesulam suggests, meaning that the patient appears most of the time to be "spaced-out." Vivid colors answer a primary need for a form of stimulation that helps reconnect the patient to the outer world.

28. Mesulam remarks that memories, even recent ones, "with high emotional impact can be recollected relatively well" (264). The stronger emotional component of childhood memories is another factor in their greater resilience for the Alzheimer's patient.

29. As he lists the deficits that occur in the intermediate stages of Alzheimer's, Mesulam mentions the emergence of psychiatric symptoms (delusions and hallucinations) and remarks as well on "the disturbances of the sleep-wake cycle" (465). As "observers" of the illness, both Jonathan Franzen and Jürgs are struck by the sleeping-dreaming aspect of Alzheimer's patients. Franzen writes of a patient that "his life in a nursing home appeared to be an endless troubled dream populated by figments from his past and by his deformed and brain-damaged fellow inmates" (103). "With the diminution of acetylcholine and the corresponding heightening levels of serotonin," Jürgs explains, "the brain sinks into sleep" (316). Further, "What we know in states of healthy dreaming becomes for the Alzheimer's patient, because of this deficit, a perpetual state of madness, a dream that cannot be recognized or controlled and cannot be influenced. They, as it were, never awaken from their dream and cannot acknowledge its existence. At some point there is no functioning brain: reality is unreality, and conversely" (316–17). In *The Forgetting*, Shenk quotes the description of Emerson in the middle stages of the disease in the description of his biographer: "Outlines and edges were no longer perceptible, and he dwelt in a dreamlike mist which hid from his vision everything that was not intimate and immediately recognizable" (103).

30. I would not assume that the landscape architect, gardener, or head nurse involved in the planting of a memory garden is consciously referring to Proust's text. As I have argued in the introduction to this book, Proustian memory is now an implicit and often unacknowledged part of our understanding of how memory works.

31. Neurological research has suggested that the olfactory sense is the most closely related to emotions because the neural pathways that lead to odor perception

are mostly those of the more primitive brain (the amygdala, the hippocampus) in which emotions get processed. An odor stimulus reaches the "amygdala and enthorinal cortex without passing first through the filtering thamalus and is thus particularly effective at triggering emotional and mnemonic response (although more so for the former than the later)," writes Shane Smith (10).

32. Rachel S. Herz has shown that episodic memories evoked by smell are not more accurate than memories evoked by other senses. Summarizing her argument in "The Scent of Lost Time," S. Smith writes that "the difference lies not in the type of memory that is retrieved, but rather in the manner of its retrieval. Upon their retrieval, memories evoked by odorous cues are infused with affective weight, and it is the added emotional quality that causes them to seem more rich and accurate than memories cued differently" (6). See Herz, "Are Odors the Best Cues to Memory?"; Herz and Schooler, "A Naturalistic Study of Autobiographical Memories Evoked by Olfactory and Visual Cues: Testing the Proustian Hypothesis."

33. I am grateful to Ravit Reichman for inviting me to press further on the paradox that underlies the Proustian experience. She points out that Proust's thesis that "reality takes shape in memory alone" ultimately leads to the claim that "memory is (ironically), the very thing that prevents the past from becoming 'past'" ("Memory-Gardens." May 3, 2004, e-mail to the author).

34. "Retrogenesis," Shenk explains in *The Forgetting,* "is not a perfect reversal—not literally the unwiring of the brain, neuron by neuron. . . . But the deconstruction is remarkably similar to the construction" (124). On p. 122, Shenk reproduces the chart established in 1980 by Barry Reisberg. It shows, with chilling accuracy, how the seven main stages of child development are mirrored in reverse in the degenerative process of Alzheimer's disease.

35. In their discussion of reminiscence from a therapeutic and social perspective, the two psychologists Cohen and Taylor come closest to offering a definition for the type of remembrance that is encouraged in memory gardens. It bears on a distant past, serves a biographical purpose, and occurs more often among institutionalized older people. They emphasize the difference between ordinary autobiographical remembrance and reminiscence, by quoting the words of Rubin and Schulkin that "reminiscence refer[s] to conscious recollections seemingly done for their own purposes rather than those requested by another or sued for the retrieval of specific information" (602). This emphasis on the seemingly gratuitous and solipsistic nature of reminiscence helps us understand why the Proustian "recipe" for remembrance might have a therapeutic value: it triggers a mechanism of recollection that is part of the experience of natural aging, but needs to be artificially "boosted" among the forgetting.

36. The elements of this controversy (linguistic, philosophical, and scientific) lie much beyond the scope of this book. For an overview as well as a convincing standpoint on the issue of language, memory, and consciousness, see Gerald Edelman, chapter 15, "Philosophical Issues: Qualified Realism," in *The Remembered Present,* in particular pp. 265–68.

37. David Pillemer's book *Momentous Events, Vivid Memories* offers many insights into the social function of shared memories and thus of reminiscence, as he

notes: "Contemporary functions served by remembering specific episodes in expansive detail, and by sharing the memories with others, are explored throughout this book" (62).

38. Pierre Janet, the French psychologist and neurologist, uses the image of a sentinel or messenger (who comes back to the camp to alert fellow soldiers about some significant happening) to illustrate his narrative conception of memory, which he sums up in a provocative definition: "Memory consists in a social reaction in a condition of absence" (*L'Evolution*, 221). In Janet's theory, remembrance begins with the need "to tell someone" about an event. Gradually, this "someone" can become ourselves. The argument for a gradual transition that takes the child from externalized forms of awareness to an inner consciousness (where memories are first pure acts of narration and gradually become a form of consciousness) is presented in great detail by Lev Vygotski in *Thought and Language*.

39. The argument is made by Emile Benveniste in "Subjectivity in Language," which focuses on the use of the grammatical persons "I" and "you." Benveniste writes: "Now we hold that 'subjectivity,' whether it is placed in phenomenology or in psychology . . . is only the emergence in the being of a fundamental property of language. 'Ego' is he who *says* 'ego.' That is where we see the foundation of 'subjectivity,' which is determined by the linguistic status of 'person'" (224).

40. Daniel Schacter gives a probing overview of neuroimaging techniques that can be used for the study of memory in "Scanning the Brain," pp. 52–56 of *Searching for Memory*.

41. *Le Temps retrouvé*, 3:725. This notion is often repeated in the work, as Proust's aesthetic is fundamentally vested in the idea that literature can represent the singular, phenomenal qualities of the subject's experience. The hero of the *Recherche* thus teaches his lover, Albertine, that what defines an artist's genius is "this unknown quality of a unique world and that no other . . . has ever made us see." Proust often expresses this same idea, for example in the early essay *Contre Sainte Beuve* and in an interview published in 1913 in *Le Temps*, in which he states: "style . . . is a certain quality of vision, the revelation of the particular universe seen by each of us, and that the others do not see" (*Recherche*, 3:893, n. 152).

42. Quoted by Harold Bloom, 52.

43. This distinction resembles that which Freud sketched out in his discussion of "word presentation" and "thing presentation." More recently, partly in the wake of neuroscientific research on implicit or nonconscious memory, Pillemer has defended "the idea of separated but interacting imagistic and narrative memory systems" (see in particular pp. 99–108).

44. The French author Nathalie Sarraute experiments, similarly, with the idea of *tropismes*, in representing in her fiction passing moods that obey unconscious, unidentifiable mental currents.

45. For a probing discussion of the ineffable element in the act of communication, see George Steiner's *After Babel*, particularly the chapter "Understanding Translation," 46–48.

46. The idea that there is an inexpressible dimension to our perceptions or mem-

ories contributes to the myth of "the mystery of consciousness," which Dennett identifies (and tries to demote) in *Consciousness Explained.*

47. Similarly, the "architect of memory" runs counter to Dennett's philosophical argument: he represents another version of the homunculus around which the Cartesian theater of consciousness revolves.

48. For a survey of this position, see Daniel Schacter's summary presentation of the connectionist theory (*Searching for Memory,* 71) and the more developed philosophical presentation by John Sutton, in "Wriggle-work: the Quick and Nimble Animal Spirits" (chap. 2, pp. 25–49) and "Appendix: Memory and Connectionism" (pp. 19–20) of *Memory Traces.*

49. For a discussion of this topic, see chapter 3, "Reading the Past: Childhood Memories."

50. Quoting George Eliot's celebration of the world as memory garden in *The Mill on the Floss:* "We could never have loved the earth so well if we had had no childhood in it, if it were not the earth where the same flowers come up again every spring that we used to gather with our tiny fingers as we sat lisping to ourselves on the grass—the same hips and haws on the autumn hedgerows—the same *redbreasts that we used to call 'God's birds'"* (94).

51. Echoing Sacks's conclusion in "The River of Consciousness": "So it is not just perceptual moments, simple physiological moments. . . , but moments of an essentially personal kind, which seem to constitute our very being" (44).

Chapter 7

1. I owe the inspiration for this chapter, as well as much of my historical understanding of nostalgia, to Jean Starobinski's groundbreaking article on the history of an emotion, "The Idea of Nostalgia." He cites Balzac in a note on page 86, and Kant on page 94.

2. "Nostalgia is to memory like kitsch is to art," Charles Maier declares in a statement that vividly expresses our current unease and easy dismissal of nostalgia as a naive and thus "cheap" emotion (quoted in Svetlana Boym, *The Future of Memory,* xiv). In "Back through the Future," Leo Spitzer gives a very useful historical overview of nostalgia, and remarks: "the overall practice of nostalgia itself, and societal function and effects of nostalgic memory in general, have been the subject of sharp reproach by many social critics" (91). Like Spitzer, I believe that nostalgia "plays a significant role in . . . the continuity of individual and collective identity" (92).

3. Prefacing *The Man Who Mistook His Wife for a Hat,* Oliver Sacks suggests that "clinical tales" are the only way of unraveling diseases that are as closely connected to identity as are some of the neurological/psychological cases that he encountered in his practice.

4. "Inventer, au fond, c'est se ressouvenir," Nerval writes in his preface to *Les Filles du feu,* where he defends himself against the indictment of madness. For an enlightening commentary on this preface, see Felman, *Writing and Madness,* 62–66.

5. In building an autobiographical self on the foundations of memory, Raymond Jean argues, Nerval resembles Proust (82). Béatrice Didier similarly compares Nerval to Proust in their use of "memory signs." "But," she adds, "although Nerval intuited in 'Sylvie' that the whole work could be built thanks to this mechanism, Nerval's project does not have the systematic character found in Proust" (15). More recently, the connection between "Sylvie" and the *Recherche* is discussed by Anne Simon in her excellent article "De *Sylvie* à la *Recherche*"; Richard Sieburth explores the same connection in his introductory note to "Sylvie" in Nerval's *Selected Writings*.

6. Nerval's madness has been amply studied and discussed. But my discussion owes most to the work of Jean Richer, *Nerval: Expérience et création*; Michel Jeanneret, *La Lettre perdue: Ecriture et folie dans l'oeuvre de Gérard de Nerval*; Shoshana Felman, and Sarah Kofman, *Nerval: Le charme de la répétition*.

7. This is how, on his way to the Princesse de Guermantes, the Proustian rememberer encounters the first of a famous succession of involuntary memories (*Le Temps retrouvé*, 3:702–4).

8. Such freezing is for Proust the mark of a strong impression, whether it occurs as a perception—as is the case with the hawthorns encountered early in the work (*Swann's Way*, 151–53), or a memory, as is the case here.

9. This episode could be read allegorically, as showing a rememberer who, in his or her eagerness to plunge into this specular surface, expresses an overwhelming attraction for the wellsprings of memory. However, this interpretation would still not account for the storyteller's odd interest in ducks.

10. I discuss in chapter 3, "Reading the Past: Childhood Memories," Woolf's similarly striking unmitigated preference for memory images, in focusing on her acknowledgment, in "A Sketch of the Past," that images of the nursery or the beach are more real than what lies in front of her eyes, a garden peopled by her gardener and her charwoman.

11. LeDoux presents the principle of mood congruity of memory and how the content of memory is influenced by emotional states in *The Emotional Brain*, 211–13. David Pillemer discusses the relation between mood and memory, to show not only how mood affects remembrance, but also how memories can assume "an active rather than passive role in emotional regulation" (172–76).

12. I am quoting from the "Introductory Note to 'Angélique' and 'Sylvie' by Richard Sieburth, in Nerval, *Selected Writings*, 63.

13. For Jean Richer suggests that the two works "Sylvie" and *Aurélia* constitute together one "autobiographie romancée": they were written over the same period and may have been originally conceived as "one unique continuous narrative" (303).

14. Many exegetes and biographers have commented on this remarkably innovative therapeutic gesture, but for a detailed study see Laure Murat, *La Maison du Dr. Blanche*.

15. I show in chapter 4, "George Eliot's Movie-in-the-Brain," how the construction of mnemonic scenes depends on contextualization. "Context makes memories autobiographical, locating them in space and time," LeDoux writes in *The Emo-*

tional Brain, drawing on the work that J. O'Keefe and L. Nadel developed on sensory-independent spatial representations (199). It would seem then that our ability to imagine spaces is an essential component of autobiographical recall.

16. Pillemer writes: "The argument is for two memory systems, one encoding a structural description of perceptual input, the other representing the event itself in its episodic content" (103).

17. I quote Pillemer, who provides the most useful of summaries on the question of explicit and implicit memories (104–5). I have relied essentially on Schacter (*Searching for Memory* and "Implicit Memory: History and Current Status") and LeDoux *(The Emotional Brain)* for psychological and neuroscientific discussion of these two systems. However, as Pillemer (105–6) and Schacter ("Implicit Memory," 317–18) both point out, there is no full consensus among psychologists and cognitive scientists about this division of memory into these two systems.

18. I am actually quoting from Poulet's *L'espace proustien,* 9. The relevance of this commentary on Proust for Nerval's conception of memory implies the existence of deep affinities between these authors, which I explore in the next chapter, "Textures of the Past."

19. Translating Nerval, Kendall Lappin mistakenly "affixes" to the modern mirror the idyllic picture of a shepherd and a shepherdess, turning it into an example of kitsch. But for Nerval, this image of a lost idyll properly belongs to nostalgia; it justifies the regret for the past and is not part of the cheap clichés of modern life.

20. "Where are the rosebush hedges that used to encircle the hillock? What's left of them, a few plants reverting to the wild state, is overrun by eglantine and raspberry canes.—As for the laurels, have they been cut down, as in the song about the girls who won't go to the woods any more?" (132).

21. Thus in the seventh and central chapter of "Sylvie," the narrator wonders: "As I retrace these details, I begin to ask myself whether they are real, or whether I have dreamed them up" and wonder furthermore "whether this memory is perhaps an obsession" (126; translation amended).

22. The correspondence following the publication of Py-Lieberman's article appeared in the January 2000 issue of *Smithsonian.*

23. Proust discusses this "method of abrupt transition" in his early article, published in 1920, "A propos du style de Flaubert" (quoted in Jean, 58). It is easy to see how this technique would have inspired Proust, and we can only trust him when he says that representing this aspect of mental functioning in a convincing fashion takes unusual skill.

24. I am quoting Sieburth again. I show, in chapter 6, "Proustian Memory Gardens," that consciousness cannot happen in the present alone.

25. See his letter to Gaston Gallimard, dated November 8, 1912, quoted by Tadié in Pléiade, 1044.

26. *Les Intermittences du coeur* is the subtitle given to the section of *Sodome et Gomorrhe II* where Proust's hero is suddenly reminded of his grandmother's death. This involuntary memory surges up in the midst of "a bout of cardiac fatigue" (*Cities of the Plain,* 783), leading the narrator to conclude that memory troubles and intermittences of the heart are related ("aux troubles de la mémoire sont liées les

intermittences du coeur"). I discuss the topic of "body memory" in chapter 9, "The Rememberer's Task."

27. LeDoux focuses on memory and mood on pages 203 and 212. Schacter discusses what psychologists call "mood-congruent retrieval" in his chapter "Emotional Memories," *Searching for Memory,* 211. See also Pillemer's discussion, "Memory as Cause of Emotional Upheaval" in *Momentous Events, Vivid Memories,* which assumes that "affectively salient memories can be retrieved purposefully in order to alter one's mood" (174).

28. The first publication in 1999 of Nerval's *Selected Writings,* in the Penguin Classics edition, translated by Richard Sieburth, suggests that his prose might have an appeal that extends beyond the French-speaking world.

29. Drawing on the work done on implicit memory, this documentary spoke of the "psycho-somatic" underpinnings of drug addiction. It is not enough to cure the body of addictive substances; the mind or the brain needs to be cured as well of a "nostalgia" for places associated with the drug experience. The proceedings of a meeting organized by the National Institute of Health on the subject of emotional memory and drug abuse thus state: "Because some drugs of abuse induce intense euphoria, and because it is considered that recall of drug-related emotional experiences elicited by cues associated with past drug use plays an important role in relapse to drug seeking . . . , the topic of how emotional memories are acquired and how emotional experiences and the memory of them are represented in the brain have become topics of interest" (Pollock et al., 1). In her article "The Hardest Habit to Break," Denise Grady reports: "Although a relapse can occur for no apparent reason, many addicts say that cravings are brought on by cues or reminders of past drug use, like seeing a needle or crack pipe or visiting a place where they used to get high" (9).

Chapter 8

1. Whereas the amygdala seems to deal with affect alone, the hippocampus involves both the cognitive and the emotional dimensions of memory. The temporal regions and the cortex, meanwhile, serve the higher conceptual demands of memory. This is, in a summary, the map for memories that LeDoux draws on the basis of the most recent research into the localization of forms of memory and consciousness in the brain (see in particular pp. 189–204).

2. Evoking the need to validate our memories, Pillemer writes: "Public expression of personal event memories depends on the spoken or written word. A person recounting a memory must translate the initial perceptual and sensory registration of a momentous event into a shared, narrative representation" (99). For more on this subject, see my introduction, as well as chapter 6, "Proustian Memory Gardens."

3. Measuring the skin's electroconductance is one of the finest, most discriminating ways of deciphering emotion in the body. On the registration of emotion through this method, see, for example, Damasio, *Feeling of What Happens,* 50 and 151–52.

4. "Gérard de Nerval," in *Contre Sainte-Beuve*, 188–89.

5. In introducing the notion of "emotional memory" I am following the distinction made by LeDoux, who writes: "We are going to call the implicit, fear-conditioned memory an 'emotional memory' and the explicit declarative memory a 'memory of an emotion'" (182). However, the type of emotional memory I envisage is not necessarily fear-conditioned.

6. Maine de Biran, who develops this theory of memory-signs in his essay *Influence de l'habitude sur la faculté de penser*, first published in 1804, influenced both Pierre Janet and Henri Bergson, as mentioned by Schacter, "Implicit Memory," 320. As has been pointed out by his modern editor, Pierre Tisserand, de Biran was himself inspired by Jean-Jacques Rousseau, and may have drawn from him the notion of *signes mémoratifs*.

7. Procedural memory is memory for skills, such as riding a bicycle, playing the piano, or tying one's shoes.

8. De Biran discusses the influence that words hold over our passions and emotions in the section of his book devoted to "mémoire sensitive" (pp. 137 and 144). "Language abounds in metaphors," he writes, and it "provides us with weapons as well as talismans" (144).

9. See the concluding section of chapter 2, "Painting the Past: Virginia Woolf's Memory Images" for a discussion of this passage, from the philosophical perspective of "qualia."

10. These are the words or thoughts ascribed by Woolf to Clarissa Dalloway in the opening pages of *Mrs Dalloway*, 3.

11. Proust's receptiveness to the poetry of proper names in "Sylvie" prepares the ground for his own later disquisition, in *Swann's Way*, on the same subject. Thus, we learn in the last section, "Place-Names," that all the rememberer needs in order to produce "dreams of the Atlantic and of Italy" is to "pronounce the names Balbec, Venice, Florence, within whose syllables had gradually accumulated the longing inspired in [him] by the places for which they stood" (420). Here however, an important distinction between Proust and Nerval emerges. Whereas Proust regularly emphasizes the value of such toponymies for the future (as my example shows, names, for him, create anticipation and shape his desire), they are deeply embedded in Nerval's nostalgia.

12. In showing that the mere sound of words creates association leading to recollection, Proust announces what will be a major aspect of his treatment of music and memory, around Vinteuil's sonata and septuor, in *La Recherche*. Proust's ideas on music, emotion, and memory are so complex that they deserve a separate treatment.

13. I am referring to Hofstader's article entitled "Analogy as the Core of Cognition," anthologized in *The Best American Science Writing 2000*, ed. by James Gleick. All subsequent references are to this text.

14. "What we have here is one of those picture of an unreal coloring, which we never see in reality, that words even do not evoke, but that a dream sometimes or music can evoke," writes Proust in *Contre Sainte-Beuve*, focusing in a revealing fashion on the musical nature of Nerval's representation ("Gérard de Nerval," 185).

"[The inexpressible] is not to be found in the words, it is not expressed; it is entirely in-between the words, like the morning haze in Chantilly" (192).

15. I briefly discuss Damasio's conception of "dispositional memories" in chapter 6, "Proustian Memory-Gardens."

16. "Pregnant memories" are phenomenally vivid and emotionally significant memories. Thus LeDoux, a neuroscientist, explains that "without the emotional arousal elicited through the implicit system, the conscious memory would be emotionally flat," analyzing how the implicit system gives "an emotional flavoring to the conscious memory" (201). Pillemer, a psychologist, similarly argues that "memory's vividness is related to the perceived strength of affective reactions: the stronger the emotions, the more vivid the memories" (149).

17. "Je dis: une fleur! et, hors de l'oubli où ma voix relègue aucun contour, en tant que quelque chose d'autre que les calices sus, musicalement se lève, idée même et suave, l'absente de tous bouquets," Mallarmé writes in "Crise de vers" (358). The quotation is truncated in my text: Mallarmé thus makes a difference between the experience of a flower and its abstracted, scientifically established identity, as a chalix. See my introduction for a broader discussion of this aphorism by Mallarmé.

18. This statement is to be found among the collected notes of Nerval, which Richer gathered in the Pléiade edition under the rubric "Autres notes" (*Oeuvres*, 439). In the next line, the "rememberer" writes: "[Superiority] of intelligence articulated around the past over intelligence articulated around the present."

19. See *Swann's Way*, 29–46.

20. The scene presents indeed the crucial turning point from which the *Künstler-roman* will develop (the indulged, neurotic child will become the artist).

21. This wedding scene seems to have "haunted" Nerval, writes Béatrice Didier, who shows that it exists in four other texts that he wrote, including *Aurélia*, where the hero witnesses Aurélia's marriage to his double (396).

22. Nerval reveals a number of biographical details in the section "Juvenalia" of his "Promenades et souvenirs." In this text, part of which was published posthumously, Nerval writes about his mother with perceptible emotion (*Oeuvres*, 135). "There is an age in which memories are reborn so vividly, in which certain forgotten drawings reappear under the crumpled texture *(trame)* of life!" (130).

23. Relying on a grammar that may well surprise contemporary readers, Woolf depends on the masculine gender to establish a universal point that is nevertheless born from her own experience in writing her memoir.

24. Chapter 10, "Virginia Woolf's Life-Writing," presents a further development of this maternal complex.

25. The affect remains unconscious, but the emerging image, one might say drawing on Freud's first topography, belongs to the subconscious.

26. Freud elaborates on this metaphor in his famous essay on the *Wunderblock*, the mystic writing-pad (cf. *SE*, 19:227–32).

27. The volume edited by Daniel Schacter, *Memory Distortion*, captures many elements of the current debate. Pillemer's discussion of the accuracy of vivid memories (55–59) provides a useful summary from a psychological perspective. For the Freudian view, see chapter 5, "Screen Memories."

28. For recent discussions of photography and memory, see Sylviane Agacinski, *Le Passeur de temps,* 96, as well as Linda Haverty Rugg, *Picturing Ourselves,* and Marianne Hirsch, *Family Frames.*

29. I discuss memory and mood in the previous chapter, in the wake of LeDoux's notion that the presence of implicit memories explains how we can find ourselves "in the throes of an emotional state that exists for reasons [we] do not quite understand" (203).

30. The wedding scene in Othys combines, very transparently, an idealized vision of a primal scene showing a happy parental union, and the son's love for his mother. At the core of Nerval's nostalgia, we find, just as we did in Proust, an Oedipal complex, as if the nostalgia expressed by these men were at first destined to unite a mother and her male child. But beyond this Oedipal drama, nostalgia, I argue, harks back to a preoedipal era, where it matters little whether the child is a boy or a girl.

Chapter 9

1. Freud's essay on transience exists in translation in volume 14 of the *Standard Edition* but in a style that is antiquated and lacks precision. I rely, in this instance, on my own translation, and the page references correspond to the German text, "Vergänglichkeit," in *Bildende Kunst und Literatur,* 225–27.

2. The importance that an aesthetic perception of the world holds for an artist is vividly illustrated by "The Case of the Colorblind Painter," which we owe to Oliver Sacks. Having lost all sense of color, the painter Jonathan I. is not only deprived of a full visual perception of the world, he has also lost "the world of art . . . that had absorbed his profoundly visual and chromatic talents and sensibilities" (*Anthropologist,* 33). Falling into deep depression, the painter reinvents himself as an artist who paints in the shades of grays. In learning to paint in a different phenomenal, colorless universe, Jonathan eventually regains his mental balance.

3. Throughout her essay, Salomé refers to writers as *Dichters,* thereby emphasizing the creative, poetic (and not the descriptive or narrative) nature of their work. Freud's essay known in English as "Creative Writers and Day-Dreaming" is similarly entitled "Der Dichter und das Phantasieren." The meaning of *Dichtung* also reaches back to Goethe's major work on the relation between the biographical and the aesthetic, *Dichtung and Wahrheit,* with its focus on fiction versus truth. The discussion I develop in this chapter must be understood in light of this crucial distinction between writing as creation and writing as mimesis, which German renders more visible in the contrast between the *Dichter* (a creative writer or poet) and the *Schriftsteller* (the man of letters).

4. In comparing Woolf's philosophical impulse to Pascal's, I situate her writing in an existentialist tradition where Pascal features as a precursor. See "Existentialism," *Encyclopaedia Britannica,* 2004, Encyclopaedia Britannica Online, April 5, 2004, http://www.search.eb.com/article? Eu=115432.

5. Woolf's *Diary* bears rich testimony to her lifelong quest for happiness against

deep depressive tendencies. The words I omitted in the diary entry are distressed indeed: "My depression is a harassed feeling—I'm looking; but that's not it—that's not it." Writing as I am, on the life-enhancing nature of aesthetic-mnemonic experiences, I want to quote here from an entry written by Woolf on her return to Cassis, shortly after she finished *Mrs Dalloway*. Steeped in Proust, Woolf expresses his admiration for his "sensibility" and "tenacity," noting that "he searches out these butterfly shades to the last grain." Pondering over ways of "commemorating" the happiness she felt in Cassis ("I am waiting to see what form of itself Cassis will finally cast up in my mind"), Woolf concludes, "Nobody shall say of me that I have not known perfect happiness" and adds, quasi-prophetically, "but few could put their finger on the moment, or say what made it" (April 8, 1925, *Diary*, vol. 3). The editor of Woolf's diaries, Anne Olivier Bell, appropriately quotes a letter Woolf wrote at the same time to Gwen Raverat (May 1, 1925), which says "But enough to death; it is life that matters." It is this relentless focus on what "living" means that gives Woolf's search as a rememberer its striking existential features.

6. In "Les Moments de Marcel Proust," Michel Butor traces across the *Recherche* a series of "moments of revelation"—impressions and memories—that resemble the epiphany that Woolf is describing in her diary (*Essais sur les modernes*, 111–28). Gilles Deleuze develops a compelling argument for the relation between signs and truth in his groundbreaking philosophical essay *Proust et les signes*.

7. For a discussion of memory and reality in Proust, see chapter 6, "Proustian Memory Gardens." "Truth" is also part of Proust philosophical vocabulary and the aim of this "search," as is made clear, for example, in this letter to A.-J. Rivière: "I have found it more honest and delicate as an artist not to reveal, not to announce that it was precisely on a search for Truth that I had started, nor to say in what it consisted" (quoted by Henry, 20). The chapter "Là où la vie emmure, l'intelligence perce une issue" of Henry's book provides an excellent overview of Proust's philosophical project.

8. It seems that Woolf's philosophical stance comes closest to existentialism in that it is founded on the particularity of her existence and yet reaches toward a universal "meaning of Being." It also corresponds to existentialist views in originating in a concrete historical situation that becomes the ground for an intersubjective, pedagogical "sharing" of the human condition. The entry "Existentialism" in *Encyclopaedia Britannica* usefully brings together the "diverse and contrasting directions" of philosophical trends that are indeed "in the air" as Woolf elaborates her own philosophy.

9. For an overview of this concept see "Deferred Action," in *The Language of Psychoanalysis* as well Adam Phillips's discussion in "Freud and the Uses of Forgetting," in *On Flirtation*, 33–35.

10. I discuss the overlap between memory and consciousness in light of Edelman's theory in the chapter "Proustian Memory Gardens."

11. For a discussion of the time lapse between event and memory, see my article "Intervals and Their Truths in Marcel Proust and Virginia Woolf."

12. This entry (March 14, 1927, *Diary*, vol. 3) makes it clear that the contemplating mind embraces here the space of memory. Looking at the flower, the subject

travels freely through the channel of time (Woolf uses other similar metaphors for this process, and speaks of "an avenue into the past" or of "tunneling her way into the past"). In this context, it might be worth recalling that Woolf's first memory, according to her autobiographical account in "A Sketch of the Past," is of flowers on her mother's dress.

13. "A flower, a tulip for example, is considered beautiful, because we apprehend in it, through our judgment, the purposiveness without purpose of the beautiful object," writes Immanuel Kant in *Kritik der Urteilskraft*, 155.

14. "I shall here write the first pages of the greatest book in the world. This is what the book would be that was made entirely solely & with integrity of one's thoughts," Woolf writes in the summer of 1926 (n.d.) (*Diary*, 3:102). I am assuming that the project for the book on a flower is an outgrowth of this literary absolute.

15. For this definition I paraphrase Gerald Edelman's definitions (*Bright Air*, 114–16). For a discussion of qualia, see chapter 2, "Painting the Past: Virginia Woolf's Memory Images."

16. For other references in her project for *The Moths*, see "there must be a flower growing" (June 23, 1929, as well as May 28, 1929, *Diary*, vol. 3). This flower also appears in "Time Passes," the middle section of *To the Lighthouse*, and in *The Years*. The most developed version of this scene is found in Woolf's philosophical essay "On Being Ill," where a stretch of about twenty lines, beginning with "Let us examine the rose," is devoted to the examination of flowers (*Essays*, 321–22).

17. Lesley Stephen bought Talland House in St. Ives in 1881, before Virginia was born. She spent her summers there until her early teens (see Lee, *Virginia Woolf*, 25–31). Woolf sees herself as a child in this memory.

18. Among them: the loss of a brother, Toby, in *Jacob's Room* and *The Waves*; psychotic episodes in *Mrs Dalloway* and *The Waves*; her mother's death in *To the Lighthouse* and *The Waves*; sexual trauma evoked at the beginning of *The Years* and turned into a story in the autobiographical narrative "22 Hyde Park Gate."

19. The psychoanalyst Stanley A. Leavy, who translated her essay, speaks unequivocally of the challenges that a reader of Salomé's "labored and turgid prose" must face (see pp. 2 and 12 of his introduction to *The Freud Journal of Lou Andreas-Salomé*). Given my interest in highlighting the philosophical as well as psychoanalytical currents of Salomé's thought, I am relying here mostly on my own, more literal translation of her text. In *Lou Andreas-Salomé: L'alliée de la vie*, Stéphane Michaud observes that "the Freudian rigor is much blunted in narcissism as she conceives of it," while noting that Salomé is often inclined "to reformulate [psychoanalysis] in her own language" and particularly through images (238).

20. My reading bears mainly on the last two sections of Salomé's essay.

21. "Intellectual in the richest sense of the word, Lou is above all a shaper of life *(une plasticienne du vivant)*. This is why her essays represent outlines of existence," Stéphane Michaud writes (162), underlining, as I do, the existential dimensions of Salomé's philosophical thinking, which she owes partly to the influence of German *Lebensphilosophie*.

22. Salomé's definition of autobiographical memory, to which she gives the name *Erinnerung*, focuses on the notion of impression, as an event that unites an

inner experience (*Innen-Erlebniss*) and an outer event *(Aussen-Vorfall)* ("Narziss-mus als Doppelrichtung," 213). Thus her conception matches that of Woolf, as well as, more broadly, the phenomenological model that I have relied on in my discussion of memory images. What Salomé means by *Erinnerung* is discussed further below and in the next chapter.

23. For Jean Laplanche, for whom narcissism represents a vital psychic function, the maxim "I live for my own love, for the love of the ego" summarizes the narcis-sist stance (*Life and Death in Psychoanalysis*, 83).

24. In the original, Salomé writes: "Gewiss ist unser Narzissmus selbst nichts weiter als das im Gefühlerlebnis noch dunkel festgehaltene Wissen um unseres Sub-jektivstes als unsere objektive Anschlussstelle" ("Narzissmus als Doppelrichtung," 205).

25. This is how Stanley Leavy defines Salomé's project (*The Freud Journal of Lou Andreas-Salomé*, introduction, 3).

26. What I mean by experience here is best defined in terms of the distinction that Walter Benjamin draws, in his essay "On Some Motifs in Baudelaire," between *Erfahrung* and *Erlebnis*. Whereas *Erfahrung* represents cumulative knowledge (as in "life experience"), *Erlebnis* means "a certain hour of one's life" or "a moment that has been lived" (163). I speak of autobiographical memory in terms of *Erlebnis* claiming that it corresponds to an event that happened to a subject.

27. The richest account of their relationship is to be found in Michaud, *Lou Andréas-Salomé*.

28. Paul Roazen, the author of *Freud and His Followers*, suggested, in a private communication, that the unknown poet was in fact Rainer Maria Rilke. But I have not been able to find confirmation for this information. In "Entre Rilke and Freud," Michael Molnar expresses skepticism but does not fully eliminate the possibility of this encounter, which would have followed (too closely he thinks) a first encounter on September 8, 1913 (82–83 n. 2).

Lou Andreas-Salomé had indeed introduced Rilke to Freud at the Munich con-gress (1913), and they met for an evening in 1915. Even in the absence of compelling evidence for this joint excursion to the countryside, it remains a tantalizing thought that the unidentified *Dichter* may have been Rilke, who, precisely in those years, was beginning his slow work toward the *Duino Elegien,* gradually emerging from the difficult, unproductive times that followed his semiautobiographical text, *The Note-books of Malte Laurids Brigge.* It was during this period that Rilke had sought advice concerning the advisability of undertaking psychoanalytic treatment, and had been told unambiguously, by Salomé, that it would mean the end of this creative work. Assuming, for a moment, that Freud and Rilke did take that walk together, one must be grateful for an exchange that led Rilke neither toward psychoanalysis nor a naive and immediate response to the beauties of the world—else, these remark-able elegies would never have been written.

29. For a glimpse of the pain undergone by Rilke, see for example his letter to Lou Andreas-Salomé of January 24, 1912: "I know now that psychoanalysis would make sense for me only if I were really serious about the strange possibility of *no longer* writing, which during the completion of *Malte* I often dangled in front of my

nose as a kind of relief. Then one might let one's devils be exorcised, since in daily life they are truly just disturbing and painful. And if it happened that the angels left too, one would have to understand this as a further simplification and tell oneself that in the new profession (which?), there would certainly be not use for them" (cited by Stephen Mitchell in *The Selected Poetry of Rainer Maria Rilke,* 312). In Woolf one finds a similar complaint against the pain of having to feel and write: "Lord how I suffer! What a terrific capacity I possess for feeling with intensity. . . . I'm screwed up into a ball; . . . wonder how a year or 20 perhaps is to be endured. Think, yet people do live" (May 25, 1932, *Diary,* vol. 4). But there is no hint here of a desire for "simplification" or a "new profession."

30. "A Sketch of the Past" provides us with a striking instance of such a narcissistic threat, as Virginia Woolf looks into a mirror, this time literally, and sees in it a monstrous apparition ("I dreamt that I was looking in a glass when a horrible face—the face of an animal—suddenly showed over my shoulder," 69). For a discussion of this moment see my article "Intervals and Their Truths."

31. The last two lines of Rilke's poem thus say, "For, when I lose myself in my gaze / I could think it is murderous" (translation mine).

32. In *Narcissisme de vie et de mort,* André Green evokes similarly the dangers of a narcissism that he defines as "negative": "Negative narcissism tends towards inexistence, asthenia, emptiness, a blank space (from the English 'blank' translated as the category of the neutral), whether this blank invests affect (as indifference), representations (as negative hallucination), or thought (as psychosis)" (39). He thus provides a persuasive development to Salomé's (and Rilke's) intuition of the risk incurred by the narcissistic subject.

33. I am quoting from Jean Laplanche's "The Ego and the Vital Order," in *Life and Death in Psychoanalysis,* 51–54.

34. Rilke, "Narziss (2)," 56.

35. As we saw in studying nostalgia, this original happiness may be nothing more than a retroactive projection.

36. On first appearances, the rememberer's desire in "Sylvie" focuses on the three women, Adrienne, Sylvie, and Aurélie, whom he encounters in his peregrinations. Yet, as has been brilliantly demonstrated by Sarah Kofman, *Nerval: le charme de la répétition,* what emerges from this dazzling, bewildering play of similarities and doublings (all women end up looking alike, or are perceived as contrasting imprints of each other) is the presiding figure of Gérard's mother. In *Gérard de Nerval: Expérience et création,* Jean Richer similarly argues that the mother is the source of all nostalgia in Nerval's work.

37. A brief incursion into phenomenology might be enlightening here, because it spells out the philosophical implications of Proust's idea. In *Being and Nothingness,* Sartre discusses, under the rubric of "affective images," the notion of a "psychical body" that carries our subjective history. "As the body is the contingent and indifferent matter of all our psychical events," he writes, "this body defines a *psychical space.*" In this psychical space constituted by our bodily awareness, Sartre finds a justification for a psychoanalytical model of mind: the psychical body "justifies psychological theories such as that of the unconscious, and questions such as that of the

preservation of memories" (386–87). Overlapping with Proust's ideas, Sartre's theory suggests that the body is ultimately the keeper of our memories.

38. For a recent discussion of the role of the body in Proust, see Anne Henry, " 'Exister en soi c'est vouloir': présence du corps," in *La Tentation de Marcel Proust*, 101–11.

39. In the first few pages of the *Recherche*, cheeks represented twice—first as perception and then as memory—constitute a privileged site of pleasure: "I would lay my cheeks gently against the comfortable cheeks of my pillow, as plump and blooming as the cheeks of babyhood *(les joues de notre enfance)*" *(Swann's Way,* 4). The English translation evokes more powerfully than the original how the oldest of memories (reemerging from "babyhood") underwrite current pleasurable sensations. For Proust mnemonic images seem to inhabit the body, as is shown when he writes on the next page that after dreaming of intercourse with a woman, "my cheek was still warm from her kiss" (5).

40. See in particular *La Fugitive*, 3:429–38. In a striking passage, which seems to unwittingly echo psychoanalytical theories, Proust writes about a hysterical body where symptoms symbolize lost memories. Thus Proust writes: "I ended up wondering whether the return of my pain was not due to merely pathological causes and whether what I took to be the rebirth of a memory and the final stage of my love was not rather the beginning of a heart complaint" (431). Proust suggests here, as he does in the "Intermittences of the heart," that lost memories can reappear in the forms of symptoms. In this instance, too, the heart is the site of such involuntary recollection.

41. The concept of body memory has been recently explored in different contexts. The neuroscientist Israel Rosenfield, for example, develops, in *The Strange, Familiar, and Forgotten*, the thesis that the body is the ultimate and indispensable frame of reference for our memories and for consciousness. Rosenfield elicits the notion of body memory from a text by John Hull, who wrote about the changes in the mechanism of recollection brought about by his blindness (see 64–67). Combining a phenomenological and a psychoanalytical perspective, Monique David-Ménard argues, in *Hysteria from Freud to Lacan*, that our most significant autobiographical memories ultimately go back to bodily sites of pleasure and pain.

42. I discuss the distinction between *Gedächtnis* (recollection) and *Erinnerung* (reminiscence) in "The Color of the Past: A Postscript."

43. For writers, however, this is possible, and it enables them to reach the space of childhood—the place of greatest coincidence between inner experience and outer event. *Die Kinderstube* (the nursery) is the place where creative writers ultimately like to return. Salomé's idea coincides with Woolf's, who also believed in gathering first impressions from the nursery.

44. In a letter to Anna Freud of August 1923, Salomé further specifies what she means by form. "Form is, from an artistic point of view, the content of unconscious, inexpressible traces, that is, it is always symbol" ("Aus Briefen an Anna Freud," 228). This line of argument, it turns out, offers an implicit response to the fear expressed in Rilke's poem: aesthetic form binds the flesh that seeps out of the kernel.

In other words, it gives the necessary outline to the ego image (or autobiographical image, as we might say) sought by Narcissus.

45. "I've forced myself to work at R[oger Fry] this morning. . . . if one cared for R. this is a way to show it" (October 20, 1938, *Diary*, vol. 5).

Chapter 10

1. Hermione Lee quotes a revealing statement from a letter to Hugh Walpole: "In fact I sometimes think only autobiography is literature—novels are what we peel off, and come at last to the core, which is only you and me" (637). From this, Lee concludes, as I do, that fiction and autobiography are profoundly interrelated in Woolf's work.

2. For the notion of remembrance and intervals, see my article "Intervals and Their Truths."

3. This was written on February 7, 1941. Before her death Woolf wrote another four entries (*Diary*, vol. 5). On March 24, Woolf describes her husband's gardening, "L[eonard] is doing the rhododendrons . . ." These are her last words (followed by suspension marks) in her diary; she died four days later. This notation is all the more suggestive for providing a counterpart to the important scene (which I discuss in chapter 2) where the rememberer finds that her perception of the gardener vanishes in light of her childhood memories.

4. "I am simply recording the various emotional experiences which marked me for life, both the earliest ones and those which occurred subsequently and linked to them," Althusser explains in his autobiography *L'Avenir dure longtemps* (Phillips, "Childhood Again," 148). This definition of autobiography is at the center of Phillips's essay.

5. Phillips explains that the repetitions constitutive of autobiography "gradually transform, through symbolic transformation, the irruption of infancy into a pattern" ("Childhood Again," 153).

6. Here is how Woolf herself puts it in a memoir she addresses to her nephew Julian Bell under the title "Reminiscences" (she is twenty-five): "If what I have said of her has any meaning you will believe that her death was the greatest disaster that could happen" (39).

7. See Freud, *Beyond the Pleasure Principle*, 13–17.

8. Thomas Cottle writes about his mother, the pianist Gitta Gradova, in *When the Music Stopped*. The citation comes from the preface, xii. "Bioautographies are life narratives . . . that write and read the self through the representation of another's life," Janet Beizer writes in her book *Vicarious Life*, forthcoming from Cornell University Press.

9. Two texts by Sigmund Freud connecting memory and pain or loss are part of crucial importance in this chapter, "Remembering, Repeating, and Working Through," and "Mourning and Melancholia." In the latter text, Freud reflects on the time frame involved in mourning and concludes that there this duration cannot

be determined objectively, given that each cathexis (or affectively charged mnemonic scene) needs to be revisited in turn until the rememberer comes to the end of her journey (see pp. 252–56).

10. Freud, it will be recalled, developed a first understanding of hysteria as a memory disorder in declaring that "hysterics suffer mainly from reminiscences" in his early *Studies in Hysteria* published in collaboration with Breuer (*SE* 2:2). Pierre Janet's work focused, meanwhile, on hypermnesia, as an "exaggeration of memory," a concept he develops at length in his famous case study on Irène published separately under the title "L'Amnésie et la dissociation des souvenirs par l'émotion." In *La Querelle de l'hystérie*, Pierre-Henri Castel offers an excellent summary of Janet's rich, but lesser-known theory: "Hysteria is defined as an inability to reactualize representations and to create the necessary contact with the active, attentive side of the mind. . . . instead these representations, which escape the patient's willpower and attention, function in a subconscious and automatic manner, in occasionally creating new aggregates [i.e. hallucinations] that emerge outside of consciousness" (138–39).

11. For a rich discussion of Woolf and psychoanalysis, see Elizabeth Abel, *Virginia Woolf and the Fictions of Psychoanalysis*.

12. Discussing the impossibility of establishing what caused Woolf's mental illness, Hermione Lee adds a resonant description of the place held by writing in Woolf's existence: "We can only look at what it did to her, and she did with it. What is certain is her closeness, all her life, to a terrifying edge, and her creation of a language which faces it and makes something of it. This is a life of heroism, not of oppression, a life of writing wrestled from illness, fear, and pain" (199).

13. In *Studies on Hysteria*, Freud and Breuer compare the presence of an unresolved trauma to a "foreign body" or a "cyst" lodged in the psyche.

14. In "Remembering, Repeating, and Working-Through," Freud provides us with an explanation of Woolf's oxymoronic definition: "When the patient talks about these 'forgotten' things he seldom fails to add: 'As a matter of fact I've always known it; only I've never thought of it.' He often expresses disappointment at the fact that not enough things come into his head that can be called 'forgotten'—that he has never thought of it since it happened" (148).

15. September 12, 1934, *Diary*, vol. 4. Woolf's transcription in French of Maupassant's text says: "never to suffer, think, love, feel like everyone else, just frankly, simply, without analyzing oneself after each joy and after each sob."

16. This indifference is clearly at odds with Woolf's acknowledged sensitivity; see note 29 of the previous chapter, "The Rememberer's Task."

17. *The Complete Letters of Virginia Woolf*, vol. 3, May 22, 1927.

18. For a discussion of this type of symbolization from a phenomenological perspective see the chapter Jean-Jacques Wunenburger's "La profondeur symbolique," 15–25.

19. Woolf expresses her resistance to easy sentiment in a formulation that evokes the presence of a hysterical (?) knot in her throat: "The word sentimental sticks in my gizzard," she writes in her diary (July 10, 1925, *Diary*, vol. 3).

20. These colors, "bathed in resplendent light" or endowed with an aura *(ray-*

onnement), might trace the child's earlier fascination with the maternal figure, as Maurice Blanchot suggests: "It is because the child is fascinated that the mother fascinates, and this is also why all the impressions from infancy carry some of that fixedness *(ont quelque chose de fixe)* that derives from this fascination" (*L'espace littéraire,* 26–27).

Whereas in Woolf's phenomenal universe the aura appears when the mother disappears, William Wordsworth, in a famous passage of *The Prelude,* tells us that for the poet who has "gather[ed] passion from his mother's eye," the world is endowed with an intensity connected to maternal presence: "From this beloved Presence, there exists / A virtue which irradiates and exalts / All objects through all intercourse of sense."

21. The mystery that Henry James explores in his famous allegorical tale "The Figure in the Carpet" is the same one that I am facing, namely to what extent the figures I see in Woolf's text are the result of an act of literary projection.

22. A compromise formation is the symbolic form taken by a repressed content (see "Compromise formation" in Laplanche and Pontalis, *The Language of Psychoanalysis*). While such formations enable the rememberer to move out of the hysterical dissociation I analyzed earlier, they represent only the beginnings of a recovery to the extent that their signification remains obscure and barely communicable. For a literary author, there might be as well another dimension to this compromise; it might obey a desire for privacy. Thus while Woolf reveals her most intimate emotions, she hides them behind the screen of a very private symbolism.

23. In *Les Maladies de la mémoire,* Jean Delay argues that "social memory" normally inhibits "autistic memory" (16). In the importance he gives to the social imprinting of memory, Delay draws on the work of Pierre Janet as well as of Maurice Halbwachs; he thus explains that social memory depends on narrative, defined by Janet as "the language created by society to overcome a condition of absence" (*L'Evolution,* 221). In the broader framework of a reflection on the therapeutic efficacy of Woolf's memory work, it may be worth bearing in mind that for Delay psychoanalysis effects the transfer of memories from the plane of affects to that of representation, that is, from autistic to social memory (20).

24. For a discussion of narcissism and autobiography, see the previous chapter, "The Rememberer's Task."

25. "But perhaps it might be properly be said that there are three times, the present of things past, the present of things present, the present of things future. . . .The present of things past is in memory," writes Augustine in book 11, chap. 44 of his *Confessions.* Commenting on this passage in *Narrative Crossings,* Alexander Gelley writes: "Augustine's 'present of things past' suggests a conception of memory as a process of blending and transforming different modes of temporal experience for the sake of present consciousness" (108). In *The Strange, the Familiar, the Forgotten,* the neuroscientist Israel Rosenfield defines recollection in similar ways, in writing that "a conscious image of the past is created from an integration of past experience and present reality in terms of the self" (66). I will emphasize throughout my commentary on Woolf that it is in the present and for the sake of the present that the rememberer gives shape to mnemonic scenes.

26. Jacques Lacan's discussion of such a cry in *Le séminaire VII, L'Ethique de la Psychanalyse* provides an indirect commentary on this scene (56–70). It could indeed be argued that the cry uttered in *To the Lighthouse* marks the encounter with "an object *(das Ding)* that represents an absolute Other for the subject, and that must be found again" (65).

27. In *Gradus, les procédés littéraires* Bernard Dupriez emphasizes the psychological underpinnings of prosopopoeia in his commentary: it "is a strange figure. . . . the person becomes a real interlocutor, hence the apostrophe and the dialogism. The absent is placed in the present . . . and the figure belongs to the same family as hallucination" (365). I will argue, however, that through writing Woolf substitutes. a constructed, fictive hallucination for another form (which she describes as an obsession) that might have been fatal to her mental life. To that extent her fiction amounts to play—but serious play in the sense that Winnicott might ascribe to this activity. For Freud, meanwhile, hallucinations are part of mourning, as he suggests in describing "hallucinatory wishful psychosis" ("Mourning and Melancholia," 244).

28. As Damasio demonstrates, recognizing faces is a highly specialized mental skill; see his discussions of patients who have lost their memory for faces and suffer from "face agnosia" in *The Feeling of What Happens* (see 162–66 and 300–301).

29. In his article "Hypogram and Inscription," Paul de Man ascribes this property of reference to all signifiers (48). I suggest here that the referent of a memory is a product of the phenomenal and sensory properties of the figure.

30. For this conception of scene, see Schneider, "Temporalité, inconscient et répétition," in *Mythes et représentations du temps,* 28ff.

31. I am invoking here the definition of remembrance that is Lou-Andreas Salomé's, which I discuss in the previous chapter, "The Rememberer's Task."

32. Woolf's remembering naturally belongs to a Freudian conception that attributes a therapeutic value to narrative. As is well known, Breuer and Freud developed in *Studies in Hysteria* the first elements of this theory in speaking of a "talking cure" or of "chimney sweeping" and suggesting that the act of narration can release the patient from her reminiscences. However, Freud's work on transference and countertransference shows that he developed over time a much more complex understanding of narrative in psychoanalysis. *In Retelling a Life: Narration and Dialogue in Psychoanalysis* Roy Schafer discusses extensively the various dimensions of the relation between narration and psychoanalytic cure.

33. While working on *To the Lighthouse* and approaching mental exhaustion, Woolf comments on the special image-making abilities of writers: "*Returning health.* This is shown by the power to make images: the suggestive power of every sight & word is enormously increased. Shakespeare must have had this" (July 31, 1926, *Diary,* vol. 3).

34. "I have an idea that I will invent a new name for my books to supplant 'novel.' A new—by Virginia Woolf. But what? Elegy" (June 27, 1925, *Diary,* vol. 3). To write one "elegy" (this is how she defines *To the Lighthouse* in an early, prescient diary entry) is not enough. As we are seeing, there seems to be no end, for Woolf, to

mourning and remembering her mother. But what changes, however, are the forms taken by her remembrance.

35. For a discussion of these two forms of remembrance, see chapter 4, "George Eliot's Movie-in-the-Brain."

36. In "Conceptions of Affect," André Green writes: "The whole question seems to me to lie in the wasteland between two types of affects . . . in respect of which I have put forward a theoretical reformulation: affect with a semantic function as an element in the chain of signifiers *(chaîne signifiante)*, and affect overflowing the concatenation and spreading as it breaks the links of the chain" (208). Our discussion of Woolf has taken us to a place in her writing where affect is most clearly endowed "with a semantic function" in the signifying chain that defines her narrative. Eschewing the sentimentality she abhors, Woolf writes about memories that involve feeling as an awareness of emotions and of primitive bodily perceptions.

37. This episode, which belongs to the earliest drafts of the *Recherche*, now appears in *Cities of the Plain*, 783–90. "Intermittences" is a significant concept in Proust's conception of mind and body. Anne Henry argues that the author was inspired to use the term "intermittence" by the work of the famous doctor Bichat, the author of *Recherches physiologiques sur la vie et la mort* (*Proust*, 189). For a more detailed discussion, see Antoine Compagnon's notes in the Pléiade edition, 3:1225–27.

38. For a rich analysis of the difficulty of representing affects that "come too early," see Laplanche, 35–45.

39. As many critics have shown, often identifying very definite autobiographical features in the literary representation, the figure of the mother and the grandmother in *A la Recherche du temps perdu* are given overlapping features, suggesting that Proust "spread" one maternal image over these two distinctive figures.

40. In his notes to volume 3 of the Pléiade edition of *A la Recherche du temps perdu*, Antoine Compagnon richly discusses *les Intermittences du coeur*, and concludes that "this theme predates the theories of involuntary memory that structure the novel" (1225–27).

41. Walter Benjamin highlights this aspect of Proustian remembrance in "The Image of Proust," 204–5.

42. Describing the process that relegates some memories "in the back of" others, Proust uses the term *refoulé*, which is, coincidentally, the standard French term for "repressed." In his authoritative biography of Proust, Jean-Yves Tadié summarily dismisses any idea of an overt influence between these two authors, who neither know each other nor were aware of each other's work, in writing: "Freud, dont Proust ignore tout et réciproquement" (1:765).

It would be tempting, meanwhile, to give the name "unconscious" to that "unknown region" that Proust evokes in his first description of an involuntary memory. Memories, he thus tells us, lie in wait until they are "recaptured" through the coincidence of sensation. The subject retains them "in a virtual state" *(un état virtuel)* until, as is the case here, a sudden encounter with a sensation brings them to consciousness.

43. The last two sentences of this paragraph are filled with quotations marks because I am citing what are, in fact, Proust's own resounding words in this key passage.

44. It would be a mistake, however, to erase all differences between them. As the "intermittences of the heart" confirm, Proust tells us the story, in his *Recherche,* of the emergence of memory *in the body.* This choice commits him, however, to conceal the crucial function of writing (of his style) in the presentation of mnemonic contents. Woolf, on the contrary, begins her inquiry into remembrance from the standpoint of writing: she makes us thus aware of a literary performance that is designed to produce (sometimes, but not always) the remembering body. In other words, Proust and Woolf move in contrary directions, but within the same epistemological framework, where memories are defined as body and mind and where writing is the instrument of their creation.

45. See, for example, Beryl Schlossman, "The Descent of Orpheus," as well as Diana Knight "The Woman without a Shadow," 136–37, and Colin McCabe, "The Ontology of the Image," 73–75.

46. Jacques Derrida addresses this question in "Les Morts de Roland Barthes," 272 and 282–83. See also Elissa Marder's commentary on both Barthes and Derrida in "Nothing to Say," 26–28. In *Family Frames,* Marianne Hirsch writes: "If reference is, as Barthes says, the 'founding order' of photography, a picture may be the optimal medium for such a process of consolidating the past and bringing it into the present" (202).

47. While acknowledging Proust's influence (63), Barthes argues that photography kills memory: "Not only is the Photograph never, in essence, a memory. . . , but it actually blocks memory, quickly becomes a counter memory" (91). But *Camera Lucida* shows repeatedly that photographs (provided they have punctum) prompt memories, through what Marianne Hirsch has aptly called the "illusion of depth" (119). Speaking of "photographic *ecstasy*" in the last pages of *Camera Lucida,* Barthes makes it clear that he experiences, through the medium of photography, memories that are analogous to those presented in "A Sketch of the Past" (119).

48. It might be worth putting this remark in a different context, not merely phenomenological but literary. As rememberers we are, forever, looking for works of art that will produce lasting traces of our memories. Horace developed the conventions of *aere perennium* that endow writing with the privileged ability to keep everlasting traces of human experiences.

49. Jean-Michel Rabaté quotes from Jean-Paul Sartre, *L'Imaginaire,* 371.

The Color of the Past

1. See Jean Starobinski, "Le Style de l'autobiographie," 261.

2. For a discussion of this difference in Hegel, see Chase, "Getting Versed," 116–24.

3. Throughout her essay, Salomé relates the subject to "nature," whereas in the

conception we developed around Woolf and, more generally, from a phenomenological perspective, the relation is between the subject and the world more generally.

4. Quoted by Pillemer in *Momentous Events, Vivid Memories*. In fact, memories remain generally consistent over long stretches of time, as Pillemer further specifies: "Most studies reveal some instances of memory distortion, but at the same time have shown reasonably high overall levels of consistency over months or years" (57).

Bibliography

Abel, Elizabeth. *Virginia Woolf and the Fictions of Psychoanalysis*. Chicago: University of Chicago Press, 1989.

Aciman, André. "Letter from Illiers-Combray: In Search of Proust." *New Yorker*, December 21, 1998, 81–85.

———. "Shadow Cities." In *False Papers: Essays on Exile and Memory*. New York: Farrar, Straus and Giroux, 2000.

Agacinski, Sylviane. *Le Passeur de temps: Modernité et nostalgie*. Paris: Seuil, 2000.

Alphen, Ernst Van. *Caught by History: Holocaust Affects in Contemporary Art, Literature, and Theory*. Stanford: Stanford University Press, 1997.

Andreas-Salomé, Lou. "Aus Briefen an Anna Freud." In *Das "Zweideutige" Lächeln der Erotik*. Freiburg i.Br.: Kore, 1990.

———. "The Dual Orientation of Narcissism." Trans. Stanley A. Leavy. *Psychoanalytic Quarterly* 31 (1962): 1–31.

———. "Mein Dank an Freud." In *Das "Zweideutige" Lächeln der Erotik*. Freiburg: Kore, 1990.

———. "Le Narcissisme comme double direction." In *L'Amour du narcissisme: Textes psychanalytiques*. Trans. Isabelle Hildenbrand. Paris: Gallimard, 1980.

———. "Narzissmus als Doppelrichtung." In *Das "Zweideutige" Lächeln der Erotik*. Freiburg: Kore, 1990.

Ashton, Rosemary. *The Mill on the Floss*. Boston: Twayne, 1990.

Augustine. *The Confessions of St. Augustine*. Trans. John K. Ryan. Garden City, New York: Image Books, 1960.

Bal, Mieke. "Memories in the Museum." In *Acts of Memory: Cultural Recall in the Present*. Ed. Mieke Bal et al. Hanover: University Press of New England, 1999.

Bal, Mieke, Jonathan Crewe, and Leo Spitzer, eds. *Acts of Memory: Cultural Recall in the Present*. Hanover: University Press of New England, 1999.

Barthes, Roland. *Camera Lucida: Reflections on Photography*. Trans. Richard Howard. New York: Farrar, Straus and Giroux, 1981.

———. "L'effet de réel." In *Littérature et réalité*. Paris: Seuil, 1982.

———. "Longtemps, je me suis couché de bonne heure." In *Oeuvres complètes*, vol. 2. Paris: Seuil, 1995.

Baudelaire, Charles. *Paris Spleen 1869*. Trans. Louise Varèse. New York: New Directions, 1970.

Beckett, Samuel. *Proust*. New York: Grove Press, 1957.

Benjamin, Walter. "The Image of Proust." In *Illuminations*. Ed. Hannah Arendt. Trans. Harry Zohn. New York: Schocken, 1968.

———. "On Some Motifs in Baudelaire." In *Illuminations*. Ed. Hannah Arendt. Trans. Harry Zohn. New York: Schocken, 1968.

———. "The Work of Art in the Age of Mechanical Reproduction." Ed. Hannah Arendt. Trans. Harry Zohn. New York: Schocken, 1968.

Benstock, Shari. "Authorizing the Autobiographical." In *The Private Self: Theory and Practice of Women's Autobiography*. Ed. Shari Benstock. London: Routledge, 1988.

Benveniste, Emile. "Subjectivity in Language." In *Problems in General Linguistics*. Trans. Mary E. Meek. Coral Gables, Fla.: University of Miami Press, 1971.

Biran, Maine de. *Influence de l'habitude sur la faculté de penser*. Ed. Pierre Tisserand. Paris: Presses Universitaires de France, 1954.

Bizub, Edward. *La Venise intérieure: Proust et la poétique de la traduction*. Neuchâtel: La Baconnière, 1991.

Blanchot, Maurice. *L'Espace littéraire*. Paris: Gallimard, 1955.

Bloom, Harold. *Poetry and Repression*. New Haven: Yale University Press, 1976.

Bowie, Malcolm. *Lacan*. Cambridge: Harvard University Press, 1991.

———. *Proust among the Stars*. New York: Columbia University Press, 1998.

Boym, Svetlana. *The Future of Memory*. New York: Basic Books, 2001.

Breuer, Josef, and Sigmund Freud. *Studies on Hysteria*. Trans. James Strachey with the collaboration of Anna Freud. New York: Basic Books, 1955.

Brewer, William F. "What Is Autobiographical Memory?" in *Autobiographical Memory*. Ed. David C. Rubin. Cambridge: Cambridge University Press, 1986.

Bronowski, Jacob. "Knowledge as Algorithm and as Metaphor." In *The Origins of Knowledge and Imagination*. New Haven: Yale University Press, 1978.

Butor, Michel. *Essais sur les modernes*. Paris: Gallimard, 1963.

———. *Répertoire II*. Paris: Les Editions de Minuit, 1964.

Butters, Nelson, and Laird S. Cermak. "A Case Study of the Forgetting of Autobiographical Knowledge: Implications for the Study of Retrograde Amnesia." In *Autobiographical Memory*. Ed. D. C. Rubin. Cambridge: Cambridge University Press, 1986.

Caruth, Cathy. *Unclaimed Experience: Trauma Narrative and History*. Baltimore: Johns Hopkins University Press, 1996.

———, ed. *Trauma: Explorations in Memory*. Baltimore: Johns Hopkins University Press, 1995.

Castel, Pierre-Henri. *La Querelle de l'hystérie: La formation du discours psychopathologique en France (1881–1913)*. Paris: Presses Universitaires de France, 1998.

Chase, Cynthia. "Getting Versed: Reading Hegel with Baudelaire." In *Decomposing Figures: Rhetorical Reading in the Romantic Tradition*. Baltimore: Johns Hopkins University Press, 1986.

Chu, Simon, and John J. Downes. "Proust Nose Best: Odors Are Better Cues of Autobiographical Memory." *Memory & Cognition* 30, no. 4 (2002): 511–18.

Cohen, Elizabeth. *The House on Beartown Road: A Memoir of Learning and Forgetting*. New York: Random House, 2003.

Cohen, Gillian, and Stephanie Taylor. "Reminiscence and Aging." *Aging and Society* 18, no. 5 (1998): 601–10.

Compagnon, Antoine. "La *Recherche du temps perdu* de Marcel Proust." In *Lieux de mémoire*. Ed. Pierre Nora. Vol. 3. Paris: Quarto Gallimard, 1997.

Conway, Martin A. *Autobiographical Memory: An Introduction.* Milton Keynes: Open University Press, 1990.

Corvol, Andrée. "La forêt." In *Lieux de mémoire*. Vol. 2. Ed. Pierre Nora. Paris: Gallimard, 1997.

Cottle, Thomas. *When the Music Stopped: Discovering My Mother.* Albany: State University of New York Press, 2004.

Craig, Edward, ed. *Routledge Encyclopedia of Philosophy.* London: Routledge, 1998.

Crews, Frederick. *The Memory Wars: Freud in Dispute.* New York: New York Review of Books, 1995.

Damasio, Antonio R. *Descartes' Error: Emotion, Reason, and the Human Brain.* New York: Avon, 1994.

———. *The Feeling of What Happens: Body and Emotion in the Making of Consciousness.* New York: Harcourt Brace, 1999.

———. "How the Brain Creates the Mind." *Scientific American,* December 1999, 112–17.

David-Ménard, Monique. *Hysteria from Freud to Lacan: Body and Language in Psychoanalysis.* Trans. Catherine Porter. Ithaca: Cornell University Press, 1989.

De Bolla, Peter. *Art Matters.* Cambridge: Harvard University Press, 2001.

De Botton, Alain. *How Proust Can Change Your Life: Not a Novel.* New York: Pantheon, 1997.

Delay, Jean. *Les Maladies de la mémoire.* Paris: Presses Universitaires de France, 1961.

Deleuze, Gilles. *Bergsonism.* Trans. Hugh Tomlinson and Barbara Habberjam. New York: Zone, 1988.

———. *Proust et les signes.* Paris: Presses Universitaires de France, 1971.

de Man, Paul. "Autobiography as De-facement." In *The Rhetoric of Romanticism.* New York: Columbia University Press, 1984.

———. "Hypogram and Inscription." In *The Resistance to Theory.* Minneapolis: Minnesota University Press, 1986.

Dennett, Daniel C. *Consciousness Explained.* Boston: Little, Brown, 1991.

Derrida, Jacques. "Les Morts de Roland Barthes." *Poétique* 12, no. 47 (1981): 269–92.

Didier, Béatrice. "Le Voyage, le livre, l'écriture." Preface to *Les Filles du feu suivi de Aurélia.* Paris: Folio, 1972.

Dupriez, Bernard. *Les Procédés littéraires.* Paris: Union Général d'éditions, 1984.

Edelman, Gerald M. *Bright Air, Brilliant Fire: On the Matter of the Mind.* New York: Basic Books, 1992.

———. *The Remembered Present: A Biological Theory of Consciousness.* New York: Basic Books, 1989.

Eliot, George. *The Mill on the Floss.* Harmondsworth: Penguin, 1986.

Ender, Evelyne. "Intervals and Their Truths in Marcel Proust and Virginia Woolf." *Comp(a)rison* 1 (1995): 59–78.

———. " 'Speculating Carnally' or, Some Reflections on the Modernist Body." *Yale Journal of Criticism* 12, no. 1 (1999): 113–30.

Erickson, Lynn M., and Kathryn Leide. "Taste, Touch, and Smell the Memories." *Activities, Adaptation, and Aging* 16, no. 3 (1991): 25–39.

Felman, Shoshana. *Writing and Madness (Literature/Philosophy/Psychoanalysis)*. Trans. Martha Evans with the assistance of Brian Massumi. Palo Alto: Stanford University Press, 2004.

Felman, Shoshana, and Dori Laub. *Testimony: Crises in Witnessing in Literature, Psychoanalysis, and History*. New York: Routledge, 1992.

Ferrer, Daniel. *Virginia Woolf and the Madness of Language*. Trans. J. Bennington and R. Bowlby. London: Routledge, 1990.

Franzen, Jonathan. "My Father's Brain." In *The Best American Essays*. Ed. Stephen Jay Gould. Boston: Houghton Mifflin, 2002.

Freud, Sigmund. *The Standard Edition of the Complete Psychological Works of Sigmund Freud*. Trans. under the direction of James Strachey. 24 vols. London: Hogarth Press, 1959–72. Cited throughout as *SE*.

———. *Beyond the Pleasure Principle*. Trans. James Strachey. London: Norton, 1961.

———. "Constructions in Analysis." *SE*, vol. 13.

———. *The Interpretation of Dreams*. Trans. James Strachey. New York: Avon Books, 1965.

———. "Mourning and Melancholia." *SE*, vol. 14.

———. "On Narcissism: An Introduction." *SE*, vol. 14.

———. *The Psychopathology of Everyday Life*. Trans. James Strachey. New York: Norton, 1989.

———. "Remembering, Repeating and Working-Through." *SE*, vol. 12.

———. "Screen Memories." *SE*, vol. 3.

———. *Three Essays on the Theory of Sexuality*. Trans. James Strachey. New York: Basic Books, 1962.

———. "The Uncanny." *SE*, vol. 17.

———. "Vergänglichkeit." In *Bildende Kunst und Literatur*. Frankfurt am Main: Fischer Verlag, 1969.

Gelley, Alexander. *Narrative Crossings: Theory and Pragmatics of Prose Fiction*. Baltimore: Johns Hopkins University Press, 1987.

Good, Michael. "Screen Reconstructions." *Journal of the American Psychoanalytic Association* 46, no. 1 (1998): 149–83.

Craig, Edward, ed. *Routledge Encyclopedia of Philosophy*. London: Routledge, 1998.

Grady, Denise. "The Hardest Habit to Break: Memories of the High." *New York Times*, October 27, 1998, Science section.

Green, André. "Conceptions of Affect." In *On Private Madness*. London: Hogarth Press and the Institute of Psychoanalysis, 1986.

———. "L'Enfant modèle." *L'Enfant.* Special issue, *Nouvelle Revue de Psychanalyse* 19 (1979): 27–47.

———. *Narcissisme de vie, narcissisme de mort.* Paris: Editions de Minuit, 1983.

Greenacre, Phyllis. "A Contribution to the Study of Screen Memories." *Psychoanalytic Study of the Child* 3–4 (1949): 73–84.

Guillaumin, Jean. *La Genèse du souvenir: Essai sur les fondements de la psychologie de l'enfant.* Paris: Presses Universitaires de France, 1968.

Hacking, Ian. *Rewriting the Soul: Multiple Personality and the Sciences of Memory.* Princeton: Princeton University Press, 1995.

Hall, Stephen S. "Our Memories, Our Selves." *New York Times Magazine,* February 15, 1998, 26–33, 49, 56–57.

Hartman, Geoffrey H., ed. *Holocaust Remembrance: The Shape of Memory.* Oxford: Blackwell, 1994.

Heer, Jeet. "Haunted." *Boston Globe,* April 4, 2004, "Ideas," D1.

Hegel, Georg Wilhelm Friedrich. *Vorlesungen über die Aesthetik.* Stuttgart: Friedrich Frommann Verlag, 1964.

Henry, Anne. *La Tentation de Marcel Proust.* Paris: Presses Universitaires de France, 2000.

Herz, Rachel S. "Are Odors the Best Cues to Memory? A Cross-Modal Comparison of Associative Memory Stimuli." *Annals of the New York Academy of Sciences* 855 (1998): 670–74.

Herz, Rachel S., and Jonathan W. Schooler. "A Naturalistic Study of Autobiographical Memories Evoked by Olfactory and Visual Cues: Testing the Proustian Hypothesis." *The American Journal of Psychology* 115, no. 1 (spring 2002): 21–32.

Hirsch, Marianne. *Family Frames: Photography, Narrative, and Postmemory.* Cambridge: Harvard University Press, 1997.

Hirst, William, and Michael S. Gazzaniga. "Present and Future of Memory Research and Its Applications." In *Perspectives in Memory Research.* Ed. Michael S. Gazzaniga. Cambridge: MIT Press, 1988.

Hofstader, Douglas R. "Analogy as the Core of Cognition." In *The Best American Science Writing, 2000.* Ed. James Gleick. New York: HarperCollins, 2000.

Holloway, Marguerite. "The Ascent of Scent." *Scientific American,* November 1999, 42–44.

Honderich, Ted, ed. *Oxford Companion to Philosophy.* Oxford: Oxford University Press, 1995.

Hume, David. *Treatise of Human Nature.* Ed. L. A. Selby-Bigge and P. H. Nidditch. Oxford: Clarendon Press, 1978.

Huyssen, Andreas. *Twilight Memories: Marking Time in a Culture of Amnesia.* New York: Routledge, 1995.

Janet, Pierre. "L'Amnésie et la dissociation des souvenirs par l'émotion." *Le Journal de Psychologie Normal et Pathologique* 5 (1904): 1–37.

———. *L'Evolution de la mémoire et de la notion du temps.* Paris: A. Chahine, 1928.

Jankélévich, Vladimir. *L'Irréversible et la nostalgie.* Paris: Flammarion, 1974.

Jansari, Ashok, and Alan J. Parkin. "Things That Go Bump in Your Life: Explaining the Reminiscence Bump in Autobiographical Memory." *Psychology and Aging* 11, no. 1 (1996): 85–91.

Jean, Raymond. *Nerval par lui-même*. Paris: Seuil (Ecrivains de toujours), 1964.

Jeanneret, Michel. *La Lettre perdue: Ecriture et folie dans l'oeuvre de Gérard de Nerval*. Paris: Flammarion, 1978.

Joseph, Edward D. "Sense of Conviction, Screen Memories, and Reconstruction—a Clinical Note." *Bulletin of the Menninger Clinic* 37, no. 6 (1973): 565–77.

Jürgs, Michael. *Alzheimer Spurensuche im Niemandsland*. Munich: List, 1999.

Kant, Immanuel. *Kritik der Urteilskraft*. Frankfurt am Main: Suhrkamp, 1974.

Keats, John. "Endymion." In *The Complete Poems*. Harmondsworth: Penguin Books, 1973.

Kety, Seymour S. "A Biologist Examines the Mind and Behaviour." In *Medical Behavioral Science*. Ed. Theodore Million. Philadelphia: W. B. Saunders, 1975.

Knight, Diana. "The Woman without a Shadow." In *Writing the Image after Roland Barthes*. Ed. Jean-Michel Rabaté. Philadelphia: University of Pennsylvania Press, 1997.

Kofman, Sarah. *Nerval: Le charme de la répétition*. Lausanne: L'Age d'homme, 1979.

Kristeva, Julia. *Soleil noir: Dépression et mélancolie*. Paris: Gallimard, 1987.

Lacan, Jacques. *Le séminaire VII: L'Ethique de la psychanalyse*. Paris: Seuil, 1986.

Lacey, A. R. "Mind and Body: Non-reductionist Theories." In *The Handbook of Western Philosophy*. Ed. G. H. R. Parkinson. London: Routledge, 1998.

LaGuardia, Eric. "The Return of Childhood in Autobiography." *Psychoanalysis and Contemporary Thought* 5, no. 2 (1982): 293–305.

Lane, Anthony. "Telling Time." Review of Antonio Ruiz, *Time Regained*. *New Yorker*, June 19 and 26, 2000, 187–89.

Langer, Lawrence L. *Holocaust Testimonies: The Ruins of Memory*. New Haven: Yale University Press, 1991.

Laplanche, Jean. *Life and Death in Psychoanalysis*. Trans. Jeffrey Mehlman. Baltimore: Johns Hopkins University Press, 1976.

Laplanche, Jean, and Jean-Bertrand Pontalis. *Vocabulaire de la psychanalyse*. Paris: Presses Universitaires de France, 1967.

Lappin, Elena. "The Man with Two Heads." *Granta: Truth and Lies* 66 (1999): 9–65.

Leavy, Stanley A. Introduction to *The Freud Journal of Lou Andreas-Salomé*. New York: Basic Books, 1964.

LeDoux, Joseph. *The Emotional Brain: the Mysterious Underpinnings of Emotional Life*. New York: Simon and Schuster, 1998.

Lee, Hermione. *Virginia Woolf*. London: Chatto and Windus, 1996.

Levin, Janet. "Qualia." In *Routledge Encyclopedia of Philosophy*, vol. 7. Ed. Edward Craig. London: Routledge, 1998.

Leys, Ruth. *Trauma: A Genealogy*. Chicago: University of Chicago Press, 2002.

Linton, Marigold. "Ways of Searching and the Contents of Memory." In *Autobio-*

graphical Memory. Ed. David C. Rubin. Cambridge: Cambridge University Press, 1986.

Luckhurst, Nicola. *Science and Structure in Proust's A la recherche du temps perdu.* Cambridge: Cambridge University Press, 2000.

Lukacher, Ned. *Primal Scenes: Literature, Philosophy, Psychoanalysis.* Ithaca: Cornell University Press, 1986.

Luria, A. R. *The Mind of a Mnemonist.* New York: Basic Books, 1968.

Mahon, Eugene, and Delia Battin-Mahon. "The Fate of Screen Memories in Psychoanalysis." *Psychoanalytic Study of the Child* 38 (1983): 459–79.

Mallarmé, Stéphane. "Crise de vers." Paris: Gallimard (Pléiade), 1945.

Marder, Elissa. "Nothing to Say: Fragments of the Mother in the Age of Mechanical Reproduction." *L'Esprit créateur* 40 (2000): 25–35.

Margalit, Avishai. *The Ethics of Memory.* Cambridge: Harvard University Press, 2002.

McCabe, Colin. "The Ontology of the Image." In *Writing the Image after Roland Barthes.* Ed. Jean-Michel Rabaté. Philadelphia: University of Pennsylvania Press, 1997.

McDonald, Christie. *The Proustian Fabric: Associations of Memory.* Lincoln: University of Nebraska Press, 1991.

McKee, George, and Larry Squire. "On the Development of Declarative Memory." *Journal of Experimental Psychology* 19 (1993): 397–404.

"Memory Gardens Stimulating for People with Alzheimer's." *Advances: Progress in Alzheimer Research and Care* (Alzheimer's Association), fall 2000, 2.

Mesulam, M.-Marsel. "Aging, Alzheimer's Disease, and Dementia: Clinical and Neurobiological Perspectives." In *Principles of Behavioral and Cognitive Neurology.* Oxford: Oxford University Press, 2000.

Michaud, Stéphane. *Lou Andreas-Salomé: L'alliée de la vie.* Paris: Seuil, 2000.

Mitchell, Stephen. *The Selected Poetry of Rainer Maria Rilke.* New York: Random House, 1980.

Mitchell, W. J. T. *Iconology: Image, Text, Ideology.* Chicago: University of Chicago Press, 1987.

Molnar, Michael. "Entre Rilke et Freud." In *Rilke et son amie Lou Andreas-Salomé à Paris.* Ed. Stéphane Michaud and Gerald Stieg. Paris: Presses de la Sorbonne Nouvelle, 2000.

Montaigne, Michel de. "On Practice." In *Essays,* vol. 2. Trans. M. A. Screech. London: Allen Lane, 1991.

Murat, Laure. *La Maison du docteur Blanche: Histoire d'un asile et de ses pensionnaires, de Nerval à Maupassant.* Paris: J-C. Lattès, 2001.

Neisser, Ulric, ed. *Memory Observed: Remembering in Natural Contexts.* New York: W. H. Freeman, 1992.

———. "Nested Structure in Autobiographical Memory." In *Autobiographical Memory.* Ed. David C. Rubin. Cambridge: Cambridge University Press, 1986.

Nerval, Gérard de. "A Alexandre Dumas" (preface to *Les Filles du feu*). In *Oeuvres,* ed. Albert Béguin and Jean Richer, vol. 1. Paris: Gallimard (Pléiade), 1974.

———. *Oeuvres*. Ed. Albert Béguin and Jean Richer. Vol. 1. Paris: Gallimard (Pléiade), 1974.

———. *Promenades et souvenirs*. In *Oeuvres de Gérard de Nerval*. Paris: Gallimard, 1966.

———. *Selected Writings*. Trans. Richard Sieburth. New York: Penguin, 1999.

———. "Sylvie." In *Aurélia Followed by Sylvie*. Trans. Kendall Lappin. Santa Maria: Asylum Arts, 1993.

Phillips, Adam. *The Beast in the Nursery: On Curiosity and Other Appetites*. New York: Vintage, 1998.

———. "Childhood Again." In *Equals*. New York: Basic Books, 2002.

———. "Freud and the Uses of Forgetting." In *On Flirtation*. Cambridge: Harvard University Press, 1994.

———. "On Being Bored." In *On Kissing, Tickling, and Being Bored: Psychoanalytic Essays on the Unexamined Life*. Cambridge: Harvard University Press, 1993.

Picon, Gaëtan. *Lecture de Proust*. Paris: Gallimard, 1963.

Pillemer, David B. *Momentous Events, Vivid Memories*. Cambridge: Harvard University Press, 2000.

Pollack, Robert. "Memory and the Unconscious." In *The Missing Moment: How the Unconscious Shapes Modern Science*. Boston: Houghton Mifflin, 1999.

Pollock, Jonathan D., et al. "Summary of Meeting on 'Molecular and Cellular Basis of Emotional Memory.'" Rockville (MD): National Institute of Health and National Institute on Drug Abuse, 1998.

Poulet, Georges. *L'Espace proustien*. Paris: Gallimard, 1982.

———. *Etudes sur le temps humain: Mesure de l'instant*. Paris: Plon, 1968.

———. *The Interior Distance*. Trans. Elliot Coleman. Baltimore: Johns Hopkins University Press, 1959.

———. Introduction to *Etudes sur le temps humain*, vol. 1. Paris: Editions du rocher, 1989.

———. "The Phenomenology of Reading." Trans. Richard Macksey. *New Literary History* 1, no. 1 (1969): 53–68.

Proust, Marcel. *A la Recherche du temps perdu*. Ed. Jean-Yves Tadié. 4 vols. Paris: Gallimard (Pléiade), 1987.

———. *A la Recherche du temps perdu*. 3 vols. Paris: Robert Laffont, 1987.

———. *Cities of the Plain*. In *Remembrance of Things Past*, vol. 2. New York: Vintage, 1982.

———. "Gérard de Nerval." In *Contre Sainte-Beuve*. Paris: Gallimard, 1954.

———. *Swann's Way*. Trans. C. K. Scott Moncrieff and Terence Kilmartin. New York: Vintage, 1989.

Py-Lieberman, Beth. "The Colors of Childhood." *Smithsonian*, November 1999, 32–36.

———. "Letters to the Editor." *Smithsonian*, January 2000, 16–17.

Rabaté, Jean-Michel, ed. *Writing the Image after Roland Barthes*. Philadelphia: University of Pennsylvania Press, 1997.

Rees, Geraint, Gabriel Kreiman, and Christof Koch. "Neural Correlates of Consciousness in Humans." *Neuroscience* 3 (2002): 261–70.

Ribot, Théodore. *Diseases of Memory: An Essay in Positive Psychology*. New York: D. Appleton and Company, 1882.

Richer, Jean. *Nerval: Expérience et création*. Paris: Hachette, 1970.

Rilke, Rainer Maria. "Narziss (2)." In *Gedichte 1910 bis 1926*. Frankfurt am Main: Insel Verlag, 1996.

Robinson, John A. "Autobiographical Memory." In *Aspects of Memory*. Ed. Michael Gruneberg and Peter Morris. New York: Routledge, 1992.

Rosenfield, Israel. *The Strange, Familiar, and Forgotten: An Anatomy of Consciousness*. New York: Vintage, 1993.

Rosolato, Guy. *La Relation d'inconnu*. Paris: Gallimard, 1978.

Rousseau, Jean-Jacques. *The Reveries of a Solitary*. Trans. John Gould Fletcher. New York: Burt Franklin, 1971.

Rubin, David C., ed. *Autobiographical Memory*. Cambridge: Cambridge University Press, 1986.

Rugg, Linda Haverty. *Picturing Ourselves: Photography and Autobiography*. Chicago: University of Chicago Press, 1997.

Sacks, Oliver. *An Anthropologist on Mars: Seven Paradoxical Tales*. New York: Vintage, 1995.

———. "In the River of Consciousness." *New York Review of Books,* January 15, 2004, 41–44.

———. *The Man Who Mistook His Wife for a Hat, and Other Clinical Tales*. New York: Simon and Schuster, 1998.

———. "Neurology and the Soul." *New York Review of Books,* November 22, 1990, 44–50.

Salaman, Esther. "A Collection of Moments." In *Memory Observed: Remembering in Natural Contexts*. Ed. Ulric Neisser. New York: W. H. Freeman, 1992.

Santner, Eric L. *Stranded Objects: Mourning, Memory, and Film in Post-war Germany*. Ithaca: Cornell University Press, 1990.

Sartre, Jean-Paul. *L'Etre et le néant: Essai d'ontologie phénoménologique*. Paris: Gallimard, [1943] 1993.

———. *L'Imaginaire: Psychologie phénoménologique de l'imagination*. Paris: Gallimard, [1966] 1940.

———. *L'Imagination*. Paris: Alcan, 1936.

Scarry, Elaine. *Dreaming by the Book*. New York: Farrar, Straus and Giroux, 1998.

Schactel, Ernest G. "On Memory and Childhood Amnesia." In *Memory Observed: Remembering in Natural Contexts*. Ed. Ulric Neisser. New York: W. H. Freeman, 1992.

Schacter, Daniel L. "Implicit Memory: History and Current Status." In *Human Memory: A Reader*. Ed. David R. Shanks. London: Arnold, 1997.

———. *Searching for Memory: the Brain, the Mind, and the Past*. New York: Basic Books, 1996.

———, ed. *Memory Distortion: How Minds, Brains, and Societies Reconstruct the Past*. Cambridge: Harvard University Press, 1995.

Schafer, Roy. *Retelling a Life: Narration and Dialogue in Psychoanalysis.* New York: Basic Books, 1992.

Schechtman, Marya. "The Truth about Memory." *Philosophical Psychology* 7, no. 1 (1994): 3–18.

Schlossman, Beryl. "The Descent of Orpheus: On Reading Barthes and Proust." In *Writing the Image after Roland Barthes.* Ed. Jean-Michel Rabaté. Philadelphia: University of Pennsylvania Press, 1997.

Schneider, Monique. "Temporalité, inconscient et répétition: Du mythe à l'élaboration théorique." In *Mythes et représentations du temps.* Ed. D'Orian Tiffeneau. Paris: Editions du CNRS, 1985.

Searle, John R. *The Mystery of Consciousness.* New York: New York Review of Books, 1997.

Shanks, David R., ed. *Human Memory: A Reader.* London: Arnold, 1997.

Shenk, David. *The Forgetting, Alzheimer's: Portrait of an Epidemic.* New York: Anchor, 2001.

Silverman, Kaja. *Threshold of the Visible World.* New York: Routledge, 1996.

Simon, Anne. "De *Sylvie* à la *Recherche*: Proust et l'inspiration nervalienne." *Romantisme* 95, no. 1 (1997): 39–49.

Smith, Paul. *Discerning the Subject.* Minneapolis: University of Minnesota Press, 1998.

Smith, Shane. "The Scent of Lost Time: Proust and the Odor-Cued Involuntary Memory in a Biopsychological Context." Boston University, 2002, 1–13. Typescript.

Sorabji, Richard. *Aristotle on Memory.* London: Duckworth, 1972.

Spiro, Joanna E. "Facing Texts: Autobiographical Reckonings with the Second World War in Woolf, Duras, H.D., and Perec." Ph.D. diss., Yale University, 1996.

Spitzer, Leo. "Back through the Future: Nostalgic Memory and Critical Memory in *Refuge from Nazism.*" In *Acts of Memory: Cultural Recall in the Present.* Hanover: University Press of New England, 1999.

Squire, Larry R. *Memory and Brain.* Oxford: Oxford University Press, 1987.

Squire, Larry, and Eric Kandel. *Memory from Mind to Molecules.* New York: Scientific American Library, 1999.

Stamelman, Richard. *Representations of Death and Absence in Modern French Poetry.* Ithaca: Cornell University Press, 1990.

Starobinski, Jean. "The Idea of Nostalgia." *Diogenes* 54 (summer 1966): 81–103.

———. "Le Style de l'autobiographie." *Poétique* 3 (1970): 257–65.

Steiner, George. *After Babel: Aspects of Language and Translation.* Oxford: Oxford University Press, 1975.

Sutton, John. *Philosophy and Memory Traces: Descartes to Connectionism.* Cambridge: Cambridge University Press, 1998.

Tadié, Jean-Yves. *Marcel Proust: Biographie.* 2 vols. Paris: Gallimard, 1996.

Tadié, Jean-Yves, and Marc Tadié. *Le Sens de la mémoire.* Paris: Gallimard, 1999.

Tereshchuk, David. "An Unreliable Witness." *New York Times Magazine,* January 28, 2001, 66.

Tulving, Endel. "Relations between Encoding Specificity and Levels of Processing." In *Human Memory: A Reader.* Ed. David R. Shanks. London: Arnold, 1997.

Vernière, Paul. "Proust et les deux mémoires." *Revue d'histoire littéraire: Marcel Proust* 5–6 (1971): 936–49.

Vygotsky, Lev. *Thought and Language.* Cambridge: MIT Press, 1986.

Weber, Bruce. "It's All about Me, Especially the Ugly Parts." *New York Times,* January 18 2004, WK 12.

Weiner, Richard. "Amnesia." In *Signs and Symptoms of Psychiatry.* Ed. J. O. Covenar and Keith H. Brodie. Philadelphia: Lippincott, 1983.

Wetzler Scott E., and John A. Sweeney. "Childhood Amnesia: An Empirical Demonstration." In *Autobiographical Memory.* Ed. David C. Rubin. Cambridge: Cambridge University Press, 1986.

Wieviorka, Annette. "On Testimony." In *Holocaust Remembrance: The Shape of Memory.* Ed. Geoffrey H. Hartman. Oxford: Blackwell, 1994.

Winterson, Jeanette. *Written on the Body.* London: Vintage, 1993.

Woolf, Virginia. *The Diary of Virginia Woolf.* 5 vols. Ed. Anne Olivier Bell. Harmondsworth: Penguin, 1983.

———. *Mrs Dalloway.* Oxford: Oxford University Press, 1992.

———. "On Being Ill." In *The Essays of Virginia Woolf.* London: Hogarth Press, 1994.

———. "Reminiscences." In *Moments of Being.* Ed. Jeanne Schulkind. London: Harcourt Brace, 1985.

———. "A Sketch of the Past." In *Moments of Being.* Ed. Jeanne Schulkind. London: Harcourt Brace, 1985.

———. *To the Lighthouse.* London: Harcourt Brace, 1981.

———. *The Waves.* Oxford: Oxford University Press, 1992.

Wunenburger, Jean-Jacques. "La Profondeur symbolique." In *La Vie des images.* Strasbourg: Presses Universitaires de Strasbourg, 1995.

Young, Allan. *The Harmony of Illusions: Inventing Post-traumatic Stress Disorder.* Princeton: Princeton University Press, 1995.

Zeisel, John, and Martha M. Tyson. "Alzheimer's Treatment Gardens." In *Therapeutic Gardens: Therapeutic Benefits and Design Recommendations.* Ed. Clare Cooper Marcus and Marni Barnes. New York: John Wiley and Sons, 1999.

Ziman, J. M. "What Is Science?" In *Public Knowledge.* Cambridge: Cambridge University Press, 1968.

Index